Foundations of Music Education

OTHER BOOKS BY DAVID WHITWELL

Philosophic Foundations of Education
Foundations of Music Education
Music Education of the Future
The Sousa Oral History Project

The History and Literature of the Wind Band and Wind Ensemble Series
A Concise History of the Wind Band
Volume 1 *The Wind Band and Wind Ensemble Before 1500*
Volume 2 *The Renaissance Wind Band and Wind Ensemble*
Volume 3 *The Baroque Wind Band and Wind Ensemble*
Volume 4 *The Wind Band and Wind Ensemble of the Classic Period (1750–1800)*
Volume 5 *The Nineteenth-Century Wind Band and Wind Ensemble*

For a complete list of the currently available works of David Whitwell visit:
whitwellbooks.com

David Whitwell

Foundations of Music Education

EDITED BY CRAIG DABELSTEIN

WHITWELL BOOKS • AUSTIN, TEXAS, USA

FOUNDATIONS OF MUSIC EDUCATION
DAVID WHITWELL
EDITED BY CRAIG DABELSTEIN
WWW.WHITWELLBOOKS.COM

WHITWELL BOOKS
P.O. BOX 342673
AUSTIN, TEXAS, USA

Copyright © David Whitwell 2011
All rights reserved

Cover Photo
A school of music in Amarna, Egypt, ca. 1,580 BC

Composed in Bembo Book
Published in the United States of America

FOUNDATIONS OF MUSIC EDUCATION (PAPERBACK) ISBN 978-1-936512-10-2

Contents

Foreword vii
Preface x
1 *Music Education Before Plato* 1
2 *Plato on Music Education* 21
3 *Aristotle on Music Education* 49
4 *Greek Views on Music Education After Aristotle* 69
5 *Music Education in Ancient Rome* 87
6 *How the Church Reinvented Music Education* 101
7 *Music Education in the Dark Ages* 121
8 *Music Education in the Pre-Renaissance* 141
9 *Music Education in the Fourteenth Century* 165
10 *Music Education in the Fifteenth Century* 175
11 *Music Education in Sixteenth-Century Italy* 193
12 *Music Education in Sixteenth-Century France* 209
13 *Music Education in Sixteenth-Century Germany* 219
14 *Music Education Treatises of Sixteenth-Century Germany* 227
15 *Martin Luther on Music Education* 245
16 *Music Education in Sixteenth-Century England* 253
17 *On Music Education in Baroque Italy* 265
18 *On the Philosphical Roots of German Music Education* 277
19 *The Music Education Scene in Baroque Germany* 293
20 *On the Philosophical Roots of French Music Education* 301
21 *The Music Education Scene in Baroque France* 317
22 *The Music Education Scene in Jacobean England* 331
23 *On Music Education in Restoration England* 347
24 *Schumann on Music Education* 361
25 *Chopin on Music Education* 369
26 *Mendelssohn on Music Education* 373
27 *Liszt on Music Education* 381
28 *Berlioz on Music Education* 387
29 *Wagner on Music Education* 395
Illustrations 401
About the Author 405

Foreword

There are lots of books on music education.

During the last fifty years there has been a plethora of scholarship and research into this subject. Sometimes it seems that not a week goes by without the latest expert releasing a new book or band method that will 'guarantee results for your ensemble'. Entire curricula have been written to professionalize and legitimize the school music class—to make it the equal of other subjects at school (forgetting that music was in the privileged position of *not* being like all other subjects at school, and that is what made it special).

The sheer body of work available on music education is a testimony to the hard work of many enthusiastic and talented music teachers who believe passionately in what they do. Consequently, a huge industry has developed around music education: software companies, publishing companies, retail companies—enormous businesses that rely on the budgets of primary and secondary school instrumental music departments around the world for their profits. They rely on music teachers and conductors who believe their ensembles would sound better with the latest method book, the most up-to-date software, or the most advanced rehearsal techniques.

Foundations of Music Education is also a book on music education, one that you can add to that ever increasing pile on your desk. But this book is unlike the countless other texts that have been written on the subject: it is not pedagogical (like almost every other source), it is philosophical, and it has the potential to change your music teaching and your students in a way that no method book can. As it traces the development of music education, from Ancient Egypt to Richard Wagner, you will discover in these pages what many thinkers and writers—most considered the greatest intellects of their time, or of all time—thought about the purpose of music, the principles of music, and the point of music.

Themes run through these chapters: similarities that occur between different cultures and different eras. For about three thousand years music was taught experientially—it was taught by doing and not by following a concept-laden text book. Three thousand years ago there was no choice—there was no music notation, there were no method books, and yet for three thousand years the human race still managed to teach, learn and perform music. In the last one thousand years, since the introduction of music notation, we have become adept at teaching theory and concepts and our students have lost many of the benefits of experiential learning.

Another theme flowing through these pages is the emphasis that writers put on the quality of repertoire. As far back as the Ancient Greeks there was commentary on distinguishing between good and bad music. From Plato to Berlioz, enlightened writers through two and a half thousand years have promulgated students being instructed with only the highest quality music.

How does this theory translate to modern education? At the high school where I teach the students only get to rehearse with their ensemble once a week after school, so each student learns about twelve to fifteen band pieces each year. During their five years of high school, therefore, those students will get to play only sixty pieces. Do I really want to waste even one of those pieces on something that was only composed last week to satisfy a list of 'educational' standards? It worries me that huge sums of money are spent on publishing and purchasing music that will only be played a handful of times before it is relegated to the back of the storeroom cupboard to make room for the latest composition, cleverly composed to be played by those of limited technical ability, but also devoid of any emotional or artistic content.

The great composers are remembered for the emotional and artistic quality of their work. How many modern band composers will be remembered in fifty, one hundred, or one thousand years' time? Is that even possible anymore?

I am not saying that the masters composed good music and modern band composers create bad music. And I appreciate as much as anyone that there are times when music composed to conform to technical standards is important. A beginning band, for example, needs literature they can play with a limited amount of technique. What I am saying though, is that band conductors, especially those like me with limited time to help their students experience the beauty of music, need to be extremely judicious in what they select for their students to play. Every piece in the students' folders needs to be thought about seriously. There can be no room for buying new band works every year just because they conform to your band's technical standard or the blurb sounded interesting. As the philosophers and writers quoted in this book believed, the music must be worthwhile, artistic, and *must* reach the listener on an emotional level.

Another topic, commented on by many over the centuries, is that music is credited with having the power to influence the character of the student, for better *and* worse (hence the emphasis placed on using only the best repertoire, for poor music could influence the students' character negatively). World media decry the lowering standards of young peoples' behaviour and morals. Could the introduction of universal music education arrest the decline in behavioural standards? Thousands of years of intellectual thought says it can.

Ensemble conductors are in a unique position to positively influence students' character by giving students tasks of responsibility, chances to practice leadership skills, and opportunities to cooperate and negotiate with others (think chamber music and sectionals). These are positive side effects of studying music in a modern high school, but *playing music* can have the most profound effect on the *character* of the musician, something that cannot be totally explained by science or philosophy, but which exists nonetheless. In simple terms, as Dr. Whitwell quotes William Revelli: 'The boy who blows a horn will never blow a safe.'

In this text, David Whitwell has outlined the 'big picture' of the historical development of music education. As an advocacy tool for music directors under siege from budget and program cuts it is indispensible. As a philosophical template for altering your attitude to the purpose and benefits of *every* student learning music, it is priceless.

Craig Dabelstein
Brisbane, 2011

Preface

Nikaure and Rewer were both music teachers in ancient Egypt during the Fifth Dynasty (2,563 to 2,433 BC). Why has history preserved their names from a period when even the names of the kings and the dates of their reigns are not fully understood? Why, in the tomb paintings of ancient Egypt, do you find scenes of actual music education in progress? Was music education really that important?

The reader may be quite surprised to find, in the following pages, that the values and principles of good music education were discussed and set in place far before any form of written language. Plato (428–348 BC) suggested that once the values of good music education were understood and established no changes were allowed for the next 10,000 years! What were these values and what constituted good music education among the ancient Egyptians, the most ancient culture we know much about?

First, the whole value of music education, they felt, was in the development of character and this depended on the use of only the best repertoire and no other. Second, they found no need for notation because they had discovered that music must be taught by personal, present tense experience. And third, they believed good music education must be accompanied by strict discipline. This included the discipline of the teachers and when the ancient music education system seemed to break down by the first century BC, Plutarch blames the teachers. The reader will find in the following pages centuries of experience during which these values are reconsidered and redefined.

The early views on music education in ancient Greece all came from Egypt and in Plato we see the subject of the use of music to form the character of the student expanded now to require discussion of the emotions, the realization that genetic information exists and the entire concept of the 'soul.' The means by which music does this Plato describes as catharsis, a subject that Aristotle will later clarify. Both Plato and Aristotle discuss at length the actual pedagogy of music education.

Plato also discusses the music education appropriate for the musician, or as we might say the music major. Here he points out that what we mean by music theory is not what we mean by being a musician. The student must be taught how the emotions in music affect the listener and that he must love his teacher!

For the rest of the ancient Greek period the reader will be surprised how frequently these aspects of music education are discussed by the society at large. The great military historian, Polybius (203–120 BC), for example, wrote at length on the subject of the influence of music on society. But, Polybius specifies, 'I mean real music.'

In ancient Rome music education at first followed the model of Greece and was just as highly valued. Music teachers were paid more than reading teachers and Terence observed that the study of music was necessary for the 'well-brought-up young gentleman.' Even a number of the emperors were musicians and even one of the most evil, Caligula (12–41 AD), gave private recitals singing and performing on instruments.

Not everyone agreed, however, and Cicero (106–43), for one, had doubts about the study of music and complained about the cost. In both Rome and in the last 'Roman Period' of ancient Greece the gradual wealth of the aristocracy resulted in performance being given over to slaves and therefore the performance of music was no longer part of aristocratic practice.

With the coming of the Christian Era, there were more philosophers who doubted the value of music in general and they helped set the stage for one of the Church's problems when it reestablished the schools. The Church's first objective was to create a new kind of Roman citizen and one of their chief goals was to remove emotion from the citizen's life, reasoning that emotion was the first step toward sin. But it had to be clear to even the Church officials that Music is synonymous with the emotions, so how do you include music in the school? The reader will see that the eventual scheme was to make Music a branch of mathematics and thus making it a rational subject rather than a subjective one. This allowed the Church to pronounce that in church music it is the words which are important, not the music. And if there is emotion involved, it too is related only to the words, hence St. Augustine describing crying as he listened to the words of a hymn.

Only a few educated persons still wrote of the importance of music education in forming character. One was the Emperor Julian (360–363 AD) who divided studies into those which were related to the body and those related to the emotional part of man. Even the mathematician Boethius (480–524) admitted that music had the capacity for 'radical transformation' in the listener's character.

The reader will also find here the struggles of education, including music education, during the lowest point of modern history, The Dark Ages. The Church closed the schools but a few Church people struggled to keep education alive and some, like Cassiodorus (480–573 AD) collected early manuscripts and paid to have others copied. The glory of Charlemagne (768–814 AD) was in his efforts to restart education in Europe.

Eventually the Church reopened its schools but the damage had been done in so far as music education was concerned. For the Church, music was now theory and not practice. But common sense rejected this and in a tenth-century play, written by a nun, a teacher is teaching a class in music and lectures on theory. The students cry, 'What has this got to do with music?' From this point on the reader will be on familiar ground. It was in this Church environment that our modern notation system was created, a system with not a single symbol representing the emotions. More important was the shift in psychology: music now existed on paper, not live. The creation of music shifted to the composer whereas earlier it lay with the performer.

With the twelfth century the dark cloud began to lift and the reader will see the strong movement toward the Renaissance. The Crusades opened the Western world to the East, which at this moment had progressed far ahead in all fields of knowledge and to whom credit is owed for saving the works of Aristotle and the other 'pagan' writers whom the Church had tried to destroy. The modern universities are founded, but important ones such as the University of Paris remained firmly under the control of Rome. One university, that of Bologna, had a reputation of being free of church domination in the fourteenth century and so the students joked that if a professor came from Paris he had to 'unlearn' everything he had been taught and then return to Paris to 'unteach' it.

Music education during the Renaissance begins firmly under the definition created by the Church, the separation between *musica theoretica* (or *speculative*) and *musica practica*. But the great flaw in this academic scheme is that *musica theoretica* is not music and the reader will find the authors of treatises on music education written during the Renaissance struggling with this fact. It is because this academic nonsense prevailed in intellectual circles that Western music owes so much to the minstrel—he kept real music alive as he traversed across Europe.

It is only by the sixteenth century that Music fully returned to a life of performance and not the subject of treatises. The long tradition of improvisation in Church music reached a very high artistic point at this time, although the reader will not read of this in traditional history texts. Music education took a renewed and important place at court as part of the necessary preparation of the 'well-educated man.' Court and civic music became richly musical and we have for the first time significant extant repertoire which is a testimony to the musicianship of this century.

No period of history is so falsely presented to the music student as is the Baroque Period. It is withheld from the student of traditional studies that the Baroque was in fact a period absorbed with returning emotions to music. Scholars, music teachers and musicians alike searched for the key to making music musical, that is, a vehicle which communicates feelings to the listener. The reader will be amazed in what he reads.

This rich atmosphere set the stage for the arrival of Italian Opera which swept Europe and was in great demand everywhere. Being the stage equivalent of daytime television, the weeping and wailing young heroine single-handedly forced music to become melody oriented for the first time. This, in turn, set the stage for the Classic Period and for melodies which were remembered and sung by ordinary people on the street and resound undiminished two hundred years later.

The nineteenth century, of course, centered on the emotions in music and the values which these emotions brought to the development of man. In the personal reflections found here by Schumann, Chopin, Mendelssohn, Liszt and Wagner the reader will see the greatest musicians translating these values into the study of music. Wagner was actually commissioned by the government in 1865 to create a new curriculum for the

Bavarian National School of Music. Wagner did this and at every turn he emphasizes that the basis of music education be performance. The proposed music school, he writes,

> can be of profit only when it rigidly confines its work to the fostering of the art of performance.

The reader will we hope find a personal resonance when he finds that Wagner draws our attention to the very word, 'conservatory.' It means, he writes, an institution to conserve something, which of course he says is classical music. In this discussion he adds, 'we possess classical works, but as yet no classic [rules of] performance for them.' This is the fundamental fault which he finds responsible for the German audiences of his time being ill-educated and often satisfied with mere entertainment.

And, finally, the reader must wonder how music educators today think they can afford to ignore Wagner's warnings that music education must not substitute worthless music for aesthetic music.

> The acceptance of the empty for the sound is desensitizing everything we possess in the way of schools, tuition, academies and so on, by ruining the most natural feelings and misguiding the faculties of the rising generation ... But that we should pay for all this, and have nothing left when we come to our senses ... is abominable!

Finally, I wish to acknowledge the many contributions of Craig Dabelstein in making this volume available to the public.

David Whitwell
Austin, 2011

A lack of culture is a serious thing.
Thales (640–546 BC)

The three musicians, Tomb of Nakht, Thebes, Egypt, ca. 1422–1411 BC

1   *Music Education Before Plato*

THE TOMB PAINTINGS OF ANCIENT EGYPT provide us with the oldest names of music teachers: Nikaure, 'instructor of the singers of the pyramid of King Userkaf,' and Rewer, 'teacher of the royal singers,' who lived during the Fifth Dynasty (2563–2423 BC). During the Sixth Dynasty (2345–2183 BC) we find several musicians named Snefrunufer, one of whom had a tomb at Giza which identifies him as 'instructor of singers in The Great House.'

From the most ancient of times it was the custom for most professions to be handed down from father to son, thus as Herodotus suggests, that some professions such as music were maintained by family birthright.

> Their heralds and aulos players, and cooks inherit the craft from their fathers ... no others usurp their places ... they ply their craft by right of birth.[2]

Regarding the tomb of Nufer and Kaha, Manniche points to Nufer as being the head of such a family of music educators.

> Kaha was both 'director' and 'instructor' of singers. He also held a title as priest of the 'southern Merit,' the music goddess, and the inscriptions mention that he was 'unique' among the singers and had a beautiful voice. Nufer, as well as being director of singers, was also instructor in the royal artisans' workshops. Three of his sons were 'instructors of singers,' and a fourth was 'director of singers in the palace.' Four other male relatives were 'instructors of singers,' and two of them were also priests of Merit.[3]

In addition, there are extant a few ancient tomb paintings which portray the actual music education environment. A remarkable painting from the Middle Kingdom tomb of an 'instructor of singers' and 'overseer of prophets' named Khesuwer, located at Kom el-Hisn in the Delta, pictures the instructor actually teaching. We see him teaching ten ladies in sistrum-playing and in another scene teaching ten ladies in hand-clapping.

---

[1] Quoted in Giovanni Reale, *A History of Ancient Philosophy* (Albany: State University of New York Press, 1987), 143.

[2] Herodotus, *Histories*, II, 59.

[3] Lise Manniche, *Music and Musicians in Ancient Egypt* (London: British Museum Press, 1991), 122.

Another ancient painting, dating from 1,580 BC in Amarna, Egypt, shows an actual music school, with teachers teaching, students practicing and four rooms to store instruments not in use [*see cover photo*].

But, what was the nature of this music education? To begin with, one must remember that ancient Egypt fell into that long period of time without measure when music did not yet have a corresponding notational system. But this, of course, does not mean that there was no music theory or rules of composition, it only means teaching was done by example, as even today most studio teaching is still practiced. And the rules, which had been learned from experience, not from written or notated examples, were, once arrived at, not susceptible to change, as Plato (428–348 BC) recalled:

> Long ago they appear to have recognized the very principle of which we are now speaking—that their young citizens must be habituated to forms and strains of virtue. These they fixed, and exhibited the patterns of them in their temples; and no painter, no other representative artist is allowed to innovate upon them, or to leave the traditional forms and invent new ones. To this day, no alteration is allowed either in these arts, or in music at all. And you find that their works of art are painted or molded in the same forms which they had ten thousand years ago;—this is literally true and no exaggeration,—their ancient paintings and sculptures are not a bit better or worse than the works of today, but are made with just the same skill.[4]

4 *Laws*, trans., B. Jowett (Oxford: Clarendon Press, 1953), 656d.

The reason why no change was permitted in the musical materials and in their educational use was hinted at in Plato's first sentence above. Strabo, writing during the first years of the Christian Era, made this point a bit more clear. He wrote that the Egyptians instructed their children with music established by the government and that musicians were in charge of the development of character in the young.

> The musicians in giving instruction in singing and playing the lyre or aulos considered this virtue as essential, since they maintain that such studies are destined to create discipline and develop the character.[5]

5 Quoted in Manniche., 41.

Thus the Egyptians were the oldest society we know of who believed that music education was fundamental in forming the character of the young, a philosophy of music education which was followed for the next four thousand years. Why is this not discussed by music educators today? The reason is that the field of music education has abandoned this idea in favor of a new philosophy which says, 'all music is equal.' Any thinking person will understand that you cannot have it both ways.

Toward the end of the ancient Egyptian society changes appear to have taken place. According to Diodorus Siculus, first century BC, the 'virtues' of this kind of education were no longer respected.

> Music was not, in those days, a part of normal education, since it was thought not only useless but morally injurious, in that it created effeminacy.[6]

[6] Quoted by. Henry G. Farmer, 'The Music of Ancient Egypt,' *New Oxford History of Music* (London: Oxford University Press, 1966), 265.

According to Athenaeus, third century AD, the city of Alexandria would appear to have been an exception. There, at least, he found a remarkable knowledge in music which extended to everyone.

> I would have you know that there is no record in history of other people more musical than the Alexandrians, and I am not speaking merely of singing to the harp, for even the humblest layman among us, even one who has never learned his ABC's, is so familiar with that, that he can immediately detect the mistakes which occur in striking the notes; no, even when it comes to pipes, they are most musical.

It seems clear in retrospect that much of the musical culture of both the ancient Hebrews and the ancient Greeks came from Egypt. In the case of the ancient Hebrews, the constant references in the Old Testament to the importance of the performance of instruments in the Temple by the Temple officials presupposes some ongoing discipline of instruction. The scholar, Sendrey, believes there must have been organized 'schools' of music, carrying on musical traditions many of which the Hebrews may have first learned in Egypt.

> One cannot help assuming the existence of one or several such 'schools' when one finds in the biblical text a sudden and unexplained upsurge of large choirs and orchestras, consisting of thoroughly organized and trained musical groups, which would be virtually inconceivable without lengthy, methodical preparation. Similar schools of music are known to have existed among other nations of Antiquity, far back in times of Sumeria.[7]

[7] Alfred Sendrey, in *Music in the Social and Religious Life of Antiquity* (Rutherford: Fairleigh Dickinson University Press, 1974), 95–97, where Sendrey speculates on the nature of this music education.

It also seems clear that the ancient Hebrews, as the Egyptians before them, also lacked a notational system for their music. The teaching would once again be experiential and by oral process. This appears confirmed in 1 Chronicles 15:16, where we are told that Chenaniah, a leader of the Levites in music, should direct the music 'because he understood it.' A reference in one of the apocryphal books also points to an oral tradition:

> Leaders of the people by their counsels, and by their knowledge of learning meet for the people, wise and eloquent in their instructions: Such as found out musical tunes, and recited verses in writing.[8]

[8] Ecclesiasticus 44:4ff.

The book of 1 Chronicles also documents the maintenance of the music teaching profession within the family.

> God had given Heman fourteen sons and three daughters. They were all under the direction of their father in the music in the house of the Lord with cymbals, harps, and lyres.[9]

[9] 1 Chronicles 25:5ff.

In one place in the Old Testament there is a clear reference to teaching music to the people at large. Moses is told, 'write this song, and teach it to the people of Israel.' And indeed we are told he did this in the same day![10] A similar command is found in Jeremiah,[11] 'teach to your daughters a lament, and each to her neighbor a dirge,' although perhaps this is meant rhetorically.

[10] Deuteronomy 31:19, 22.
[11] Jeremiah 9:20.

There are also two references in the Psalms which go beyond the general contention that music forms character in the young, to actually teaching specific moral principles, and even laws, through music.

> I will sing of loyalty and of justice.[12]
>
> ...
>
> Thy statutes have been my songs.[13]

[12] Psalm 101.

[13] Psalm 119.

With respect to ancient Greece, one can find references to specific people who journeyed to Egypt to study. Pythagoras (580–500 BC), for example, spent twelve years in Egypt where he studied 'arithmetic, music and all the other sciences.'[14] For

[14] Porphyry (c. 233–305 AD), 'Life of Pythagoras,' trans., in Kenneth Guthrie, *The Pythagorean Sourcebook* (Grand Rapids: Phanes Press, 1987).

this reason, most modern scholars agree that much of the early Greek musical culture came from Egypt, including the absence of a notational system.[15]

We wish we had more original extant material from the centuries before Plato and Aristotle, but one must remember that the burning of the library in Alexandria, and our bombing some key monasteries during WWII together with other assorted wars and earthquakes, etc., have taken much more than half of ancient Greek literature from us. Nevertheless, on the basis of the material before Plato which has survived, in addition to passed down information from later Greek philosophers, we can gain some idea of the nature of music education in the earliest Greek period.

We believe it is possible to identify five basic ideas which were at the foundation of ancient Greek music education before Plato:

1. The formation of character was the most important purpose of music education and they carefully monitored the effect of music education on society.
2. The most ancient Greeks were aware that music could be understood on more than one level.
3. They understood the difference between experiential music education and conceptual music education and they rejected the latter.
4. They believed only the best music should be used in music education.
5. They believed education must be accompanied by strict discipline.

Nearly all philosophers of ancient Greece were convinced that the purpose of music education in the schools should be to form a higher character in the student. Most attributed music's ability to do this to the ear's ability to bring sounds directly to the soul. Plutarch describes this action as follows:

> Of this Theophrastus affirms, that [hearing] is the most sensitive of all the senses. For the several objects of sight, tasting and feeling do not excite in us so great disturbances and alterations as the sudden and frightful noises which assault us only at the ears. Yet in reality this sense is more rational than sensitive. For there are many organs and other parts of the body which serve as avenues and inlets to the soul to give admission to vice; there is but one passage of virtue into young

[15] At least through the 'Golden Era' of ancient Greece. The few fragments which show an alphabetical-based notational system all come from a very recent period, probably the first century BC, the so-called 'Roman Period of ancient Greece.'

minds, and that is by the ears, provided they be preserved all along free from the corruptions of flattery and untainted with lewd discourses. For this reason Xenocrates was of the opinion that children ought to have a defense fitted to their ears rather than fencers or prize-fighters, because the ears only of the latter suffered by the blows, but the morals of the former were hurt and maimed by words.[16]

[16] 'Of Hearing.'

This power of music to affect character seemed taken for granted, as the Leader of the Chorus in Aristophanes' (448–380 BC) play, *The Frogs*, concludes:

> So with men we know for upright, blameless lives and noble names,
> Trained in music and palaestra, freemen's choirs and freemen's games,[17]

[17] Lines, 728.

The belief in the importance of music education and the general health of the student led some philosophers to use the lyre as a metaphor for the 'complete' person. One of these was Pythagoras' follower, Euryphamus.

> Human life resembles a properly tuned and cared for lyre. Every lyre requires three things: apparatus, tuning, and musical skill of the player. By apparatus we mean preparation of all the appropriate parts: the strings, the plectrum and other instruments cooperating in the tuning of the instrument. By tuning we mean the adaptation of the sounds to each other. The musical skill is the motion of the player in consideration of the tuning. Human life requires the same three things. Apparatus is the preparation of the physical basis of life, riches, renown, and friends. Tuning is the organizing of these according to virtue and the laws. Musical skill is the mingling of these according to virtue and the laws, virtue sailing with a prosperous wind and no external resistance.[18]

[18] Quoted in Guthrie, op. cit., 245.

So obvious did it seem to the most ancient Greeks that music education was inseparable from the development of the person that it followed that one's music making was a mirror of the person. A character in Aristophanes' play, *The Thesmophoriazusae*, tells us that one's choice of music reveals one's character.

> Answer me. But you keep silent. Oh! just as you choose; your songs display your character quite sufficiently.

In a famous anecdote, Archytas (428–350 BC), who was also a musician, upon being reproached for not advertising himself more, had the same meaning when he responded, 'It is my instrument which speaks for me.'

The basis of this, of course, is because music is experiential and what one expresses through music is a form of Truth, which cannot be hidden, nor can the listener be fooled. As a result, throughout history there have been some philosophers who turned this around and asked, 'Can a bad man be a good musician?' Strabo raised this question with respect to the poet, and we remind the reader that at this time poets were singers.

> Of course we do not speak of the excellence of a poet in the same sense as we speak of that of a carpenter or a blacksmith; for their excellence depends upon no inherent nobility and dignity, whereas the excellence of a poet is inseparably associated with the excellence of the man himself, and it is impossible for one to become a good poet unless he has previously become a good man.[19]

[19] Strabo, *On Geography*, I.2.5.

The great early Greek playwright, Euripides (484–407 BC), makes an interesting observation based on this same principle. He suggests that the composer who does not enjoy his own music cannot expect others to enjoy his music.

> He who maketh songs should take a pleasure in their making; for if it be not so with him, he will in no wise avail to gladden others, if himself have sorrow in his home; nay, 'tis not even right to expect it.[20]

[20] *The Suppliants*, 174.

Finally, in one of his comedies, Aristophanes satirizes this same idea by suggesting that even the dress of the poet will be in direct relationship with the character of his poetry.

> Besides, it is bad taste for a poet to be coarse and hairy. Look at the famous Ibycus, at Anacreon of Teos, and at Alcaeus, who handled music so well; they wore head-bands and found pleasure in the lascivious dances of Ionia. [And on the other hand] And have you not heard what a dandy Phrynichus was and how careful in his dress? For this reason his pieces were also beautiful, for the works of a poet are copied from himself.[21]

[21] *The Thesmophoriazusae*, 161.

The early Greek philosophers were also aware that music could be understood on more than one level. Later, this same distinction was made by Aristotle between a type of stage production known as 'spectacle,' in which one was vastly entertained, and tragedy, which reached the observer on a deeper level resulting in catharsis. Athenaeus made a similar distinction in music. He recalls a performance he heard which was a perfect example of the kind of music, or performance, which affords 'delight':

> He entered, and after drinking he took up his lyre and delighted us to such an extent that all were amazed at his playing, fluency being combined with correct technique, as well as at the tunefulness of his voice.

But Athenaeus describes another kind of music and listening experience in quite different language. In one place he concludes, 'It is plain to me also that music should be the subject of philosophic reflection.'[22] In another place he quotes a remark by Eupolis, 'Music is a matter deep and intricate,' adding his own observation that music is always supplying something new for those who can perceive.[23] This, in a word, is aesthetic music.

For the ancient Greeks, however, aesthetic music had yet another additional expectation. In addition to 'artistic beauty,' it also had to offer the listener, as part of the process of contemplation, an educational dimension. Even in the case of the better banquet entertainers this aspect was present. They were, Athenaeus says, required

> to offer a beautiful song for the common enjoyment. They believed that the beautiful song was the one which seemed to contain advice and counsel useful for the conduct of life.[24]

In another place, Athenaeus broadens this educational purpose to include manners.

> It is plain that Homer observes the ancient Greek system when he says, 'We have satisfied our souls with the equal feast and with the lyre, which the gods have made the companion of the feast,' evidently because the art is beneficial also to those who feast. And this was the accepted custom, it is plain, first in order that every one who felt impelled to get drunk and stuff himself might have music to cure his

[22] Athenaeus, op. cit., XIV, 632.

[23] Athenaeus, op. cit., XIV, 623.

[24] ibid., XV, 694.

violence and intemperance, and secondly, because music appeases surliness; for, by stripping off a man's gloominess, it produces good-temper and gladness becoming to a gentleman ... It is plain, therefore, that while most persons devote this art to social gatherings for the sake of correcting conduct and of general usefulness, the ancients went further and included in their customs and laws the singing of praises to the gods by all who attended feasts, in order that our dignity and sobriety might be retained through their help. For, since the songs are sung in concert, if discourse on the gods has been added it dignifies the mood of every one ... It is plain, therefore, in the light of what we have said, that music did not, at the beginning, make its way into feasts merely for the sake of shallow and ordinary pleasure, as some persons think.[25]

[25] ibid., XIV, 627ff.

To Plutarch, this educational purpose in listening to good music was the point at which one could call music 'useful' to mankind.

Therefore, if it be the aim of any person to practice music with skill and judgment, let him imitate the ancient manner; let him also adorn it with those other sciences, and make philosophy his tutor, which is sufficient to judge what is in music decent and useful.[26]

[26] 'Concerning Music.'

For the education of the musician, it followed that there were also two levels: a more practical education in performance, which would be all that would be required for creating 'delight,' and an aesthetic education which went beyond the 'details' of music. This detailed practical knowledge is one thing, Plutarch says, but understanding *how to use* this knowledge is something quite different.

He then that has both judgment as well as skill is to be accounted the most complete musician. For he that understands the Dorian mode, not being able withal to discern by his judgment what is proper to it and when it is fit to be made use of, shall never know what he does; nay, he shall quite mistake the nature and custom of the mode. Indeed it is much questioned among the Dorians themselves, whether the enharmonic composers be competent judges of the Dorian songs. The same is to be said concerning the knowledge of rhythm. For he that understands a paean may not understand the proper use of it, though he know the measure of which it consists. Because it is much doubted among those that make use of paeans, whether the bare knowledge make a man capable to determine concerning the proper use of those rhythms; or, as others say, whether it aspires to presume so far. Therefore it behooves that person to have two sorts of knowledge, who will undertake to judge of what is proper and what improper; first, of the custom and manner of elegancy for which such a composition was intended, and next of those things of which the composition consists. And thus, that neither the bare knowledge of harmony, nor of rhythm, nor of any other things that singly by themselves are but a part of the whole body of music, is sufficient to judge and determine either of the one or the other, what has been already said may suffice to prove.[27]

[27] ibid.

Therefore Plutarch concludes that musicians trained only in the details of music are not even capable of judging music. He is absolutely correct and we make the same mistake in the twenty-first century: We train musicians in skills and concepts, but not in the *meaning* of the music itself. To say it more accurately, we teach the grammar of music, but not music.

We are next to consider whether the masters of music are sufficiently capable of being judges of it. Now I aver the negative. For it is impossible to be a perfect musician and a good judge of music by the knowledge of those things that seem to be but parts of the whole body, as by excellency of hand upon the instrument, or singing readily at first sight, or exquisiteness of the ear, so far as the extends to the understanding of harmony and time. Neither does the knowledge of time and harmony, pulsation or elocution, or whatever else falls under the same consideration, perfect their judgment. Now for the reasons why a musician cannot gain a perfect judgment from any of these, we must endeavor to make them clear. First then it must be granted that, of things about which judgment is to be made, some are perfect and others imperfect. Those things which are perfect are the compositions in general, whether sung or played, and the expression of those, whether upon the instruments or by the voice, with the rest of the same nature. The imperfect are the things to these appertaining, and for whose sake they are made use of. Such are the parts of expression. A second reason may be found in poetry, with which the case is the same. For a man that hears a consort of voices and instruments can judge whether they sing or play in tune, and whether the language be plain or not. But every one of these are only parts of instrumental and vocal expression; not the end itself, but for the sake of the end. For by these things of the same nature shall the elegancy of elocution be judged, whether it be proper to the poem which the performer undertakes to sing. The same is to be said of the several passions expressed in the poetry.[28]

[28] ibid.

As the reader can see, Plutarch here finds it difficult to put into words the *meaning*, or the *important* part, of music. The closest he comes is when he suggests the elements of performance are the means, but not the end. For Plutarch, and for us, it is difficult to explain in words the meaning and most important aspect of music, for the simple reason that the musical experience is in the right hemisphere of the brain, which is mute and can not speak or write, and the words are in the left hemisphere of the brain, which knows nothing of music except the conceptual parts. But there is another problem. Music is for the ears and the world of words is for the eye and our five senses are designed in such a way that one usually takes control; they do not work well in ensemble. This very concern was familiar to the earliest Greek philosophers, as we see in Gorgias, who flourished ca. 425 BC. How, he asks, can language even express what we perceive through our senses?

> For how could any one communicate by word of mouth that he has seen? And how could that which has been seen be indicated to a listener if he has not seen it? For just as the sight does not recognize sounds, so the hearing does not hear colors but sounds; and he who speaks, speaks, but does not speak a color or a thing. When, therefore, one has not a thing in the mind, how will he get it there from another person by word or any other token of the thing except by seeing it, if it is a color, or hearing it, if it is a noise? For he who speaks does not speak a noise at all, or a color, but a word; and so it is impossible to conceive a color, but only see it, nor a noise, but only to hear it.[29]

[29] Quoted in Giovanni Reale, op. cit., 167.

And there we have the precise reason why modern American music education is failing so ignominiously. For music education to be meaningful to the student it must be personal (which means interior) and experiential. The means are the teaching of pure musicianship in dialog with the emotional makeup of the student. Because this is difficult to do, and requires genuine musicianship on the part of the teacher, American music education as a profession has given up and elected to teach what is easy to teach: concepts *about* music. But this is left hemisphere of the brain and as such cannot have anything to do with what the word 'music' really means to the rest of the world. That the students are not interested in conceptual music teaching is documented in the small percentage of the total student population which takes music classes—even though *all* students come to school *already* loving music!

The earliest Greek philosophies of music education were clearly based on a belief that the quality of the musical literature must be carefully controlled. This is made very clear by Aristophanes in his *The Clouds*. 'No ignoble music,' he says and if a student and teacher attempt to introduce such music they will be punished, 'Hard stripes and heavy would reform his taste.'

> CHORUS. Applaud the discipline of former days,
>   On you I call; now is your time to show
>   You merit no less praise than you bestow.
> DICAEOLOGOS. Thus summon'd, I prepare myself to speak
>   Of manners primitive, and that good [old] time
>   Which I have seen, when discipline prevail'd.
>   And modesty was sanctioned by the laws,
>   No babbling then was suffer'd in our schools;
>   The scholar's test was silence. The whole group
>   In orderly procession sallied forth
>   Right onwards, without straggling, to attend
>   Their teacher in harmony; though the snow
>   Fell on them thick as meal, the hardy brood
>   Breasted the storm uncloak'd: their lyres were strung
>   Not to ignoble melodies, for they were taught
>   A loftier key, whether to chant the name
>   Of Pallas, terrible amidst the blaze
>   Of cities overthrown, or wide and far
>   To spread, as custom was, the echoing peal.
>   There let no low buffoon intrude his tricks,
>   Let no capricious quavering on a note,
>   No running of variations high and low
>   Break the pure stream of harmony; no Phrynis
>   Practicing wanton warblings out of place—
>   Woe to his back that so was found offending!
>   Hard stripes and heavy would reform his taste.[30]

30 *Clouds*, 961ff.

The music most preferred for use in education by the ancient Greeks was the epic song, which praised the values and actions of earlier heroes. This is mentioned, together with the use of movement, in a discussion of the education of the ancient Arcadians by Athenaeus.

> It was not by chance that the earliest Arcadians carried the art of music into their entire social organization, so that they made it obligatory and habitual not only for boys but also for young men up to thirty years of age, although in all other respects they were most austere in their habits of life. It is only among the Arcadians, at any rate, that the boys, from infancy up, are by law practiced in singing hymns and paeans, in which, according to ancestral custom, they celebrate their national heroes and gods. After these they learn the tunes of Timotheus and Philoxenus and dance them annually in the theaters with Dionysiac aulos players, the

boys competing in the boys contests, the young men in the contests of adult males. And throughout their whole lives, in their social gatherings they do not pursue methods and practices so much with the aid of imported entertainments as with their own talents, requiring one another to sing each in his turn. As for other branches of training, it is no disgrace to confess that one knows nothing, but it is deemed a disgrace among them to decline to sing. What is more, they practice marching-songs with aulos accompaniment in regular order, and further, they drill themselves in dances, and display them annually in the theaters with elaborate care and at public expense.

All this, therefore, the men of old taught them, not to gratify luxury and wealth, but because they observed the hardness in every one's life and the austerity of their character, which are the natural accompaniment of the coldness of their environment and the gloominess prevailing for the most part in their abodes; for all of us human beings naturally become assimilated to the character of our abode; hence it is also differences in our national position that cause us to differ very greatly from one another in character, in build, and in complexion. In addition to the training just described, their ancestors taught the Arcadian men and women the practice of public assembly and sacrifice, also at the same time choruses of girls and boys, eager as they were to civilize and soften the toughness of their natures by customs regularly organized.[31]

[31] Athenaeus, op. cit., XIV, 626ff.

By the time Plutarch (46–127 AD) was writing he found that the Greek music education system had broken down and that in his period interest in music for the theater had replaced concern for music education.

> Among the more ancient Greeks, music in theaters was never known, for they employed their whole musical skill in the worship of the Gods and the education of youth ... But in our age is such another face of new inventions, that there is not the least remembrance or care of that use of music which is related to education; for all our musicians make it their business to court the theater Muses, and study nothing but compositions for the stage.[32]

[32] 'Concerning Music.'

Where he finds music education, he finds it is being done more by chance than by a well thought out system.

> First therefore we are to consider that all musical learning is a sort of habituation, which does not teach the reason of her precepts at one and the same time to the learner. Moreover, we are to understand that to such an education there is not requisite an enumeration of its several divisions, but every one learns by chance what either the master or scholar, according to the authority of the one and the liberty of the

other, has most affection for. But the more prudent sort reject this chance-medley way of learning, as the Lacedaemonians of old, the Mantineans, and Pallenians, who, making choice either of one single method or else but very few styles, used only that sort of music which they deemed most proper to regulate the inclinations of youths.[33]

This phrase by Plutarch, 'But the more prudent sort reject this *chance-medley way of learning*,' reminds us of one fairly recent American approach to music education which holds the silly view that music education should be a 'buffet table' allowing the students to select whatever they want. Of what other science would a professor make the suggestion of letting the student decide what is Truth?

Plutarch warns his readers not to blame music itself for the current failures in its use, but rather one should blame the teachers for how they use it.

In brief therefore, a rational person will not blame the sciences themselves, if any one make use of them amiss, but will adjudge such a failing to be the error of those that abuse them. So that whoever he be that shall give his mind to the study of music in his youth, if he meet with a musical education, proper for the forming and regulating his inclinations, he will be sure to applaud and embrace that which is noble and generous, and to rebuke and blame the contrary, as well in other things as in what belongs to music. And by that means he will become clear from all reproachful actions, for now having reaped the noblest fruit of music, he may be of great use, not only to himself but to the commonwealth; while music teaches him to abstain from every thing indecent both in word and deed, and to observe decorum, temperance, and regularity.[34]

Strabo agreed with this viewpoint, noting,

if music is perverted when musicians turn their art to sensual delights at symposiums and in orchestric and scenic performances and the like, we should not lay the blame upon music itself, but should rather examine the nature of our system of education, since this is based on music.[35]

The reader will recall, above, that Aristophanes mentioned the application of the whip to enforce discipline in the school environment. One wonders how prevalent this was, for it is mentioned again by Cicero.

33 ibid.

34 ibid.

35 *The Geography of Strabo*, trans., H. L. Jones (Cambridge: Harvard University Press, 1960), X.3.9.

The laws of the Cretans, in accordance with Jupiter's wishes, as the poets tell, and those of Lycurgus too, train the young men by making them toil, hunting and running, going hungry and thirsty, feeling cold and heat. At Sparta, in fact, boys are received at the alter with such blows that,
much blood flows from the flesh,
sometimes even, as I heard when I was there, to the death. Not only did none of them ever cry out, none even groaned.[36]

Aristophanes, in *The Knights*, mentions an uncooperative student who was simply expelled.

You also know what a pig's education he has had; his school-fellows can recall that he only liked the Dorian style and would study no other; his music master in displeasure sent him away saying; 'This youth, in matters of harmony, will only learn the Dorian style because it is akin to bribery.'[37]

We have saved Pythagoras (580–500 BC) for last, because he is so difficult to classify. Heraclitus (ca. 500 BC) called him 'the captain of swindlers,'[38] but on another occasion wrote more admiringly, 'Phythagoras, the son of Mnesarchus, was the most assiduous enquirer.'[39]

The most fundamental problem we have in judging the man is that we possess not a single word actually written by him. What we have instead are mostly accounts by his disciples and followers, who often picture him as a mythological figure with powers above those of normal men. They said of him, for example, that he had the ability to be seen in different cities at the same time, that he gave predictions of earthquakes, chased away a pestilence, suppressed violent winds and hail and calmed storms on the seas, for the comfort and safe passage of his friends.[40] They portrayed him as a figure like Jesus (six centuries before Jesus), saying that he restored life to a dead woman and that he vanished bodily from the world to become a god.[41] Like Jesus, he sometimes spoke in parables. Porphyry wrote of Pythagoras that 'none was allowed to become his friend or associate without being examined in facial expression and disposition.'[42]

Who was this man? He was a Greek, a native of Samos and said to have been a pupil of Pherecydes, although Porphyry tells us that Pythagoras' first study was with a lyre

[36] Cicero, *Tusculan Disputations*, II, 34.

[37] *The Knights*, 990. Note the reference here to Dorian as a style, not a scale. Also the reference to bribery (dorodokos, 'taker of bribes') involves a play on words with the term Doristi ('in the Dorian style'). A French translator captured it best in referring to it as the 'Louis d'or-ian mode.'

[38] Fragment 81a, quoted in T. M. Robinson, *Heraclitus* (Toronto: University of Toronto Press, 1987).

[39] Quoted in *Encyclopedia Britannica* (1951), XVIII, 802.

[40] Porphyry (ca. 233–305 AD), 'Life of Pythagoras,' in Kenneth S. Guthrie, *The Pythagorean Sourcebook* (Grand Rapids: Phanes Press, 1987).

[41] Empedocles, quoted in Stuart Isacoff, *Temperament* (New York: Vintage Books, 2001), 29.

[42] ibid.

player, a gymnast and a painter. He apparently traveled widely throughout the Mediterranean, including Egypt, according to Isocrates. Another biographer tells us he spent twelve years in Egypt where he studied 'arithmetic, music and all the other sciences.'[43]

[43] Iamblichus (ca. 250–325 AD), 'The Life of Pythagoras,' in ibid.

Driven from Samos by the evil Polycrates, he arrived in Croton, a Dorian community in southern Italy, in about 529 AD. It was here that he developed his 'school,' a kind of religious brotherhood which aimed at the moral reformation of society. When the members of this school became actively involved in politics, in mid sixth century, its meeting houses were sacked and burned. One account, of the 'house of Milo' in Croton, tells of more than fifty Pythagoreans being surprised and slain. A number of his followers fled to Thebes, but as a school of philosophy it did not survive the fourth century. Some of the individual contributions of Pythagoras, especially in the field of mathematics, remain valid today.

Everything we know of the 'School of Pythagoras' is second-hand, passed down by his followers. Perhaps it was for this reason that Aristotle never referred to Pythagoras, only to Pythagoreans. Of the many anecdotes told of this school, some are very attractive, as for example his idea that one should preserve what one has learned from a teacher with the same sense of value that one saves a gift of money. Another thing he got right was his imposition of a term of five years of silence upon new students who came to study with him[44] before they were allowed to talk! Porphyry summarized the general nature of his teaching in this passage:

[44] 'Of Inquisitiveness into Things Impertinent.'

> He taught the following. A cultivated and fruit-bearing plant, harmless to man and beast, should neither be injured nor destroyed. A deposit of money or of teachings should be faithfully preserved by the trustee.
>
> There are three kinds of things that deserve to be pursued and acquired: honorable and virtuous things, those that conduce to the use of life, and those that bring pleasures of the blameless, secure and solemn kind, and not the vulgar intoxicating kinds. Of pleasures there are two kinds: one that indulges the stomach and lusts by a profusion of wealth, which he compared to the murderous songs of the Sirens; the other kind consists of things honest, just, and necessary to life, which are just as sweet as the first, without being followed by repentance, and these pleasures he compared to the harmony of the Muses.
>
> …

His utterances were of two kinds, plain or symbolical. His teaching was twofold: of his disciples some were called Students (*mathematikoi*), and other Hearers (*akousmatikoi*). The Students learned the fuller and more exactly elaborate reasons of science, while the Hearers heard only the summarized instructions of learning, without more detailed explanations.

Porphyry tells us that Pythagoras' first study was with a lyre player, a gymnast and a painter and that as an adult, Pythagoras continued his activity as a musician on a daily basis.

> He himself held morning conferences at his residence, composing his soul with the music of the lyre, and singing certain ancient paeans of Thales. He also sang verses of Homer and Hesiod, which seemed to soothe the mind. He danced certain dances which he thought conferred on the body agility and health.

Regarding this reference to 'composing his soul' with music, Iamblichus gives us a very interesting, and more detailed, account of Pythagoras' use of music in relationship to health. It is no doubt this passage which has caused some more recent scholars to regard Pythagoras as 'the Father of Music Therapy.'

> Pythagoras conceived the first attention that should be given to men should be addressed to the senses, as when one perceives beautiful figures and forms, or hears beautiful rhythms and melodies. Consequently he laid down that the first erudition was that which subsists through music's melodies and rhythms, and from these he obtained remedies of human manners and passions, and restored the pristine harmony of the faculties of the soul. Moreover, he devised medicines calculated to repress and cure the diseases of both bodies and souls. Here is also by Zeus, something which deserves to be mentioned above all: namely, that for his disciples he arranged and adjusted what might be called 'preparations' and 'touchings,' divinely contriving mingling of certain diatonic, chromatic and enharmonic melodies, through which he easily switched and circulated the passions of the soul in a contrary direction, whenever they had accumulated recently, irrationally, or clandestinely—such as sorrow, rage, pity, over-emulation, fear, manifold desires, angers, appetites, pride, collapse or spasms. Each of these he corrected by the rule of virtue, attempering them through appropriate melodies, as through some salutary medicine.
>
> In the evening, likewise, when his disciples were retiring to sleep, he would thus liberate them from the day's perturbations and tumults, purifying their intellective powers from the influxive and effluxive waves of corporeal nature, quieting their sleep, and rendering their dreams pleasing and prophetic. But when they arose again in the morn-

ing, he would free them from the night's heaviness, coma and torpor through certain peculiar chords and modulations, produced by either simply striking the lyre, or adapting the voice.[45]

Unfortunately, none of the followers of Pythagoras went into more detail regarding their Master's thoughts on music education.

[45] Iamblichus, op. cit.

2 *Plato on Music Education*

AFTER THE PERSIAN WARS OF 490–470 BC, when Sparta and Athens combined to defeat the efforts of Darius and Xerxes to colonize Greece, there follows a century of remarkable intellectual growth in science, mathematics, philosophy and the arts. In philosophy we have one of the great contributions to the literature of Western Europe in the writings of Plato together with his representation of Socrates.

Plato (427–347 BC) was born in comfort, was an experienced soldier, and had won prizes for physical feats in the Isthmian games. His coming into contact with Socrates changed his life and he would later observe, 'Thank God I was born Greek and not barbarian, freeman and not slave, man and not woman; but above all, that I was born in the age of Socrates.'[1]

After the death of Socrates, Plato, a young man of twenty-eight, began a period of travel, first to Egypt for a period of study at Heliopolis, then to Sicily, Italy and finally returning to Greece where he visited the members of the school founded by Pythagoras. He returned to Athens in 387 BC, a man of forty years of age and fully prepared to begin his historic writing.

As everyone knows most, and perhaps all, of the writings of Plato are composed as if the author were Socrates, as if they were notes taken from the classes of Socrates. We will use the name of Plato, who, after all wrote the works. In the end, whether the reference is to Socrates or Plato is perhaps not so important to the reader, as both represent a common philosophical perspective of a particular time and place twenty-four centuries in the past.

Plato is not easy to read for two main reasons. First, his intellectual perspective was quite different from the reader's today and this entailed kinds of discussion we no longer hear. Second, many of the most basic ideas, on the topic of music education in particular, are spread across a large number of separate dialogs, or treatises. Our purpose in this essay is to organize this material in a way that the reader can follow the arguments of Plato. We will present his views on music education in the following order:

Opposite page: Herm représentant Plato. Marble, Roman copy after a Greek original from the last quarter of the fourth century.

[1] Quoted in Will Durant, *The Story of Philosophy* (New York: Simon & Schuster, 1926), 13.

- On the Purpose of Music Education
- On the Goals of Music Education for the Regular Student
- On the Goals of Music Education for the Musician
- On the Pedagogy of Music Education

Opposite page: Bust of Socrates, marble, Roman copy after a Greek original from the fourth century BC.

Before considering the views of Plato on music education it is necessary to give the reader some sense of the intellectual perspective the man held. In particular, we must touch on a few topics which formed the background for his thoughts on music.

First, Plato, like all early philosophers, was unaware of the separate faculties of our brain. But, they were aware of the brain and made the basic conclusion that the brain was the source of all things rational. On the other hand, nearly all early philosophers were aware that there is more to the story, in particular how do you explain experience and what we gain from it, and where is the center for the information we gain from the senses and what about the emotions? If the brain is the source of Reason, where do you put all these other things?

For Plato the other 'location' for all the things that make up man other than Reason was the 'soul.' But, because he placed so much importance on the soul, he assumed that Reason must also play some role there. Although he was aware of the presence of the emotions in men, he had great difficulty in all his writings trying to find a place for the emotions and in trying to give them a rational explanation. In a typical passage one can see him in this struggle:

> And are there not many other cases in which we observe that when a man's desires violently prevail over his reason, he reviles himself, and is angry at the violence within him, and that in this struggle, which is like the struggle of factions in a State, his spirit is on the side of his reason … ?
>
> …
>
> But a further question arises: Is passion different from reason also, or only a kind of reason; in which the latter case, instead of three principles in the soul, there will only be two, the rational and the concupiscent? …
> Yes, he said, there must be a third.
> Yes, I replied, if passion, which has already been shown to be different from desire, turns out also to be different from reason.[2]

[2] *Republic*, IV, 439d and following. Our quotations are taken from *The Dialogues of Plato*, B. Josett, ed. (Oxford: Clarendon Press, 1953).

As Plato never did come to understand the importance of the role emotions play in our lives, neither was he comfortable about the value of experience, although in some cases it seemed to him obvious, as when he has Socrates admitting that a woman should not be a mid-wife unless she has had the experience of child birth.[3] The perceptions we gain from our senses was an even bigger obstacle for Plato. How can perception be considered knowledge when different persons have different perceptions?[4] Plato quotes a Socrates illustration of how men with differing perceptions can *both* be correct.

[3] *Theaetetus*, 149c.

[4] This discussion is found in ibid., 151e and following.

> SOCRATES. To the sick man his food appears to be and is bitter, and to the man in health it is and appears the opposite. Now I cannot conceive that one of these men can be or ought to be made wiser than the other: nor can you call the sick man foolish because he has one impression, and say that the healthy man because he has another is wise.[5]

[5] ibid., 166e.

In spite of Plato's hesitancy in trying to 'rationalize' these other faculties, it is interesting that he did seem to take it for granted that man possesses a certain amount of genetic knowledge. One discussion of this subject deals with an uneducated slave boy belonging to Meno. Socrates observes that the boy knows certain things which he has obviously not been taught. Socrates concludes that everyone, like this slave boy, has a certain amount genetic 'notions' in the soul, 'which only need to be awakened into knowledge by putting questions to him.'[6]

[6] *Meno*, 85e.

The most interesting discussion of this topic is found in a dialogue which Socrates had with Ion, a rhapsodist who performed in some kind of sung/speech epic poetry, such as Homer. Socrates presents a brilliant analogy of magnets and their shared attraction to explain how the 'divinity' speaks to the poet, who then communicates with the performer and then through him to the audience.

> SOCRATES. The gift which you possess of speaking excellently about Homer is not an art, but, an inspiration; there is a divinity moving you, like that contained in the stone which Euripides calls a magnet, but which is commonly known as the stone of Heraclea. This stone not only attracts iron rings, but also imparts to them a similar power of attracting other rings; and sometimes you may see a number of pieces of iron and rings suspended from one another so as to form

> quite a long chain: and all of them derive their power of suspension from the original stone. In like manner the Muse first of all inspires men herself; and from these inspired persons a chain of other persons is suspended, who take the inspiration.
>
> ...
>
> Do you know that the spectator is the last of the rings which, as I am saying, receive the power of the original magnet from one another? Yourself, and the actor, are intermediate links, and the poet himself is the first of them.[7]

[7] *Ion*, 533d, 535e.

It was possibly this passage which inspired Wagner to create a similar analogy explaining, again through magnets, how the 'quintessence' of an emotion passes from composer to performer to the audience.

Another topic which presented much difficulty to Plato was the nature and importance of pleasure. He found so many apparent contradictions, as for example his observation that most pleasurable things are bad.[8] Other things, like gymnastic exercises and military service are painful, but good.[9] It is curious, but typical of Plato, that his discussion of pleasure is concerned with the body, yet omits any discussion of the arts in this regard. His only reference to music when discussing this topic is very interesting and contains a memorable phrase. At the end of his life, waiting in prison, Socrates is described as taking up the topic of pleasure and pain. At this time he confides having a reoccurring dream that he should 'Set to work and make music.' But while he apparently did compose at least one hymn in prison, he curiously interpreted his dream as meaning he should concentrate on philosophy.

[8] *Philebus*, 13b.
[9] *Protagaoras*, 353e.

> I had imagined that this was only intended to exhort and encourage me in the study of philosophy, which has been the pursuit of my life, and is the noblest and best of music.[10]

[10] *Phaedo*, 60e. It would have been interesting to hear him argue this with Beethoven, who said 'Music is a more lofty revelation than all wisdom and philosophy!'

This passing reference to music can only mean that Plato was aware that some music performance invited, and perhaps demanded, contemplation. It is too bad that he made no attempt here to relate this kind of experience to knowledge.

The final area of background we think it important to offer the reader has to do with Plato's difficulty in understanding and discussing beauty. He takes it for granted that we can recognize beauty, whatever it is, and this form of beauty he calls 'Absolute Beauty.' Other than 'Absolute Beauty,' if we find something beautiful it means that the object partakes of Absolute Beauty. If he finds something beautiful, he does not want anyone to talk to him about its color, its form, etc. Such discussion, he says, is 'confusing to me.'[11] It is the same as when you are moved by the performance of a masterpiece of music—you do not want the person sitting next to you to start talking about chords, harmony and form, etc. In a word, forget the grammar.

[11] ibid., 100b.

Another important discussion of the definition of beauty is found in *Greater Hippias*, 290d, where Socrates leads poor Hippias around and around in circles on this subject. In the course of this discussion, however, Plato quotes one very important conclusion which Socrates reached, that utility plays no role in the beautiful. It is the basic principle we recognize in music and in art, and that is that the highest art has no purpose.

It has been our intent here to help the reader understand where Plato was coming from with respect to some of the important general philosophical subjects which form an important background for his perspective and conclusions on music education. But, we have one more subject which needs to be discussed before we consider Plato's views on music education and that is the general environment of music performance which he knew. Everyone has heard some form of the expression, 'the younger generation is going to the dogs.' The fact that one finds expressions of this sort at the dawn of written history makes one wonder if perhaps there were remarkable civilizations long before the invention of writing. In any case, we find Plato, five centuries BC, complaining that 'modern' music has become licentious, lawless and vulgar. In this remarkable discussion he describes the musical environment of the past, when laws and overseers monitored composers and performers, when music was closely tied to the gods and when the audience sat in silence, a respectful silence enforced by officials with sticks!

The decline of this tradition of noble music came in the wake of the public being allowed to decide for themselves what was good, in other words music moved toward entertainment goals. This point reminds us of the ancient Greek philosophers' horror of the idea of government by democracy, allowing the ignorant mob to elect its officials, etc. In this case, the horror is in letting the ignorant public decide what is good and what is truth in music.

> AN ATHENIAN STRANGER. Let us speak of the laws about music,—that is to say, such music as then existed,—in order that we may trace the growth of the excess of freedom from the beginning. Now music was early divided among us into certain kinds and manners. One sort consisted of prayers to the Gods, which were called hymns; and there was another and opposite sort called lamentations, and another termed paeans, and another, celebrating (I believe) the birth of Dionysus, called 'dithyrambs.' And they used the actual word 'laws' for another kind of song; and to this they added the term 'citharoedic.' All these and others were duly distinguished, nor were the performers allowed to confuse one style of music with another. And the authority which determined and give judgment, and punished the disobedient, was not expressed in a hiss, nor in the most unmusical shouts of the multitude, as in our days, nor in applause and clapping of hands. But the directors of public instruction insisted that the spectators should listen in silence to the end; and boys and their tutors, and the multitude in general, were kept quiet by a hint from a stick. Such was the good order which the multitude were willing to observe; they would never have dared to give judgment by noisy cries. And then, as time went on, the poets themselves introduced the reign of vulgar and lawless innovation. They were men of genius, but they had no perception of what is just and lawful in music; raging like bacchanals and possessed with inordinate delights—mingling lamentations with hymns, and paeans with dithyrambs; imitating the sounds of the aulos on the lyre, and making one general confusion; ignorantly affirming that music has no truth, and, whether good or bad, can only be judged of rightly by the pleasure of the hearer. And by composing such licentious works, and adding to them words just as licentious, they have inspired the multitude with lawlessness and boldness, and made them fancy that they can judge for themselves about melody and song. And in this way the theaters from being silent have become vocal, as though they had understanding of good and bad in music and poetry; and instead of an aristocracy, an evil sort of theatrocracy has grown up. For if there had been a democracy in music alone, consisting of free men, no fatal harm would have been done; but in music there first arose the universal conceit of omniscience and general lawlessness;—freedom came following afterwards, and men, fancying that they knew what they did not know, had no longer any fear, and the absence of fear begets shamelessness. For what is this shamelessness, which is so evil a thing, but the insolent refusal to regard the opinion of the better by reason of an over-daring sort of liberty?[12]

[12] *Laws*, 700ff.

These insights into what Plato recognized as the highest aesthetic of music, together with his tendency to judge everything by its affect on the soul, form a very important background for the reader to keep in mind when reading Plato's thoughts on music education. We might only add that the highest art music known to Plato were the lyric and epic poets who sang to their own accompaniment on the lyre.

On the Purpose of Music Education

Perhaps the most quoted sentence by Plato on the subject of music education reads,

> Education has two branches,—one of gymnastic, which is concerned with the body, and the other of music, which is designed for the improvement of the soul.[13]

[13] ibid., 795d.

Here he is speaking of the young child and in another place he specifies that what he means by music is not the conceptual, or theoretical, aspects of music.

> Music, as you will remember, was the counterpart of gymnastic, and trained the guardians by the influences of habit, by harmony making them harmonious, by rhythm rhythmical, but not giving them science.[14]

[14] *Republic*, VII, 522.

On the contrary, by music education Plato meant something much more personal and experiential. The goal was the alignment of the soul.

> Harmony, which has motions akin to the revolutions of our souls, is not regarded by the intelligent votary of the Muses as given by them with a view to irrational pleasure, which is deemed to be the purpose of it in our day, but as meant to correct any discord which may have arisen in the courses of the soul, and to be our ally in bringing her into harmony and agreement with herself; and rhythm too was given by them for the same reason, on account of the irregular and graceless ways which prevail among mankind generally, and to help us against them.[15]

[15] *Timaeus*, 47d.

This experiential form of music education included movement and we get a more detailed look at this in Athenaeus. The Damon of Athens he refers to here was the teacher of Socrates.

> Music contributes also to the exercise and the sharpening of the mind; hence all Greeks as well as those barbarians [those who do not speak Greek well!] with whom we are acquainted make use of it. With good reason Damon of Athens and his school say that songs and dances are the result of the soul's being in a kind of motion; those songs which are noble and beautiful produce noble and beautiful souls, whereas the contrary kind produce the contrary. Whence also came that witty remark of Cleosthenes, the ruler of Sicyon, which reveals his cultivated mind. For, as they say, after seeing one of his daughter's suitors dancing in vulgar posture he declared that he had 'danced away' his marriage, probably believing that the young man's soul was also vulgar. For, whether in dancing or in walking, decency and dignity of bearing are beautiful, whereas immodesty and vulgarity are ugly. For this reason, in fact, from the very beginning, the poets arranged dances for freemen, and they used the dance figures only to illustrate the theme of the songs, always preserving nobility and manliness in them ... But if any one arranged his figures with undue exaggeration, or when he came to his songs said anything that did not correspond to the dance, he was discredited.[16]

[16] Athenaeus, *Deipnosophistae*, XIV, 628.

This vivid illustration of how music and movement reflect the soul of the person helps us understand the importance which Plato assigned to the soul as the object of music education. Indeed, in another place, Socrates, in a dialog with Glaucon, a brother to Plato, suggests that music is 'a more potent instrument than any other' in the education of the soul.[17] Such is the power of music education over the soul that the one danger which Plato cautions about is too much music, or for that matter too much experience in gymnastic activities.

[17] *Republic*, 401d.

> Yes, he said, I am quite aware that the mere athlete becomes too much of a savage, and that the mere musician is melted and softened beyond what is good for him.[18]

[18] ibid., III, 410c.

This is an early example of a concern which will be expressed frequently in the coming five centuries, that music creates effeminacy.

On the Goals of Music Education for the Regular Student

It is possible to generalize on Plato's conclusions on the contribution music education made to the student who becomes a normal adult. This, of course, applies to the music student mentioned below, as these values are gained in the lower levels of music education. Socrates makes this clear, saying a student should learn

> the same way you learned the arts of the grammarian, or musician, or trainer, not with the view of making any of them a profession, but only as a part of education, and because a private gentleman and freeman ought to know them.[19]

[19] *Protagoras*, 312b.

Perhaps thinking of the very young student, Plato identifies as a goal of music education that it, through a kind of catharsis, creates calm minds in children who would otherwise be fearful, and it produces a 'sound mind in place of their frenzy.'

> The affection both of the Bacchantes and of the children is an emotion of fear, which springs out of an evil habit of the soul. And when someone applies external agitation to emotions of this sort, the motion coming from without gets the better of the terrible and violent internal one, and produces a peace and calm in the soul, and quiets the restless palpitation of the heart, which is a thing much to be desired, sending the children to sleep, and making the Bacchantes, although they remain awake, to dance to the pipe with the help of those gods to whom they offer acceptable sacrifices, and producing in them a sound mind, which takes the place of their frenzy.[20]

[20] *Laws*, 791.

It is with respect to general music education, especially, that we see Plato's concern for the soul. In fact, Plato refers here to music education as the true education of the inner being. Who could phrase a better definition of music education?

First, music education creates a man who is graceful, who perceives the omissions or faults in art and nature and develops a soul characterized by the noble and good.

> Rhythm and harmony find their way into the inward places of the soul, on which they mightily fasten, imparting grace, and making the soul of him who is rightly educated graceful, or of him who is ill-educated ungraceful; and also because he who has received this true education of the inner being will most shrewdly perceive omissions or faults in art and nature, and with a true taste, while he praises and rejoices over and

receives into his soul the good, and becomes noble and good, he will justly blame and hate the bad, now in the days of his youth, even before he is able to know the reason why; and when reason comes he will recognize and salute the friend with whom his education has made him long familiar.

Yes, he said, I quite agree with you in thinking that it is for such reasons that they should be trained in music.[21]

[21] *Republic*, 401d.

Aside from those formidable accomplishments, Plato continues with additional side-effects of music education and they are that a man becomes characterized by self-discipline, courage, liberality and magnanimity.

Even so, as I maintain, neither we nor the guardians, whom we say that we have to educate, can ever become musical until we and they know the essential forms of temperance [self-discipline], courage, liberality, magnanimity, and their kindred, as well as the contrary forms, in all their combinations, and can recognize them and their images wherever they are found, not slighting them either in small things or great, but believing them all to be within the sphere of one art and study.

Later in this book Plato continues in his description of the ideal civic man, now focusing on the combined contributions of music education and gymnastic classes.

The blending of music and gymnastic will bring them into accord, nerving and sustaining the reason with noble words and lessons, and moderating and soothing and civilizing the wildness of passion by harmony and rhythm?

Quite true, he said.

And these two, thus nurtured and educated, and having learned truly to know their own functions, will rule over the concupiscent, which in each of us is the largest part of the soul and by nature most insatiable of gain; over this they will keep guard, lest, waxing great and strong with the fullness of bodily pleasure, as they are termed, the concupiscent soul, no longer confined to her own sphere, should attempt to enslave and rule those who are not her natural-born subjects, and overturn the whole life of man?

Very true, he said.

Both together will they not be the best defenders of the whole soul and the whole body against attacks from without; the one counseling, and the other going out to fight as the leader directs, and courageously executing his commands and counsels?

True.

Likewise it is by reference to spirit that an individual man is deemed courageous, because his spirit retains in pleasure and in pain the commands of reason about what he ought or ought not to fear?

Right, he replied.[22]

[22] ibid., 442. Regarding the 'blending of music and gymnastic,' which Plato mentions here, Athenaeus, op. cit., XIV, 629ff, gives an extensive catalog of specific dances used for exercise with music. Through these, he says, the students acquired courage.

Finally, the normal adult, while not a professional musician, can nevertheless sing and dance as a result of his education. Not only that, but he will recognize the good from the bad and will have good taste. This, in fact, is the answer for Socrates when it comes to accountability. As he contends in the last paragraph below, if we know the good, we are well-educated; if we do not, we are not well-educated. That difference, he says, is the 'safeguard of education.'

> AN ATHENIAN STRANGER. And the uneducated is he who has not been trained in the chorus, and the educated is he who has been well trained?
> CLEINIAS. Certainly.
> AN ATHENIAN STRANGER. And the chorus is made up of two parts, dance and song?
> CLEINIAS. True.
> AN ATHENIAN STRANGER. Then he who is well educated will be able to sing and dance well?
> CLEINIAS. I suppose that he will.
> AN ATHENIAN STRANGER. Let us see; what are we saying?
> CLEINIAS. What?
> AN ATHENIAN STRANGER. He sings well and dances well; now must we add that he sings what is good and dances what is good?
> CLEINIAS. Let us make that addition.
> AN ATHENIAN STRANGER. We will suppose that he knows the good to be good, and the bad to be bad, and makes use of them accordingly: which now is the better trained in dancing and music—he who is able to move his body and use his voice in what he understands to be the right manner, but has no delight in good or hatred of evil; or he who is scarcely correct in gesture and voice and in understanding, but is right in his sense of pleasure and pain, and welcomes what is good, and is offended at what is evil?
> CLEINIAS. There is a great difference, stranger, in the two kinds of education.
> AN ATHENIAN STRANGER. If we know what is good in song and dance, then we truly know also who is educated and who is uneducated; but if not, then we certainly shall not know wherein lies the safeguard of education, and whether there is any or not.[23]

[23] *Laws*, 654b.

Developing musical taste in the normal adult is, then, by the process of conditioning. Plato returns to this explanation in a discussion of the organization of civic choral festivals and the music appropriate to them.

Now the irregular strain of music is always made ten thousand times better by attaining to law and order, and rejecting the honeyed Muse—not however that we mean wholly to exclude pleasure, which is characteristic of all music. And if a man be brought up from childhood to the age of discretion and maturity in the use of the orderly and severe music, when he hears the opposite he detests it, and calls it illiberal; but if trained in the sweet and vulgar music, he deems the severer kind cold and displeasing. So that while he who hears them gains no more pleasure from the one than from the other, the one has the advantage of making those who are trained in it better men, whereas the other makes them worse.[24]

[24] ibid., 802.

On the Goals of Music Education for the Musician

To begin with, in a brief discussion in *Philebus*, Socrates gives us a profile of what we might call the 'music major,' the basic expectations for the music student. First he must have a good ear and understand theory (systems compounded out of pitches). But he hastens to qualify this by observing that this is not what we mean by being a musician.

> SOCRATES. But you would not be a real musician if this was all that you knew; though if you did not know this you would know almost nothing of music.[25]

[25] *Philebus*, 17c.

Second, he must understand how emotions appear and 'come to be in the movements of bodies.'
Third, in another place Plato adds the basic requirement of knowing how to tune. Here he also mentions that the musician speaks 'in a gentle and harmonious tone of voice.'[26]
Fourth, the music student loves his teacher.

[26] Phaedrus, 268e.

> And as to the artists, do we not know that he only who has love for his instructor emerges into the light of fame?—he whom Love touches not walks in darkness.[27]

[27] *Symposium*, 197.

Plato gives additional goals for the performing musician in his dialog with Ion, one of the rhapsodists who sung from memory extended poetic works, such as Homer, before the public.[28] First, Plato thought the performing musician should

[28] *Ion*, 530c and following. As far as can be determined their performance was in a kind of sung/speech, a medium which no longer exists. The rhapsodists single-handedly kept the works of Homer and his contemporaries extant until such time as the written form of the Greek language was invented.

look presentable, wearing fine clothes 'to look as beautiful as you can.' This, perhaps, was due to the divine association which music enjoyed in Plato's view.

Second, one must keep company with fine poets and memorize their works. For how can one otherwise understand and interpret their works before the public, Plato asks? All this, he says, is to be greatly envied. By this he means that one grows and is educated by one association with great minds. It is a fundamental argument in music education which has been thrown over board today in the desperate search for popularity with the students, in the consequence replacing works by great minds with those of the lowest character.

Third, the performance must be inspired. Here Plato first speaks of the poet, but since the poet was both the creator of both poetry and music, as a singer, one could as well include the composer here. The poet/composer does not create from 'the rules,' but from the inspiration of divine power. Not only do they not depend on the 'rules,' but Plato correctly and forever ends this discussion by calling them non-rational, 'bereft of reason.'

Then the performer, affected by this divine power, is also inspired, his 'soul is in ecstasy.' And, last but not least, the audience is similarly affected by this and emotionally respond. This passage is followed by the magnet analogy which we have cited above. This is a very important discussion of the highest ideals of performance in music.

> SOCRATES. Many are the noble words in which poets speak concerning the actions of men; but like yourself when speaking about Homer, they do not speak of them by any rules of art: they are simply inspired to utter that to which the Muse impels them, and that only; and when inspired, one of them will make dithyrambs, another hymns of praise, another choral strains, another epic or iambic verses, but not one of them is of any account in the other kinds. For not by art does the poet sing, but by power divine; had he learned by rules of art, he would have known how to speak not of one theme only, but of all; and therefore God takes away reason from poets, and uses them as his ministers, as he also uses the pronouncers of oracles and holy prophets, in order that we who hear them may know them to be speaking not of themselves, who utter these priceless words while bereft of reason, but that God himself is the speaker, and that through them he is addressing us.
>
> ...

> I wish you would frankly tell me, Ion, what I am going to ask you: When you produce the greatest effect upon the audience in the recitation of some striking passage, such as the apparition of Odysseus leaping forth on the floor, recognized by the suitors and shaking out his arrows at his feet, or the description of Achilles springing upon Hector, or the sorrows of Andromache, Hecuba, or Priam,—are you in your right mind? Are you not carried out of yourself, and does not your soul in an ecstasy seem to be among the persons or places of which you are speaking … ?
>
> ION. That proof strikes home to me, Socrates. For I must frankly confess that at the tale of pity my eyes are filled with tears, and when I speak of horrors, my hair stands on end and my heart throbs.
>
> SOCRATES. Well, Ion, and what are we to say of a man who at a sacrifice or festival, when he is dressed in an embroidered robe, and has golden crowns upon his head, of which nobody has robbed him, appears weeping and panic-stricken in the presence of more than twenty thousand friendly faces, when there is no one despoiling or wronging him;—is he in his right mind or is he not?
>
> ION. No indeed, Socrates, I must say that, strictly speaking, he is not in his right mind.
>
> SOCRATES. And are you aware that you produce similar effects on most of the spectators?
>
> ION. Only too well; for I look down upon them from the stage, and behold the various emotions of pity, wonder, sternness, stamped upon their faces when I am performing.[29]

[29] *Ion*, 534c–535e.

This is perhaps the appropriate place to reflect on Plato's definition of a good composition, for this was at the time inseparable from performance. We begin with three isolated observations. First, Plato declares 'Musically' is the very 'name for correctness in the art of music.'[30] Second, we know Plato was assuming a contemplative listener when he writes of 'musical instruments used to charm the souls of men.'[31] Third, Plato seemed perfectly aware of the importance that compositions be composed with 'wonderful care.'

[30] *Alcibiades I*, 108d.

[31] *Symposium*, 215c.

> AN ATHENIAN STRANGER. Because all discourses and vocal exercises have preludes and overtures, which are a sort of artistic beginnings intended to help the music which is to be performed; lyric measures and music of every other kind have preludes framed with wonderful care.[32]

[32] *Laws*, 722d.

We have mentioned above Plato's contention that composers write not from rules but from inspiration. He mentions this again in the *Apology*.

> I learnt that not by wisdom do poets write poetry, but by a sort of genius and inspiration.[33]

[33] *Apology*, 22c.

Another characteristic of good music must be the contemplation of the beautiful.

> For what should be the end of music if not the love of beauty?[34]

[34] *Republic*, III, 403c.

Closely related to this, Plato makes a very important aesthetic statement when he contends that we cannot call a composition good if its purpose is merely to offer pleasure. 'Pleasure,' he says is a 'doctrine which cannot be admitted.' Instead, the goal is the 'good,' and most important, 'Truth.'

> AN ATHENIAN STRANGER. When anyone says that music is to be judged by pleasure, his doctrine cannot be admitted; and if there be any music of which pleasure is the criterion, such music is not to be sought out or deemed to have any real excellence, but only that other kind of music which is an imitation of the good, and bears a resemblance to its original.
> CLEINIAS. Very true.
> AN ATHENIAN STRANGER. And those who seek for the best kind of song and music ought not to seek for that which is pleasant, but for that which is true.[35]

[35] *Laws*, 668b.

There is a striking similarity between this passage and a statement made in Los Angeles by the famous conductor, Sergiu Celibadache.

> Anyone who still hasn't got past the stage of the beauty of music still knows nothing about music. Music is not beautiful. It has beauty as well, but the beauty is only the bait. Music is truth.[36]

[36] Quoted in *Los Angeles Philharmonic Notes*, April, 1989.

In his *Gorgias*, Plato takes this idea even further for here the discussion centers on the soul. Repertoire is not just a matter of Truth versus pleasure, but good versus evil.

> SOCRATES. I would have you consider ... whether there are not other similar activities which have to do with the soul—some of them activities of art, making a provision for the soul's highest interest; others despising the interest, and as in the parallel case considering only the pleasure, of the soul, and how this may be acquired, but not considering what pleasures are good or bad, and having no other

aim but to afford gratification, whether good or bad. In my opinion, Callicles, there are such activities, and this is the sort of thing which I term flattery, whether concerned with the body or the soul or anything else on which it is employed with a view to pleasure and without any consideration of good and evil. And now I wish that you would tell me whether you agree with us in this notion, or whether you differ.

CALLICLES. I do not differ.[37]

And when we provide the audience with the best repertoire it is not a matter of chance, but the result of Truth and art.

SOCRATES. Listen to me, then, while I recapitulate the argument: Is the pleasant the same as the good? Not the same. Callicles and I are agreed about that. And is the pleasant to be pursued for the sake of the good, or the good for the sake of the pleasant? The pleasant is to be pursued for the sake of the good. And that is pleasant at the presence of which we are pleased, and that is good by the presence of which we are good? To be sure. And we are good, and all good things whatever are good, when some virtue is present in us or them? That, Callicles, is my conviction. But the virtue of each thing, whether body or soul, instrument or creature, when given to them in the best way comes to them not by chance but as the result of the order and truth and art which are imparted to them: am I not right? I maintain that I am. And is not the virtue of each thing dependent on order or arrangement? Yes I say. And that which makes a thing good is its appropriate order inhering in each thing? Such is my view.[38]

It is interesting, by the way, that in another place Plato in planning his Utopia, the Republic, says that painting and poetry will not be admitted because they are only imitations and not Truth.[39] He specifically does not mention music in this discussion. This is apparently because he regarded art music as Truth,[40] and it was apparently for this reason that he observed that experienced singers can immediately know if a composition is a 'good or bad imitation of a good or bad soul.'[41] Plato does not hold quite so high an ideal for the amateur performer of music. Plato describes them as people so busy running around hearing concerts, and presumably performing concerts, that they never stop to contemplate on the higher meaning of the music they are playing. In fact, he says, very few artists are capable of both attaining beauty *and* contemplating on it.

[37] *Gorgias*, 501b.

[38] ibid., 506d.

[39] *Republic*, X, 595b through 602b.

[40] *Laws*, 668b.

[41] ibid., 812b.

> Musical amateurs, too, are a folk strangely out of place among philosophers, for they are the last persons in the world who would come to anything like a philosophical discussion if they could help it; while they run about at the Dionysiac festivals as if they had let out their ears for the season to hear every chorus, and miss no performance either in town or country. Now are we to maintain that all these and any who have similar tastes, as well as the professors of quite minor arts, are philosophers?
>
> Certainly not, I replied; they are only an imitation.
>
> ...
>
> And this is the distinction which I draw between the sight-loving, art-loving, practical class which you have mentioned, and those of whom I am speaking, and who are alone worthy of the name of philosophers.
>
> How do you distinguish them? he said.
>
> The lovers of sounds and sights, I replied, are, as I conceive it, fond of fine tones and colors and forms and all the artificial products that are made out of them, but their mind is incapable of seeing or loving absolute beauty.
>
> The fact is plain, he replied.
>
> Few are they who are able to attain to this ideal beauty and contemplate it.
>
> Very true.[42]

[42] *Republic*, 476c.

When Plato speaks of 'Truth' in music he is, of course, thinking of experiential Truth and specifically that regarding emotion. He makes this clear in his discussion, *Symposium*, where he defines music as 'a science of the phenomena of love in [its] application to harmony and rhythm.'[43] He follows this immediately with the following:

> Again, in the constitution of a harmony as of a rhythm there is no difficulty in discerning love, and as yet there is no sign of its duality. But when you want to use them in actual life, either in the kind of composition to which the term 'lyrical' is applied or in the correct employment of melodies and meters already composed, which latter is called education, then indeed the difficulty begins, and the good artist is needed.

[43] *Symposium* 187b. Pliny the Younger, at the end of the first century AD. He writes of the daughter of Calpurnia Hispulla,
> She has even set my verses to music and sings them, to the accompaniment of her lyre, with no musician to teach her but the best of masters, love.

By 'lyrical' music we think he means the music a musician might create on a lyre when he is setting a poem by someone else to music, for this is generically known as 'lyric poetry.'

The next kind of music, 'the employment of melodies and meters already composed,' refers to what we might think of as a concert performance today, the performance of pre-composed music. But to do this well, he warns, requires education. And here, he says, the difficulty begins for the educator must be a good artist.[44]

Ahem!

On the Pedagogy of Music Education

Unfortunately, Plato was not as descriptive in discussing the actual pedagogy of music education as he was its goals. Before we examine the actual music education process, we might mention that Plato recommends the music teachers be elected[45] and he also provides a few additional details regarding them.

> In these several schools let there be dwellings for teachers, who shall be brought from foreign parts by pay, and let them teach them who attend the schools the art of war and the art of music, and the children shall come not only if their parents please, but if they do not please.[46]

With regard to pedagogy, first, it seems clear that the central vehicle for music education, in his view, was the voice.

> AN ATHENIAN STRANGER. The whole choral art is also in our view the whole of education; and of this art, rhythms and harmonies form the part which has to do with the voice.
> CLEINIAS. Yes.
> AN ATHENIAN STRANGER. The movement of the body has rhythm in common with the movement of the voice, but gesture is peculiar to it, whereas song is simply the movement of the voice.
> CLEINIAS. Most true.
> AN ATHENIAN STRANGER. And the sound of the voice which reaches and educates the soul, we have ventured to term music.[47]

Before vocal experience, however, and apparently in part for the purpose of ear training, Plato recommends the study of the lyre.

> AN ATHENIAN STRANGER. And now that we have done with the teacher of letters, the teacher of the lyre has to receive orders from us.
> CLEINIAS. Certainly.
> AN ATHENIAN STRANGER. I think that we have only to recollect our previous discussions, and we shall be able to give suitable regulations touching all this part of instruction and education to the teachers of the lyre.

---

[44] We once observed one of the most famous doctors of music education in America humiliate himself before a large audience of music educators when he was asked to sing a G minor scale and could not do so.

[45] *Laws*, 813.

[46] ibid., 804d.

[47] *Laws*, 672e.

CLEINIAS. To what do you refer?

AN ATHENIAN STRANGER. We were saying, if I remember rightly, that the sixty years old choristers of Dionysus were to be specially quick in their perceptions of rhythm and musical composition, that they might be able to distinguish good and bad imitation, that is to say, the imitation of the good or bad soul when under the influence of passion, rejecting the one and displaying the other in hymns and songs, charming the souls of youth, and inviting them to follow and attain virtue by the way of imitation.

CLEINIAS. Very true.

AN ATHENIAN STRANGER. And with this view the teacher and the learner ought to use the sounds of the lyre, because its notes are pure, the player who teaches and his pupil rendering note for note in unison; but complexity, and variation of notes, when the strings give one sound and the poet or composer of the melody gives another,—also when they make concords and harmonies in which lesser and greater intervals, slow and quick, or high and low notes, are combined—or, again, when they make complex variations of rhythms, which they adapt to the notes of the lyre,—all that sort of thing is not suited to those who have to acquire a speedy and useful knowledge of music in three years; for opposite principles are confusing, and create a difficulty in learning, and our young men should learn quickly, and their mere necessary acquirements are not few or trifling, as will be shown in due course. Let the director of education attend to the principles concerning music which we are laying down.[48]

[48] ibid., 812b.

Next, Plato tells us the music which the lyre teacher uses must also be appropriate to children.

The teachers of the lyre take similar care that their young disciple is temperate and gets into no mischief; and when they have taught him the use of the lyre, they introduce him to the poems of other excellent poets, who are the lyric poets; and these they set to music, and make their harmonies and rhythms quite familiar to the children's souls, in order that they may learn to be more gentle, and harmonious, and rhythmical, and so more fitted for speech and action; for the life of man in every part has need of harmony and rhythm. Then they send them to the master of gymnastic.[49]

[49] *Protagoras*, 326b.

What kind of music is Plato describing here? First, the musical style must be simple and in a single style. More complex 'mixed styles' Plato did not permit in education, although he admits this type of music was more popular with both children and the general public.

You would agree with me in saying that one [style] is simple and has but slight changes; and that if an author expresses this style in fitting harmony and rhythm, he will find himself, if he does his work well, keeping pretty much within the limits of a single harmony (for the changes are not great), and in like manner he will make a similar choice of rhythm?

That is quite true, he said.

Whereas the other requires all sorts of harmonies and all sorts of rhythms if the music and the style are to correspond, because the style has all sorts of changes.

That is also perfectly true, he replied.

And do not the two styles, or the mixture of the two, comprehend all poetry and every form of expression in words? No one can say anything except in one or other of them or in both together.

They include all, he said.

And shall we receive into our State all the three styles, the one only of the two unmixed styles? Or would you include the mixed?

I should prefer only to admit the pure imitator of virtue.

Yes, I said, Adeimantus; and yet the mixed style is also charming: and indeed the opposite style to that chosen by you is by far the most popular with children and their attendants, and with the masses.

I do not deny it.[50]

[50] *Republic*, III, 397c.

Second, in a frequently quoted passage regarding Plato's views on music, we are told the choice of 'modes' are to be strictly limited. The origin of these Greek modes were in the musical styles of specific peoples. The only extant early theoretical information comes from much later and consequently we really know nothing with respect to what Plato is talking about here. What he meant, when he refers to Lydian as 'relaxed,' we can never know.

The harmonies which you mean are the mixed or tenor Lydian, and the full-toned or bass Lydian, and such-like.

These then, I said, must be banished; even to women who have a character to maintain they are of no use, and much less to men.

Certainly.

In the next place, drunkenness and softness and indolence are utterly unbecoming the character of our guardians.

Utterly unbecoming.

And which are the soft and convivial harmonies?

The Ionian, he replied, and some of the Lydian which are termed 'relaxed.'

Well, and are these of any use for warlike men?

Quite the reverse, he replied; and if so the Dorian and the Phrygian are the only ones which you have left …

> If these and only these are to be used in our songs and melodies, we shall not want multiplicity of strings or a panharmonic scale?
>
> I suppose not.[51]

[51] ibid., III, 398e. In *Laches*, 188d, Plato remarks that the Dorian is the true Hellenic mode.

Third, musical instruments which perform more complex music shall not be allowed.

> But what do you say to aulos-makers and aulos-players? Would you admit them into our State when you reflect that in this composite use of harmony the aulos is worse than any stringed instrument; even the panharmonic music is only an imitation of the aulos?
>
> Clearly not.
>
> There remain then only the lyre and the harp for use in the city, and the shepherds in the country may have some kind of pipe.[52]

[52] ibid., 399d.

Fourth, the rhythmic structure of music, like the harmonic structure, must be simple. Here, Plato seems to lack expertise.

> Next in order to harmonies, rhythms will naturally follow, and they should be subject to the same rules, for we ought not to seek out complex systems of meter, and a variety of feet, but rather to discover what rhythms are the expressions of a courageous and harmonious life; and when we have found them, we shall adapt the foot and the melody to words having a like spirit, not the words to the foot and melody. To say what these rhythms are will be your duty—you must teach me them, as you have already taught me the harmonies.
>
> But, indeed, he replied, I cannot tell you. I know from observation that there are some three principles of rhythm out of which metrical systems are framed, just in sounds there are four notes [strings on the lyre] out of which all the harmonies are composed. But of what sort of lives they are severally the imitations I am unable to say.
>
> Then, I said, we must take Damon into our counsels; and he will tell us what rhythms are expressive of meanness, or insolence, or fury, or other unworthiness, and what are to be reserved for the expression of opposed feelings. And I think that I have an indistinct recollection of his mentioning a complex Cretic rhythm; also a dactylic or heroic, and he arranged them in some manner which I do not quite understand, making the rhythms equal in the rise and fall of the foot, long and short alternating; and, unless I am mistaken, he spoke of an iambic as well as of a trochaic rhythm, and assigned to them short and long quantities. Also in some cases he appeared to praise or censure the movement of the foot quite as much as the rhythm; or perhaps a combination of the two; for I am not certain what he meant. These matters, however, as I was saying, had better be referred to Damon himself, for the analysis of the subject would be difficult, you know?
>
> Rather so, I should say.

> But it does not require much analysis to see that grace or the absence of grace accompanies good or bad rhythm.
> None at all.
> And also that good and bad rhythm naturally assimilate to a good and bad style; and that harmony and discord in like manner follow style; for our principle is that rhythm and harmony are regulated by the words, and not the words by them ...
> Then beauty of style and harmony and grace and good rhythm depend on simplicity,—I mean the true simplicity of a rightly and nobly ordered mind and character, not that other simplicity which is only a euphemism for folly.[53]

[53] *Republic*, 400.

Plato discusses at some length the relationship which the character of music has on the development of one's character. First, children need truth. While he admits that the very young are told fictitious tales, these, he says, are not suitable for school-age children.

> Shall we just carelessly allow children to hear any casual tales which may be devised by casual persons, and to receive into their minds ideas for the most part the very opposite of those which we shall wish them to have when they are grown up?[54]

[54] ibid., 377b.

Even the classic tales of Homer are unsuitable, because he observes that the young can not distinguish whether they are supposed to have an allegorical meaning or not.[55]

[55] ibid., 378d.

In the same way, music teachers must not be allowed to give the students merely whatever they desire, because the quality of the music will have a direct impact on the development of the character of the child, says Plato.

> AN ATHENIAN STRANGER. And is any harm done to the lover of vicious dances or songs, or any good done to the approver of the opposite sort of pleasure?
> CLEINIAS. I think that there is.
> AN ATHENIAN STRANGER. 'I think' is not the word, but I would say, rather, 'I am certain.' For must they not have the same effect as when a man associates with bad characters, whom he likes and approves rather than dislikes, and only censures playfully because he has but a suspicion of their badness? In that case, he who takes pleasure in them will surely become like those in whom he takes pleasure, even though he be ashamed to praise them. This result is quite certain; and what greater good or evil can a human being undergo?
> CLEINIAS. I know of none.

> AN ATHENIAN STRANGER. Then in a city which has good laws, or in future ages is to have them, bearing in mind the instruction and amusement which are given by music, can we suppose that the poets are to be allowed to teach in the dance anything which they themselves like, in the way of rhythm, or melody, or words, to the young children of any well-conditioned parents? Is the poet to train his choruses as he pleases, without reference to virtue or vice?
> CLEINIAS. That is surely quite unreasonable, and is not to be thought of.
> ...
>
> AN ATHENIAN STRANGER. The inference at which we arrive is that education is the constraining and directing of youth toward that right reason, which the law affirms, and which the experience of the eldest and best has agreed to be truly right. In order, then, that the soul of the child may not be habituated to feel joy and sorrow in a manner at variance with the law, and those who obey the law, but may rather follow the law and rejoice and sorrow at the same things as the aged—in order, I say, to produce this effect, chants appear to have been invented, which really enchant, and are designed to implant that harmony of which we speak. And, because the mind of the child is incapable of enduring serious training, they are called plays and songs, and are performed in play; just as when men are sick and ailing in their bodies, their attendants give them wholesome diet in pleasant meats and drinks, but unwholesome diet in disagreeable things, in order that they may learn, as they ought, to like the one, and to dislike the other. And similarly the true legislator will persuade, and, if he cannot persuade, will compel the poet to express, as he ought, by fair and noble words, in his rhythms, the figures, and in his melodies, the music of temperate and brave and in every way good men.[56]

[56] *Laws*, 656f and 659d.

In perhaps some of his most important recommendations, Plato discusses the quality of the music used in music education.

> Most persons say, that the excellence of music is to give pleasure to our souls. But this is intolerable and blasphemous.[57]

[57] ibid., 655d.

By 'excellence' of music, he means that of the highest value and since he believes the highest value of music is in promoting the highest virtue, therefore he regards any reference to mere pleasure as 'intolerable.' Plato's principal concern was that amusement in any form, aside from the immediate pleasure, had a potential for harming the soul.

SOCRATES. I would have you consider ... whether there are not other similar activities which have to do with the soul—some of them activities of art, making a provision for the soul's highest interest; others despising the interest, and as in the parallel case considering only the pleasure, of the soul, and how this may be acquired, but not considering what pleasures are good or bad, and having no other aim but to afford gratification, whether good or bad. In my opinion, Callicles, there are such activities, and this is the sort of thing which I term flattery, whether concerned with the body or the soul or anything else on which it is employed with a view to pleasure and without any consideration of good and evil.[58]

[58] *Gorgias*, 501b.

And, of course, he was especially concerned with the educational environment.

Then, I said, our guardians must lay the foundations of their fortress in music?
    Yes, he said; the lawlessness of which you speak too easily steals in.
    Yes, I replied, in the form of amusement, and as though it were harmless.
    Why, yes, he said, and harmless it would be; were it not that little by little this spirit of license, finding a home, imperceptibly penetrates into manners and customs; whence issuing with greater force it invades contracts between man and man, and from contracts goes on to laws and constitutions, in utter recklessness, ending at last, Socrates, by an overthrow of all rights, private as well as public.
    Is that true? I said.
    That is my belief, he replied.
    Then, as I was saying, our boys should be trained from the first in a stricter system, for if childish amusement becomes lawless, it will produce lawless children, who can never grow up into well-conducted and virtuous citizens.[59]

[59] *Republic*, IV, 424d.

Finally, there were apparently also contests held in the realm of music education, in both instrumental and choral music. Plato provides an interesting discussion on the goals and organization of such contests.

It will be proper to appoint directors of music and gymnastic, two kinds of each—of the one kind the business will be education, of the other, the superintendence of contests ... In speaking of contests, the law refers to the judges of gymnastics and of music; these again are divided into two classes, the one having to do with music, the other with gymnastics; and the same who judge of the gymnastic contests of men, shall judge of horses; but in music there shall be one set of judges of solo singing, and of imitation—I mean of rhapsodists, players on the harp, the aulos and the like, and another who shall judge of choral songs. First of all, we must choose directors for the choruses of boys, and men, and maidens, whom they shall follow in the amusement of the dance, and for our other musical arrangements;—one director will be enough for the choruses, and he should be not less than forty years of age. One director will also be enough to introduce the solo singers, and to give judgment on the competitors, and he ought to be less than thirty years of age. The director and manager of the choruses shall be elected after the following manner:—Let any persons who commonly take an interest in such matters go to the meeting, and be fined if they do not go, but those who have no interest shall not be compelled. Any elector may propose as director someone who understands music, and he in the scrutiny may be challenged on the one part by those who say he has no skill, and defended on the other hand by those who say that he has. Ten are to be elected by vote, and he of the ten who is chosen by lot shall undergo a scrutiny, and lead the choruses for a year according to law. And in like manner the competitor who wins the lot shall be leader of the solo and concert music for that year; and he who is thus elected shall deliver the award to the judges.[60]

[60] *Laws*, 764d.

3 Aristotle on Music Education

WILL DURANT CALLED ARISTOTLE a one-man 'Encyclopedia Britannica of Greece.'[1] That is not a bad description for the subjects of Aristotle's extant writings include politics, every branch of science known at the time, the arts, government, the art of public speaking, philosophy and ethics. And we must not fail to mention that he invented the philosophical branch of study we call Aesthetics.

Fortunately, Aristotle was born (in 384 BC) into circumstances which made possible the fulfillment of his genius. His father was a physician to the King of Macedonia, the grandfather to Alexander the Great, whom Aristotle would tutor. At age fifty-three, Aristotle founded in Athens his own school, known as the Lyceum. It is assumed that the many students who were drawn to this school shared in the burden of his work, collecting data, carrying out observations and experiments, and perhaps even in the actual writing. This must have been the case if some ancient writers were correct in attributing to him between four hundred and one thousand books.

In subjects such as logic or rhetoric, where Aristotle needed only his native intelligence and his love for step-by-step rational analysis, his writings must still impress every modern reader. In the field of science, our perspective after two thousand years of discoveries makes it more difficult to appreciate his pronouncements. Even if we keep in mind that the man had none of the modern tools for scientific measurement and that many basic concepts, including gravitation, the nature of chemical and electrical phenomena, etc., were as yet unknown, still we are startled at some of the 'Weird Science' we find in his pages. We can understand how someone of his epoch could believe the earth was stationary and did not move (how else would we see the same stars tomorrow night that we see tonight?). But, considering he knew the basics of anatomy, how could he have concluded that the brain is cold, bloodless, and *fluid* in nature, or that the delay in the closure of the cranial bone in infants has to do with the need for 'evapora-

[1] Will Durant, *The Story of Philosophy* (New York: Simon & Schuster, 1961 edition), 46.

Aristotle teaching Alexander the Great

Opposite page: Bust of Aristotle, marble, Roman copy after a Greek bronze original by Lysippos from 330 BC

tion?'² And how could he have not guessed that it is in the brain that we experience the senses, concluding instead that it is in the heart?

> For the passages of all the sense-organs ... run to the heart.³
>
> ...
>
> Because the source of the sensations is in the heart, therefore this is the part first formed in the whole animal.⁴

Sometimes he seems to have believed, and passes on, observations which he must have received second-hand, such as, 'More males are born if copulation takes place when north rather than south winds are blowing.' In this case, he tells us that shepherds confirm that the direction of the wind influences the production of males and females in animals if an animal even *looks* in one direction or the other while copulating!⁵

His understanding of the physical nature of musical sounds seems to have been the result of casual observation and consequentially results in some curious conclusions.

> In the case of oboes and other instruments of the same class, the sounds produced are clear when the breath emitted from them is concentrated and intense. For the impacts on the external air must be of that kind, and it is in this way that they will best travel to the ear in a solid mass.
>
> ...
>
> The reeds of oboes must be solid and smooth and even, so that the breath may pass through smoothly and evenly, without being dispersed. Therefore mouthpieces which have been well steeped and soaked in grease give a pleasant sound, while those which are dry produce less agreeable notes.⁶

Aristotle was also an interested observer of music and musicians. He recognized the difference between the musical and the unmusical performance⁷ and he noticed that quality of birth or wealth was not the factor that resulted in a good player.⁸ In various places, Aristotle mentions the institution of the chorus, how it is supported,⁹ that the conductors should be elected,¹⁰ and the modes in which their music was composed.¹¹ The breadth of observations which he lists in his *Problemata*, in a chapter devoted to music, is very impressive. Among them are,

---

² *De Partibus Animalium*, II.6. Unless otherwise noted, all translations are from *The Works of Aristotle* (Oxford: Clarendon Press).

³ *De Generatione Animalium*, V.2.

⁴ ibid., II.6.

⁵ ibid., IV.2.

⁶ *De Audibilibus*, 802a.9, and 802b.19.

⁷ *Coming-to-be and Passing-away*, II.6.

⁸ *Politica*, 1283a.

⁹ *Atheniensium Respublica*, 56.2.

¹⁰ *Politica*, 1299a.17.

¹¹ *Problemata*, 922b.10. He says they do not use Hypodorian or Hypophrygian, but like everyone else in ancient Greece, he assumes the reader knows what these terms mean. He only reminds us that the first was 'magnificent and steadfast,' and that the second had 'the character of action.'

> A sound made by a chorus travels farther than that of a solo singer.
> Most people prefer hearing music they already know.
> Most people prefer to hear an accompanied singer, rather than a solo singer.
> Low notes which are out of tune are more noticeable than high notes which are out of tune.
> A large chorus keeps better time than a smaller one.

The interesting thing is, while we have numerous observations of, and references to, music throughout his writings, and while he once specifically mentions the concert hall in Athens,[12] he never once mentions a specific musical performance nor does he ever speak of music in personal terms.[13] We believe the reason for this is that, like his teacher Plato, the world of *reason* was where he felt most comfortable and that he sensed correctly that music did not belong to that world.

Before we look at Aristotle's comments on music education, we should like to mention his views on a few topics which will help the reader understand the perspective from which he viewed music and music education. Like Plato before him, Aristotle attributes to the 'soul' everything in the nature of perception, the senses, etc. He also concluded that the soul must be both rational and non-rational, a discovery which he attributes to his teacher Plato.[14] And like his teacher, Aristotle had a strong bias toward the rational, but in the way he described this it almost seems that he spoke of the 'soul' as we might speak of the 'mind' as being something other than the physical nature of the brain.

> Now the soul of man is divided into two parts, one of which has a rational principle in itself, and the other, not having a rational principle in itself, is able to obey such a principle. And we call a man in any way good because he has the virtues of these two parts. In which of them the end is more likely to be found is no matter of doubt to those who adopt our division; for in the world both of nature and of art the inferior always exists for the sake of the better or superior, and the better or superior is that which has a rational principle.[15]

---

[12] *Metaphysica*, 1010b.12.

[13] While it is assumed that many of Aristotle's books are lost, we believe that given the many opportunities where he could have discussed these things in the extant books and did not, suggests that even given another hundred books, he would not have altered his reticence on this subject.

[14] *Magna Moralia*, 1182a.25.

[15] *Politica*, 1333a.17.

It is also quite interesting that he concluded, correctly, that everything of a rational nature, or as we might say today, everything in the left hemisphere of the brain, is 'second-hand' knowledge. He states this in the very first sentence of his *Posterior Analytics*.

> All teaching and learning that involves the use of reason proceeds from pre-existent knowledge.[16]

[16] Trans., Hugh Tredennick (Cambridge: Harvard University Press, 1960).

In another place,[17] he expands on the twin rational and non-rational soul. Here, while Aristotle suggests that the rational includes the intellect, the non-rational includes 'character.' Character has to do with moral 'virtue' and while Aristotle does not use the word, it is clear that he believed that this kind of learning is largely *experiential* (thus, non-rational) in nature.

[17] *Ethica Nicomachea*, 1138b.35.

> Of all the things that come to us by nature we first acquire the potentiality and later exhibit the activity (this is plain in the case of the senses; for it was not by often seeing or often hearing that we got these senses, but on the contrary we had them before we used them, and did not come to have them by using them); but the virtues we get by first exercising them, as also happens in the case of the arts as well. For the things we have to learn before we can do them, we learn by doing them, e.g. men become builders by building and lyre players by playing the lyre; so too we become just by doing just acts, temperate by doing temperate acts, brave by doing brave acts ...
> It is from the same causes and by the same means that every virtue is both produced and destroyed, and similarly every art; for it is from playing the lyre that both good and bad lyre players are produced ... For if this were not so, there would have been no need of a teacher, but all men would have been born good or bad at their craft. This, then, is the case with the virtues also ... Thus, in one word, *states of character arise out of like activities*. This is why the activities we exhibit must be of a certain kind; it is because the states of character correspond to the differences between these. It makes no small difference, then, whether we form habits of one kind or another from our very youth; it makes a very great difference, or rather *all* the difference.[18]

[18] ibid., 1103a.25 and following.

It is also most interesting that Aristotle recognized that the voice is in some way also the voice of the soul.

> Voice is a kind of sound characteristic of what has soul in it; nothing that is without soul utters voice, it being only by a metaphor that we speak of the voice of the aulos or the lyre or generally of what (being

without soul) possesses the power of producing a succession of notes which differ in length and pitch and timbre. The metaphor is based on the fact that all these differences are found also in voice.[19]

[19] *De Anima*, 420b.5.

The voice is also one representation of the emotions of the soul, something which Aristotle finds universal in character.

Words spoken are symbols or signs of emotions or impressions of the soul; written words are the symbols of words spoken. As writing, so also is speech not the same for all races of men. But the emotions themselves, of which these words are primarily signs, are the same for the whole of mankind.[20]

[20] *On Interpretation*, I, trans., Harold P. Cook (Cambridge: Harvard University Press, 1962).

Regarding universality, in his *Politica* Aristotle makes an interesting observation, which he felt was not necessary of explanation.

The many are better judges than a single man of music and poetry.[21]

[21] *Politica*, III, 1281b.8.

With this background we can understand how Aristotle associated the language of words and the language of music as being somehow similar. To the extent that both of them represented something real, they themselves are ends and not means.

Knowledge, the genus, we define by a reference to something beyond it, for knowledge is knowledge *of* something. Particular branches, however, of knowledge are not thus explained. For example, we do not define by a reference to something external a knowledge of grammar or music. For these, if in some sense relations, can only be taken for such in respect of their genus or knowledge. That is to say, we call grammar the knowledge, *not* grammar, of something, and music we call, in like manner, the knowledge, *not* music, of something.[22]

[22] *Categories*, VIII. In *Topica*, I, x, Aristotle again says that grammar and music 'seem to be similar and akin.'

As Aristotle found emotions to be universal, it should be no surprise that he found music to also be universal. Why, he asks, do all men love music? Aristotle, always seeking the rational rather than the experiential explanation, seemed to find his answer partly in nature and partly as an expression of his theory of 'Opposites.'

Is it because we naturally rejoice in natural movements? This is shown by the fact that children rejoice in [rhythm and melody] as soon as they are born. Now we delight in the various types of melody for their

> moral character, but we delight in rhythm because it contains a familiar and ordered number and moves in a regular manner; for ordered movement is naturally more akin to us than disordered, and is therefore more in accordance with nature ... We delight in concord because it is the mingling of contraries which stand in proportion to one another. Proportion, then, is order, which, as we have said, is naturally pleasant.[23]

[23] *Problemata*, 920b.28.

He associated music with the soul, but he was perplexed at how changes in the soul could take place.

> How [can] 'alterations' in the soul take place? How, for example, could the change from being musical to being unmusical occur, or could memory or forgetfulness occur?[24]

[24] *Coming-to-be and Passing-away*, 6.

The answer to this, he says, is the task for another investigation—which, unfortunately, we do not possess.

Among his comments on the subject of pleasure, Aristotle notes that pleasure is always associated with some activity, from which follows several observations. Since no one is capable of continuous activity, there can be no such thing as continuous pleasure. Next, every man is most active about 'those things and with those faculties that he loves most, thus the musician is active with his hearing in reference to melodies, etc.'[25] Thus it also follows that when we are enjoying pleasure we love, our concentration with that sense can prevent pleasures of the other senses.

[25] ibid., 1175a.10.

> This will be even more apparent from the fact that activities are hindered by pleasures arising from other sources. For people who are fond of playing the aulos are incapable of attending to arguments if they overhear some one playing the aulos, since they enjoy aulos playing more than the activity in hand; so the pleasure connected with aulos playing destroys the activity concerned with argument.[26]

[26] ibid., 1175b. Aristotle, rather unwittingly, here hits upon the fundamental problem of music for the voice: the listener simply can not concentrate on the 'music' (right hemisphere) and the words (left hemisphere) at the same time equally with both hemispheres. The whole era of the recitative and aria was one solution, or perhaps we should say avoidance, for the 'solution' was to merely take turns.

Those activities are most desirable which are desirable in themselves and from which nothing is sought beyond the activity.[27] Pleasant amusements are of this nature; we choose them not for the sake of other things.

[27] ibid., 1176b.5.

Finally, he returns to character and contends that the best pleasures are those which contribute to the virtuous life.

> The happy life is thought to be virtuous; now a virtuous life requires exertion, and does not consist in amusement. And we say that serious things are better than laughable things and those connected with amusement, and that the activity of the better of any two things ... is the more serious.[28]

[28] ibid., 1177a.

Finally, before considering Aristotle's thoughts on music education, it is important that the reader understand a few of his beliefs about music in general. This is a subject which, unfortunately, Aristotle does not address at length. We wish he had devoted the same careful attention to the definition of aesthetic music that he gave to drama, or perhaps he did and the book has been lost.

First, he establishes his definition of art: Art is not the object itself, but the *creation* of the object. It is also quite interesting to read that he also believed a certain unpredictability is inherent in the process of creation.

> All art is concerned with coming into being, i.e., with contriving and considering how something may come into being which is capable of either being or not being, and whose origin is in the maker and not in the thing made; for art is concerned neither with things that are, or come into being, by necessity, nor with things that do so in accordance with nature (since these have their origin in themselves). Making and acting being different, art must be a matter of making, not of acting. And in a sense chance and art are concerned with the same objects; as Agathon says, 'art loves chance and chance loves art.' Art, then, as has been said, is a state concerned with making, involving a true course of reasoning, and lack of art on the contrary is a state concerned with making, involving a false course of reasoning; both are concerned with the variable.[29]

[29] ibid., 1140a.

One definition of *good art*, he points out, is that art in which 'it is not possible either to take away or to add anything.'[30] Another definition of good art is that it must be 'good,' in the sense of moral virtue, the standard by which Aristotle measures everything.

[30] ibid., 1106b.8.

> We must see that every science and art has an end, and that too a good one; for no science or art exists for the sake of evil. Since then in all the arts the end is good, it is plain that the end of the best art will be the best good.[31]

[31] *Magna Moralia*, 1182a.33.

Aristotle gives us an illustration of this with respect to music, and at the same time a definition of 'a musical man.'

> A good man is one that delights in virtuous actions and is vexed at vicious ones, as a musical man enjoys beautiful melodies but is pained at bad ones.[32]

[32] *Ethica Nicomachea*, 1170a.9.

In another place where Aristotle addresses the good, or the virtuous, in art, he separates the *art* from the *end* and observes that in some cases the end may be good (high in character), but not the art that creates it ('the activity').

> Every art and every inquiry, and similarly every action and pursuit, is thought to aim at some good; and for this reason the good has rightly been declared to be that at which all things aim. But a certain difference is found among ends; some are activities, others are products apart from the activities that produce them. Where there are ends apart from the actions, it is the nature of the products to be better than the activities.[33]

[33] ibid., 1094a.

What he means here, in the case of music, is that while music is a 'good,' the musician himself is of a lower order (often he was a slave). This is a reflection of the way many people at the top of Greek society thought at this time. Plutarch states this view very vividly in his biography of Pericles.

> Many times ... when we are pleased with the work, we slight and set little by the workman or artist himself, as, for instance, in perfumes and purple dyes, we are taken with the things themselves well enough, but do not think dyers and perfumers otherwise than low and sordid people. It was not said amis by Antisthenes, when people told him that one Ismenias was an excellent aulos player, 'It may be so,' said he, 'but he is but a wretched human being, otherwise he would not have been an excellent aulos player.'[34]

[34] Plutarch, *Lives*, 'Pericles.'

There is no question that Aristotle shared this view.

Why is it that some men spend their time in pursuits which they have chosen, though these are sometimes mean, rather than in more honorable professions? Why, for example, should a man who chooses to be a conjurer or an actor or an aulos player prefer these callings to that of an astronomer or an orator?[35]

There are only two places where Aristotle hints at what his concept of high art might have been with respect to the actual musical literature. The first is his observation that we get the most pleasure in hearing music which is 'expressive of meaning.'[36] The second is his judgment that 'a woeful and quiet character and type of music' is 'more human.'[37]

[35] *Problemata*, 917a.5.

[36] ibid., 918a.33.
[37] ibid., 922b.20.

On Music Education

In Aristotle we find a surprisingly long discussion of Music Education. Unlike his treatment of most other subjects, where he usually has a very clear idea to present, here[38] we find him struggling with the idea itself. It is as if we are observing him in the act of talking to himself, trying out arguments and testing his deductions. Or, to say it a different way, he goes to great lengths to frame the question and since the expression, 'our discussion,' appears, perhaps this entire discussion may even be formed from notes taken by one of his students. One must read the original very carefully, for after these long 'pros and cons' Aristotle will then sometimes slip in his answer in the briefest of comments.

[38] The discussion is found in the *Politica*, beginning with line 1337.

He begins by stating that education is too important to be left to the parents. Since the effectiveness of the education of the young affects the entire community in the end, it should be available to everyone and it should be public and not private ('not as at present, when everyone looks after his own children separately, and gives them separate instruction of the sort which he thinks best').

The first problem, he observes, is that people do not agree on what the object of education itself should be. Is it to make someone useful in life? Is it to teach virtue? Is it to provide higher knowledge for its own sake? Of these three viewpoints, the first seems to him most questionable.

> There can be no doubt that children should be taught those useful things which are really necessary, but not all useful things; for occupations are divided into liberal and illiberal; and to young children should be imparted only such kinds of knowledge as will be useful to them without vulgarizing them. And any occupation, art, or science, which makes the body or soul or mind of the freeman less fit for the practice or exercise of virtue, is vulgar; wherefore we call those arts vulgar which tend to deform the body, and likewise all paid employments, for they absorb and degrade the mind.[39]

[39] ibid., 1337b.3.

Some additional conclusions seem clear to Aristotle at this point. First, the same danger of degrading the mind will also occur if one studies a particular subject too much. He may well have been thinking of music here, for in later centuries it was a frequent criticism that becoming proficient in music required too much work, too much time taken away from important occupations.

> There are also some liberal arts quite proper for a freeman to acquire, but only in a certain degree, and if he attend to them too closely, in order to attain perfection in them, the same evil effects will follow.[40]

[40] ibid., 1337b.15.

Aristotle also points out that if one learns anything for the sake of his own improvement he will be applauded, but if he learns for the sake of others he will be viewed menial and servile.

Aristotle now lists the customary branches of education as: [1] reading and writing, [2] gymnastic exercises, [3] music, to which is sometimes added [4] drawing. Of these he finds reading and writing are the most useful for daily life; gymnastic exercises are thought to infuse courage; but concerning music 'a doubt may be raised.' By this Aristotle reflects his concern regarding the role of music in society, its role after the period of education. He believed its purpose should be for the sake of the 'intellectual enjoyment' of leisure time, whereas he found most men enjoy music only as entertainment.

> In our own day men cultivate it for the sake of pleasure, but originally it was included in education, because nature herself, as has been often said, requires that we should be able, not only to work well, but to use leisure well.[41]

[41] ibid., 1337b.28.

For Aristotle, 'leisure' was a very basic concept.

> The first principle of all action is leisure. [Work and leisure] are both required, but leisure is better than work and is its end; and therefore the question must be asked, what ought we to do when at leisure?

This leads Aristotle to pause a moment to consider the nature of leisure itself, resulting at the following conclusions:

- Leisure should not be merely amusing ourselves, for then amusement would be the purpose of life.
- However, amusement and relaxation are needed as a relief from occupation. 'But only at suitable times, and they should be our medicines, for the emotion which they create in the soul is a relaxation, and from the pleasure we obtain rest.'[42]
- Leisure gives pleasure; happiness is an end, since all men deem it to be accompanied with pleasure and not pain.
- This pleasure is regarded differently by different persons.

From this Aristotle concludes that the best pleasure is the pleasure of the best man, and springs from the noblest sources.[43] Therefore, education must include some

> branches of learning and education which we must study merely with a view to leisure spent in intellectual activity, and these are to be valued for their own sake ...
>
> And therefore our fathers admitted music into education, not on the ground either of its necessity or utility, for it is not necessary, nor indeed useful in the same manner as reading and writing, which are useful in moneymaking, in the management of a household, in the acquisition of knowledge and in political life, nor like drawing, useful for a more correct judgment of the works of artists, nor again like gymnastic, which gives health and strength; for neither of these is to be gained from music. There remains, then, the use of music for intellectual enjoyment in leisure; which is in fact evidently the reason of its introduction.[44]

Before discussing the place of music in education further, Aristotle first makes three very important prerequisite conclusions:

[42] ibid., 1337b.40.

[43] ibid., 1338a.8.

[44] ibid., 1338a.9 and 14.

1. It is evident that there is a sort of education in which parents should train their sons, not as being useful or necessary, but because it is liberal or noble.[45]
2. This much we are now in a position to say, that the ancients witness to us; for their opinion may be gathered from the fact that music is one of the received and traditional branches of education.[46]
3. It is clear that in education practice must be used before theory.[47]

[45] ibid., 1338a.30.

[46] ibid., 1338a, 35.

[47] ibid., 1338b.5.

But, Aristotle now wonders, what exactly does music contribute to society? 'It is not easy,' he says, 'to determine the nature of music, or why anyone should have a knowledge of it.'

- Is it for the sake of amusement and relaxation, like sleep and drinking, which are not good in themselves, but are pleasant, and at the same time 'make care to cease,' as Euripides says?[48] And for this end men also appoint music, and make use of all three alike, sleep, drinking, music, to which some add dancing.
- Or shall we argue that music conduces to virtue, on the ground that it can form our minds and habituate us to true pleasures?
- Or does it contribute to the enjoyment of leisure and mental cultivation? Now obviously youths are not to be instructed with a view to their amusement, for learning is no amusement, but is accompanied with pain. Neither is intellectual enjoyment suitable to boys of that age, for it is the end, and that which is imperfect cannot attain the perfect or end. But perhaps it may be said that boys learn music for the sake of the amusement which they will have when they are grown up.

[48] *Bacchae*, 381.

Accepting for now this definition, Aristotle next raises an important question: Do you have to actually learn to *perform* music in order to *learn* music?[49] Is it not possible to obtain the values of music without actually being a musician? Certainly, he says, it is absurd to say that we must learn cooking, just because we need to eat! Aristotle seems to be pondering the dimensions of this question relative to music education, when he asks the following questions:[50]

[49] Beginning, *Politica*, 1339a.

[50] Beginning, ibid., 1339a.34.

- Why, like kings, can they not just listen to other musicians and not learn to play themselves?
- Even granting that music may form the character, the objection still holds: 'why should we learn ourselves?'
- Why cannot we attain true pleasure and form a correct judgment from hearing others? Why should we learn ourselves instead of enjoying the performances of others?
- Zeus does not himself sing or play on the lyre. Nay, we call professional performers vulgar; no freeman would play or sing unless he were intoxicated or in jest.

'We leave these unanswered for the present,' says Aristotle. Now Aristotle returns to the original question: Should Music be part of education?

> The first question is whether music is or is not to be a part of education. Of the three things mentioned in our discussion, which does it produce?—education or amusement or intellectual enjoyment, for it may be reckoned under all three, and seems to share in the nature of all of them.[51]

[51] ibid., 1339b.10.

The intellectual enjoyment of music, Aristotle observes, is universally acknowledged to contain not only an element of the noble, but is also pleasant and results in happiness.

> Amusement for the sake of relaxation is sweet and is a remedy of pain caused by toil. All men agree that music is one of the pleasantest things, whether with or without song. This is why it is introduced into social gatherings and entertainments, because it makes the hearts of men glad. On that ground alone we may assume that the young ought to be trained in it. It is an innocent pleasure which provides relaxation. It is good, when men are resting from their labor, to let them find refreshment in music.

But, he cautions, pleasure and relaxation are relative to the past, to past toils, etc. and are not for the sake of future good. Hence, he implies, man should not make amusement the purpose of life.

In addition to this common pleasure, which all people find in music, may it not have also some influence over the character and soul? It must have some influence if characters are affected by it, admits Aristotle. And that they are so affected is proved in many ways. 'This,' he has observed, 'is obvious in the example of the Olympus festival songs. Beyond question they inspire enthusiasm, and enthusiasm is an emotion of the ethical part of the soul.' When we hear the imitation of emotions in music our feelings move in sympathy.

> Rhythm and melody supply imitations of anger and gentleness, and also of courage and temperance, and of all the qualities contrary to these, and of the other qualities of character, which hardly fall short of the actual affections, as we know from our own experience, for in listening to such strains our souls undergo a change. The habit of feeling pleasure or pain at mere representations is not far removed from [the real feelings].[52]

[52] ibid., 1340a.19. In our view, what Aristotle is talking about here comes very close to what we think the core of music education should be.

Next, Aristotle observes, even the basic materials of music contain important elements of character. Here, of course, he is talking about the ancient Greek's belief in the characters of the various modes. Aristotle accepts this without question.

> Even in mere melodies there is an imitation of character, for the musical modes differ essentially from one another, and those who hear them are differently affected by each. Some of them make men sad and grave, like the so-called Mixolydian, others enfeeble the mind, like the relaxed modes, another, again, produces a moderate and settled temper, which appears to be the peculiar effect of the Dorian; the Phrygian inspires enthusiasm. The whole subject has been well treated by philosophical writers on this branch of education, and they confirm their arguments by facts.[53]

[53] ibid., 1340a.40. The 'facts' Aristotle refers to here are unknown to us.

We need to remind the reader that no one knows what Aristotle is talking about here. The ancient Greek modes were originally names representing the *styles of the music* of various distinct peoples and had nothing whatsoever to do with music theory as we know it. But as there was no notation, and would not be any so far as we know for several more centuries, and no extant theoretical commentary, we simply have no alternative but to take descriptions such as these at face value. But there is some significance in that, for it tells us that the Greeks of this time gave careful thought to repertoire. He goes on to suggest that even rhythm has an effect on character.

> Some [rhythms] have a character of rest, others of motion, and of these latter again, some have a more vulgar, others a nobler movement.[54]

Now, after this discussion, Aristotle presents his conclusion.

> Enough has been said to show that music has a power of forming the character, and should therefore be introduced into the education of the young.[55]

In another place, Aristotle attributes one key to this as being hearing itself. He makes the interesting observation that of everything perceived by all our senses, only that perceived by hearing, specifically music, influences character.

> Why is it that of all things which are perceived by the senses that which is heard alone possesses moral character? For music, even if it is unaccompanied by words, yet has character; whereas a color and an odor and a savor have not.[56]

He touches on this in the *Politica* as well, observing that 'the objects of no other sense, such as taste or touch have any resemblance to moral qualities; in visible objects there is only a little.'[57]

In his *Prior Analytics*, in discussing facial expressions, Aristotle once again makes reference to his firm belief that the study of music influences character.

> It is possible to judge men's character from their physical appearance, if one grants that body and soul change together in all natural affections. No doubt after a man has learned music his soul has undergone a certain change.[58]

It follows, Aristotle says, that we must now return to the question whether children should be *themselves* taught to sing and play or not, for 'Clearly there is a considerable difference made in the character by the actual practice of the art.' He finds two immediate reasons why children should indeed actually learn to perform music. First, 'It is difficult, if not impossible, for those who do not perform to be good judges of the performance of others.'[59] 'Besides,' he says, 'children need

[54] ibid., 1340b.7.

[55] ibid., 1340b.10.

[56] *Problemata*, 919b.26.

[57] *Politica*, 1339b.29.

[58] *Prior Analytics*, II, xxvii.

[59] *Politica*, 1340b.25.

something to do.' As an illustration, he mentions the rattle given to infants, which prevents them 'from breaking things in the house, etc.'

At this point Aristotle offers his conclusion to this question: yes, students should be taught actually to perform.

> We conclude then that they should be taught music in such a way as to become not only critics but performers.[60]

[60] ibid., 1340b.31.

Still, Aristotle admits, there are some who say that performance should not be taught in the schools as performing on an instrument is vulgar. Here he is referring to the fact that in his society the actual performance of music was being taken over by slaves. For this he offers two answers, the first being that as an adult you really are not capable of judging performance unless you yourself have been a performer when you were young.[61]

[61] ibid., 1340b.35.

Second, the extent to which there is a 'vulgarizing effect' on the student depends on questions such as how much music education freemen should pursue, what melodies and rhythms they are allowed to use and what instruments are employed in teaching them to play, for even the instrument makes a difference. Without further discussion of these three qualifications here, he states that

> it is quite possible that certain methods of teaching and learning music do really have a degrading effect. It is evident then that the learning of music ought not to impede the business of riper years, or to degrade the body or render it unfit for civil or military training.[62]

[62] ibid., 1341a.5.

Again, after not giving us any further information about this critical concern about teaching methods, he simply observes,

> The right measure will be attained if students of music stop short of the arts which are practiced in professional contests, and do not seek to acquire those fantastic marvels of execution which are now the fashion in such contests, and from these have passed into education.[63]

[63] ibid., 1341a.10.

His final word seems to be, Yes, teach performance in the schools—but not too much. Almost as an after thought, he adds to this a quality of repertoire requirement.

> Let the young practice even such music as we have prescribed, only until they are able to feel delight in noble melodies and rhythms, and not merely in that common part of music in which every slave or child and even some animals find pleasure.[64]

Now, Aristotle turns to the question of which instruments should be used in the schools. He finds the aulos and the lyre [harp], the usual instruments of professional players, simply too difficult for students. With regard to the aulos, he has three additional concerns which make this instrument unsuitable for public education.

> The aulos is not an instrument which is expressive of moral character; it is too exciting. The proper time for using it is when the performance aims not at instruction, but at the relief of the passions.[65]
> ...
> Another objection is that when you play aulos you cannot at the same time sing—thus detracting from its educational value. The ancients therefore were right in forbidding the aulos to youths and freemen, although they had once allowed it.[66]
> ...
> Also it distorts the face, as the old myth goes.

Finally, because the professional player, in Aristotle's experience, cannot resist being influenced by the popular taste of the audience, the subsequent influence of this dimension on the character of the player represents yet another reason why an emphasis on a high level of performance is not appropriate to public education.

> Thus then we reject the professional instruments and also the professional mode of education in music (and by professional we mean that which is adopted in contests), for in this the performer practices the art, not for the sake of his own improvement, but in order to give pleasure, and that of a vulgar sort, to his hearers ... The result is that the performers are vulgarized, for the end at which they aim is bad. The vulgarity of the spectator tends to lower the character of the music and therefore of the performers.[67]

Aristotle now considers the question of which 'rhythms and modes' are to be used in education.[68] Since these modes, as we explained above, referred to the kinds of music particular to specific peoples, the subject of this discussion is in effect, reper-

[64] ibid., 1341a.12.

[65] ibid., 1341a.21.

[66] ibid., 1341a.25. Aristotle gives a lengthy paragraph here regarding the use of the aulos by the higher classes of Greece. Then, without explanation, he simply says,
> 'Later experience enabled men to judge what was or was not really conducive to virtue, and they rejected both the aulos and several other old-fashioned instruments.'

[67] ibid., 1341b.9.

[68] This discussion begins at ibid., 1341b.20.

toire. It is a very important topic, perhaps the most important topic with respect to Greek music practice. Unfortunately for us, and no doubt due to his own lack of knowledge and experience in music, Aristotle omits this entire question by saying that everyone has access to this [now lost!] information.

> But as the subject has been very well treated by many musicians of the present day, and also by philosophers who have had considerable experience of musical education, to these we would refer the more exact student of the subject.

He then provides us with a single insight regarding these lost contemporary views. He tells us he agrees with the current practice of distinguishing melodies [meaning probably music] as to their being either ethical, melodies of action or emotional melodies ['passionate or inspiring']. And, he says, each of these melodies has specific modes associated with them.

Now, Aristotle says, we should not study just one of these in school, but many for the purposes of education, catharsis[69] and intellectual enjoyment. You use them all, but not in the same manner.

> In education the most ethical modes are to be preferred, but in listening to the performances of others we may admit the modes of action and passions also. For feelings such as pity and fear, or, again, enthusiasm, exist very strongly in some souls, and have more or less influence over all. Some persons fall into a religious frenzy, whom we see as a result of the sacred melodies—when they have used the melodies that excite the soul to mystic frenzy—restored as though they had found healing and purgation. Those who are influenced by pity and fear, and every emotional nature, must have a like experience, and others in so far as each is susceptible to such emotions, and all are in a manner purged and their souls lightened and delighted. The purgative melodies likewise give an innocent pleasure to mankind.[70]

After this discussion of catharsis, Aristotle adds that it would be a good idea if musicians also used these modes in the theater.

> Such are the modes and the melodies in which those who perform music at the theater should be invited to compete. But since the spectators are of two kinds—the one free and educated, and the other a vulgar crowd composed of mechanics, laborers, and the like—there ought to be contests and exhibitions instituted for the relaxation of the second class also. And the music will correspond to their minds; for as

[69] He says here that he will discuss this later in a book on poetry [meaning playwriting], and he does.

[70] ibid., 1342a. Some of these modes were apparently so associated with particular forms, that Aristotle cites [1342b.] an instance of a performer who attempted to perform a dithyramb, 'acknowledged to be Phrygian,' in the Dorian and could not do it.

their minds are perverted from the natural state, so there are perverted modes and highly strung and unnaturally colored melodies. A man receives pleasure from what is natural to him, and therefore professional musicians may be allowed to practice this lower sort of music before an audience of a lower type.[71]

[71] ibid., 1342a.17.

Returning to the subject of education, and particularly the subject of character building, Aristotle limits the appropriate styles.

But for education the ethical modes should be used, such as Dorian ... All men agree that the Dorian music is the gravest and manliest. And whereas we say that the extremes should be avoided and the mean followed, and whereas the Dorian is a mean between the other modes, it is evident that our youth should be taught the Dorian music.[72]

[72] ibid., 1342a.27 and 1342b.14.

Finally, Aristotle defines two general principles to keep in mind: 'what is possible [technically], what is becoming.' By 'what is possible,' he is thinking of the example of older people who can no longer sing the 'high-strung modes,' and should thus 'practice the gentler modes, such as Lydian. The Lydian, he adds,

above all others appears to be, which is suited to children of tender age, and possesses the elements both of order and of education.

In closing, Aristotle proposes,

Thus it is clear that [music] education should be based upon three principles—the mean, the possible, the becoming, these three.

Before leaving the subject of education, we might mention that in his book, *Ethica Nicomachea*, Aristotle briefly mentions the question of the monetary value of education. Should the value of the education be established by the teacher or the student? While he indicates this should probably be a fixed fee, he mentions an anecdote about Protagoras, who allowed the students to judge what the instruction was worth.

Whenever he taught anything whatsoever, he bade the learner assess the value of the knowledge, and accepted the amount.[73]

[73] *Ethica Nicomachea*, 1164a.22.

A practice we might find risky today!

Female musician playing an aulos from a mosaic of a street scene with musicians from the Villa del Cicerone in Pompeii.

4 Greek Views on Music Education After Aristotle

WE HAVE A STARK TESTIMONIAL to the extent of the loss of ancient Greek literature in the case of Aristotle's student, Aristoxenus (b. ca. 379 BC), who specialized in writing treatises on music. Among the books which are entirely lost are *On Aulos Players*, *On The Aulos and Musical Instruments*, *On Aulos Boring*, *On Music*, and *Brief Notes*, all titles mentioned by Athenaeus. All that has come down to us is one chapter of his book, *Elements of Rhythm*, and three chapters of another, *Elements of Harmony*. Plutarch, who knew the now lost books on music by Aristoxenus, also mentions that the latter spoke on the value of music in forming character. Indeed, Plutarch quotes Aristoxenus from one of these lost books on the importance of early education in music. The illustration which confirms this contention is one in which the early education in good music stayed with the child and as a man it made it impossible for him to compose bad music.

> Now that the right molding or ruin of ingenuous manners and civil conduct lies in a well-grounded musical education, Aristoxenus has made apparent. For, of those that were contemporary with him, he gives an account of Telesias the Theban, who in his youth was bred up in the noblest excellences of music, and moreover studied the works of the most famous lyric poets, Pindar, Dionysius the Theban, Lamprus, Pratinas, and all the rest who were accounted most eminent; who played also to perfection upon the aulos, and was not a little industrious to furnish himself with all those other accomplishments of learning; but being past the prime of his age, he was so bewitched with the theater's new fangles and the innovations of multiplied notes, that despising those noble precepts and that solid practice to which he had been educated, he betook himself to Philoxenus and Timotheus, and among those delighted chiefly in such as were most depraved with diversity of notes and baneful innovation. And yet, when he made it his business to make verses and labor both ways, as well in that of Pindar as that of Philoxenus, he could have no success in the latter. And the reason proceeded from the truth and exactness of his first education.[1]

[1] Quoted by Plutarch in 'Concerning Music.'

In the only surviving fragments of Aristoxenus' writing which mentions the ability of music to affect the child's character, he seems a bit more hesitant than his teacher Aristotle, who took this for granted.

> Some consider Harmonie a sublime science, and expect a course of it to make them musicians; nay some even conceive it will exalt their moral nature. This mistake is due to their having run away with such phrases in our preamble as ... 'one class of musical art is hurtful to the moral character, another improves it'; while they missed completely our qualification of this statement, 'in so far as musical art can improve the moral character.'[2]

[2] Aristoxenus, *The Elements of Harmony*, 16, trans., Henry S. Macran (Hildesheim: Georg Olms Verlag, 1974), 31.

In the following century we find a philosopher, Eratosthenes (276–194 BC), who takes the position that the role of music is to entertain, not instruct. The philosopher Strabo (63 BC–24 AD) attacked him for this viewpoint, which suggests that Eratosthenes was an exception.

> Eratosthenes contends that the aim of every poet is to entertain, not to instruct. The ancients assert, on the contrary, that poetry is a kind of elementary philosophy, which, taking us in our very boyhood, introduces us to the art of life and instructs us, with pleasure to ourselves, in character, emotions, and actions ... Why, even the musicians, when they give instruction in singing, in lyre playing, or in aulos playing ... maintain that these studies tend to discipline and correct the character.[3]

[3] *The Geography of Strabo*, trans., Horace L. Jones (Cambridge: Harvard University Press, 1960), I.2.3.

The Alexandrian Period philosopher, Crates of Thebes (fl. 326 BC), a member of the Cynic School of Diogenes, for one, appreciated the musical education he had received, for he reflected that he valued not his money, which 'is prey to vanity,' but rather that which he has learned and thinks, 'The noble lessons taught me by the Muses.'[4]

It is also in the generation after Aristotle that we find a few extant records of actual instruction in music. First, Diogenes Laertius (fourth century BC) mentions one of the techniques of choral conductors:

[4] Quoted in Diogenes Laertius, *Lives of the Eminent Philosophers*, trans., R. D. Hicks (Cambridge: Harvard University Press, 1950), II, 89. Pyrrho, in ibid., II, 511, arrives at the conclusion that there is no such thing as motion. Another Diogenes (ca. 404–323 BC), founder of the Cynic School of philosophy, on hearing a similar statement, answered by simply getting up and walking around the room!

> He used to say that he followed the example of the trainers of choruses; for they too set the note a little high, to ensure that the rest should hit the right note.[5]

[5] ibid., II, 37.

Second, Zeno (333–261 BC) tells an anecdote about the educational philosophy of an aulos teacher named Caphisius. When one of his students began playing too loudly, the teacher gave him a slap and said, 'Good playing consists not in bigness, but bigness depends upon good playing.'[6]

Athenaeus records that Stratonicus (fourth century BC), as a teacher, had only two students, but in his studio he had statues of the nine Muses as well as one of Apollo. Thus, when someone asked him how many pupils he had, he would answer, 'With the assistance of the gods, around a dozen.'[7] We are also told he had a tablet on the wall of his studio which read, 'In protest against all bad harpists.'

Once when he heard a recital by the students of another harp teacher, who himself was not a very good player, Stratonicus told those present, 'The man who cannot teach himself to play because he is so bad, is seen at his worst when he tries to teach others.'

Two more views of Stratonicus as a teacher are provided by Athenaeus:

> While giving a harp lesson to a Helvetian pupil, he became enraged at the pupil's failure to do as he was told and cried out, 'To hell-veta with you!'
>
> ...
>
> To a student of music who had formerly been a gardener and who got into an argument with him on a question of music, he quoted, 'Every man should tend the art he knows.'

No early writer addresses the topic of the influence music plays on character development as an important byproduct of music education with more heartfelt passion than the historian Polybius (203–120 BC). He departs from his description of the internal wars of the period 220–216 BC to give a fervent testimonial to the role music plays in shaping the character of entire peoples. He offers the illustration of the Cynaetheans and what happened to them when they neglected music education, together with a plea that they return to this use of music to save themselves. In addition to some detail not found elsewhere in ancient Greek literature, he gives us one of the most extraordinary pictures of the educational use of music ('I mean *real* music,' he says) in ancient Greece.

---

[6] ibid., II, 133. This is retold in Athenaeus, *Deipnosophistae*, XIV, 629.

[7] Athenaeus, op. cit., VIII, 348 and following.

It is worth while to give a moment's consideration to the question of the savagery of the Cynaetheans, and ask ourselves why, though unquestionably of Arcadian stock, they so far surpassed all other Greeks at this period in cruelty and wickedness. I think the reason was that they were the first and indeed the only people in Arcadia to abandon an admirable institution, introduced by their forefathers with a nice regard for the natural conditions under which all the inhabitants of that country live.

For the practice of music, I mean real music, is beneficial to all men, but to Arcadians it is a necessity. For we must not suppose, as Ephorus, in his Preface to his History, making a hasty assertion quite unworthy of him, says, that music was introduced by men for the purpose of deception and delusion; we should not think that the ancient Cretans and Lacedaemonians acted at haphazard in substituting the aulos and rhythmic movement for the bugle in war, or that the early Arcadians had no good reason for incorporating music in their whole public life to such an extent that not only boys, but young men up to the age of thirty were compelled to study it constantly, although in other matters their lives were most austere.

For it is a well-known fact, familiar to all, that it is hardly known except in Arcadia, that in the first place the boys from their earliest childhood are trained to sing in measure the hymns and paeans in which by traditional usage they celebrate the heroes and gods of each particular place; later they learn the measures of Philoxenus and Timotheus, and every year in the theater they compete keenly in choral singing to the accompaniment of professional aulos players, the boys in the contest proper to them and the young men in what is called the men's contest. And not only this, but through their whole life they entertain themselves at banquets not by listening to hired musicians but by their own efforts, calling for a song from each in turn. Whereas they are not ashamed of denying acquaintance with other studies, in the case of singing it is neither possible for them to deny a knowledge of it because they all are compelled to learn it, nor, if they confess to such knowledge can they excuse themselves, so great a disgrace is this considered in that country. Besides this the young men practice military parades to the music of the aulos and perfect themselves in dances and give annual performances in the theaters, all under state supervision and at public expense.

Now all these practices I believe to have been introduced by the men of old time, not as luxuries and superfluities but because they had before their eyes the universal practice of personal manual labor in Arcadia, and in general the toilsomeness and hardship of the men's lives, as well as the harshness of character resulting from the cold and gloomy atmospheric conditions usually prevailing in these parts—conditions to which all men by their very nature must perforce assimilate themselves; there being no other cause than this why separate nations and peoples dwelling widely apart differ so much from each other in character, feature, and color as well as in the most of their pursuits. The primitive Arcadians, therefore, with the view of softening and tempering the stubbornness and harshness of nature, introduced all the practices I mentioned, and in addition accustomed the people, both men and women, to frequent festivals and general sacrifices, and dances of young men and maidens, and in fact resorted to every contrivance to render more gentle and mild, by the influence of the customs they instituted, the extreme hardness of the national character.

The Cynaetheans, by entirely neglecting these institutions, though in special need of such influences, as their country is the most rugged and their climate the most inclement in Arcadia, and by devoting themselves exclusively to their local affairs and political rivalries, finally became so savage that in no city of Greece were greater and more constant crimes committed …

I have said so much on this subject firstly in order that the character of the Arcadian nation should not suffer for the crimes of one city, and secondly to deter any other Arcadians from beginning to neglect music under the impression that its extensive practice in Arcadia serves no necessary purpose. I also spoke for the sake of the Cynaetheans themselves, in order that, if Heaven ever grant them better fortune, they may humanize themselves by turning their attention to education and especially to music; for by no other means can they hope to free themselves from that savagery which overtook them at this time.[8]

[8] Polybius, *The Histories*, IV.20.5ff, trans., W. R. Paton (Cambridge: Harvard University Press, 1954).

Athenaeus confirms the point Polybius makes about the Cynaetheans.

But the people of Cynaetha came at the end to neglect these customs [the use of music in education], although they occupied by far the rudest part of Arcadia in point of topography as well as climate; when they plunged right into friction and rivalry with one another they finally became so brutalized that among them alone occurred the gravest acts of sacrilege.[9]

[9] Athenaeus, op. cit., XIV, 626.

The final chapter of ancient Greece is known as the Roman Period and includes the era 146 BC–529 AD. During this period we have much extant information in the works of Plutarch (46–127 AD). He was one of the few ancient philosophers who seemed to understand the necessary coordination of the rational and 'irrational' in the way we understand it today. He arrived at this purely by deduction, not knowing anything, of course, of the true nature of our left and right brain hemispheres. He was quite aware, however, that earlier philosophers were concerned primarily with the rational. His reference to a comment about music by Pythagoras in this regard is particularly interesting, as this information survives in no other source.

> Pythagoras, that grave philosopher, rejected the judging of music by the senses, affirming that the virtue of music could be appreciated only by the intellect. And therefore he did not judge of music by the ear, but by the harmonical proportion.[10]

[10] 'Concerning Music.'

Having acknowledged this, Plutarch now attempts to demonstrate the necessity of *both* kinds of knowing. He begins by explaining how the intellect (left hemisphere) created 'reason' out of mere sounds. It is interesting that he is so close to the view of philologists today that it was a form of musical sounds in early man which eventually led to language.

> Now then, as voice, merely voice, is only an insignificant and brutish noise, but speech is the expression of the mind as significant utterance; as harmony consists of sounds and intervals,—a sound being always one and the same, and an interval being the difference and diversity of sounds, while both being mixed together produce melody;—thus the passive nature of the soul was without limits and unstable, but afterwards became determinate, when limits were set and a certain form was given to the divisible and manifold variety of motion. Thus having comprised the Same and the Other, by the similitudes and dissimilitudes of numbers which produce concord out of disagreement, it becomes the life of the world, sober and prudent, harmony itself, and reason overruling necessity mixed with persuasion.[11]

[11] 'Of the Procreation of the Soul.'

He also discussed the emotions played in creating judgment[12] as well as the value of experience. He makes the interesting confession that it was his experience which gave meaning to words, not the other way around.

[12] ibid.

> But for me, I live in a little town, where I am willing to continue, lest it should grow less; and having had no leisure, while I was in Rome or other parts of Italy, to exercise myself in the Roman language, on account of public business and of those who came to be instructed by me in philosophy, it was very late, and in the decline of my age, before I applied myself to the reading of Latin authors. Upon which that which happened to me, may seem strange, though it be true; for it was not so much by the knowledge of words, that I came to understanding of things, as by my experience of things I was enabled to follow the meaning of words.

In his 'Life of Pericles,' he makes reference to the ancient Greek belief that the emotions in music are the key to the soul.

> Rhetoric, or the art of speaking, is ... the government of the souls of men, and that her chief business is to address the affections and passions,[13] which are as it were the strings and keys to the soul, and require a skillful and careful touch to be played on as they should be.

[13] One is reminded of a contemporary of Rousseau, who said of him at the time of the French Revolution, 'He made madmen of people who would otherwise only have been fools.'

A contemporary of Plutarch, Epictetus (55–135 AD), refers to a social change in music which one begins to see after the period of Plato. Basically, it was the tendency of the Greek aristocracy to love music but have little desire to associate with the musician.

> Every art, when it is being taught, is tiresome to one who is unskilled and untried in it. The products of the arts indeed show at once the use they are made for, and most of them have an attraction and charm of their own; for though it is no pleasure to be present and follow the process by which a shoemaker learns his art, the shoe itself is useful and a pleasant thing to look at as well. So too the process by which a carpenter learns is very tiresome to the unskilled person who happens to be by, but his work shows the use of his art. This you will see still more in the case of music, for if you are by when a man is being taught you will think the process of all things the most unpleasant, yet the effects of music are pleasant and delightful for unmusical persons to hear.[14]

[14] *The Discourses of Epictetus*, trans., P. E. Matheson (New York: Random House, 1957), 308. In another place, p. 372, he says, 'for it is being a child to be unmusical in musical things, ungrammatical in grammar.'

Epictetus, in the opening sentence of his *Discourses*, makes the point that only the rational truly exists in a form by which one can comprehend its nature. In explaining this, it is interesting that he makes an association of the character of music and grammar.

> Of our faculties in general you will find that none can take cognizance of itself; none therefore has the power to approve or disapprove its own action. Our grammatical faculty for instance: how far can that take cognizance? Only so far as to distinguish expression. Our musical faculty? Only so far as to distinguish tune. Does any one of these then take cognizance of itself? By no means. If you are writing to your friend, when you want to know what words to write grammar will tell you; but whether you should write to your friend or should not write grammar will not tell you. And in the same way music will tell you about tunes, but whether at this precise moment you should sing and play the lyre or should not sing nor play the lyre it will not tell you. What will tell you then? That faculty which takes cognizance of itself and of all things else. What is this? The reasoning faculty: for this alone

of the faculties we have received is created to comprehend even its own nature; that is to say, what it is and what it can do, and with what precious qualities it has come to us, and to comprehend all other faculties as well.[15]

Today, of course, we understand that an analogy can be made between the *notated* form of music and grammar. But this notated form is the *least* important aspect of music, while the *most* important aspect of grammar.

In the writings of Athenaeus (ca. second century AD) one still finds the kind of respect for music that one finds in the more ancient literature. In one place, for example, he concludes, 'It is plain to me also that music should be the subject of philosophic reflection.'[16] In another place he quotes a remark by Eupolis, 'Music is a matter deep and intricate,' adding his own observation that music is always supplying something new for those who can perceive.[17] This, in a word, is aesthetic music. What they are saying is that in addition to 'artistic beauty,' music also had to offer the listener the process of contemplation, an educational dimension. Even in the case of the better banquet entertainers this aspect was present. They were, Athenaeus says, required

> to offer a beautiful song for the common enjoyment. They believed that the beautiful song was the one which seemed to contain advice and counsel useful for the conduct of life.[18]

From the writer known as Aristides Quintilianus (third century AD) we have an extensive discussion of music education. This discussion, which is a portion of his larger treatise, *De Musica*,[19] clearly follows the thinking of Plato, but is much more detailed. It is, therefore, valuable not only for filling in philosophical details, but because of its very existence it seems to suggest that these ideas may have been continuously held by Greek philosophers for six or seven centuries. He begins with the following promise:

> We ought to investigate whether it is possible to educate by means of music or not; whether such education is useful or not; whether it can be given to all or only to some; and whether it can be given through just one kind of composition or through several. We must inquire whether the kinds thought unsuitable for education have no use at all, or whether even these can sometimes be found beneficial.

[15] ibid., 224.

[16] Athenaeus, op. cit., XIV, 632.

[17] ibid., XIV, 623.

[18] ibid., XV, 694.

[19] Aristides discussion begins Book II. All our quotations are from the translation by Andrew Barker, *Greek Musical Writings* (Cambridge: Cambridge University Press, 1989), II, 457ff.

But first, he says, 'we must give some account of the soul.' Aristides then makes a few comments relative to the soul's relationship with the body. It is a brief discussion, because he assumes the reader is familiar with these ideas which had been discussed at length by many Greek philosophers, as we have seen in the course of this book. Like earlier philosophers, Aristides was aware of the rational and irrational aspects of our nature, which he relates to the soul, much as we might say similar things of the 'mind,' as follows, 'He who orders the universe' gave the soul two basic parts. One, reason, is associated with the divine and was given to the soul for the purpose of bringing order to the world. The other, the irrational, is attached to desire and through this the soul seeks 'after things in this world.' 'God' gave the soul memory, so the soul would not forget the beauties of 'the other world' and become interested in things less worthy than itself.

Now it follows that there are two different kinds of branches of learning. One branch deals with the rational part, it keeps this part pure by 'gifts of wisdom.' The other branch deals with the irrational part, 'as though it were some savage beast that is moved without order,' taming it, allowing it neither 'excesses nor to be wholly subdued.' The 'leader and high priest' of the first branch of learning is philosophy, the 'ruler' of the second is music.

This second branch of education is especially important for children, for they would reject mere words, as they contain no pleasure, and it permits education 'which does not stir up the rational part before its time.' Everyone understands that children are by nature attracted to music.

> Song always comes readily to all children, as we can see, and so do patterns of joyful movement: nor would anyone in his senses forbid them the pleasure they get from such things ...
>
> Since all this is so, we have a reply to those who doubt whether everyone is moved by melody. To begin with, they have failed to realize that learning is for children, all of whom, as we can see, are naturally overcome by this kind of delight. Secondly, they have not noticed that even if it does not at once capture those whose way of life makes them less amenable to it, nevertheless it enslaves them before long. Just as one and the same drug applied to the same kind of complaint in several bodies does not always work in the same way, depending on the

slightness or severity of the condition, but cures some more quickly, others more slowly, so music too arouses those more open to its influence immediately, but takes longer to capture the less susceptible.

Aristides gives two reasons why music 'captures' children so successfully, as he has just described, and in doing so he very accurately defines the true nature of music. First, unlike painting which appeals first only to the eye, music appeals to several senses. Second, while the other arts cannot *quickly* bring us to a conception of the actions they represent, music does so immediately. This is because music is not a representation of the 'characters and emotions of the soul,' but is rather *synonymous* with those characters and emotions.

> Music persuades most directly and effectively, since the means by which it makes its imitation [*mimesis*] are of just the same kind as those by which the actions themselves are accomplished in reality.

It is this character of music, Aristides says, which makes it so valuable in achieving the general aim of education, the moral education through music, as was so clearly understood by the 'ancients.'

> Hence education of this sort should attend most especially upon children, so that through the imitations and likenesses they encounter when they are young they may come, through familiarity and practice, to recognize and to desire the things which are accomplished in earnest in adult life.
>
> Why then are we surprised to find that it was mostly through music that people in ancient times produced moral correction?—for they saw how powerful a thing it is, and how effective its nature makes it. Just as they applied their intelligence to such other human attributes as health and bodily well-being, seeking to preserve one thing, working to increase another, limiting to what is beneficial anything that tended towards excess, so also with the songs and dances to which all children are naturally attracted. It was impossible to prohibit them without destroying the children's own nature: instead, by cultivating them, little by little and imperceptibly, they devised an [educational] activity both decorous and delightful, and out of something useless made something useful.

Aristides next observes that music is especially valuable in dealing with the emotions, something which the rational part of us is noticeably unsuccessful at.

> No cure could be found in Reason alone for those who were burdened by these emotions; for pleasure is a very powerful temptation, captivating even the animals that lack reason, and grief which remains unsolaced casts many people into incurable illnesses; while inspired ecstasies, if not kept in moderation ... bring on superstition and irrational fears.

The practical importance of this is for the restoration of the soul, which, he adds, has a relationship with age and sex. Children sing of pleasure; women of grief, and old men of divine possession. Thus the ancients made everyone cultivate music from childhood throughout their lives in order that the proper kind of music would have a positive impact on the soul. The effectiveness of music in doing this he compares to the 'diverting of a stream, which was rushing through impassable crags or dispersing itself in marshy places, into an easily trodden and fertile plain.'

The only ancients who had anxieties about the use of music were two kinds of people: those who were poor musicians, and popular musicians.

> Those who neglected music, melody and unaccompanied poetry alike, were utterly crude and foolish; [and second] those who had involved themselves in it in the wrong way fell into serious errors, and through their passion for worthless melodies and poetry stamped upon themselves ugly idiosyncrasies of character.

It was for these concerns that the ancients so carefully controlled the kinds of music used in education. Therefore, he notes, they 'assigned educational music to as many as a hundred days, and the relaxing kind [of music] to no more than thirty.' Unfortunately we do not know for sure what he was referring to by this statement. Most likely it was a reference to the great tradition of spring festivals, for he adds,

> Through the serious songs and dances they educated persons of the better sort—audiences and performers alike—while through the pleasurable kind they gave recreation to the common people.

With this observation, he pauses to consider for a moment the question of entertainment music in general. He notes, with disapproval, that some people dismiss entertainment music in entirety.

> Some of them have treated melodies that are conducive to pleasure as completely worthless, without distinguishing the people for whom they are suitable and the manner in which they are used.

But this is wrong, he says, and 'I say this without condoning those melodies which are altogether discreditable.' Rather the point is, as in everything else, to 'separate out the best from the worst,' while keeping in mind the true purpose of music, the moral education of the student.

> We should not avoid song altogether just because it gives pleasure. Not all delight is to be condemned, but neither is delight itself the objective of music. Amusement may come as it will, but the aim set for music is to help us toward virtue.

By 'the aim of music to help us toward virtue,' Aristides specifically means the use of music to form the character. 'Music,' he says, 'is the most powerful agent of education, rivaled by no other, [and it can be shown] that our characters commonly deteriorate if they are left undisciplined, lapsing into base or brutal passions.' Here he points to the success of the Greeks in using music for forming character. Other cultures, in failing to do this have arrived, in his view, at a rather alarming condition.

> So far as education is concerned, there are two undesirable conditions, lack of culture and corruption of culture. The first comes from absence of education, the second from poor teaching. Now the soul is found to contain two generic varieties of emotion, spirit and appetite. Hence of the races that have never tasted the beauties of music at all, those that truckle to their appetites are insensitive and bovine, as are the peoples of Opicia and Leucania, while those that encourage their spirited side are savage, like wild beasts, as are the peoples of Garamantis and Iberia. Of those among whom music has been perverted against its nature into depravity and cultural corruption, the peoples that cultivate the appetites have souls that are too slack, and improper bodily affectations, like those who live in Phoenicia and their descendants in Africa; while those that are ruled by the spirited part lack all mental discipline—they

are drunkards, addicted to weapon-dances no matter whether the occasion is right, excessive in anger and manic in war, like the Thracian peoples and the entire Celtic race. But the races that have embraced the learning of music and dexterity in its use, by which I mean the Greeks and any there may be who have emulated them, are blessed with virtue and knowledge of every kind, and their humanity is outstanding. If music can delight and mold whole cities and races, can it be incapable of educating individuals? I think not.

It is surprising to the modern reader to find how much importance Aristides assigns to this larger civic role of music. 'No other activity,' he says, 'has so great a capacity both for establishing a community and for sustaining it once it is established.' It was his understanding that music performed this role of moral education even in the pre-historic period of Greece.

> Thus it was that in the earliest times, when political institutions were nowhere firmly established, the cultivation of music in association with virtue corrected civil discord and put an end to hostilities with neighboring cities and races. It specified set times for communal assemblies, and through the celebrations and revels customary at such occasions it restrained their aggressiveness towards one another, replacing it with kindliness.

'Now,' Aristides says, 'it is time to explain what kinds of melody and rhythm will discipline the natural emotions.' Here he promises to not only set forth the principles written down by the great philosophers, but to reveal to us some of the things they did not write about—those 'esoteric secrets' they reserved 'for their discussions with one another.' The subject he is thinking of here is the way music is the key to the education of the emotions and hence the key to music education. He must do this, he says, because now,

> indifference to music (to put it politely) is so widespread, we cannot expect people with only a mild interest in the subject to tolerate being faced with a book in which not everything is explicitly spelled out.

Like all earlier Greek philosophers, Aristides assigns the emotions to the soul, where he divides them into male and female qualities. This same duality he finds in nature as well, in plants, minerals, and spices, expressed through their qualities of color or texture and their opposites.

> Passions arise in the soul out of its affinity with the male or the female or with both. Thus the female is seriously lacking in restraint, and with it the appetitive part [of the soul] is in accord, while the male is violent and energetic, and the spirited part [of the soul] resembles it. In the female—both the female type of soul and the female branch of humanity—griefs and pleasures are rife, anger and recklessness in the male. Couplings of these passions arise too: of griefs with pleasures and of anger with recklessness, of recklessness with pleasure and grief, of anger with both, and indeed of each with any one or more of the others. One could find a thousand different varieties of these emotions if one studied them in all their complexity.

Aristides acknowledges that each person has his own unique emotional makeup and that this affects perception. Also the objects of our perception have their own emotional characteristics. Thus when the soul encounters an object, through perception, it 'obtains an impression' of the object and compares it to the emotions of itself. By this he means first comparing it to the male and female natures.

> We distinguish as belonging to the female those colors and shapes that are vivid and decorative, and to the male those that are subdued and conducive to mental reflection. Secondly, among the objects of hearing, we associate sounds that are smooth and gentle with the female, rougher ones with its opposite. To avoid mentioning everything individually, one may assert that it is quite generally true, in all cases, that those objects of perception which naturally invite us to pleasure and to the gentle relaxation of the mind are to be adjudged female, those that stimulate us to thought and arouse activity are to be assigned to the province of the male.

This duality Aristides finds in the simplest elements of music, even in single notes, or sounds. 'Some of them are hard and male, others relaxed and female.' It is because of this that some melodies are suitable for the harp which would be inappropriate on the aulos, as he will explain below.

To demonstrate how character is found in melody, Aristides provides a lengthy discussion of the male and female qualities of vowels, diphthongs, consonants, etc., which reveals little to the modern reader. Although he says these same principles apply to melody with respect to instruments, he does not explain this.

It is the identification of these emotional characters in a melody which is the first step in affecting character through music education. Unfortunately he does not explain this process beyond indicating that one selects a melody of a desired character in order to introduce this character into children, 'and older people too,' in which this character is missing.

> If it is obscure and hard to diagnose, you should begin by applying whatever melody comes to hand. If this is effective in influencing the soul, you should persist with it, but if the patient remains unaltered you should introduce a modulation [meaning introducing another style of music]; for it is likely that someone who is resistant to one sort of melody will be attracted by its opposite.

Aristides next turns to rhythm, which he also considers in terms of emotion and character. Like all ancient Greeks, he associates the beginning of rhythm with the rise and fall of marching feet: those rhythms associated with the *arsis* are restless and those associated with the *thesis* are more peaceful. Rhythms composed of short syllables are faster and 'more passionate,' those composed only of long syllables are slower and calm and mixtures have the qualities of both. Compound rhythms are more emotional and 'the impression they give is tempestuous, because the number from which they are constructed does not keep the same order of its parts in each position.' Running rhythms inspire us to action, other are supine and flabby.

Since Aristides finds that rhythm is so closely associated with character, it follows that one can judge a person by his manner of walking.

> We find that people whose steps are of good length and equal, in the manner of the spondee, are stable and manly in character: those whose steps are long but unequal, in the manner of trochees or paions, are excessively passionate: those whose steps are equal but too short, in the manner of the pyrrhic, are spineless and lack nobility: while those whose steps are short and unequal, and approach rhythmical irrationality, are utterly dissipated. As to those who employ all the gaits in no particular order, you will realize that their minds are unstable and erratic.

Here too, movement is an important aspect of education, to the degree that it is an element which can be imitated.

> Concerning the art of delivery the following must be said. Of the bodily movements in which delivery consists, those which imitate ideas, diction, melodies and rhythms of a reverent and male character, and which incite us to manliness, should be seen and copied by everyone. Those whose nature is the opposite may be watched and imitated by the common people—but not all of them, and not by everyone. At any rate, people of noble nature and sound character should refrain from imitating and watching them altogether.

Musical instruments also have character, which explains why a particular listener will 'love and admire the instruments that are suited to them.' Thus he finds the trumpet to be male, because of its vehemence, and the aulos female, 'since it has a mournful and dirge-like sound.' Similarly, among the strings, he finds the lyra to be male, because of its extreme deepness and roughness and the *sambyke* to be female, 'since it lacks nobility and incites people to abandonment because of its very high pitch.'

> Are not those who have heard all these things filled more than ever with a desire to discover why it is so, and to find out what it is that makes the soul so easily captivated by the melody of instruments? The account I shall give is an ancient one, but its exponents were wise men, and it is to be trusted. Even if other considerations might lead us to doubt it, its truth is indisputably attested by experience; for the fact that the soul is naturally stirred by the music of instruments is one that everybody knows.

This ancient explanation which he promises to give us turns out to be the same point he made with respect to perceptions. Here, since each instrument has its own inherent character, and so does our soul, it follows that we are attracted to, or are influenced by, those instruments whose character conforms with that of our soul. Before continuing his argument, Aristides reminds us,

> There are two useful forms of music-making, one valuable for the benefit it brings to the best of men, the other for the harmless relaxation it gives to the common run of mankind, and to anyone there may be still less exalted than they.

Putting these two ideas together, he takes the example of the aulos, which he tells us the goddess threw away, 'on the grounds that the pleasure the instrument gave was unsuitable for those who desire wisdom,'[20] although he says it might have some value for those 'worn out by the exertions of constant physical labor.' In this regard, Aristides quotes something of Pythagoras which is not found elsewhere.

[20] In the form of this myth which has come down to us today, the goddess threw the aulos away when she discovered, by looking into a pond while she was playing, that the exertion of playing disfigured her face.

> This was also the sense of the advice Pythagoras is said to have given his disciples: that if they heard the aulos they should wash out their ears because the breath had defiled them, but that they should use well-omened melodies sung to the lyra to cleanse their souls of irrational impulses. The aulos, he said, serves the thing that is master of our worse part, while the lyra is loved and enjoyed by that which cares for our rational nature.

Aristides concludes this idea, and his essay on music education, by projecting this idea to cosmic proportions never before expressed.

> Learned men of all nations also bear witness for me that it is not our souls alone that are constituted in this way, but also the soul of the whole universe. Some of them worship the region below the moon, which is full of breaths and has a moist constitution, and yet derives its activity from the life of the region of aether: these people make propitiation to it with both kinds of instruments, wind and stringed. Others worship the pure and aetherial region: they reject all wind instruments as defiling the soul and tempting it towards earthly things, and sing their hymns and praises with the kithara and lyra alone, because these are purer. Wise men imitate and emulate the aetherial region.

Roman music was really Greek, transformed to Roman soil and adapted to Roman condition.[1]

5 Music Education in Ancient Rome

AMONG THE ROMAN PHILOSOPHERS of the Republic Period (240–27 BC) the debt of Roman culture to ancient Greece must have been a familiar topic of debate. One philosopher, Lucretius (99–55 BC), frankly admitted this debt, which, by the way, everyone today recognizes.

[1] Albert Trevor, *History of Ancient Civilization* (New York, 1939), II, 590.

> O glory of the Greeks, the first to raise
> The shining light out of tremendous dark
> Illumining the blessings of our life,
> You are the one I follow; in your steps
> I tread, not as a rival, but for love
> Of your example. Does the swallow vie
> With swans? Do wobbly-legged little goats
> Compete in strength and speed with thoroughbreds?[2]

[2] Lucretius, *The Way Things Are*, III.

But, another Roman philosopher, Sallust (86–34 BC), had quite a contrary view, declaring that the fame of ancient Greece's cultural achievements was just due to the fact that she had better historians.

> There can be no question that Fortune is supreme in all human affairs. It is a capricious power, which makes men's actions famous or leaves them in obscurity without regard to their true worth. I do not doubt, for instance, that the exploits of the Athenians were splendid and impressive; but I think they are much overrated. It is because she produced historians of genius that the achievement of Athens is so renowned all the world over; for the merit of successful men is rated according to the brilliance of the authors who extol it. The Romans never had this advantage, because at Rome the cleverest men were also the busiest.[3]

[3] Sallust, *The Conspiracy of Catiline*, 8.

Cicero tended to agree and emphasized the need for Roman philosophy to be independent.

> It would redound to the fame and glory of the Roman people to be made independent of Greek writers in the study of philosophy, and this result I shall certainly bring about if my present plans are accomplished.[4]

[4] Cicero, *De Divinatione*, II, ii, 5.

In arguing that philosophy was the most reputable of the disciplines of study, he makes a passing suggestion that one cannot be a musician unless he is educated.

> For philosophy does not resemble the other sciences—for what good will a man be in geometry if he has not studied it? Or in music? He will either have to hold his tongue or be set down as a positive lunatic; whereas the contents of philosophy are discovered by intellects of the keenest acumen in eliciting the probable answer to every problem.[5]

[5] Cicero, *De Oratore*, III, xx, 79.

As a matter of common sense one would suppose that education of some kind would be necessary in any of the arts. Indeed, Pliny the Elder once expressed a sense of surprise in learning that a sculptor named Silanion had 'became famous without having had any teacher.'[6]

[6] Pliny the Elder, *Natural History*, XXXIV, xix, 51.

A poem by Ovid mentions 'young men and shy girls' participating in the rituals.[7] This leads us to suppose that the children of the nobles of Rome had some music education. We note, for example, that one motion before the Senate relative to the funeral for Augustus was that, 'boys and girls of the nobility should sing his dirge.'[8] An indication of an even more challenging achievement is found in a procession in honor of Antiochus of Commagene organized by Caligula which called for 'children of noble birth chanting an anthem in praise of his virtues.'[9]

[7] *Amores*, III, 13

[8] Suetonius, *The Twelve Caesars* (New York: Penguin, 1989), 110.

[9] ibid., 161.

While there are only occasional hints at the existence of music schools, there is somewhat more evidence of the private education of dilettante singers. An important scholar of the music of ancient Rome mentions these singers in his survey of the general musical scene.

> In general, contemporary records indicate that the tendency to practice music prevailed, at least in public life, in gigantic proportions. Music teachers and music schools furnished dilettantes *en masse*; it belonged to the *bon ton* of every bourgeois family to give their daughters instruction in lyre playing. Rich people employed multitudes of slaves, who made music day and night, to the despair of their neighbors. At banquets there was no longer any conversation, since music drowned out every attempt at it. A veritable invasion of virtuosi of all kinds flooded the theaters and concert halls, bringing with them all their idiosyncrasies, vanities, and intrigues.[10]

[10] Alfred Sendrey, *Music in the Social and Religious Life of Antiquity* (Rutherford: Fairleigh Dickinson University Press, 1974), 379.

This Roman craze for the dilettante singer, something one finds little trace of in ancient Greece, extended to the members of the highest level of society. For example, Sulla, though a harsh ruler, was a good singer. The consul Lucius Flaccus (fl. ca. 19 AD) was a diligent trumpet player, practicing daily it would appear.[11] And while we know nothing specific of Julius Caesar's interest in music, perhaps his sympathy for it is reflected in the fact that upon his death and ritual cremation, the musicians of Rome threw their professional clothes onto the fire as an expression of grief.[12] And, in one place, Cicero mentions a conversation in which he heard of a knight who had studied music as a boy and was still practicing his singing.[13]

As Sendrey mentioned above, this dilettante activity included the female members of society, although the philosopher, Sallust, grumbles that a lady should not have too much skill.

> Among their number was Sempronia, a woman who had committed many crimes that showed her to have the reckless daring of a man. Fortune had favored her abundantly, not only with birth and beauty, but with a good husband and children. Well educated in Greek and Latin literature, she had greater skill in lyre playing and dancing than there is any need for a respectable woman to acquire.[14]

On the other hand, there is evidence that the value of music education in ancient Rome was not that of ancient Greece. We see this, for example, in a passage where Cicero is writing of Epicurus.

> You are pleased to think him uneducated. The reason is that he refused to consider any education worth the name that did not help to school us in happiness. Was he to spend his time in perusing poets, who give us nothing solid and useful, but merely childish amusement? Was he to occupy himself like Plato with music and geometry, arithmetic and astronomy, which starting from false premises cannot be true, and which moreover if they were true would contribute nothing to make our lives pleasanter and therefore better? Was he to study arts like these, and neglect the master art, so difficult and correspondingly so fruitful, the art of living?[15]

[11] Sendrey, op. cit., 391.

[12] Suetonius, *Lives of the Caesars*, Book I, lxxxiv.

[13] Cicero, *De oratore*, III, xxiii, 87.

[14] *The Conspiracy of Catiline*, 25, 5.

[15] Cicero, *De Finibus*, I, xxi, 72.

No doubt Cicero was influenced in his thinking by the fact that in ancient Rome, as was the case at this chronological time in Greece, much of the music making was done by slaves. It was for this reason that the historian Nepos (100–22 BC) wrote that the practice of music and singing was not appropriate to a man of distinction.[16] And Cicero once criticized a member of the aristocracy, Chrysogonos, whom he felt supported too much slave music.

[16] Sendrey, op. cit., 407.

> But what am I to say about his vast household of slaves and the variety of their technical skill? I say nothing about such common trades, such as those of cooks, bakers, litter-bearers: to charm his mind and ears, he has so many artists, that the whole neighborhood rings daily with the sound of vocal music, stringed instruments, and auloi, and with the noise of banquets by night. When a man leads such a life … can you imagine his daily expenses, his lavish displays, his banquets? Quite respectable, I suppose, in such a house, if that can be called a house rather than a manufactory of wickedness and a lodging house of every sort of crime.[17]

[17] Cicero, *Pro Sexto Roscio Amerino*, XLVI, 134.

On the other hand, the vast number of these slaves made possible some very large performing forces. A procession in the time of Ptolemaeus Philadelphus (283–246 BC), for example, included no fewer than six hundred singers and three hundred kithara players.[18] A similar report by Horace reports numerous aulos and lyres accompanying songs in the temple of Venus.[19] Many of these musicians were Greeks who fled to Rome after the conquest of Macedonia in 167 BC and the destruction of Corinth in 144 BC.[20]

[18] ibid., 411.

[19] *Carmina*, IV, 1, 22.

Apart from the slave music and dilettante singers there are a few hints of music education in schools after the Greek tradition, but unfortunately no information regarding pedagogy that we know of. Music education seems to have been available, but not required, in the schools of Rome from a very early period. We know that in the late third century BC, for example, the music teachers were more highly paid than those of reading or gymnastics. This education consisted of instruction in music theory and performance on the kithara, with examinations at the end of the school term.[21]

[20] Their instruments went with them, but changed names. Marcus Varro, in *On the Latin Language*, VI, 75 and VIII, 61, gives *tuba* for trumpet and *tubicines* for the players (*liticines* and *bucinator* for the other types of trumpet); *cornicines* for 'horn blowers'; *tibiae* for auloi and *tibicines* for the players; and *cithara* for lute.

[21] Sendry, op. cit., 404.

Music education on a private basis was also highly organized, as we know from a papyrus dating from 206 BC. This document is a contract between a music teacher and a young slave named Narcissus and details specific amount of repertoire to be learned, as well as specifying study on two kinds of aulos, panpipes, and kithara.[22]

In the second century BC there were also private academies specializing in singing and dance instruction, which were attended by the aristocracy. A reference to the study of music in *The Eunuch*, by Terence, suggests that such study was a social expectation.

> *Parmeno*
> Inspect him, please.
> Examine his Literature. Music. Athletics.
> Guaranteed performance in all the pursuits deemed fit and proper
> For a well-brought-up young gentleman.

During the next period of ancient Rome, the Augustian Age (27 BC–14 AD), one begins to find references to the epic poet, the ancient Greek tradition of the singer who sang of great men and events for the purpose of the education of the listeners. In Horace (66–8 BC), for example:

> Let us by ancient custom recall great men
> In song sustained by Lydian auoli: let us
> Of Troy and Anchises sing, and
> Bountiful Venus's high descendants.[23]

Virgil (70–19 BC) also mentions the age of this tradition, dating it from the earliest period of Roman history.

> Then the Salian priests sang songs
> Round the burning altars, their brows twined with poplar branches.
> On this side the chorus of youths, on that side the old men
> Sang praises of Hercules and of his deeds.[24]

In one place Horace mentions that such performances were sometimes heard outdoors by large crowds.[25] We might also presume that songs relating great battles were accompanied by the aulos, which had become a stronger and coarse instrument in Rome, for Horace mentions that such topics are ill-suited 'for the tender lyre.'[26] Virgil, faced with the desire to craft such a song, calls on one of the Muses for support.

[22] ibid., 404.

[23] Horace, *Odes*, IV, 15, 1 and 29.

[24] Virgil, *Aeneid*, VIII, 305.

[25] Horace, *Odes*, II, 13, 30.

[26] ibid., II, 12, 4.

> O you, Calliope, breathe grace upon
> The singer, and you, Muses, tell what slaughter,
> What deaths were wrought by Turnus' sword, which man
> Each fighter sent to Orcus, and unroll
> With me the lengthy tale of this great war:
> For you recall and you can tell the story.[27]

[27] Virgil, op. cit., IX, 541.

Following this ancient tradition of epic poetry, the poet Propertius (50–16 BC) attempts this kind of poem in a modern context, in praise of Caesar Augustus. In the following poem he suggests this is a new experience for him and that perhaps this kind of poetry should be done by older men, the younger poets specializing in love poetry. This, he says, is more serious, requiring a 'graven frown,' and he leaves the implication that this kind of epic poetry was accompanied by a type of lute new to him as well. He concludes with an apology that if his work is not lofty enough, it is because his art is still inspired by the goddess of love.

> The time comes for a new dance on the mountain,
>   a new rite on Helicon;
> The time comes to chant horsemen under the hill,
>   and I will now sing of battle,
>   and squads of heroes, & Caesar's Roman camp;
> And if my strength fails, still, a laudable essay
>   To try the great song brings its own commendation.
> In a man's early years, his tune is a love tune;
>   let age sing of swordplay;
>   War will be my canticle
>   when Cynthia's beauty is well inscribed in my books.
> I would now wear a graven frown & learn a new lute,
>   my spirit rising from the low song
>   taking strength out of heaven,
>   for the work needs a booming voice.
> Now the Euphrates rolls unguarded by Parthians,
>   & Persia grieves to have cut down the Crassi;
>   India kneels before Caesar,
>   & virgin Arabia trembles in her tent;
> For Caesar's hand will soon menace the rims of the wide earth,
>   & I will follow along tall among camp poets;
>   may fate reserve me that honor.
> But when we cannot reach a great statue's pinnacle
>   we lay our wreaths at the foot;
>   and so now, without means to lift up a crown of song
>   I put my myrrh in the fire with the simple ceremony of poverty,

for my verses are not yet baptized in the fountain of Hesiod,
but their tune still flows
from the bright stream holy to Aphrodite.[28]

[28] ibid., II, 10.

And in another poem, Propertius seems to imply that love poetry, such as that which he excels in, is not as highly esteemed as the work of the epic poets. But, he counters, writing love poetry is a special art, it does not come by itself. When one finds oneself in need of this ability he has, then one will have respect for him. So, he says to the epic poet, don't look down on love poetry!

And you will wish to bind down more supple verses
 without much luck, love being insufficient
 to lift up its own canticles;
 and you will then take great notice,
 & I will seem no mean versemaker then;
 indeed you may have me at the head
 of that whole not ungifted pack,
 and I do not think the young will stand mute
 at my graveside, but they will call me
 the poet of their flame who lies there.
Beware of hauteur, epic poet; despise no love songs;
 Love coming late is dearly bought.[29]

[29] ibid., I, 7.

This repertoire of love poetry is known as lyric poetry and it became so popular at this time that Horace complains that everyone is writing such poetry, even those who know nothing about it.

The fickle public has changed its taste and is fired throughout with a scribbling craze; sons and grave sires sup crowned with leaves and dictate their lines. I myself, who declare that I write no verses, prove to be more of a liar than the Parthians: before sunrise I wake, and call for pen, paper, and writing-case. A man who knows nothing of a ship fears to handle one; no one dares to give southernwood to the sick unless he has learnt its use; doctors undertake a doctor's work; carpenters handle carpenters' tools; but, skilled or unskilled, we scribble poetry, all alike.[30]

[30] Horace, *Epistles*, II, 1, 117.

Moreover, like epic poetry, this poetry was sung, as we know, for example, from Propertius' comment that he 'took to the lyre & sang.'[31] Horace is even more specific.

[31] Propertius, *Poems*, I, 3.

> You have no cause to think that *the words which I,*
> By far-resounding Aufidus born, *compose*
> *For singing to the lyre*, in meters
> All but unknown before mine, will perish.

We will give one example of this kind of lyric poetry, although it is not related to education. In this work by Propertius, which he refers to as a 'tune,' not a poem, we are reminded again that these poems were sung. He says at the end that this is no epic poetry ('you need not celebrate the Teutonic wars') and instead mentions Apollo, who in addition to being a god of music was also the god of the bow. Apollo urges the poet to abandon his love poetry as something of little value. The Muse, Calliope, however, comes to his support, telling him to continue on the path he is on.

> Apollo watched from the trees before a cave
>   leaning on his golden lyre & said:
>   'Lunatic, who asked you to muddy the fountain?
> Your glory lies elsewhere,
>   so roll your small wheels on softer terrain.
> Your book will be the lonely reading
>   of a nervous girl awaiting her lover
>   & will be put down at his arrival.
> Propertius, why do your tunes
>   revolve in wrong orbits?
> Your skiff is fast and light,
>   let your oars flash close to shore;
>   avoid the trackless sea.'
> So spoke Phoebus Apollo, & with ivory plectrum
>   he pointed out a footpath
>   moss-grown on the forest floor
>   and a sea-green cave
>   studded with chrysoprase,
>   tambourines hanging from the walls,
>   from soft stone concavities.
> And the mysteries of the Muses
>   floated among the rocks,
>   & a clay idol of father Silenus stood there,
>   & Cytherean pigeons crowded their red beaks
>   into the Hippocrene cistern

    & the nine delicate-fingered deities
    were about their work,
    winding ivy on the staff,
    measuring song to the lyre,
    lacing roses into wreaths,
    whereupon Calliope, the fiery beauty,
    touched me, & spoke:
    'Be content to follow the path
    of the bright swan always;
    shun the road of the rattling cavalry,
    shiver no airs with brass-throated war note;
Keep the stain of war from the leaves of Helicon.
    The standards of Marius stand without your help,
    & you need not celebrate
    Teutonic wars reddening the dismal Rhine,
    clotting its waters with corpses.
You will sing instead of the lover in laurel
    waiting before his true love's lintel,
    you will sing the passwords
    of drunken night flights,
    and through your artful incantations
    guarded girls may be sung loose
    from their suspicious proprietors.'[32]

During the final period of ancient Rome, the Empire 14–476 AD, in what one normally thinks of as the period of decline, one is surprised by the significant numbers of the aristocracy who still had a serious interest in music. Among the members of the Senate, for example, we know of Caius Calpurnius Piso, one of the conspirators against Nero in 65 AD, who was an accomplished lyre player.[33] The musical accomplishments of many of the emperors is also surprising.[34] Caligula (12–41 AD) received an education which included both vocal and instrumental music and used to perform in private concerts before the aristocracy. Caligula once asked a famous singer, Apelles, whether he considered he or Jupiter the greater. When the singer unfortunately hesitated in his answer, Caligula had him scourged, but complimented his voice as being attractive even in his cries of pain! We are also told that 'if anyone made even the slightest sound while his favorite was dancing, he had the person dragged from his seat and scourged him with his own hand.'[35]

[32] Propertius, op. cit., III, 3.

[33] Sendrey, op. cit., 391.

[34] ibid., 392ff.

[35] Suetonius, *Lives of the Caesars*, Book IV, lv.

Nero (37–68 AD), the most debauched and cruel of the emperors (he murdered his mother when age 22!), considered himself a serious singer and studied the lyre, with which he accompanied his singing, with the foremost teacher of his time, Terpnos. We will mention here only some of the specific educational theories under which he practiced, as is described by Suetonius.

> He little by little began to practice himself, neglecting none of the exercises which artists of that kind are in the habit of following, to preserve or strengthen their voices. For he used to lie upon his back and hold a leaden plate on his chest,[36] purge himself by the syringe and by vomiting, and deny himself fruits and all foods injurious to the voice ... So far from neglecting or relaxing his practice of the art, he never addressed the soldiers except by letter or in a speech delivered by another, to save his voice; and he never did anything for amusement or in earnest without an elocutionist by his side, to warn him to spare his vocal organs and hold a handkerchief to his mouth.[37]

[36] This information comes from Pliny the Elder, *Natural History*, XXXIV, xliv, 167, who says,
> Nero, whom heaven was pleased to make emperor, used to have a plate of lead on his chest when singing songs *fortissimo*, thus showing a method for preserving the voice.

[37] Suetonius, op. cit., Book VI, xxff.

It is from this final period that we have the only extant significant discussion on music education in ancient Rome. The author, Quintilian (30–96 AD), was born in Spain and was sent to Rome to study by his well-educated father. There he studied law and rhetoric and eventually opened his own school of rhetoric and among his students were Pliny the Younger and perhaps Tacitus. While his discussion of music education is only a part of a larger work, his knowledge of the Greek's emphasis on music education suggests that this tradition was not unknown to the Romans. It is a review of that tradition which begins his discussion.[38]

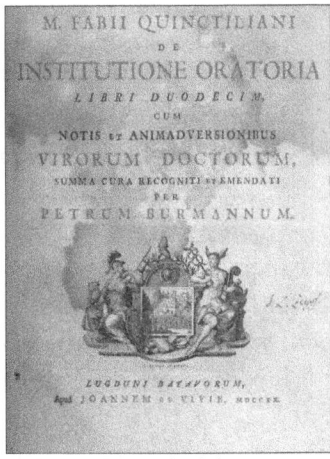

Title page of Quintilian's 'Institutio oratoria', ed. by Pieter Burman the Elder, Leiden, 1720

[38] Quintilian, *The Education of an Orator* (Institutio Oratoria), trans., H. E. Butler (London: Heinemann, 1938), I, x, 9ff.

> For myself I should be ready to accept the verdict of antiquity. Who is ignorant of the fact that music was in ancient times the object not merely of intense study but of veneration: in fact Orpheus and Linus, to mention no others, were regarded as uniting the roles of musician, poet and philosopher. Both were of divine origin, while the former, because by the marvel of his music he soothed the savage breast, is recorded to have drawn after him not merely beasts of the wild, but rocks and trees. So too Timagenes asserts that music is the oldest of the arts related to literature, a statement which is confirmed by the testimony of the greatest poets in whose songs we read that the praise of heroes and gods were sung to the music of the lyre at the feasts of kings ...

There can in any case be no doubt that some of those men whose wisdom is a household word have been earnest students of music: Pythagoras for instance …

But why speak only of the philosophers, whose master, Socrates, did not blush to receive instruction in playing the lyre even when far advanced in years? It is recorded that the greatest generals played on the lyre and the aulos, and that the armies of Sparta were fired to martial ardor by the strains of music. And what else is the function of the horns and trumpets attached to our legions? The louder the concert of their notes, the greater is the glorious supremacy of our arms over all the nations of the earth. It was not therefore without reason that Plato regarded the knowledge of music as necessary to his ideal statesman or politician, as he calls him; while the leaders even of that school, which in other respects is the strictest and most severe of all schools of philosophy, held that the wise man might well devote some of his attention to such studies. Lycurgus himself, the founder of the stern laws of Sparta, approved of the training supplied by music.

Quintilian now turns to this relationship between music and literature. He also reminds his reader that the most ancient of Romans also emphasized music.

Archytas and Euenus held that [letters] are subordinate to [music], while we know that the same instructors were employed for the teaching of both from Sophron, a writer of farces, it is true, but so highly esteemed by Plato, that he is believed to have had Sophron's works under his pillow on his deathbed: the same fact is proved by the case of Eupolis, who makes Prodamus teach both music and literature, and whose Maricas, who was none other than Hyperbolus in disguise asserts that he knows nothing of music but letters. Aristophanes again in more than one of his plays shows that boys were trained in music from remote antiquity, while in the *Hypobolimaeus* of Menander an old man, when a father claims his son from him, gives an account of all expenses incurred on behalf of the boy's education and states that he has paid out large sums to musicians and geometricians. From the importance thus given to music also originated the custom of taking a lyre round the company after dinner, and when on such an occasion Themistocles confessed that he could not play, his education was (to quote Cicero) 'regarded as imperfect.' Even at the banquets of our own forefathers it was the custom to introduce the aulos and lyre, and even the hymn of the Salii has its tune. These practices were instituted by King Numa and clearly prove that not even those whom we regard as rude warriors, neglected the study of music, at least in so far as the resources of that age allowed.

He concludes his introduction by suggesting that the importance of music education is so universally understood that he is fearful that in saying too much he risks the impression that the idea needs defense. These comments are particularly interesting in their suggestion that music education was much more the norm in Roman education than extant literature suggests.

> If there were anything novel in my insistence on the study of music, I should have to treat the matter at greater length. But in the view of the fact that the study of music has, from those remote times when Chiron taught Achilles down to our own day, continued to be studied by all except those who have a hatred for any regular course of study, it would be a mistake to seem to cast any doubt upon its value by showing an excessive zeal in its defense.

But if music were so fundamental to education as he suggests, Quintilian was nevertheless worried by the implications of the changes in musical style familiar to him. In this passage he also gives several vivid examples of the power of music over behavior. He also documents here the decay in the quality of music that others mention and he pleas for a return to the ideals of the past.

> I think I ought to be more emphatic than I have been in stating that the music which I desire to see taught is not our modern music, which has been emasculated by the lascivious melodies of our effeminate stage and has to no small extent destroyed such manly vigor as we still possessed. No, I refer to the music of old which was employed to sing the praises of brave men and was sung by the brave themselves. I will have none of your psalteries and viols, that are unfit even for the use of a modest girl. Give me the knowledge of the principles of music, which have power to excite or assuage the emotions of mankind. We are told that Pythagoras on one occasion, when some young men were led astray by their passions to commit an outrage on a respectable family, calmed them by ordering the aulos player to change her strain to a spondaic meter, while Chrysippus selects a special melody to be used by nurses to entice their little charges to sleep. Further I may point out that among the fictitious themes employed in declamation is one, doing no little credit to its author's learning, in which it is supposed that an aulos player is accused of manslaughter because he had played a tune in the Phrygian mode as an accompaniment to a sacrifice, with the result that the person officiating went mad and flung himself over a precipice.

Copper engraving by F. Bleyswyk showing Quintilian teaching rhetorics. Frontispiece of Quintilian's 'Institutio oratoria', ed. by Pieter Burman the Elder, Leiden, 1720.

In another place, Quintilian makes the curious statement,

> It is held that schools corrupt the morals. It is true that this is sometimes the case.[39]

[39] ibid., I, ii, 4.

It is perhaps in this light that he expresses concern over the types of poetry introduced in school.

> The reading of tragedy also is useful, and lyric poets will provide nourishment for the mind, provided not merely that the authors be carefully selected, but also the passages from their works which are to be read. For the Greek lyric poets are often licentious and even in Horace there are passages which I should be unwilling to explain to a class. Elegiacs, however, more especially erotic elegy, and hendecasyllables, which are merely sections of Sotadean verse, should be entirely banished, if possible; if not absolutely banished, they should be reserved for pupils of a less impressionable age.[40]

[40] ibid., I, viii, 6.

6   *How the Church Reinvented Music Education*

THE NEW CHRISTIAN CHURCH had big problems with music. For the first several centuries, as an outlaw organization meeting in secret, it could not afford to have instrumental music for obvious reasons. But, the Old Testament is full of descriptions of instrumental music in the service. How, the early Church fathers wondered, do we explain that? The answer was, we will say that all those references are only metaphors and not descriptions of real musical instruments. And so the New Testament mentions no instrumental music in the service whatsoever.

And then there is the problem of emotion, the communication of which is obviously the whole point of music. But the Church fathers were going to great lengths to create a new Christian citizen devoid of emotions. Don't even laugh, said St. Basil, for laughter is a form of emotion! But how can you have music education without emotion? The answer is, we will perform a little slight of hand and make music education a branch of mathematics—a branch of the most rational subject they knew. And that is what they did and for the next one thousand years all music treatises were written by mathematicians.

With such problems, the early Church fathers would probably have liked to just get rid of music entirely, but they couldn't, their hands were tied. Not only did the angels sing at the birth of Jesus, but Jesus himself is described as singing in the New Testament. So they couldn't leave out music entirely, but they could restrict it to vocal music. And they were able to hold that line for fifteen centuries.

The remarkable feat by which the Church reinvented music education was prepared to some degree by several schools of philosophy which emerged near the end of the ancient Greek Period which began to question the fundamental importance assigned to music by Plato and Aristotle. One of these was a school founded by Epicurus (341–270 BC) two generations after Aristotle which held that what is good is that which is pleasurable and what is bad is that which is painful. This philosophy largely eliminated the old Greek arguments about 'the Good' and introduced a general mood of skepticism about earlier foundations of Greek philosophy.

Skepticism itself became a branch of philosophy personified by the second century physician, Sextus Empiricus, to whom we shall return below. This branch of philosophy was largely concerned with the conflicting information given by the senses, as for example in their observation that honey seems pleasant to the tongue but unpleasant to the eyes; so that it is impossible to say whether it is absolutely pleasant or unpleasant. Empiricus, in one of his similar circumlocutions, arrives at the announcement that music does not even exist.

This fragmentation of ancient Greek philosophy in its last chapter led to considerable weakening in the great body of thought constructed by Plato and Aristotle. It is in this environment that we encounter Philodemus (110–35 BC), a very rare ancient Greek philosopher who was distinctly hostile toward music. We make that judgment on the basis of the surviving portion of the fourth volume of his *De Musica*, thought to have been originally in five volumes. In any case, we know of no other early philosopher who maintains, for example, that music lacks even the power to arouse or soothe emotions![1]

Among Philodemus' list of indictments against music are musicians who 'produce pieces which are devoid of significance [such as] instrumental music and trilling'[2] and the fact that music naturally 'equates with disorderliness and lack of restraint.'[3]

Music, he says, has no serious value, 'on the contrary, most of it ends up at dinner parties.'[4] Its function, he continues, must therefore be to give pleasure. But it is only a very simple and low level of pleasure,

> a direct titillation of the ear in which the mind has no share, analogous to the taste of pleasant food and drink.[5]

If there is any value in such a primitive level of pleasure, it would be one appropriate only to the common masses.

> The conclusion that music is profitable does not obtain. If it actually does profit any group, that group is the common people. And the common people are not profited by every kind of music; nor is this true of

---

[1] Quoted in L. P. Wilkinson, 'Philodemus in Ethos in Music,' *Classical Quarterly* 32 (1938), 174. An extant poem by Philodemus demonstrates that the philosopher was not immune to love. Here he seems to give testimony to the power of romantic music, although he notes he does not understand how it works!

> Xanthippe's touch on the lyre, and her talk, and her speaking eyes, and her singing, and the fire is just alight, will burn thee, my heart, but from what beginning or when or how I know not. Thou, unhappy heart, shalt know when thou are smoldering. [*Greek Anthology*, V, 131.]

[2] Wilkinson, op. cit., 175.

[3] Quoted in Warren D. Anderson, *Ethos and Education in Greek Music* (Cambridge: Harvard University Press, 1966), 163.

[4] ibid., 167.

[5] Wilkinson, op. cit., 179.

the quantity of very elaborate music that is heard ... and not by all but some Greeks, and under certain circumstances, and ... now through hired performers.⁶

⁶ Anderson, op. cit., 166.

Certainly a man of the upper class should not spend his time going to hear concerts—they last too long, wasting valuable time, and they are exhausting and cause our attention to wander. And, in addition, there is no point in actually learning to perform music when there are already so many concerts available.

> It is a sign that men are poor-spirited and have nothing worth while with which to occupy themselves—for why should I say, 'make themselves happy?'—if they labor to learn music for the sake of providing pleasure for themselves in the future, and do not realize what a wealth of recitals is provided publicly, and the chance that we have of sharing in them continually in the city, if we wish; and if they fail to consider that when it goes on for long it exhausts our powers and begins to pall, so that often when performances are long drawn out our attention wanders. Not to mention the fact that the pleasure is not necessary, and that the process of learning and practice that our enjoyment involves is laborious, and cuts out the things most important to our well-being; nor the impropriety of singing like any boy or actively playing the lyre.⁷

7 Wilkinson, op. cit., 180. No history text for the pre-Christian era suggests such an active concert schedule.

Philodemus also sees no social value for the educated person in even acquiring an understanding of music. In his opinion, it doesn't even serve to make a good topic for conversation!

> To have something to say and start the ball rolling at parties and other gatherings is not a peculiar gift (of musical knowledge), and it is not, as we decided, a thing valued by all; perhaps it might even provoke laughter if a philosopher were to indulge in it; and the theoretical side is not understood by most people, and, if it is to be mastered, demands trouble, which is a departure from the things that make for happiness.⁸

⁸ ibid., 181.

As a philosopher, Philodemus did make two important observations regarding the universality of music. First, he seemed to have come to the correct view that there is a genetic aspect of music and he found significance for this in the fact that an infant (presumed to have no Reason) was clearly affected.

> We have an innate affinity with the Muses, one which does not have to be learned. This is clearly shown by the way infants are lulled to sleep with wordless singing.[9]

[9] Anderson, op. cit., 173.

It was his next observation which led Philodemus down a wrong path. We know today that music does communicate on both a general and an individual basis. Philodemus' error was that he was aware of only the latter. He had noticed that, 'not everyone will be moved in the same way by the same music.'[10] He believed that the differing reactions which listeners had to music was due not to the music itself, or anything in it, but simply to the varying moods of the listeners themselves. He failed to understand that it is the experience of the listener which affects his perception.

[10] ibid., 172.

> Now with regard to these things it is possible for varying impressions to be received corresponding to predispositions; but with regard to the actual hearing there is no difference whatsoever, all having the same perceptions of the same melody and deriving like pleasure from it; thus both in the case of the Enharmonic and the Chromatic scale people differ, not in respect of the irrational perception, but in respect of their opinions, some, like Diogenes, saying that the Enharmonic is solemn and noble and straightforward and pure, and the Chromatic unmanly and vulgar and mean, while others call the Enharmonic severe and despotic, and the Chromatic mild and persuasive; both sides importing ideas which do not belong to either scale by nature. Whereas the more scientific [modern] thinkers bid us cull from each what pleases the ear, thinking that none of the qualities imputed belongs to either by its nature.[11]

[11] Wilkinson, op. cit., 177.

He assumed, therefore, that music must not communicate anything real or anything of substance. If it did, everyone would receive the same communication. He is wrong, of course, for music could not communicate anything, even pleasure, were it not through the actual musical materials themselves.

In any case, we can see here the perspective from which he wrote his book, which is primarily a strong attack against the long held educational idea that music can influence character. Indeed, the very pretext for writing this book seems to have been a rebuttal to a book by the Stoic philosopher, Diogenes, who had lived a century earlier, and who had contended that the correct use of music, 'will create a disposition which is harmonious and rhythmic in the highest degree.'¹² Regarding this well-known Greek association of music and character, Philodemus quotes an anecdote, for which Diogenes was apparently the source, of a painter who could only capture the correct character of his subject through listening to music as he worked. Perhaps in seeking another opportunity to denounce the ideas of Diogenes, Philodemus pretends to miss the real point.

> Presumably Diogenes did not suppose that music endows men with added technical proficiency. If he did, he was simpleminded.¹³

Philodemus was, in fact, well acquainted with the Greek association of music and character, as the following demonstrates.

> (They have proposed the theory) that every mode has a Tonos which relates to the emotions assumed to be present [in it]. Melodic composition, rhythms, and the rest are dealt with similarly. Therefore, as they maintain, our inner attitudes become familiarized with the modes in a kind of rapture (literally, 'in the manner of one who is *entheos*,' who has the god within him).¹⁴

For Philodemus these kinds of ideas could not be supported by Reason. This entire body of Greek philosophical claims, he pronounces, is 'filled full of "divine" inspiration and varnishing over, in a way that has no reason or order.'¹⁵ Indeed, he says, they were attempting to credit music with something which only Reason can accomplish.

> As for those who say that music makes us gentle, softening our spirit and taking away its savageness, one must consider them utter fools; for it is only the instruction of reason which accomplishes this.¹⁶

He is particularly enthusiastic in his denunciation of any notion that music can promote action.

> And therefore the musical specialist who seeks the kind of understanding that will enable him to discern the nature of the various kinds of sense perception is looking for precise knowledge in things which do not have it, and his teaching on this matter is empty of meaning. The fact is that no melody, as melody (that is, with an irrational nature),

---

[12] Anderson, op. cit., 159.

[13] ibid., 167. A first-century poem by Lucilius tells of another painter who had a somewhat similar difficulty, 'Eutychus the painter was the father of twenty sons, but never got a likeness even among his children.' [*Greek Anthology*, IV, 215]

[14] ibid., 158.

[15] ibid., 171.

[16] ibid., 168.

rouses the soul from immobility and repose and brings it toward its natural ethical disposition, any more than it soothes or sets at rest the soul that is carried away by frenzy ... Nor does melody have the power to divert the soul from one impulse to another or to cause intensification or lessening of the state in which the soul may find itself. For music is not an imitative thing, as some foolishly claim; nor does it, as Diogenes supposes, contain ethical likenesses that are non-imitative while showing in full all such ethical qualities ... as magnificence and humbleness of spirit, or manliness and its opposite, or orderliness and boldness. This is no more true of music that it would be of cooking.[17]

[17] ibid., 164.

In another reference to this same idea, Philodemus curiously refuses to believe that even the human face is a reflection of inner emotions. Today, of course, all psychologists are aware that the face not only expresses emotions in man, prenatal man, and even animals, but that the expressions together with their associated emotions are *universal*. Philodemus writes,

> Inducing to action means impulse and choice; but melody does not, like reason, impel us rationally or implant a choice. [It is absurd to say that music] somehow affects the disposition not only of the body but of the mind as well. How can it even be claimed that the body is affected? A singer's altered facial expression does not prove this.[18]

[18] ibid., 165, the final two sentences being paraphrases by Anderson.

In the view of Philodemus, if music could be said to have any effect on man whatsoever, it was not the music itself but the words which the music accompanied, particularly in the case of the use of music by the Greeks to inculcate religious attitudes in the young.

Philodemus attacks even Diogenes' suggestion that in erotic poetry music has the power to stimulate. It was not the melodies of Ibycus, Anacreon and others who corrupted the young, says, Philodemus, but their words.[19]

[19] ibid., 170.

Thus one can understand how Philodemus could find no independent place in education for music. He would have us believe that his view was widely shared.

> Many say that those who lack natural capacity are not made one whit better by music.[20]

[20] ibid., 174.

Regarding music's place in education, he proposes that while music itself cannot educate, it can serve as a vehicle to aid rational processes.

It is not the theoretical knowledge of good and bad or suitable and unsuitable melodies that educates, but philosophy working through literary and musical training.[21]

[21] ibid., 175.

The second treatise which we have mentioned which is thoroughly negative toward music, is the 'Against the Musicians,' by the second-century philosopher, Sextus Empiricus. Empiricus begins by noting that at his time the term 'Music' was used in three meanings. First, as a science 'dealing with melodies and notes and rhythm-making and similar things.' Second, to connote instrumental skill, 'as when we describe those who use flutes and harps as musicians.'

It is with these significations that the term 'Music' is properly and generally used.

And, finally, as an adjective referring to the other arts. 'Thus we speak of a work as "musical," even though it be a piece of painting.'[22]

The plan of this treatise is to first list the characteristics which most people praise in music, the views, he admits, the majority of people hold. He will then set out to prove that each of these views is false. Two of these are of particular interest to our present topic.[23]

[22] Sextus Empiricus, 'Against the Musicians,' in *Against the Professors*, trans., R. G. Bury (Cambridge: Harvard University Press, 1949), VI, 1.

[23] ibid., VI, 7ff.

One is that, like philosophy, most people believe that music helps in 'regulating human life and repressing the passions of the soul.' Here he quotes the often related story that Pythagoras once calmed some youths, who 'were in a state of Bacchic frenzy' from drinking, by having an aulos player perform a 'spondean' melody, whereupon they suddenly became sober.

The second characteristic of interest is the role of music in education, in forming character. Here he quotes the anecdote of Socrates who began the study of music as an old man. When someone made fun of him, he responded, 'that it was better to be accused of being late-learned than unlearned.'

Now Empiricus begins his refutation of all these attributions,[24] beginning with the notion that music helps in 'regulating human life and repressing the passions of the soul.' Here he says he does not concede that any melody has, in itself, any particular quality, 'that some tunes are in their nature stimulating, others repressive.'

[24] ibid., VI, 19ff.

In the case of musical tunes it is not by nature that some are of this kind and others of that kind, but it is we ourselves who suppose them to be such. Thus the same tune serves to excite horses, but not at all to excite men who hear it in a theater.

And, he says, it may not actually excite the horses, only distract them. This becomes his principle refutation, that music only distracts. Thus the drunken youths, in the Pythagoras story, only experienced a momentarily moderating influence of the music, soon thereafter to return to their original state.

As to Pythagoras, in the first place he was foolish in desiring to render drunkards sober at the wrong moment, instead of quitting the place; and secondly, by trying to reform them in this way he confesses that aulos players have more influence than philosophers for the reforming of morals.

Sextus Empiricus

Empiricus at this point breaks off with his refutation of the positive characteristics presumed of music and instead turns his attention to the question: Does the performer benefit more from music than the non-performer who only listens to music? His real concern here is with regard to the reputed ability of music to improve the character, because if this is true, then the performer has a distinct advantage over the non-trained listener. This, again, makes no sense to Empiricus.

Firstly, the pleasure felt by ordinary people is not inevitable as are those caused by food, drink and warmth after hunger, thirst and cold; and secondly, even if they are inevitable we can enjoy them without musical skill.

He provides here the example of the infant who is 'lulled to sleep by listening to a tuneful cradle song,' yet obviously has no skill in music.

And for this reason it may be that, just as we enjoy tasting food or wine though without the art of cooking food or that of wine-tasting, so also, though without the art of music, we take pleasure in hearing a delightful melody; for though the expert musician understands that it is artistically performed better than the ordinary man, he gets from it no greater feeling of pleasure.

From this observation, Empiricus concludes that there is no evidence that music leads one either to wisdom or virtue. Indeed, he believes, music often has the effect of 'making young people easily led into incontinence and debauchery.'

One has no way of knowing how representative these anti-music views were between the first century BC and the second century AD, but one cannot help noticing that the Roman Church was also anti-music in its first two centuries. In attempting to create a new kind of citizen, a Christian, the Church tried to isolate the Christian from emotions of all kinds. But the church also included music and musical instruments in the lists of 'banned' things for Christians. As Gibbon points out,

> The unfeeling candidate for heaven was instructed, not only to resist the grosser allurements of the taste or smell, but even to shut his ears against the profane harmony of sounds, and to view with indifference the most finished productions of human art. Gay apparel, magnificent houses, and elegant furniture, were supposed to unite the double guilt of pride and sensuality; a simple and mortified appearance was more suitable to the Christian who was certain of his sins and doubtful of his salvation. In their censures of luxury the fathers are extremely minute and circumstantial; and among the various articles which excite their pious indignation we may enumerate false hair, garments of any color except white, instruments of music.[25]

[25] Edward Gibbon, *The History of the Decline and Fall of the Roman Empire* (Philadelphia: Coates), I, 547.

Because of security considerations, the Church permitted only vocal music and its subsequent philosophers were quick to point out that in vocal church music it is the words which are important, not the music. We see this in a comment by St. Basil (329–379 AD) when he writes of the benefits of having educational ideas presented through singing. When Basil says it is nice that we can learn something *useful* while singing, he is talking about the words and not about the music!

> Oh! the wise invention of the teacher who contrived that while we were singing we should at the same time learn something useful; by this means, too, the teachings are in a certain way impressed more deeply on our minds. Even a forceful lesson does not always endure, but what enters the mind with joy and pleasure somehow becomes more firmly impressed upon it.[26]

[26] St. Basil, 'Homily 10,' in *Exegetic Homilies*, trans., Sister Agnes Way (Washington, D.C.: The Catholic University of America Press), 153.

In another place, Basil speaks at greater length on the educational power of singing Psalms. While he contends here that it may appear to be music, but it is really education which is important, at least he appears to give some credit to the contributing educational power of melody.

> For when the Holy Spirit saw that mankind was ill-inclined toward virtue and that we were heedless of the righteous life because of our inclination to pleasure, what did He do? He blended the delight of melody with doctrines in order that through the pleasantness and softness of the sound we might unawares receive what was useful in the words, according to the practice of wise physicians, who, when they give the more bitter draughts to the sick, often smear the rim of the cup with honey. For this purpose these harmonious melodies of the Psalms have been designed for us, that those who are of boyish age or wholly youthful in their character, while in appearance they sing, may in reality be educating their souls ... If somewhere one who rages like a wild beast from excessive anger falls under the spell of the psalm, he straightaway departs, with the fierceness of his soul calmed by the melody.[27]

[27] St. Basil, 'Homily on the First Psalm,' quoted in Oliver Strunk, *Source Readings in Music History* (New York: Norton, 1950), 65.

There is a suggestion of some kind of ongoing musical education in the fourth century by Basil's contemporary, St. Gregory Nazianzus (330–390 AD) when he acknowledges the period of practice necessary to becoming an instrumental musician.

> There aren't any boxers who haven't had previous training and made a study in good time of contests. Do you find a track runner who hasn't exercised his legs? Did anyone in his senses ever cut pipes [for the aulos], shape them, and enter a contest all on the same day?[28]

[28] Saint Gregory of Nazianzus, 'Concerning Himself and the Bishops,' trans., Denis Meehan (Washington DC: The Catholic University of America Press), 66.

On the other hand, when St. Basil poses the question, 'How should instructors in the arts correct the blunders of the children?,' he is not thinking of the blunders of art, but the blunders of behavior.

> It is the duty of those themselves who teach the arts to reprimand the faulty technique of their pupils and correct their mistakes. All offenses, however, which arise from perversity of character, such as disobedience and the spirit of contradiction, laziness in performing tasks, idle talking, lying, or any other act forbidden to those who lead a religious life, should be referred to the person in charge of general discipline.[29]

[29] St. Basil, 'The Long Rules,' in *Ascetical Works*, trans., Sister Monica Wagner (New York: Fathers of the Church, 1950), 329.

Since the Church had taken such a clear position against 'pagan' philosophy, one does not expect to find any reference to the power of music to influence and improve the character in the writings of the fourth century Church fathers—indeed, that is now the Church's role. However, when it came to the Church's *own* music, suddenly the ancient Greek discussion of the role of music on character becomes relevant. St. John Chrysostom (349–407 AD), for example, writes,

> From strange chants harm, ruin, and many grievous matters are brought in, for those things that are lascivious and vicious in all songs settle in parts of the mind, making it softer and weaker; from the spiritual psalms, however, proceeds music of value, much utility, much sanctity, and every inducement to philosophy, for the words purify the mind.[30]

[30] St. John Chrysostom, 'Exposition of Psalm XLI,' quoted in Oliver Strunk, *Source Readings in Music History* (New York: Norton, 1950), 68ff.

In referring to David, St. Ambrose (340–397 AD) uses a number of musical metaphors. Of particular interest are the ones he chooses to represent the impact of matters of faith on character. While only speaking metaphorically, the passage does suggest a familiarity with the long-held beliefs of the Greeks in this regard.

> This is the song that holy David, the instrument of God's word and interpreter of the Lord's speech, sang on a spiritual cithara. With such measures of grace he calmed his noble soul and spirit. With such song he smoothed the roughness of this world, with such sound he softened its hardness, with such a psaltery he crushed the dread fear of death, with such sweet chords he trampled underfoot the regions that are below.[31]

[31] Saint Ambrose, 'Jacob and the Happy Life,' in *Seven Exegetical Works*, trans., Michael P. McHugh (Washington DC: The Catholic University of America Press), 171. Another lengthy use of music as a metaphor can be found in ibid., 419.

The best-known of the fourth-century Church fathers was Augustine, who follows the lead of his Church colleagues in dismissing 'pagan' philosophy. Perhaps because he sensed that the mysteries of music lay outside the realm of Reason, Augustine unfortunately fails to accept that the study of music can make any positive contribution to the mind.

> Studies that are taken up with things that are more curious than solidly worthwhile—granted even that on occasion they are not entirely useless—dissipate the mind and hence must be put in our second category.

> Just because one flute player so delighted the ears of the populace, according to Varro, that they made him a king is no reason for supposing that we can effect enlargement of the mind by flute playing.[32]

[32] *The Magnitude of the Soul*, trans., Ludwig Schopp in *Writings of Saint Augustine* (New York: CIMA), II, xx.

The only value he can recommend in the study of music is a secondary one, for learning 'order.' And even in this case only moderate study is recommended.

> Now in music, in geometry, in the movements of the stars, in the fixed ratios of numbers, order reigns in such manner that if one desires to see its source and its very shrine, so to speak, he either finds it in these, or he is unerringly led to it through them. Indeed, such learning, if one uses it with moderation—and in this matter, nothing is to be feared more than excess—rears for philosophy a soldier ... so competent that he sallies forth wherever he wishes and leads others as well, and reaches that ultimate goal, beyond which he desires nothing else, beyond which he neither ought nor can seek anything.[33]

[33] *Divine Providence and the Problem of Evil*, trans., Ludwig Schopp (New York: CIMA Publishing Co.), 289.

In the above remarks by the fourth-century Church fathers, the reader can clearly see that the ancient Greek values of music to society and to man were rapidly disappearing from view, in so far as the Church was concerned. We see a similar confirmation that the old values of music were also virtually missing among the aristocracy. The Emperor Julian (reign 360–363 AD) wrote in one place of two kinds of study: subjects related to the body and those related to the emotional part of man. Here he clearly is thinking of music and suggests that noble persons would not want to devote the effort necessary to accomplish this, for 'persistent study is disgraceful!'

> And in the next place he will also observe the first principles of certain arts by which the body is assisted to that permanence, for instance, medicine, husbandry and the like. And of such arts as are useless and superfluous he will not be wholly ignorant, since these too have been devised to humor the emotional part of our souls. For though he will avoid the persistent study of these last, because he thinks such persistent study disgraceful, and will avoid what seems to involve hard work in those subjects; nevertheless he will not, generally speaking, remain in ignorance of their apparent nature and what parts of the soul they suit.[34]

[34] Julian, 'To the Uneducated Cynics,' in *Variae*, trans., Thomas Hodgkin (London: Frowde, 1886), II, 11.

In another place, Julian is much more specific in saying that the noble class now considered it degrading to study music, and especially singing.

> The fashion of education that now prevails among the well-born deprives me of the use of the music that consists in song. For in these days men think it more degrading to study music than once in the past they thought it to be rich by dishonest means.[35]

[35] Julian, 'Misopogon,' in ibid., II, 421.

It is in the following century, the fifth century, that we find our first reference to the *Trivium* (grammar, dialectic and rhetoric) and the *Quadrivium* (geometry, arithmetic, astronomy and music [here called 'Harmony']) which represent the Church's official organization of the liberal arts. This reference comes in an important book, written between 410–429 AD, by the 'pagan' philosopher, Martianus Capella, called *The Marriage of Philology and Mercury*. At this time the Church had not yet won its final battle against the 'pagans' and it is possible that one of the purposes of this book was to attempt to fight back against the efforts of the new Church to completely shut down education. At the very least it was an attempt to keep the liberal arts alive. In a poetic passage, surely Capella is actually making reference to the dampening influence of the stern Church philosophers, as he refers to teachers who kill all pleasure and enthusiasm in education. There can be little doubt that the reference to instrumental music being stilled reflects the Church's constant attacks.

> Will learned teachers ever thwart conjugal pleasures? Lovely Pleasure, used to pampering, sits benumbed, and Cupid has a pale and glowering look. Comely Flora, whose wont it is to deck the marriage couch with garlands, sits anxiously with the Graces three. Sweet Melpomene has grown quiet; she plays no lyric tune upon her flute, nor tries to sings. In short, all revelry and youthful mirth that customarily prevail, are muffled now in awe of learned utterance.[36]

[36] *Martianus Capella and the Seven Liberal Arts*, trans., William Harris Stahl and Richard Johnson (New York: Columbia University Press, 1977), II, 345.

The observations on the decay of music by philosophers, beginning several centuries before the Christian era, are joined by Capella. He clearly believed the music of the past was better. The reader will also notice here his reference to the destruction of the schools which was proceeding.

> Having long since taken her departure from earth, harmony has rejected mortals and their desolated academies.[37]

[37] ibid., 349.

Similarly, in another place, 'Harmony' says,

> I could mention countless benefactions that I have given to mankind to show you that I did not leave the earth merely because of a desire to get away, but because I was justified in censuring ungrateful mankind for their apathetic attitude.[38]

[38] ibid., 359.

Perhaps the most interesting descriptions of music itself by Capella are his comments on rhythm. Reminding the reader that rhythm was still thought of sequentially, having its origin in the rhythmic structure of poetry, and not yet a system based on pulse, it is interesting that Capella defines a tone as something 'stretched over a space.'[39] All rhythm, he says, falls into three categories: visual, auditory, or tactual.

[39] ibid., 370.

> An example of the visual is in bodily movements; of auditory, in an appraisal of a vocal performance; of tactual, when a doctor looks for symptoms by feeling the pulse.[40]

[40] ibid., 373.

For the modern reader, perhaps his most curious contention is that rhythm is 'masculine,' melody is 'feminine,' and that it is rhythm which produces form.[41]

[41] ibid., 381.

We also do not know when the Church formally decided on its historic slight-of-hand by which it took music, a language of the emotions, and eliminated all reference to emotions by making it a branch of mathematics, but this reference by Capella to music being together with the other mathematical sciences is the earliest known documentation of this being an accomplished fact.

Before the full impact of the Dark Ages set in, three men managed to write specialized works on the subject of music which give us a brief view of the value of music and music education just before the complete closing of schools for two centuries. They were Boethius (475–524 AD), Cassiodorus (480–573 AD) and Isidore of Seville (560–636 AD) and the existence of their works in manuscript copies made possible the education of musicians for centuries, not to mention helping to preserve the liberal arts through the Dark Ages. The book by Boethius, in particular, was the most influential music treatise of the Middle Ages. This work was still a commonly studied text in the fourteenth century, although yet unpublished.

Boethius was a member of the last generation who was able to attend the Platonic Academy and for this reason we find in him alone, in the sixth century, passages which reflect the ancient Greek views on music. He was a man of great gifts, as the greatest mathematician of his time, a master of a number of languages and served Theodoric as a kind of prime minister of his government. Due to his own education in the last of the ancient Greek schools of philosophy, Boethius was alarmed as he saw the systematic destruction of the ancient books by the Church. He vowed that he would personally translate all the works of Aristotle he could find and was indeed responsible for the few books of Aristotle which remained known in the West before the general rediscovery of Greek literature in the East.

For the modern reader some of the pronouncements by Boethius are quite shocking, as for example his belief that one must judge music not just by the ear, but by Reason, by 'numbers.'

Medieval illustraion of Anicius Manlius Severinus Boëthius

> Judgment should be exercised with respect to all these consonances which we have discussed; one ought to decide by the reason, as well as by the ear, which of them is the more pleasing. For as the ear is affected by sound or the eye by a visible form, in the same way the judgment of the mind is affected by numbers or continuous quantity.[42]

[42] Boethius, *Fundamentals of Music*, trans., Calvin Bower (New Haven: Yale University Press), I, xxxii.

Nothing in that statement suggests a role for feeling in judging music. The church influence here is clearly seen, as well as in the following passage where again he says that it is Reason which is the part of music which is to be valued.

> Now one should bear in mind that every art and also every discipline considers reason inherently more honorable than a skill which is practiced by the hand and the labor of an artisan. For it is much better and nobler to know about what someone else fashions than to execute that about which someone else knows; in fact, physical skill serves as a slave, while reason, rules like a mistress. Unless the hand acts according to the will of reason, it acts in vain. How much nobler, then, is the study of music as a rational discipline than as composition and performance![43]

[43] ibid., I, xxxiv.

And what did Boethius mean by the 'nobler' aspect of music? It is music's new home in mathematics. Here is a sample for the reader who might be thinking at this point that it might be nice to think of music in this way:

> But since the nete synemmenon to the mese (3,456 to 4,608) holds a sesquitertian ratio—that is, a diatessaron—whereas the trite synemmenon to the nete synemmenon (4,374 to 3,456) holds the ratio of two tones.[44]

[44] ibid., IV, ix.

But Boethius was not entirely blind to the true nature of music, the above quotations to the contrary. He admits that we find pleasure in listening to music and in one place he even testifies to the power over us by admitting that sometimes we 'cannot be free from it even if we so desired.' This is the concluding sentence in a brief discussion on the emotions music projects, and that this is even true in the case of someone who is not a trained singer.

> Someone who cannot sing well will nevertheless sing something to himself, not because the song that he sings affects him with particular satisfaction, but because those who express a kind of inborn sweetness from the soul—regardless of how it is expressed—find pleasure. Is it not equally evident that the passions of those fighting in battle are roused by the call of trumpets? If it is true that fury and wrath can be brought forth out of a peaceful state of mind, there is no doubt that a more temperate mode can calm the wrath or excessive desire of a troubled mind. How does it come about that when someone voluntarily listens to a song with ears and mind, he is also involuntarily turned toward it in such a way that his body responds with motions somehow similar to the song heard? How does it happen that the mind itself, solely by means of memory, picks out some melody previously heard?
> From all these accounts it appears beyond doubt that music is so naturally united with us that we cannot be free from it even if we so desired.[45]

[45] ibid.

Boethius is the last direct representative of the ancient Greek belief that music has the power to shape the character of the student. In the context of the first five centuries of the Christian Era, one is pleasantly surprised to read this admission:

> There happen to be four mathematical disciplines [arithmetic, music, geometry, and astronomy], the other three share with music the task of searching for truth; but music is associated not only with speculation but with morality as well ...
> Indeed no path to the mind is as open for instruction as the sense of hearing. Thus, when rhythms and modes reach an intellect through the ears, they doubtless affect and reshape that mind according to their particular character.[46]

[46] ibid. Recent clinical research demonstrates that the brain actually changes *physically* according to the music it listens to.

He is speaking of music education and in this passage he gives us our last look at the ancient logic of the old Greek philosophers and how they imagined this music education pedagogy worked.

> For nothing is more characteristic of human nature than to be soothed by pleasant modes or disturbed by their opposites. This is not peculiar to people in particular endeavors or of particular ages. Indeed, music extends to every endeavor; moreover, youths, as well as the aged are so naturally attuned to musical modes by a kind of voluntary affection that no age at all is excluded from the charm of sweet song. What Plato rightfully said can likewise be understood: the soul of the universe was joined together according to musical concord. For when we hear what is properly and harmoniously united in sound in conjunction with that which is harmoniously coupled and joined together within us and are attracted to it, then we recognize that we ourselves are put together in its likeness. For likeness attracts, whereas unlikeness disgusts and repels.
>
> From this cause, radical transformations in character also arise. A lascivious disposition takes pleasure in more lascivious modes or is often made soft and corrupted upon hearing them. On the other hand, a rougher spirit finds pleasure in more exciting modes or becomes aroused when it hears them. This is the reason why musical modes were named after certain peoples, such as 'Lydian' mode and 'Phrygian,' for in whatever a particular people finds pleasure, by that same name the mode itself is designated. A people finds pleasure in modes because of likeness to its own character, for it is not possible for gentle things to be joined with or find pleasure in rough things, nor rough things in gentle. Rather, as has been said, similitude brings about love and pleasure. Thus Plato holds that the greatest care should be exercised lest something be altered in music of good character. He states that there is no greater ruin of morals in a republic than the gradual perversion of chaste and temperate music, for the minds of those listening at first acquiesce. Then they gradually submit, preserving no trace of honesty or justice—whether lascivious modes bring something immodest into the dispositions of the people or rougher ones implant something warlike and savage.[47]

Cassiodorus also worked for Theodoric, as his public relations man and speech writer. One reads him feeling the shadow of Boethius and indeed when Cassiodorus retired he devoted himself to preserving ancient manuscripts, including those of Boethius. We see him paying tribute to the Church's new definition of music as a branch of mathematics:

[47] ibid.

> *Arithmetic* is the science of numerable quantity considered in itself. *Music* is the science which treats measure in relation to sound.[48]

But at the same time we read in him the last fading glimpses of the respect accorded to music by the ancient Greek philosophers.

> Musical science, then, is diffused through all the acts of our life if we before all else obey the commands of the Creator and observe with pure hearts the rules which he has established. For whatever we say or whatever inward effect is caused by the beating of our pulse is joined by musical rhythms to the power of harmony. Music is indeed the science of proper modulation; and if we observe the good way of life we are always associated with this excellent science. When we sin, however, we no longer have music [we are not in 'harmony']. The sky and the earth and everything which is accomplished in them by the supernal stewardship are not without the science of music; for Pythagoras is witness to the fact that this world was founded through the instrumentality of music and can be governed by it.
>
> Music also freely permeates religion itself: witness the ten-stringed instrument of the Decalogue, the reverberations of the harp, timbrels, the melody of the organ, the sound of cymbals. There is no doubt, moreover, that the Psalter itself was named after a musical instrument because it contains the exceedingly pleasant and agreeable modulation of the heavenly virtues.[49]

He still thinks of music as a 'branch of learning,' but to guard himself against some Church official attacking him for this 'pagan' view, Cassiodorus quickly amends this to read that it is educating our ability to understand heavenly things.[50]

We mention Isidore of Seville only in passing, primarily to remind the reader that there was still no form of notation for music in Western Europe.

> The sound of [music], since it is an impression upon the sense, flows by into the past and is imprinted upon the memory ... Unless sounds are remembered by man, they perish, for they cannot be written down.[51]

By his lifetime Isidore could find the art of music with no place left in the curriculum of whatever schools he might have found still open. And perhaps he was the 'last man standing' when it came to understanding the educational value of music

[48] 'On Music,' in Cassiodorus, 'On Dialectic,' in *An Introduction to Divine and Human Readings*, trans., Leslie Jones (New York, Octagon Books, 1966).

[49] 'On Music,' in ibid., 1.

[50] ibid., 10.

[51] *Etymologiarum*, III, xv, trans., W. M. Linsay, quoted in Oliver Strunk, *Source Readings in Music History* (New York: Norton, 1950). This important work, published a dozen times in the fifteenth century, has never been translated into English.

itself, and not as the Church's silly surrogate for mathematics. At least we would like to see him that way, as he looked out on a nearly extinguished educational world with no music, he warns,

> Without music there can be no perfect knowledge, for there is nothing without it.'[52]

[52] ibid., III, XVII.

Today, in fact, neither Athens, nor Nicomedia, nor Alexandria in Egypt, nor Phoenicia, nor even the two Romes [Rome and Constantinople], nor any other State glories any longer in literary achievement. The golden streams of the past ... all are blocked and choked up: their damming is complete.[1]

Psellus, eleventh century

7   *Music Education in the Dark Ages*

AFTER THE FALL OF THE ROMAN EMPIRE, the victors, the new Roman Church, consolidated its victories by closing the schools in the sixth century. This singular action was intended to end once and for all any residual influence of 'pagan' philosophy (meaning Plato and Aristotle, etc.) and to make possible an environment in which the Church itself would supply all necessary philosophical thought and would, in effect, do the thinking for the citizens. It is this censoring of thought to which Cassiodorus (480–573 AD) refers in correspondence:

[1] Michael Psellus, *Chronographia*, trans., E. R. A. Sewter (Baltimore: Penguin Books, 1966), VI, 43.

> The most holy Fathers, moreover, not tolerating harm to upright faith, have preferred to establish ecclesiastical rules at [church] councils and have destroyed the stubborn contrivers of new heresies with the divine sword, decreeing that no one ought to trouble them with new questions, but that, content with the authority of the excellent men of old, they ought to obey the wholesome decrees without evasion and treachery.[2]

[2] 'Divine Letters,' trans., Leslie W. Jones (New York: Octagon Books, 1966), XI, 1.

And, in another place,

> if anything happens to be found out of harmony and inconsistent with the rules of the Fathers, let us decide that it should be avoided.[3]

[3] ibid., XXIV, 1.

But, of course, there was an obvious price to pay in bringing education to an end and Cassiodorus was one of those to clearly recognize this.

> I have referred disputes involving sons to the senators, that they may take thought for the careers of those affected by the advancement of education at Rome. For it is incredible that you should lack concern for something which brings honors to your offspring, and gives your assembly the counsel that comes from constant reading. Now recently I came to know by discreet reports from various people, that the teachers of eloquence at Rome are not receiving the constituted rewards for their labors, and that the trafficking of certain men has caused the sums assigned to the masters of the schools to be diminished.

Therefore, since it is clear that rewards feed the arts, I have judged it abominable that anything should be stolen from the teachers of youth; they should instead be incited to their noble studies by an increase in their fees.

For the school of grammar has primacy: it is the fairest foundation of learning, the glorious mother of eloquence, which has learnt to aim at praise, to speak without fault. As good morals view an alien crime, so it views a dissonant error in the course of declamation. For, as the musician creates the sweetest song from a choir in harmony, so, by well ordered modulations of sound, the grammarian can recite in meter.

Grammar is the mistress of words, the embellisher of the human race; through the practice of the noble reading of ancient authors, she helps us, we know, by her counsels.[4]

[4] Letter to the Senate in Rome, in ibid., IX, xxi.

In fact, Cassiodorus was one of several important Church philosophers who understood the importance of preserving the liberal arts. Indeed, he was personally active in collecting and trying to save ancient manuscripts and one modern writer states that were it not for Cassiodorus, no Latin classic except the works of Virgil would have come down to us in complete form.[5]

Other leaders of the Church were moving more slowly, but we continue to read, here and there, of more enlightened prelates. A letter of 1051 by Peter Damian, for example, praises the bishop of Numana for his study of the liberal arts.[6] There is one Church leader of this period who was quite extraordinary: the tenth century pope, Sylvester II. He was one of those enlightened Churchmen who privately paid to have manuscripts copied. In a letter of 985, for example, we read,

[5] M. R. James, quoted in William Harris Stahl, *Martianus Capella and the Seven Liberal Arts* (New York: Columbia University Press), I, 7, fn. 12.

[6] *The Letters of Peter Damian*, trans., Owen Blum (Washington, D.C.: The Catholic University of America Press, 1990), II, Letter 38.

> Just as a short time ago in Rome and in other parts of Italy, in Germany also, and in Lorraine, I used large sums of money to pay copyists and to acquire copies of authors, permit me to beg that this be done likewise in your locality.[7]

[7] *The Letters of Gerbert*, trans., Harriet Lattin (New York: Columbia University Press, 1961), Letter 50.

In another letter he observes, 'I offer to noble scholars the pleasing fruits of the liberal disciplines to feed upon.'[8]

This man was also an accomplished musician, an organist apparently, and music education teacher who offered to give lessons in music[9] and proved himself capable of explaining some of the most difficult passages found in Boethius.[10]

[8] ibid., Letter 105.

[9] ibid.

[10] ibid., Letters 3 and 5.

For such Churchmen, including Cassiodorus, the great value of the liberal arts, including music, was to produce in the Christian the intelligence necessary to understanding the sermons and sacred literature.

> Beyond any doubt knowledge of [the liberal arts], as it seemed to our Fathers, is useful and not to be avoided, since one finds this knowledge diffused everywhere in sacred literature, as it were in the origin of universal and perfect wisdom. When these matters have been restored to sacred literature and taught in connection with it, our capacity for understanding will be helped in every way.[11]

This argument, that the good Christian needed at least a minimum level of education, was the strongest available for those who fought to preserve the liberal arts. Although the seventh and eighth centuries were the darkest of the Dark Ages, and a period for which we are left with little information, it would appear that this argument continued for some time for the Venerable Bede (672–735 AD), another enlightened Churchman, presents this same plea for the contribution of the liberal arts to Christian understanding.

> We are to be initiated in *grammatica*, then in *dialectia*, afterward in *rhetorica*. Equipped with these arms, we should approach the study of philosophy. Here the order is first the quadrivium, and in this first *arithmetica*, second *musica*, third *geometria*, fourth *astronomia*, then holy writ, so that through knowledge of what is created we arrive at knowledge of the Creator.[12]

But, beyond the chaos caused by the Church, there was another reason why an environment now existed in which education, including music education, was virtually impossible. The fall of the Roman Empire also meant the removal of its armies which had served as a kind of police force for Western Europe. Now towns of all sizes were left exposed to slaughter by tribes from the North and East. Consider, for example, that Paris was pillaged in 856, 861, and burned in 865. Tours was pillaged in 853, 856, 862, 872, 886, 903, and 919. It is no wonder that Gregory of Tours, in his *History of the Franks*, wrote,

Depiction of the Venerable Bede from the Nuremberg Chronicle, 1493

[11] Cassiodorus, *Divine Letters*, op. cit., XXVII, 1.

[12] *De elementis philosophiae*, quoted in Nan Cooke Carpenter, *Music in the Medieval and Renaissance Universities* (Norman: University of Oklahoma Press, 1958), 20, fn. 12.

In fact in the towns of Gaul the writing of literature has declined to the point where it has virtually disappeared altogether. Many people have complained about this, not once but time and time again. 'What a poor period this is!' they have been heard to say. 'If among all our people there is not one man to be found who can write a book about what is happening today, the pursuit of letters really is dead in us!'[13]

[13] Gregory of Tours, *The History of the Franks*, trans., Lewis Thorpe (Harmondsworth: Penguin Books, 1974), 63.

How could there be culture? Culture requires peace, as Cassiodorus points out, 'Peace is the fair mother of all liberal arts, the softener of manners.'[14]

[14] Letter to Emperor Anastasius, in *Variae*, op. cit., I, i.

What else, but the 'Dark Ages,' can we call a Europe which one writer described in 909:

The cities are depopulated ... the country reduced to solitude ... As the first men lived without law ... so now every man does what seems good in his own eyes, despising laws human and divine ... The strong oppress the weak; the world is full of violence against the poor ... Men devour one another like the fishes in the sea.[15]

[15] H. W. C. Davis, *Medieval England* (Oxford, 1928), 266.

Rome, itself, was in total decay by 700, its great institutions forgotten (the Forum was used as a cow pasture already in the seventh century) and the great public buildings and temples were dismembered to provide building material for Christian churches and palaces.

Once the schools had been closed, the clergy remained the principal portion of the population which was literate and they served as the official scribes attending to the needs of the nobles. This became a self-perpetuating problem, for why should a noble learn to write, for example, when an inexpensive scribe was available to do the work. Consequently, for centuries most lay persons in Western Europe, including kings and emperors, could neither read or write.[16]

[16] Kenneth Clark, *Civilisation* (New York: Harper & Row, 1969), 17.

The first break in this chain of illiteracy came with the court of the greatest of medieval kings, Charlemagne (768–814 AD). A naturally brilliant man, Charlemagne, observing the appalling illiteracy of his age, called leading scholars to his court for the purpose of restoring the schools of France. In 787 he issued an historic document, *Capitulare de litteris colendis*, urging the Church to establish schools. In another document of 789, he includes music education as one of his concerns as he urged these schools to

Charlemagne by Albrecht Dürer, 1512

take care to make no difference between the sons of serfs and of freemen, so that they might come and sit on the same benches to study grammar, music, and arithmetic.[17]

The result of his efforts saw the founding of numerous schools in France and Western Germany.[18] Among these were the first examples in history of free public education.[19]

As a consequence of Charlemagne attracting so many scholars to his court, we are fortunate to have historical portraits of this man and the music of his immediate circle which are unique for these dark centuries. One of these scholars, Einhard, writes of Charlemagne's personal interest in the liberal arts.

> He paid the greatest attention to the liberal arts; and he had great respect for men who taught them, bestowing high honors upon them. When he was learning the rules of grammar he studied with Peter the Deacon of Pisa ... but for all other subjects he was taught by Alcuin ... a man of the Saxon race who came from Britain and was the most learned man anywhere to be found.[20]

Another member of the court tells of Greek envoys who came to visit the court and brought a number of musical instruments. His account includes some of the most interesting details extant regarding the early organ.

> These Greek envoys brought with them every kind of organ, as well as all sorts of other instruments. These were all examined by the craftsmen of the most sagacious Charlemagne to see just what was new about them. Then the craftsmen reproduced them with the greatest possible accuracy. The chief of these was that most remarkable of organs ever possessed by musicians which, when its bronze wind chests were filled and its bellows of ox-hide blew through its pipes of bronze, equaled with its deep note the roar of thunder, and yet which, for very sweetness, could resemble the soft tinkle of a lyre or a cymbal.[21]

A very rare eye-witness of the performance of music during these years is a description of music heard at a banquet, suggesting that even on such occasions this court heard a high level of aesthetic music.

[17] Quoted in Will Durant, *The Age of Faith* (New York: Simon and Schuster, 1950), 466.

[18] Nan Cooke Carpenter, *Music in the Medieval and Renaissance Universities* (Norman: University of Oklahoma Press, 1958), 17ff.

[19] Einhard and Notker the Stammerer, *Two Lives of Charlemagne*, trans., Lewis Thorpe (Harmondsworth: Penguin Books, 1981), 95.

[20] ibid., 79.

[21] ibid., 143.

> The bishop ordered skilled choristers to advance: they were accompanied by every musical instrument one could think of, and by the sound of their singing they could have softened the hardest hearts or turned to ice the limpid waters of the Rhine.[22]

Charlemagne also took an interest in jongleurs, the earliest of the wandering minstrels, and even rewarded them with gifts of land in Provence. One scholar points to this court as the birth of what would become the *chansons de geste*.[23] An attractive anecdote tells of a jongleur who guided Charlemagne over Mt. Cenis in 773 and was then given as a reward all the land over which his *tuba* [trumpet] could be heard when played from a hill.[24]

According to another source, Charlemagne even had prepared a collection of his hunting signals called *Frohliche Jagd*.[25] While this music is not extant, iconographic clues suggest it was performed by various animal horns, trumpet-types, flute-types, drums and bells.

Charlemagne also took an active interest in Church music. Einhard describes his actual singing.

> He made careful reforms in the way in which the psalms were chanted and the lessons read. He was himself quite an expert at both of these exercises, but he never read the lesson in public and he would sing only with the rest of the congregation and then in a low voice.[26]

It was in this regard that Charlemagne once requested that the pope send him two singers who were expert in the approved Roman style of singing to instruct the various churches of his realm. These two came, but deviously instructed each congregation in a separate style. When Charlemagne discovered this he sent them back to Rome, where they were punished with life imprisonment. Thereupon, the pope wrote Charlemagne,

> If I send you some more they will be just as blind with envy as the first ones, and they will cheat you in their turn ... Send me two of the most intelligent monks whom you have in your own entourage ... With God's help they will acquire the proficiency in this art which you are looking for.[27]

---

[22] ibid., 112.

[23] E. K. Chambers, *The Mediaeval Stage* (Oxford, 1903), I, 37, who quotes Philippe Mouskes, *de Poetis Provincialibus*,
> Quar quant li buens Rois Karlemaigne
> Ot toute mise a son demaine
> Provence, qui mult iert plentive
> De vins, de bois, d'aigue, de rive,
> As lecours, as menestreus,
> Qui sont auques luxurieus,
> Le donna toute et departi.

[24] ibid., I, 37, fn. 2.

[25] Gottfried Veit, *Die Blasmusik* (Innsbruck, 1972), 20.

[26] Einhard and Notker, op. cit., 80.

[27] ibid., 103ff.

There are also two interesting anecdotes regarding Charlemagne and his Church music. In the first,[28] a choir member appeared at an important feast somewhat drunk and intoned the final response instead of the first. This monk was fired on the spot. The monk in the second anecdote was considerably more fortunate.

[28] ibid., 98ff.

One day when Charlemagne was on a journey he came to a great cathedral. A certain wandering monk, who was unaware of the Emperor's attention to small detail, came into the choir and, since he had never learned to do anything of the sort himself, stood silent and confused in the middle of those who were chanting. Thereupon the choir-master raised his baton and threatened to hit him, if he did not sing. The monk, not knowing what to do or where to turn, and not daring to go out, twisted and contorted his throat, opened his mouth wide, moved his bottom jaw up and down, and did all that he could to imitate the appearance of someone singing. The others present had not the self-control to stop laughing. Our valiant Emperor, who was not to be moved from his serenity by even the greatest events, sat solemnly waiting until the end of the Mass, just as if he had not noticed this pretense at singing. When it was all over, he called the poor wretch to him and, taking pity on his struggles and the strain he had gone through, consoled with with these words: 'My good monk, thank you very much for your singing and your efforts.' Then he ordered him to be given a pound of silver to relieve his poverty.[29]

[29] ibid., 100ff.

For Alcuin, the leading teacher at the court of Charlemagne, the primary characteristic of art seems to have been precision. He defines elequence in rhetoric as that which 'observes the rules of grammar, and is supported by the authority of the ancients.'[30] In another place he states an aesthetic principle, which he says is of the greatest importance, that what is unbecoming can give no pleasure. Here he again quotes Tullius.

[30] Alcuin, *Rhetoric*, trans., Wilbur Howell (New York: Russell & Russell, 1965), 133. In his poem, *The Bishops, Kings, and Saint of York*, ed., Peter Godman (Oxford: Clarendon Press, 1982), 113, 121.

> The cardinal precept of art is that the sense of propriety must regulate the activity of the artist.[31]

[31] ibid., 141.

Finally, in a dialog with Charlemagne, Alcuin sets forth his concept of the Four Virtues which he associated with rhetoric, and presumably art in general.

> ALCUIN. Virtue is perfection of mind, dignity of character, reasonableness of life, excellence of habits.
> CHARLEMAGNE. How many aspects does it have?

ALCUIN. Four: Prudence, Justice, Courage, Temperance.
CHARLEMAGNE. What is Prudence?
ALCUIN. Prudence is the knowledge of things and of natures ... [Its attributes are] Memory, Intelligence, Foresight.
CHARLEMAGNE. Explain now the concept of Justice.
ALCUIN. Justice is a disposition of the mind to render to each what is his due ... [Its attributes are] Religion, Duty, Gratitude, Retribution, Respect, Truthfulness.
CHARLEMAGNE. Now I entreat you to consider Courage and its special attributes.
ALCUIN. Courage is the capacity to endure danger and hardship with an undaunted spirit. Its attributes are High-Mindedness, Confidence, Forbearance, Perseverance ...
CHARLEMAGNE. It remains for you to speak of Temperance ...
ALCUIN. Temperance may be defined as the firm and moderate rule by the reason of our desires and the other wayward passions of our souls. Its attributes are Restraint, Clemency, Moderation.[32]

[32] ibid., 147ff.

Alcuin also mentions that his own teacher, Aelberht, owned the works of both Cassiodorus and Boethius and taught his students not only rhetoric and grammar, but music.

> Some he polished with the whetstone of true speech,
> teaching others to sing in Aonian strain,
> teaching some to blow on the Castalian pipe,
> and run with lyric step over the peaks of Parnassus.
> To others this master taught the harmony of the spheres ...

Thanks to the enlightenment of Charlemagne, the Church began to engage in a broader educational role in the ninth century. These monastic schools, particularly in France, joining together with the Church's need to teach the new official body of Church music, developed into the first real schools of music of modern Europe. Because of the great flourishing of monasteries famous for the cultivation of music during the ninth through the eleventh centuries, one can say that music education emerged out of the Dark Ages before almost any other discipline.[33]

One result of the development of music pedagogy in these monastic schools are the extant treatises on music and Church singing. Several of these treatises contain hints regarding the strict discipline of these choir-boy schools. One can well imagine such an environment before the arrival of notation, when teaching would have been mostly by rote. In the tenth

[33] The growth of these monastic schools is summarized in Nan Cooke Carpenter, *Music in the Medieval and Renaissance Universities* (Norman: University of Oklahoma Press, 1954), 13-31.

century *Enchiridion musices*, by Odo of Cluny, when the teacher promises an effective new system of learning sight-singing, the student replies with relief,

> he will never [again] torment me with blows or abuse when provoked by the slowness of my sense.³⁴

34 Quoted in Oliver Strunk, *Source Readings in Music History* (New York: Norton, 1950), 109.

Similarly, Guido, in *Prologus antiphonarii sui*, eleventh century, remarking on the success of his new method of teaching music reading, recalls such teaching conditions of the past:

> Should anyone doubt that I am telling the truth, let him come, make a trial, and see what small boys can do under our direction, boys who until now have been beaten for their gross ignorance of the psalms.³⁵

35 Quoted in ibid., 118.

We get another glimpse of the rigid discipline of these monastic schools when we see the unvarying daily schedule which these young music students had to observe. Here is the schedule of one of these schools.³⁶

36 Given in Joseph Smits van Waesberghe, *Musikerziehung, Lehre und Theorie der Musik in Mittelalter* (Leipzig: VEB Deutscher Verlag fur Musik), III, Lfg. 3, 28.

23:30	Waken
24:00–2:00	Sing Matin Service
2:00	Sleep
4:30	Waken
5:00–6:30	Sing Laudes and First Mass
7:00–9:00	School Studies
9:00–10:00	Sing Mass
11:00–15:00	Sing *Hora sexta* Service
	Lunch
	Rest Period
15:00–18:00	Sing *Hora nona* Service
	School Studies
	Dinner
18:00–19:00	Sing Vesper Service
19:30	Sleep

We see this rigid environment surrounding church singing also in the reports of one Peter Damian, the leader of a group of hermits at this time. He complains about monks who hurry the singing of their psalms at night in order to get to bed sooner and worries that evil thoughts will creep into the minds of monks who may daydream while singing.³⁷ There is no pleasure in singing here! Time and time again, Damian

37 *The Letters of Peter Damian*, trans., Owen Blum (Washington DC: The Catholic University of America Press, 1990), II, Letter 50.

warns his monks against the sins of pleasure, with such exhortations as, 'In every struggle with titillating pleasure try always to evoke the memory of the grave.'[38] He even went so far as to prescribe exercises in crying, in order that the monks could develop suitably somber demeanors.

Regarding specific performance practices, in one place he recommends the practice of a monk, named Dominic, of singing twelve psalms twenty-four times with ones hands extended above the head in the form of a cross. This, he says, would compensate for one year of penance.[39] In another place, he mentions instrumental music in an interesting distinction between canticles and psalms.

> That a canticle is daily added to the psalms in the office of Lauds, seems to be redolent with mystery, namely, the mystery of both the contemplative and the active life. For the psaltery, an instrument made in the shape of a delta, vibrates through its ten strings when struck by the plectrum; a song, however, is produced only by the voice. Wherefore, the former, because it needs the use of the hands, denotes work and hence the active life, while the latter, because it related to a song of joy, indicated the contemplative life. And because we are able to experience contemplation only briefly and interruptedly, and that, scarcely for a moment, but are always engaged in the business of the active life, it is proper that we employ several psalms but only one canticle.[40]

The Church non-liturgical literature of this period remains filled with tales of new miracles and other extraordinary stories to support the faith. Music is almost never mentioned in such literature, although we find in the 'Life of Mary Magdalene,' by the ninth-century writer, Rabanus Maurus, the assertion that Mary, Martha and Lazarus were in their youth highly educated, not only in Hebrew, but 'the gifts of arts.'[41] In this romantic biography, by the way, Martha, after the death of Christ, goes to France and fights a dragon![42]

There is one very significant secular work, the play 'Paphnutius,' by the tenth-century nun, Hrotswitha, which contains a scene which captures for us an actual class on the subject of music.[43] The passage begins with a Disciple asking, 'What *is* music?' Paphnutius answers with a brief description of the place held by music among the liberal arts. The Disciples beg for more information and Paphnutius relents, 'since it is knowledge which monks don't have.'

---

[38] ibid.

[39] ibid., Letter 53.

[40] ibid., I, Letter 17.

[41] *The Life of Saint Mary Magdalene and of her Sister Saint Martha*, trans., David Mycoff (Kalamazoo: Cistercian Publications, 1989), I, 29.

[42] ibid., XL, 2365.

[43] *The Plays of Hrotswitha of Gandersheim*, trans., Larissa Bonfante (New York: New York University Press, 1979), 108ff.

Paphnutius, following the definition by Boethius, begins by telling the students that music is divided into three species: the celestial, the human, and that made with instruments.

> DISCIPLES. What does celestial music consist of?
> PAPHNUTIUS. Of the seven planets and the celestial sphere.
> DISCIPLES. How do you mean that?
> PAPHNUTIUS. Because, you see, they produce the same harmonious music as the strings of stringed instruments; For just as in the case of instruments, we find the same concordances and intervals of like number and length.
> DISCIPLES. And what are these 'intervals' you speak of?
> PAPHNUTIUS. They are the distances which exist between the planets, as between the notes of strings.

Upon further questions about the 'notes' just mentioned, Paphnutius begins to speak in the complex mathematical language of Boethius. The students object to this conceptual language and respond, 'What has this got to do with *music*?,' implying, we presume, that music has instead to do with feelings and emotions, not mathematics. The teacher's answer is one you might very well hear today, 'But that is how you *talk* about music!' The reader will notice that he introduces here the word 'symphonia,' which the Greeks had used in place of our term 'harmony.'

> PAPHNUTIUS. A tone is formed of two sounds, of which the proportion is that of an epothos number, a sesquioctave: that is of nine to eight.
> DISCIPLES. (Discouraged.) The faster we try to keep up with you and follow the basic notions you give us, and technical terms of this discussion, the more you go on adding more difficult concepts for us to take in.
> PAPHNUTIUS. But that is how this kind of discussion is carried on.
> DISCIPLES. Well at least tell us something—but only the simplest account—about what they mean by concordances, just so we will know what the word means.
> PAPHNUTIUS. A concordance or 'symphonia' is a proper combination of sounds.

The students now ask the difficult question, 'Why can't we hear the music of the spheres?' Of all early philosophers, Paphnutius now gives the most complete answer, indeed four possible explanations.

DISCIPLES. Well, why can't we hear them, then?
PAPHNUTIUS. Many different reasons are given to explain why we can't hear the music of the heavenly spheres. Some assert it can't be heard because the music never stops, and we become accustomed to its sound. Others say it is the density of the air, while there are some who claim that a sound of such grand volume cannot physically be taken in by the narrow passages of our human ears. And there are some who say that the spheres give forth a sound so sweet, of such great joy, that if men ever heard it, they would all join together, of one common accord, forget about themselves and any other interest, and be intent only on following this sound as it led them from the East to the Western regions.

Well, say the students, we have heard enough of the music of the spheres. Now tell us about 'human' music, and how it is produced.

PAPHNUTIUS. Not only, as I said before, in the harmonious connection between body and soul, and in the deep bass or high pitched soprano voices, but even in the rhythmic throbbing of our veins, and in the measure and proportion of each of our limbs, as for example in the joints of our fingers, for which we find the same proportions when we measure off their sections. These are the same proportions, if you remember, which we talked of in our discussion of the meaning of 'symphonias,' because music is in fact an agreeable combination not only of voices, but of other unlike elements as well.
DISCIPLES. (The have been looking at the joints of their fingers. They are quite frankly lost.) If we had only known before we asked, how knotty all these problems were for laymen like us, and how difficult to follow or resolve, we would have preferred never to have known about the 'lesser world' than try to learn such difficult lessons.
PAPHNUTIUS. It did you no harm to try, for now you have learned things you did not know before.
DISCIPLES. That's true. But we are exhausted from this philosophical lecture, since we are not able to understand the details of your explanation.

Perhaps because of the student's professed exhaustion, this discussion never continues on to the subject of instrumental music. The teacher brings the topic to a close by reminding the students of the true purpose of the acquisition of knowledge—to understand God.

PAPHNUTIUS. For to whose praise does knowledge of all the arts
redound more worthily and justly, if not to His, since He is the One
who created all things knowable and gave us knowledge of them?

Now we should like to visit a few of the music treatises which emerged at this time and which were envisioned, in part, as music texts for teaching students music in the final period before the invention of the modern notation system. We will consider only those passages which offer insight on music education.

Aurelian of Reome, author of the *Musica Disciplina*, ca. 843 AD, begins with a poem which demonstrates, in its reference to Pythagoras and Greek philosophy, that some information of that ancient 'pagan' period had been preserved in spite of the efforts of the Church.

> Whoever reads this, composed in the line of great authority,
> Will know that the most wholesome authors are here;
> Here is the musician Pythagoras, the fountain head of the Greeks;
> Here are the sayings of the Latin fathers.
> I, your Aurelian, have compiled, arranged, and written,
> O Pastor Bernard, this slight gift.[44]

44 Aurelian of Reome, *The Discipline of Music*, trans., Joseph Ponte (Colorado Springs: Colorado College Music Press, 1968), 1.

This initial poem to the contrary, Aurelian is more indebted to the treatises of the sixth century. In the Preface Aurelian makes the interesting observation that present day singers know the rules, but are nevertheless lacking as musicians. We take this as a complaint that the experiential teaching of music has been lacking.

> I know that very noble singers are found, but I confess that I have seen none skilled in this art save you alone; for some of our musicians know many rules of music, yet nowhere, I think, is a musician found like the old ones.[45]

45 ibid., 3.

This music treatise contends that music should not be neglected and by testifying that its power is still evident in both secular and sacred usage.

> There is much authority both in the ancient books, that is, those of the heathen, and in the holy books, affirming that the discipline of music should not be disdained, since there are to be found, both among the heathen and our own people, innumerable acts of efficacious through its power.[46]

[46] ibid., I.

Aurelian defines music as, 'the science, applicable to sound and song, of correctly controlling variations of sound.'[47] Now it is most curious that he reaches back to ancient Greek mythology, a body of literature which would have been most condemned by the Church. He remarks that music was associated with one of the daughters of Jupiter, who were also goddesses of memory, 'because this art, unless it is imprinted in the memory, is not retained.' This last remark tells us that notation has not yet arrived.

[47] ibid., II.

Following Boethius, Aurelian categorizes music in the order of importance: celestial music, human music and instrumental music.[48] Regarding 'human music,' he says first that it is music which joins 'Reason to the body.' It is only music, he believes, which unites the rational and the irrational.

[48] ibid., III.

> What else is it that binds together the parts of the soul and body of man himself, who, as Aristotle is pleased to put it, has been joined together of the rational and the irrational.[49]

[49] ibid., III. The Aristotle reference is apparently to the *Nicomachean Ethics*, I, 13.

Aurelian, in asking the question, 'What is the difference between a musician and a singer?', outlines the role of Reason in good musicianship. The nature of this discussion clearly reflects a philosophy of music education based on the conceptual views of the Church. In the last paragraph he gives us just a hint of the studio teaching pedagogy. When he uses the analogy of prisoner and judge to represent the student and teacher, one might wonder if much has changed in the following one thousand years.

> There is as much difference between a musician and a singer as there is between a grammarian and a mere reader, or between physical skill and intellect. For physical skill obeys like a servant, but reason rules like a mistress, because the hands of the worker labor in vain, unless work grows out of the intellect. Every art and discipline has naturally a more honorable character than a handicraft, which is performed by hand and toil. For it is a much greater thing to know what someone does than to

do what someone knows. Thus it is that the intellectual contemplation of work does not stand in need of any act of working, but the works of the hands are nothing unless they are directed by reason. How great the glory of the art of music is can be learned from this: that other craftsmen have received their names not from their discipline, but from the instruments themselves, as the hammerer from the hammer, the cithara player from the cithara, and each one of the others who have received their names from the instrument of their employment. But a musician is one who has with well-weighed intellect attained the science of singing not by the servitude of labor, but by the rule of contemplation. We see this antithesis particularly in the works of buildings and of wars. For buildings are inscribed with, and the triumphs of war are called by, the names not of those by whose toil and servitude they were completed, but by the names of those at whose command and inspiration they were begun: hence, the temple is called Solomon's …

Musician and singer seem to differ as much as teacher and pupil. For example, the former creates poems, the latter analyses them; and the least little thing that the pupil accomplishes with time-consuming labor, the teacher discusses and empties of difficulty in the space of a single moment through the skill of his aptitude. And the singer seems to stand before the musician like a prisoner before the judge. Whoever has any notion of music, however small it may be, can understand this fairly well. As we have said in the foreword, very noble singers are found, yet nowhere, in my opinion, is a musician found like the old ones.[50]

[50] ibid., VII.

When Aurelian begins his review of music theory, we see the Church dogma about music being a branch of mathematics.

Music has the greatest correspondence to mathematics and encompasses that part of mathematics that compares one quantity with another …[51]

[51] ibid., VI.

It is in this same context that he says if one wishes to become more versed in *music*,

let him turn his eyes to the harmony of proportions, to the contemplation of intervals, and to the exactitude of mathematics.[52]

[52] ibid., X.

On the other hand, when he speaks of the names of the Greek modes, he mentions emotions and not mathematics.

I asked a certain Greek how they would be translated into Latin. He answered that they were untranslatable, but that among the Greeks they were exclamations of one rejoicing.[53]

[53] ibid., IX.

Among his observations about the performance of chant, he offers a curious maxim which demonstrates that the spirit of the myth had not completely died.

> We pray the singer to begin concluding all the verses of the nocturnal responses from the fifth syllable before the end; and this is according to the musicians who have maintained that not more than five waves of the sea also remove all storms from the same.[54]

[54] ibid., XIX.

Although Aurelian's entire understanding of music is closely tied to Reason and mathematics, it is interesting that he apparently felt compelled to conclude his treatise on music with a brief testimonial to the ability of music to affect the emotions.

> The very world and the sky above us, according to the doctrine of philosophers, are said to bear in themselves the sound of music. Music moves the affections of men, stimulates the emotions into a different mood. In war it restores the strength of the combatants; and the stronger the blaring of the trumpet, the braver is the spirit made for battle. It influences beasts also, serpents, birds, and dolphins, at its hearing ... And what more? The art of music surpasses all other arts. If anyone doubts that the angels, too, in the starry sky, render praises to God with the practice of this discipline, he is not a reader of [the book of Revelations].[55]

[55] ibid.

Hucbald (b. ca. 840 AD) taught at several monastic schools and it seems clear that his treatise, *De harmonica institutione*, was intended for instruction in such a school. The functional premise of treatises such as this was to produce a church singer who understood music on a conceptual level as opposed to what seems to have become a traditional singer who learned only by ear. In this case, Hucbald promises such a singer that if he will just study the exercises in this treatise, he

> may at length be granted entry to the inner regions of this discipline, the darkness being gradually withdrawn from his dull eyes.[56]

[56] Hucbald, 'Melodic Instruction' in *Hucbald, Guido, and John on Music*, trans., Warren Babb (New Haven: Yale University Press, 1978), 104a/16.

Although this treatise is primarily conceptual, there are hints that Hucbald was aware of something beyond the conceptual in music. For example, we wish he would have expanded his remarks on the distinction between understanding by 'judgment' and 'ear.'

> One will generally find that melodies can close on these notes a fifth above without offending either one's judgment or ear.⁵⁷

[57] ibid., 119b/1.

The anonymous treatise, *Scholia enchiriadis*, ca. 900 AD, formerly ascribed to Hucbald, is the earliest which deals with the improvisation of a simple counterpoint to a given chant. This author is still thinking of the Church definition of the science of mathematics consisting of arithmetic, geometry, music, and astronomy. Indeed, he says 'Music is the daughter of Arithmetic.' It is in this context that he defines music.

> [Music is] the rational discipline of agreement and discrepancy of sounds according to numbers in their relation to those things which are found in sounds … Because everything comprehended by these disciplines exists through reason formed of numbers and without numbers can be neither understood nor made known.⁵⁸

[58] Anonymous, 'Of Symphonies,' in Oliver Strunk, *Source Readings in Music History* (New York: Norton, 1950), 135.

This writer clearly believed that the aim of this knowledge was 'delight,' a term he uses repeatedly, but delight for him was not aesthetic delight, but the delight of Reason.

> Whatever is delightful in song is brought about by number through the proportioned dimensions of sounds; whatever is excellent in rhythms, or in songs, or in any rhythmic movements you will, is effected wholly by number. Sounds pass quickly away, but numbers, which are obscured by the corporeal element in sounds and movements, remain.⁵⁹

[59] ibid., 137.

The important treatise by Al-Farabi, *Ihsa al-ulum*, ca. 900 AD, was the first to distinguish between 'practical music' and 'theoretical music,' a division of the art which would be observed through nearly all later treatises. In the nature of the way he defines these thoughts he also gives us a clear picture of the subjects of music education as he perceived it.

> As for the Science of Music, it comprises, in short, the investigation into the various kinds of melodies, and what they are composed of, and for what they are composed, and how they are composed, and in what forms it is necessary that they should be in order that the performance of them be made more impressive and effective. And that which is known by this name [music] comprises two sciences. One of them is the science of practical music, and the second is the science of theoretical music.

> And as for practical music, its concern is the production of the various kinds of perceptible melodies in the instruments adapted for them either by nature or by artifice ...
>
> And the science of theoretical music is divided into [two] major parts. The first of them is the discourse about principles and fundamentals ... And the second part is the discourse about the rudiments of this art.[60]

[60] Quoted in Henry George Farmer, *Al-Farabi's Writings on Music* (New York: Hinrichsen, 1934), 13ff.

Another treatise by this same writer, and one written in Latin, the *De ortu scientiarum*, ca. 900 AD, is most interesting in that we find an important passage which preserves two familiar tenets of Greek philosophy, namely the influence of music on character and the definition of dance as visible music. We remind the reader that most of the ancient Greek works we know today were preserved in the East, after the Church attempted to suppress them in the West, hence Al-Farabi's knowledge of them. He seems to lack the belief in these ancient principles, for he adds the thought that the educational purpose of music is to make man 'keener' and to prepare him for other studies.

> [Music's] utility lies in tempering the character of living beings that digress from the mean and in perfecting the fitness of those that have not yet been perfected, and in maintaining those that appear to possess the mean and have not yet gone to any of the extremes. It is also of utility to bodily health whenever the body is weakened by a languid soul and is impeded by the existence of its own impediment. Thus the cure of the body is affected by the cure of the soul through the adjustment of its own constitution, and combining this with its own substance of means of effective sounds, such as concordant sounds.
>
> To this science are three roots—meter, melody, and gesture. Meter was devised to regulate a rational comprehension of diction. Melody was devised to regulate the parts of acuteness and gravity, and to it two roots have been included in the sense of hearing. Gesture has been included in the sense of seeing which, by coincident motions and corresponding proportions, has been arranged to agree with meter and sound. This art, therefore, is included in two particular senses—hearing and seeing.
>
> And in this the educational sciences which are called the dominating sciences are completed. Therefore, it is now manifest whence the art of music emerged, and whence it arose and flowed. And these four sciences are called the dominating because they dominate their investigator, render him keener, and disclose to him the right way to become most accurately acquainted with that which comes after them.[61]

[61] ibid., 49.

This discussion has been concerned with the ninth through the eleventh centuries, centuries which truly were the 'Dark Ages.' The infusion of new information on culture and the arts which followed the Crusades, together with the rediscovery and retranslation into Western languages of works by the ancient Greeks (which had survived in Arabic translations), and the founding of the modern universities, had the result of beginning to raise the dark curtain. The twelfth and thirteenth centuries would become a pre-Renaissance in music, the arts and in culture in general. The following discussion will focus on those two centuries.

People will be self-centered and grasping; boastful, arrogant and rude; disobedient to their parents, ungrateful, irreligious; heartless and unappeasable; they will be slanderers, profligates, savages, and enemies of everything that is good; they will be treacherous and reckless and demented by pride, preferring their own pleasure to God. They will keep up the outward appearances of religion but will have rejected the inner power of it. Have nothing to do with people like that.

William of Saint-Amour, thirteenth century, in a sermon, 'On the Dangers of the New Times,' warning his congregation on the dangers in the establishment of the new universities.

8   *Music Education in the Pre-Renaissance*

THE TWELFTH AND THIRTEENTH CENTURIES are characterized by the beginnings of humanism, a final burst of freedom from the dogma of the Dark Ages. The virtual explosion of confidence in man and his works is both the hallmark of these two centuries and the harbinger of the Renaissance. What greater display of this new confidence can there be than the huge cathedrals which began to spring up everywhere. Built in cities which had only a fraction of the population they have today, they remain not only as symbols of faith, but of man himself and of the glorious final two centuries of the Middle Ages.

Many factors contributed to this period of enthusiastic renewal of society. Certainly the great Crusades introduced to the West the more advanced and more cultured civilizations of the East. International trade followed the Crusades and through it came not only a dramatic expansion of the general economy, but a great stimulus to all the arts. Consider, for example, the testimony of a priest named Theophilus. From a small monastery near Paderborn, Germany, he wrote in 1190,

> Here you shall find all that Greece possesses in the way of diverse colors and mixtures; all that Tuscany knows of the working of enamels ... all that Arabia has to show of works ductile, fusible, or chased; all the many vases and sculptured gems and ivory that Italy adorns with gold; all that France prizes in costly variety of windows; all that is extolled in gold, silver, copper, or iron, or in subtle working of wood or stone.[1]

[1] Theophilus, 'Schedule diversarum artium,' in E. Dillon, *Glass* (New York, 1907), 126.

This period saw equally dramatic progress in the intellectual life of Western Europe. Just before the dawn of the twelfth century paper mills in Germany and France began to open. The modern universities were founded at this time and the rediscovery of the works of Aristotle and the ancient philosophers provided them with an immediate challenge: to reconcile these monuments of Reason with a Church long content to rest its case on Faith.

In the profession of music something happened at this time which would forever change the nature of performance—the invention of the modern notation system. From time beyond calculation no musician had ever played from the page and the ramifications of this change are many. The concept of music existing on a page meant the music was past tense for the first time. The concept of music existing on a page gave new importance to the music theorist, as well as the composer; the composer was now the creator, not the player. The new notational system was a product of the Church and as such is a system based on mathematics. It is entirely attributable to the Church that to this very day we have no notational symbol which represents any emotion or feeling. Since the communication of emotion is what music is all about, it means we have a notational system which from the very beginning could not accurately notate music. And, of course, the concept of music to be read by the *eye*, instead of being heard by the *ear*, also changed the nature of music education. Some of the educational implications we can see in the music treatises which appeared at this time.

Odo of Cluny's treatise, *Enchiridion musices*, ca. 935 AD, is an important landmark, for it is the first in which letters are used as symbols for pitch in the modern sense, and was also written for the purpose of perfecting the ability to teach church singers to read. With his system, Odo says he has taught boys in a few days to read 'without fault anything written in music,' something which he states that until now ordinary singers could not do even after fifty years' experience.[2]

Given the purpose of this treatise, we are not surprised to find, when the Disciple asks, 'What is music?,' the Master answers, 'The science of singing correctly.' This, of course, means singing what is on the page. Singing something because it pleases the ear was no justification for Odo.

> Ordinary singers often fall into the greatest error because they scarcely consider the force of tone and semitone and of the other consonances. Each of them chooses what first pleases his ear.[3]

One very important aspect of this treatise is its confirmation of improvisation in Church music by the tenth century. Odo gives as the goal of any such changes in the music, that it 'sound better.' When he summarizes the selection of modes, his comments reflect not 'science,' but improvisation and even

[2] Odo, 'Enchiridion musices,' in Strunk, op. cit., 104.

[3] ibid., 110.

'trial and error.' He takes a small but important step away from the Church and mathematics when he says the ear must judge where the eye cannot.

> From this it is understood that the musician who lightly and presumptuously emends many melodies is ignorant unless he first goes through all the modes to determine whether the melody may perhaps not stand in one or another, nor should he care as much for its similarity to other melodies as for regular truth. But if it suits no mode, let it be emended according to the one with which it least disagrees. This also should be observed: that the emended melody either sound better or depart little from its previous likeness.[4]

[4] ibid., 111.

The important treatise, *Micrologus*, ca. 1026–1028 AD, by Guido of Arezzo, is famous for the introduction of a staff of lines and spaces for the notation of music This treatise is another educational one, directed at the training of church singers. He begins his discussion with a little anagram which refers to the disappearance of music in the schools during the Dark Ages.

> Gone from school are the Muses; there may I hope to induce them,
> Unknown yet to adults, to unveil their light to the young ones!
> Ill will's indiscriminate rage let charity frustrate;
> Dire indeed are the blights that else will ravage our planet,
> Opening letters of these five lines will spell you the author.[5]

[5] Guido of Arezzo, 'Micrologus,' 80, in Babb, op. cit.

In his Prologue, Guido immediately centers on the importance of teaching the student the ability to sing at sight. If the singer can not do this, he says, 'I do not know with what face he can venture to call himself a musician or a singer.'[6] He declares that he will discuss here only those things important to singing and then adds a comment we can only wish he had elaborated on. He says he will omit those 'things which are said but cannot be understood.'[7] He means by this those things which are said on the basis of experience but which cannot be understood in the context of mathematics. This same point he makes in another place, where he admits,

[6] ibid., 85.

[7] ibid., 86.

> In our times, of all men, singers are the most foolish. For in any art those things which we know of ourselves are much more numerous than those which we learn from a master.[8]

[8] Quoted in Strunck, op. cit., 117.

Among his comments on music theory, we find interesting his explanation for why there are seven tones of the scale as being associated with the seven days of the week.[9] It is also interesting that he gives the origin of the word 'tone' as *intonandus*, 'to be sounded.'[10] That is, the concept came from the experience, whereas in today's world of music education the experience is usually thought to come from the concept. He takes the opposite view with respect to *musica ficta*, which is clearly an appropriate aesthetic concept which grew out of experience. This violated his goal of accurate sight-singing.

> False notes also creep in through inaccuracy in singing; sometimes performers deviate from well-tuned notes, lowering or raising them slightly, as is done by untrue human voices.[11]

Guido's discussion of cadences includes a very curious statement. It strikes our attention especially as so many earlier Church philosophers had commented on the fact that music disappears after it is performed, suggesting that music exists only in its precise moment of performance. Guido presents here a thought which is quite different psychologically.

> The previous notes, as is evident to trained musicians only, are so adjusted to the last one that in an amazing way they seem to draw a certain semblance of color from it.[12]

His actual explanation of the importance of the cadence he draws from grammar, a place where Church philosophers often sought relationships with music.

> It is no wonder that music bases its rules on the last note, since in the elements of language, too, we almost everywhere see the real force of the meaning in the final letters or syllables, in regard to cases, numbers, persons, and tenses.[13]

He provides an illustration of the ability of music to affect character in an anecdote not found elsewhere. As to the explanation how music does this, he cannot say, offering only the observation that this is known only to Divine Wisdom.

---

[9] 'Micrologus,' 116, in Babb, op. cit. The number '7' was a very special number in Old Testament mythology.

[10] ibid., 116.

[11] ibid., 134.

[12] ibid., 139.

[13] ibid., 145.

Another man was roused by the sound of the cithara to such lust that, in his madness, he sought to break into the bedchamber of a girl, but, when the cithara player quickly changed the mode, was brought to feel remorse for his libidinousness and to retreat abashed.[14]

Regarding the emotions in performance, Guido makes an interesting psychological observation.

We often place an acute or grave accent above the notes, because we often utter them with more or less stress, so much so that the repetition of the same note often seems to be a raising or lowering.[15]

Finally, in an example of ignorance caused by the Church's destruction of the books by the ancient Greek philosophers, Guido refuses to believe that more ancient men could have understood music on a rational level.

In ancient times there were instruments that we are not clear about and also a multitude of singers who were, however, in the dark, for no man could by any train of thought reason out the differences between notes or a description of music.[16]

In another treatise, *Epistola de ignoto cantu*, ca. 1030–1032 AD, Guido again promises a music education system which will rapidly produce accurate sight-singers. Here he gives us an important insight on music pedagogy before the era of notation when he observes that previously singers learned by rote, after hearing the pitch on a monochord. This he calls, 'childish.'[17]

He refers to the previous treatise, which he says he has simplified for the sake of the young. He makes an implicit reference that current thinking is beginning to shift from the old Church mathematic basis of music to a more 'practical' one when he points out that he has not followed the model of Boethius, 'whose treatise is useful to philosophers, but not to singers.'[18]

An author, now known as simply John and formerly known as John Cotton, has also written a treatise intended for a choir school, called *On Music*, ca. 1100 AD. His viewpoint is again primarily a conceptual one and he clearly states that it is

[14] ibid., 160.

[15] ibid.

[16] ibid., 288.

[17] Guido, 'Epistola de ignoto cantu,' in Strunk, op. cit., 123.

[18] ibid., 125.

knowledge, the ability to judge music intellectually, which is the highest accomplishment. He dismisses the 'pleasing music' created by the jongleurs who lack this kind of education.

> Music is one of the seven liberal arts—and a natural one, as are the others. Thus we sometimes see jongleurs and actors who are absolutely illiterate composing pleasant-sounding songs. But just as grammar, dialectic, and the other arts would be considered vague and chaotic if they were not committed to writing and made clear by precepts, so it is with music …
>
> For whoever devotes unremitting labor to it, and perseveres without pausing or wearying, can gain from it this reward, that he will know how to judge the quality of song—whether it is refined or commonplace, true or false—and how to correct the faulty and compose the new.[19]

[19] John, 'On Music,' 51, in Babb, op. cit.

We see the fingerprints of the Church, and their definition that music is a branch of mathematics, when he writes that the real musician proceeds 'by calculation.' The singer who just sings on the basis of experience, and not on the basis of conceptual and mathematical knowledge, is nothing more than a drunk!

> Nor, it seems, should we omit that the musician and the singer differ not a little from one another. Whereas the musician always proceeds correctly and by calculation, the singer holds the right road intermittently, merely through habit. To whom then should I better compare the singer than to a drunken man who does indeed get home but does not in the least know by what path he returns.[20]

[20] ibid., 52.

And if his characterization of the singer as a drunk is not enough, he now goes further by quoting from Guido, that a musician who does not know what he is doing is a 'beast!'

> From the musician to the singer how immense the distance is;
> The latter's voice, the former's mind will show what music's nature is;
> But he who does, he knows not what, a beast by definition is.[21]

[21] John gives the source as the *Micrologus*, but it actually comes from the beginning of Guido's *Regulae rhythmicae*.

In another place he stipulates that by 'having a knowledge of music' he does not mean that which is derived from experience or natural talent provided by nature—even if it sounds correct and is agreeable!

> We said 'having a knowledge of music' because even if one unversed in the subject does what he does correctly, still, because he does it unwittingly, he is little esteemed, especially since both actors and precentors of dancing choruses for the most part sing agreeably, which is granted to them not by art but by nature.[22]

[22] 'On Music,' 77.

He mentions his principal music education tool, the monochord, an instrument through which he believed true pitch could be achieved. This was a goal he apparently found to be not universally appreciated.

> For there are indeed a great many clerics and monks who neither understand this discipline nor wish to understand it, and, what is worse, who avoid and abhor those that do.
> If, as sometimes happens, a musician takes them to task about a chant which they perform either inaccurately or crudely, they get angry and make a shameless uproar and are unwilling to admit the truth, but defend their error with the greatest effort …
> The monochord serves to silence their wrong-headedness, so that those who will not trust the words of a musician are refuted by the testimony of the sound itself.[23]

[23] ibid., 65ff.

In an example of how conceptual and nonmusical his logic can be, in discussing cadences, unlike Guido who found confirmation of his logic in grammar, John finds an analogy in business.

> Musicians of judgment have not unreasonably decided to base the decision as to modes on the endings, since in business affairs a singleminded regard for the outcome distinguishes the wise from the heedless.[24]

[24] ibid., 82.

In his reflection on performances at which he has heard *musica ficta*, the addition of accidentals by the performers, he makes a statement which is remarkably similar to Mahler's famous definition of 'tradition' as being 'the last bad performance.'

> We do know most assuredly that a chant is often distorted by the ignorance of men, so that we could now enumerate many corrupted ones. These were really not produced by the composers originally in the way that they are now sung in churches, but wrong pitches, by men who

followed the promptings of their own minds, have distorted what was composed correctly and perpetuated what was distorted in an incorrigible tradition, so that by now the worst usage is clung to as authentic.[25]

[25] ibid., 104.

He also has observed that the physical status of the singer can affect the performance, pointing to 'singers weighed down by weariness' singing flat and those of 'high spirits' singing sharp.[26]

[26] ibid.

John also touches on a subject which must have been a confusing and difficult problem for anyone attempting to explain music from the standpoint of Reason, not to mention mathematics. One characteristic of mathematics, for example, is that everyone agrees. Everyone has the same answer to the question, What is the sum of two plus two? The problem with the understanding of the right hemisphere of our brain, where the experiential understanding of music lies, is that everyone has a different answer, based on their personal experience. We are confident this was more confusing to John than he admits in his observation.

> Nor should it seem surprising to anyone that we say different men are attracted by different things, for by nature itself men are so endowed that not everyone's senses cherish the same desire. Thus, it often happens that while to one man what is being sung appears most delightful, by another it is pronounced ill-sounding and utterly formless. Indeed I myself remember singing a number of chants for some people, and what one praised to the heights another disliked profoundly.[27]

[27] This discussion is found in ibid., 109ff.

Therefore, he concludes, it is not the mode which affects man, rather it is the natural emotional affinity of the man which is attracted to a particular mode—thus, each man likes a different mode.

In an apparent reference to intervals, John adopts a much more subjective attitude. His conclusions are remarkably similar to those of at least one modern study of how melody communicates feeling.

> Some are pleased by the slow and ceremonious peregrinations of the first, some are taken by the hoarse profundity of the second, some are delighted by the austere and almost haughty prancing of the third, some are attracted by the ingratiating sound of the fourth, some are stirred by the well-bred high spirits and the sudden fall to the final in the fifth, some are melted by the tearful voice of the sixth, some like to hear the spectacular leaps of the seventh, and some favor the staid and almost matronly strains of the eighth.

Another observation arrives at similar subjective conclusions.

> It is obvious that men with harsh and intractable voices avoid semitones as much as possible, while those who have flexible voices relish them greatly—so much so that they sometimes produce them even where they should not be made.[28]

A comment on the modes runs in the same direction.

> The modes have individual qualities of sound, differing from each other, so that they prompt spontaneous recognition by an attentive musician or even by a practiced singer. Just as someone who has studied the manners and appearances of various peoples distinguishes expertly the nationality of any man he sees, noting, for instance, that this one is a Greek and that one a German, but that one a Spaniard and that one a Frenchman.

John's conclusion, based on such observations, is that the object of the composer, then, is to fit the character of the music to the character of the listener. It is a surprising suggestion that the aim of church music should be to 'please' the congregation member. How the composer does this, not to mention what one does in the case of a large congregation of assorted personalities, he does not say.

> Therefore, in composing chants, the duly circumspect musician should plan to use in the most fitting way the mode by which he sees those are most attracted whom he wishes his chant to please.

Later in this same treatise, however, John takes the opposite, and ancient Greek, view that it is the music itself which affects character. He begins by rhapsodizing on the wide range of purpose available in music.

> It should not pass unmentioned that chant has great power of stirring the souls of its hearers, in that it delights the ears, uplifts the mind, arouses fighters to warfare, revives the prostrate and despairing, strengthens wayfarers, disarms bandits, assuages the wrathful, gladdens the sorrowful and distressed, pacifies those at strife, dispels idle thoughts, and allays the frenzy of the demented …
>
> Music has different powers according to the different modes. Thus, you can by one kind of singing rouse someone to lustfulness and by another kind bring the same man as quickly as possible to repentance and recall him to himself.[29]

[28] ibid., 137.

[29] ibid., 114ff.

A MAJOR STEP FORWARD FOR CIVILIZATION which occurred at the end of the Middle Ages was the foundation and growth of the modern universities. The twelfth and thirteenth centuries saw the conversion of the medieval monastic schools into the first modern universities of Western Europe. This process had its origin in part in a monastic reform movement opposed to the rising secular culture, but also to the climate of intellectual enthusiasm following the relatively recent and wide spread reappearance of the works of the ancient philosophers. The rediscovery of these ancient works, in particular, brought a sense of urgency to reconciling the broad spectrum of natural philosophy with a Church which had been content to rest on Faith. The liberal arts, which had long been justified only for their role in preparing the Christian to understand the Scriptures, now received a new impetus. A modern scholar pictures what an exciting period this must have been for the student.

> For the first time in European history students and teachers at Paris and Bologna enjoyed the intoxicating experience of participating in the work of an academic community engaged in solving problems of universal importance, clarifying the principles of the Christian religion, of human behavior, and of correct reasoning, and then of adapting these principles to the organization of society. The students had the stimulus of belonging to a cosmopolitan body of men of varied backgrounds and turbulent instincts, and future importance. The masters had the stimulus of critical pupils and the daily discipline of expounding difficult subjects and solving intricate problems. And they all had the satisfaction of adding to a growing body of important knowledge.[30]

[30] R. W. Southern, *Robert Grosseteste* (Oxford: Clarendon, 1992), 50.

The great university at Bologna was characterized, among other things, by the strong role of the students in its day to day administration. Students not only paid the teachers, but hired and fired them and allotted their holidays. Students determined when lectures began and ended, their duration and the portions of the texts to be used. One can understand how, for six hundred years, we professors have tried to keep this quiet!

Perhaps related to the student influence in this university, Bologna had a reputation in the thirteenth century for being the only university which was relatively free of Church domination, indeed, there was no theological faculty at all before 1364.[31] It was in this light that a popular joke of the day among students told of a professor from Paris who came to Bolo-

[31] Will Durant, *The Age of Faith* (New York: Simon and Schuster, 1950), 918. Durant provides an extensive description of the early universities in Bologna, Paris and Oxford.

gna, where he had to 'unlearn' everything he had learned in Paris and then returned to Paris to 'unteach' it. Perhaps it was the lack of Church interference in Paris which made possible women students there in the thirteenth century and women professors in the following century.

Without question, then or now, the greatest university center of the thirteenth century was Paris. It was truly an international university and it has been suggested that so many German students were in residence that it contributed to the delay in the establishment of universities in Germany.[32]

The curriculum in Paris began with the liberal arts,[33] then proceeded to philosophy and finally to theology. The professors, clerics usually, were required to speak without notes and

[32] ibid., 920.

[33] Hence, the students of the Liberal Arts, the undergraduates, so to speak, were called 'art-ists' [artistae]. For a discussion of the role of music in the curriculum of the thirteenth-century university, see Nan Cooke Carpenter, *Music in the Medieval and Renaissance Universities* (Norman: University of Oklahoma Press, 1958), 48, 115.

Map of Medieval Universities from 'Historical Atlas' by William R. Shepherd

were forbidden to read their lectures. It is interesting that as early as the twelfth century one philosopher complained that in Paris some teachers gave easy courses to gain popularity with the students and concluded that permitting the students to choose from a wide variety of teachers and subjects resulted in a lowering of the standard.[34] It is from the question and answer format of these classes, known as *scholastica disputatio*, that we derive the term, Scholastic Philosophy.

The third great university center, Oxford, was based on the Paris model and had by 1209, according to a contemporary, already more than three thousand students and teachers.[35]

A decree issued by Pope Gregory IX in 1231 essentially gave the University of Paris relative freedom to conduct its lectures and debates free from Church interference. A century of very vibrant debate began the long struggle of trying to introduce the ancient Greek's ideas on Reason into a Church based entirely on Faith. Similarly, works by Aristotle in particular made objective science an implicit attack on Creationism. Students led protests in the streets, students were attacked by Church authorities and popular professors such as Peter Abelard had their careers destroyed by the Church.[36] Bernard of Clairvaux, 'St. Bernard,' (1090–1153) destroyed the career of Abelard because he was speaking of Reason and not Faith.

> Faith believes, it does not dispute. But this man [Abelard], apparently holding God suspect, will not believe anything until he has first examined it with his reason.[37]

There is no question that the Church felt it was under attack and its response, partly digging in the heels and partly trying to ignore philosophers like Aristotle, can be sensed in the comment by Siger de Brabant, made in Paris during the thirteenth century.

> One should not try to investigate by reason those things which are above reason or to refute arguments for the contrary position. But since a philosopher, however great he may be, may err on many points, one ought not to deny the Catholic faith because of some philosophical argument, even though he does not know how to refute it.[38]

---

[34] Lynn Thorndike, *History of Magic and Experimental Science* (New York, 1929), II, 53.

[35] H. Rashdall, *The Universities of Europe in the Middle Ages* (Oxford, 1936), III, 29fn.

[36] The book by Richard E. Rubenstein, *Aristotle's Children*, (New Work: Harcourt, 2003) offers a wonderful description of this dynamic century, as well as a fascinating account of the rediscovery and translation into Western languages of the 'lost' Greek treatises.

[37] Letter of Bernard of Clairvaux to Cardinal Haimeric, in *The Letters of St. Bernard of Clairvaux*, trans., Bruno James (Chicago: Regnery, 1953), 328.

[38] Quoted in Richard Dales, *Medieval Discussions of the Eternity of the World* (Leiden and New York: Brill, 1995), 144.

In these universities, particularly in Paris, music education was present as a member of the liberal arts. It was in arguing for the importance of the liberal arts during the Dark Ages, for the purpose of helping the citizen be equipped to understand the sermons and sacred writings of the Church, that some philosophers helped to keep some education alive. One finds this argument still present in the thirteenth century. In his treatise on 'Mathematics,' Roger Bacon (b. ca. 1214 AD) adds an educational facet to the purpose of music, in a passage in which he maintains that the theologian must have music education in order to understand the Scriptures.[39] The first reason, of course, is simply to be able to fully understand the many references to music in the Old Testament.

[39] This entire discussion is found in *Opus Majus*, 'Mathematics,' in *The Opus Majus of Roger Bacon*, trans., Robert Burke (New York: Russell & Russell, 1962), I, 259.

> According to the judgment of the sacred writers matters pertaining to music are necessary to theology in many ways. For although it is not necessary for an understanding of Scripture that the theologian should have a practical knowledge of singing and of instruments and of other musical things, yet he should know the theory of them, in order to grasp the natures and properties of these things and of the writings on this subject in accordance with their teachings of music theoretical and practical. For Scripture is full of musical terms like rejoice, shout for joy, sing, play upon the cithara, cymbals, and the like of different kinds.

The second reason Bacon gives is relative to the many kinds of meters found in the old Hebrew text. Here he notes that while the grammarian may teach the practical rules, only music gives 'the reasons and theories' for these meters. In the same manner, he points to the issue of pronunciation, as the Scripture is filled with 'accents, longs, shorts, colons, commas, and period.'

> All these belong causally to music, because of all these matters the musician states the reason, but the grammarian merely the fact.

Even though the liberal arts had in fact survived the Dark Ages and were now the foundation of the new universities, we are surprised to find very little discussion of music by the major scholastic philosophers of the thirteenth century. The most likely cause was the over-riding debates going on between Reason and the Church and its faith-based knowledge. Even though music itself, in so far as performance, was breaking new ground everywhere, in the towns, in the courts and in the Church, it almost seems, judging by the coverage it received, that music had disappeared from the list of the seven liberal arts. Perhaps, in the perspective of these philosophers, that is what happened. While they continue to refer to music as one of the liberal arts, they had come to realize that music was somehow no longer a 'science' in the way the other disciplines of the liberal arts were, and are. We wonder if perhaps this is the point made in an allegorical poem, 'The Battle of the Seven Arts' (*La Bataille des*.VII Ars), composed in about 1236 by a trouvere named Henri d'Andeli. In this work he describes a battle between Grammar and Logic. Music is present here, but stands apart and is not a participant in the 'battle.'

> Madam Music, she of the little bells
> And her clerks full of songs
> Carried fiddles and viols,
> Psalteries and small flutes;
> From the sound of the first fa
> The ascended to cc sol fa.
> The sweet tones diatessaron
> Diapente, diapason,
> Are struck in various combinations.
> In groups of four and three
> Through the army they went singing,
> They go enchanting them with their song.
> These do not engage in battle.[40]

There was another characteristic which distinguished music from the other six liberal arts—music, alone, could not be *seen*. We would therefore venture to suggest the following possibility. These philosophers, in their enthusiasm to write commentaries on the newly available works of Aristotle and the other ancient Greek philosophers, and subsequently to reconcile these ideas to those of the Church, were drawn immediately to the subjects of Reason, the Intellect, Understanding, and Metaphysics. These subjects are all of the left hemisphere domain, a world of writing and language, a world dependent on the eye. Perhaps it should be no surprise that several writers state the the eye is the most important of the senses. And music, of course, has very little to do with either the eye or Reason.

[40] Quoted in Carpenter, op. cit., 71.

The one philosopher of the thirteenth century whom we might have expected to write extensively about music was Robert Grosseteste (d. 1253). A contemporary, Matthew Paris, tells us Grosseteste was well-grounded in the Quadrivium, which included music.

> Grosseteste was born from the very humblest stock, a man of refined learning in both trivium and quadrivium, unconventional in his manner of life, following his own will and relying on his own judgment.[41]

It has always been assumed that he was a great lover of music, perhaps an inaccurate generalization based on some early poetry. In the following, we are told that he listened to music day and night because it gave him solace and sharpened his mind. When asked why he took such delight in music, he answered that the virtue in music protected one against the devil and that good skill in harp playing was closely associated with the Church.

> Y shall you tell as I have herd
> Of the bysshop seynt Roberd;
> His toname is Grosteste,
> Of Lyncolne, so seyth the geste.
> He lovede moche to here the harpe,
> For mans witte it makyth sharpe;
> Next hys chamber, besyde his study,
> Hys harpers chamber was fast the by.
> Many tymes, by nightes and dayes,
> He hadd solace of notes and layes.
> One askede hem the resun why
> He hadde delyte in mynstrelsy:
> He answered hym on thys manere
> Why he helde the harpe so dere:
> 'The virtu of the harpe, thurgh style and ryght
> Wyll destrye the fendys myght;
> And to the cros by gode skeyl
> Ys the harpe lykened weyl.'[42]

But there is no great new philosophical treatise on music by Grosseteste. In his treatise, 'De artibus liberalibus,' he places music at the head of the Quadrivium, but there is nothing new here, only the old discussions about the mathematical basis of

[41] Quoted in R. W. Southern, *Robert Grosseteste* (Oxford: Clarendon, 1992), 11. Paris, as quoted in ibid., 10, adds another dimension of Grosseteste's reputation.

> Let no one be disturbed by the violent acts which he did in his life-time ... his treatment of his canons whom he excommunicated and harassed, his savage attacks on monks, and even more savage against nuns ... They arose from zeal.

[42] William de Wadington, *Manuel des Peches*, trans., Robert Mannyng, quoted in James McEvoy, *The Philosophy of Robert Grosseteste* (Oxford: Clarendon, 1982), 43.

music, reference to the 'Music of the Spheres,' and so on.[43] His few remarks about music reveal an interest more in the practical, such as the use of music in healing.

It was clearly his interest in music which prompted him to attempt to explain the physics of sound production and the nature of hearing. His explanation, however, tied to the Church's old pronouncement that music is a branch of mathematics, was all bound up in numbers and the soul, namely that a sound is understood as a number in the ear, which is then compared to numbers stored in the soul-memory, whereupon it is judged harmonious or dissonant. Music, then, was not just a matter of hearing musical tones, but involved a broad range of faculties dealing with numbers, memory and finally Reason.[44]

The one scholar who did contribute original thought on music at this time was an Englishman, Roger Bacon. Bacon studied at Oxford and at the University of Paris, where he received a doctorate in theology and then joined the Franciscan Order in about 1247. Unlike the gentle patron of his Order, St. Francis, Bacon was very outspoken and many who read or heard him must have felt somewhat insulted. Youth, he says, has no interest in the perfection demanded by science, indeed they take pleasure in their imperfection, and older people, 'with the greatest difficulty climb to perfection in anything.'[45] He was even more outspoken in his disrespect for the masses, the 'unenlightened throng,' the 'ignorant multitude,' whom he says can never rise to the perfection of wisdom. For this reason, he maintains, the wise have always been an elite segment of society, separated from the masses. He found this true in religion ('as with Moses so with Christ the common throng does not ascend the mountain') as well as in the universities.

> We see that such is the case among the professors of philosophy as well as in the truth of our faith. For the wise have always been divided from the multitude, and they have veiled the secrets of wisdom not only from the world at large but also from the rank and file of those devoting themselves to philosophy.[46]

He cites a book by A. Gellius in which the author maintained that the great Greek philosophers had discussions among themselves at night, so as to 'avoid the multitude.'

[43] Some Latin text is quoted in Carpenter, op. cit., 82.

[44] McEvoy, ibid., 258.

[45] *Opus Majus*, 'Causes of Error,' III, in *The Opus Majus of Roger Bacon*, trans., Robert Burke (New York: Russell & Russell, 1962), 9ff.

[46] This discussion is found in ibid., 'Causes of Error,' IV.

In this book he says that it is foolish to feed an ass lettuces when thistles suffice him. He is speaking of the multitude for whom rude, cheap, imperfect food of science is sufficient. Nor ought we to cast pearls before swine.

He was also outspoken about false teaching in the schools and other forms of vice and corruption. One can suppose he did not make many friends and, in fact, was brought to trial in 1278, condemned and thrown into prison for fourteen years.

But, from our perspective today, he reads much more objectively than most philosophers of his day. We admire him for being honest enough to point out that the famous philosophers were sometimes wrong[47] and that none of us can have perfect knowledge, for what we know is far less than what we don't know.[48] And we believe he was right on the mark when he observed that the greatest barriers to truth are the 'submission to faulty and unworthy authority, influence of custom [and] popular prejudice.'[49]

In his discussion of the liberal arts, Bacon first comments that while the ancients knew of the various sciences, they only actually used two: astronomy for the calendar, and music for worship.[50] Mathematics, he calls the 'gate and key' for the other liberal arts[51] and he specifically recommends that the study of mathematics should come before music education.

> The natural road for us is to begin with things which befit the state and nature of childhood, because children begin with facts that are better known by us and that must be acquired first. But of this nature is mathematics, since children are first taught to sing, and in the same way they can learn the method of making figures and of counting, and it would be far easier and more necessary for them to know about numbers before singing, because in the relations of numbers in music the whole theory of numbers is set forth by example, just as the authors on music teach, both in ecclesiastical music and in philosophy.[52]

Sounding very much like those today who attempt to defend music in the schools by suggesting, 'Music helps Reading,' or 'Music helps Math,' Bacon gives a strong endorsement for the importance of music education in fully understanding another of the liberal arts, grammar.

---

[47] ibid., 'Causes of Error,' VII.

[48] ibid., X.

[49] ibid., I.

[50] ibid., XIV.

[51] ibid., 'Mathematics,' I.

[52] ibid., III. See also XVI for more on the relationship of music to both mathematics and theology.

Now the accidental parts of philosophy are grammar and logic. Alpharabius makes it clear in his book on the sciences that grammar and logic cannot be known without mathematics. For although grammar furnishes children with the facts relating to speech and its properties in prose, meter, and rhythm, nevertheless it does so in a puerile way by means of statement and not through causes or reasons. For it is the function of another science to give the reasons for these things, namely, of that science, which must consider fully the nature of tones, and this alone is music, of which there are numerous varieties and parts. For one deals with prose, a second with meter, a third with rhythm, and a fourth with music in singing. And besides these it has more parts. The part dealing with prose teaches the reasons for all elevations of the voice in prose, as regards differences of accents and as regards colons, commas, periods, and the like. The metrical part teaches all the reasons and causes for feet and meters. The part on rhythm teaches about every modulation and sweet relation in rhythms, because all those are certain kinds of singing, although not so treated as in ordinary singing ... Therefore grammar depends causatively on music.

In the same way logic ... Alpharabius especially teaches this in regard to the poetic argument, the statements of which should be sublime and beautiful, and therefore accompanied with notable adornment in prose, meter, and rhythm ... And therefore the end of logic depends upon music.[53]

In his discussion of music, as one of the liberal arts, Bacon contributes the most precise and interesting definition offered by any philosopher of the thirteenth century. He begins by dividing the world of music into two broad categories, 'one part of music deals with what is audible, the other with what is visible.'[54]

Audible Music he recognizes as being of two divisions, vocal music and instrumental music. In vocal music, in turn, Bacon finds four subdivisions.

For one part concerns melody, as in singing; the second concerns meters, and considers the nature and properties of all songs, meters, and feet; the third concerns rhythm, and considers every variety of relations in rhythms; the fourth concerns prose and considers accents and other aforesaid things in prose discourse. For accent is a kind of singing; whence it is called accent from accino, accinis [I sing, thou singest], because every syllable has its own proper sound either raised, lowered, or composite, and all syllables of one word are adapted or sung to one syllable on which rests the principal sound. Thus length and shortness and all other things required in correct pronunciation are reduced to music.

[53] ibid., II.

[54] ibid., XVI, in Burke, op. cit., I, 259, for this entire discussion.

This is a very interesting discussion for several reasons. First, these thoughts come at the end of two thousand years, at least, during which poetry was sung. When Bacon says 'every syllable has its own proper sound either raised, lowered, or composite,' we wonder if there was a commonly recognized, but now lost, tradition in the performance of sung poetry. Did the text, perhaps, 'compose' the music? Such a possibility adds another dimension to the ancient Rhapsodists, whose vocal technique we know nothing about, but who performed in public works such as Homer. We also find fascinating his statement, 'For accent is a kind of singing.' This comment, seven hundred years before our age, reminds us that among ancient peoples singing preceded language. Can we not see a trace here of that distant period when pitch fluctuation preceded, and perhaps turned into, the sounds we call consonants?

Bacon is not so expansive on instrumental music, noting only that the subject deals with learning 'the structure of the instruments and their use.' He also adds that the theologian must also know the 'numberless mystical meanings' of the instruments. We wish he had elaborated more, for he has made it clear in previous passages that he takes the Old Testament references to instruments literally, and not metaphorically as did many earlier medieval philosophers.

It is Bacon's recognition of a category of music which he calls 'visual music' which is of great significance. The ancient Greek philosophers never discussed this topic at length, but there are sufficient hints in their descriptions of choral performance to suggest that the inevitable movements by the singers were thought of not as a kind of dance, but as the part of music you could see. One must remember that the Greeks placed considerable significance in the fact that one cannot see music and it was for this reason that music was so closely associated with religion (whose principal mysteries also cannot be seen). The significance of Bacon's discussion is that it is the first which supplies important insights into this ancient association of music and movement.

> Music, moreover, consisting in what is visible, is necessary; and that it is such is evident from the book on the Origin of the Sciences. For whatever can be conformed to sound in similar movements and in corresponding formations, so that our delight may be made com-

plete not only by hearing, but by seeing, belongs to music. Therefore dances and all bendings of bodies are reduced to gesture, which is a branch of music, since these are conformed to sound in similar movements and corresponding formations, as the author of the aforesaid book maintains. Therefore Aristotle says in the seventh book of the Metaphysics that the art of dancing is not complete without another art, that is, without another kind of music to which the art of dancing is conformed.

Bacon mentions the Old Testament reference to the dancing by the sister of Moses and recommends that theologians need to be taught this aspect of music (dance) in order that in preaching on these passages they might

> know how to express all their properties, so that they may give utterance to all the spiritual senses of an angelic devotion.

In the end, however, Bacon returns to the old Church position that the liberal arts have their real value in bringing one to know God.

> I say, therefore, that one science is the mistress of the others, namely, theology, to which the remaining sciences are vitally necessary, and without which it cannot reach its end.[55]

He adds that whatever cannot be connected with the Gospel is therefore against it and should be shunned by the Christian.

In spite of the few philosophical comments on music education, there are some hints that a high level of music education was being carried on, at least in the higher levels of the aristocracy. Strassburg, in his thirteenth-century Romance, characterized Tristan as one who in addition to the study of languages and extensive reading of books, studied all the string instruments for seven years, practicing all day long, beginning at age seven.[56] While, of course this is fiction, Strassburg would not have written this had he not been familiar with people who had such a background.

Another insight into sophisticated singing instruction is found in a true story, the discovery of Richard I, of England, who was captured on his return from the Third Crusade and was being held captive by Austria for debts owed. He was discovered by Blondel, a fellow member of an aristocratic

[55] ibid., 'Philosophy,' I.

[56] Gottfried von Strassburg, *Tristan*, trans., Arthus Hatto (Harmondsworth: Penguin Books, 1960), 69, 91. He played harp, fiddle, organistrum, rote, lyre and sambuca.

singing society in England, who heard Richard singing an art song known only to members of this society. In the following version of this tale, written by a jongleur of Reims in 1260, we are told Blondel found a castle which reportedly held a distinguished prisoner. He offered himself as a jongleur to work in the castle, as a means of discovering the identity of the prisoner. The knight in charge of the castle 'said he would keep him gladly.'

> Then was Blondel right glad, and he went and fetched his viol and his other instruments. And he continued to serve the castellan and pleased him well. And he was on good terms with them of the castle and with all the household. So Blondel abode there all that winter; yet never could he find out who the prisoner was, until one day in Eastertide he went all alone into a garden that adjoined the tower. And he looked about him and bethought himself if by any chance he might see the prisoner. And while he was yet thinking of this, the king looked out through a loophole and espied Blondel. And he took thought how he might make himself known to him. Then did he bethink himself of a song that the two of them had made betwixt them, which none other knew save they two. So began he to sing the first words thereof, loud and clear (for he sang passing well); and when Blondel heard him, then knew he of a surety that this was his lord. And he had in his heart the greatest joy that ever yet he had had in all his days. Straightway he left the garden and went into his own chamber, where he slept; and he took his viol and began to play a strain, and as he played he rejoiced over his lord whom he had found.[57]

One of the last great philosophers of the Middle Ages was Thomas Aquinas (1224–1274 AD), who was also the most prolific Church writer of the late Middle Ages. Born to a noble family, Aquinas spent five years at the University of Naples where he came under the influence of the recently rediscovered works of the ancient Greek philosophers. As a result, Aquinas' admiration for Aristotle is apparent on nearly every page of his many books (a number of them based directly on Aristotle) and in his emphasis on Reason. His life's purpose was to try to demonstrate that the uncompromising logic of Aristotle could be reconciled to a religion based on unquestioned faith. His 'intellectualism' was not well received by the followers of St. Francis, who sought God by Augustine's mystic road of love.[58]

[57] 'La Chronique de Rains,' quoted in Edward Stone, trans., *Three Old French Chronicles of the Crusades* (Seattle: The University of Washington Press, 1939), 275.

[58] Will Durant, *The Age of Faith* (New York: Simon and Schuster, 1950), 977.

John Peckham, who followed Bonaventura in the chair of Philosophy in Paris criticized Aquinas for involving himself in the philosophy of a pagan.

As a thoroughly genuine Churchman, he followed the ancient Church definition of music, writing that music 'takes its principles from arithmetic.'[59] But, surrounded by music performance which was rapidly expanding everywhere in the thirteenth century, Aquinas could not help giving experiential education a level of recognition which the earlier Church fathers could never have done. Therefore he writes,

> For it seems impossible that anyone ... should become a harpist who has not first played the harp.[60]

This apparent confusion in Aquinas is actually a manifestation of the one academic notion which has survived the Middle Ages and is alive and well with us today: the separation of music into two branches, the speculative and the practical. University music departments still separate performance from the speculative wing (being music theory, music history, etc.). The implication, for some, is that you can play in an ensemble, but you can't learn anything about music there. It is the tenth century all over again.

For ourselves, we have two objections to this tenth-century organization of music education. First, we have the suspicion that some of the 'speculative' instruction could be better done in performance. Understanding and hearing harmony, for example, might make more sense to a modern student through experiencing this in performance, that is to say by ear, than by looking at a blackboard covered with Roman numerals. And might the modern student graduate with a better understanding of Renaissance music if he experienced playing more of it, as opposed to hearing someone lecture? How much, and how much better, we might teach speculative concepts through performance we shall probably never know, because of this tenth-century wall between the speculative and the practical.

Our second objection to this tenth-century organization of music education is that we don't think things like music theory and music history should be called 'music' courses. The word 'music,' in our view, should be reserved for live performance. Much of music theory is not music, but rather is grammar or is

[59] *Summa Theologiae* (London: Blackfriars, 1971), I, 11. See also *Commentary on Aristotle's Physics*, op. cit., 12 (184 b 15–185 a 19), 'Music is subalternated to arithmetic,' and 80 (193 b 22–194 a 11).

[60] *Commentary on the Metaphysics of Aristotle*, trans., John Rowan (Chicago: Henry Regnery, 1961), 684–685 (IX.L.7:C 1850).

a symbolic language, like Russian, where the symbols actually represent something else. We think 'music theory' is very important, we just think it should be taught in the Department of Foreign Languages. 'Music history,' of course, is not music, but history. Transfer those professors to the History Department! We are already sending students out in to a world where they will learn that maybe they can't believe everything their government tells them and that maybe they can't believe everything they see on TV (is it live, or is it not?) or read in a newspaper. Let's not add to the confusion they are going to have with reality by calling their courses something they are not.

9 *Music Education in the Fourteenth Century*

THE DOCUMENTS OF THE ARTS FACULTY of the University of Bologna no longer exist, but in a letter of 1308 by Giovanni Bonandrea, a lecturer in rhetoric and poetry, we have evidence that music was being taught.[1] There is also evidence that music was a part of the curriculum at the University of Padua during the fourteenth century. The names of several important students or teachers who were active in music at this university are still known, including Antonio Lido, a professor of medicine, whose epitaph begins, 'Musicus Artista ... '[2] Pietro Vergerio, an important humanist and professor of logic at the university in 1391, wrote a treatise, *De ingenuis moribus*, in which he recommends the study of both the theory and practice of music 'as an aid to the inner harmony of the soul.'[3]

At the University of Paris the study of music remained under its medieval Church definition as a branch of mathematics and was a required course for all students of the arts faculty.[4] French theorists of the fourteenth century continued to divide music into *musica theoretica* and *musica practica*, although the former clearly dominates their treatises. One encounters these terms everywhere, and perhaps they had passed into the common language, as we can see in Machaut, where, with respect to a lover's ability to heal his pain, he notes that she was 'like one who knew all the theory and practice needed to heal me.'[5]

We call these *music* treatises, but they were written by mathematicians. It is for this reason that one has to be disappointed that they made so few comments on what is the most important subject from our perspective today, the stylistic distinctions in *musica practica* between the *ars antiqua* and the *ars nova*.

The most famous representative of the *ars antiqua* in Paris was Jacques de Liege, who wrote his *Speculum Musicae* in about 1313. In this treatise, of which the first five of seven books are concerned with mathematics, we recognize changes were occurring rapidly because here we have a man crying out for the respect which he feels is due the older practice.

[1] Nan Cooke Carpenter, *Music in the Medieval and Renaissance Universities* (Norman: University of Oklahoma Press, 1958), 33.

[2] ibid., 39.

[3] ibid., 40.

[4] ibid., 54, 68.

[5] Guillaume de Machaut, 'Remede de Fortune,' trans., James Wimsatt and William Kibler (Athens: The University of Georgia Press, 1988), 256.

> Now in our day have come new and more recent authors, writing on mensurable music, little revering their ancestors, the ancient doctors; nay, rather changing their sound doctrine in many respects, corrupting, reproving, annulling it, they protest against it in word and deed ...
>
> ...
>
> Should the men who composed and used these [older] sorts of music, or those who know and use them, be called rude, idiotic, and ignorant of the art of singing?[6]

It had been eight hundred years since music education had been divided into the 'speculative' (theory, etc.) and the 'practical' (performance), but only now in the Renaissance do we begin to notice some recognition of the value of performance. We can see Marchetto of Padua, a choirmaster at the Padua Cathedral early in the fourteenth century, trying to bring performance into the picture.

> Nothing concerning numbers and their proportions is relevant to the musician in his capacity as musician. Rather such matters pertain exclusively to arithmetic: to consider how three is related to five is the main concern of the arithmetician, not of the musician.
>
> But to study numbers and proportions as they apply to melody does pertain to music, for the study of music alone informs about melody.
>
> To consider from which numerical proportions—setting numbered notes and syllables in melody in proportion—consonance arises from which ones dissonance arises is, therefore, the consideration of the musician.
>
> Experience shows that this can be understood only in the realm of music itself—that is, in sounding bodies.[7]

But, at the very end of his treatise, Marchetto loses courage and retreats back to the old Church dogma which held that only the student of the speculative side could be called a 'musician.' The singer here represents 'practical music.'

> The musician knows the power and nature of the musical proportions; he judges according to them, not according to sound alone.
>
> The singer is, as it were, the tool of that musician—who is an artisan in that he is occupied with a tool, but a musician inasmuch as he puts into practice what he has previously investigated through rational process.
>
> Thus the musician is to the singer as the judge is to the herald.[8]

---

[6] Quoted in Oliver Strunk, *Source Readings in Music History* (New York: Norton, 1950), 181, 185, 189.

[7] ibid., treatise 2, I, 10, v.

[8] ibid., treatise 16, I, ivff.

Jean de Muris's (ca. 1290–1350) treatise, *Ars nove musice*, although it soon replaced Boethius as the standard university text, is again basically a treatise in the old Church mathematical style. It is the old mathematical basis of music, as part of the liberal arts, which enables de Muris to say, 'no [other] science is hidden from him who knows music well.'[9]

[9] Strunk, op. cit., 179.

He seems particularly old-fashioned in his condemnation of the new musical practice of abandoning the foundation of perfection, the division of rhythm and time into units of three.[10]

[10] ibid., 173.

> All music, especially mensurable music, is founded in perfection, combining in itself number and sound. The number, moreover, which musicians consider perfect in music is ... the ternary number. Music, then, takes its origin from the ternary number.[11]

[11] ibid., 174.

As his rational support of this, he offers an extensive list of 'proofs,' including not only the Trinity, but the three aspects of time of celestial bodies, the three attributes of the stars and sun, the three attributes of the elements, the three intellectual operations, the three terms in the syllogism and many more.[12]

[12] ibid., 173.

In discussing what shapes the notes should be, de Muris again looks to the past, observing, 'the wiser ancients long ago agreed and conceded that geometrical figures should be the symbols of musical sounds.'[13] This he follows with an extraordinary omission, which, had he filled it, would be worth more to us than the rest of his entire treatise.

[13] ibid., 175.

> For reasons which we shall pass over, their symbols did not adequately represent what they sang.

In fourteenth-century England we also find new treatises by Walter Odington and Simon Tunstede which are organized on the basis of *musica speculativa* and *musica practica*.[14] Of the six books which constitute Odington's treatise, by the way, the first three are purely mathematical. But in Ockham we can find just a hint of things to come, the eventual recognition of experiential understanding. He thought there *should* be a non-conceptual form of knowledge, an experiential knowledge analogous to *musica practica*, but he had no insights, as we do from clinical brain research, to suppose that such a thing exists.

[14] Carpenter, op. cit., 86.

We note that [natural science] is a theoretical science for the most part. For a science that does not treat of what we do is speculative. But this science is the kind that is not about what we do; therefore it is speculative. But should there be some part of the philosophy of nature that provides a directive knowledge for the performance of actions, this part would be practical, not theoretical.[15]

But as the Renaissance progressed and music became more and more characterized by feeling and less and less based on mathematical principles, one begins to find passages such as one in Chaucer's, 'The Book of the Duchess,'[16] which begin to emphasize the experiential essence of the 'practical' form of music. Here, when a character is speaking of whether Jubal invented music, as related in the Old Testament, or Pythagoras, another character responds that none of that matters and as for himself, 'I put my feeling into songs, to gladden my heart.' Another Chaucer reference to the importance of *feeling* in music is most revealing. Here he makes the point that singing with feeling is more important than the old speculative theories of the famous Boethius. In the 'Nun's Priest's Tale,' a fox who has come to hear a rooster sing declares that the rooster sings with more feeling in his music than Boethius or any singer.

> Therwith ye han in musyk moore feelynge
> Than hadde Boece, or any that kan synge.[17]

Because the philosophers were not quite ready to recognize the non-rational values of music, we find references at this time to the value of music being in aiding other studies. Giorgio Valla, a fifteenth-century music theorist, distinguished between science and art (one is immutable, the other not), but took the viewpoint of some earlier philosophers that the study of music must come first.

> A knowledge of music is necessary, without a doubt, to learning the [other] liberal arts, which are all dependent on speech.[18]

We find one mention of the educational use of music to aid in learning other things in Chaucer, a reference to the use of music to learn the Latin prayers of the Church.[19] A child in the

[15] William of Ockham, 'Epistemological Problems,' in Philotheus Boehner, *Ockham, Philosophical Writings* (Edinburgh: Thomas Nelson, 1959), 15.

Opening title of 'The Dreame of Chaucer', commonly referred to as 'The Book of the Duchess', published 1532

[16] 'The Book of the Duchess,' 1172.

[17] 'Nun's Priest's Tale,' 4483

[18] Valla, 'De expetendis et fugiendis rebus' (Venice, 1501), quoted in Claude V. Palisca, *Humanism in Italian Renaissance Musical Thought* (New Haven: Yale University Press, 1985), 67, 70.

[19] 'The Prioress's Tale,' 516ff.

church school hears the older students singing the *Alma redemptoris* daily. After repeatedly hearing this, the child himself soon knows the music and the first verse by heart, but, of course, he has no idea what it means. When he asks an older child, one of the singers, what the words mean, the older child says he has heard that it is a salute to 'our blessed Lady and pray her to be our help and succor when we die.' But, he brings into question the effectiveness of using music to teach Latin by observing that he really can't say more about it, for 'I learn singing, but know little grammar.'

> I kan namoore expounde in this mateere;
> I lerne song, I kan but smal grammeere.

Other than at the universities, the most prevalent form of music education in the fourteenth century was found in the schools preparing singers for the church. We are fortunate to have an extant poem for which this kind of study is the subject. The poem is rich in detail regarding the music education pedagogy, the performance expectations of these singers (including perfect intonation), knowledge of *musica ficta* and accuracy in the reading of rhythmic and melodic notation.

> Unfit for the cloister I cower full of concern;
> I look like an idiot and, well listen to my tale.
> The song of the *si-sol-fa* makes me sick and sore
> And I sit stuttering over a song a month and more.
>
> I go wailing about as does a cuckoo.
> There is many a sorrowful song I sing in my book;
> I am held so hard at it, I scarcely dare look up.
> All the mirth of this world I gave up for God.
>
> I wail over my gradual and rore like a rook;
> Little I knew when singing I undertook!
> Some notes are short and some are long,
> Some bend a-wayward like a meat-hook.
>
> When I can sing my lesson, I go to my master
> He hears my performance and doubts I have done well.
> 'What have you been doing, Master Walter, since Saturday noon?
> You don't hold a single note, by God, in tune!'

'Oh my dear Walter, your performance is a shame,
You start and stumble as though you were lame!
Your tones are not the tones which are named;
You bite asunder the B natural, for a B flat you are blamed.'

'Oh my dear Walter, your work leaves much to wonder!
Like an old cauldron you begin to rumble!
You don't hit the notes, you sing under them.
Hold up, for shame! you sing flat.'

Then is Walter so woeful his heart nearly bleeds,
And he goes to visit William and wishes him luck.
'God knows,' says William, 'that I need it!'
Now I know how *judicare* was set in the Credo!

'I am as woeful as a bee that flounders in the water:
I work on the Psalms until my tongue tires.
I have not performed since Palm Sunday.
Are all songs as miserable as the psalms?'

'Yes, by God! You've said it, and it is worse.
I practice solfege, and sing afterwards, but I'm never better;
I hurl at the notes and heave them out of here!
Everyone who hears me knows that I error.

'Of B flat and B natural I knew nothing
When I left the secular world and, well listen to my tale—
Of *ef-fa-ut* and *e-la-mi* I knew nothing before;
I fail strongly in the *fa*, in it my fortune fails more.'

'And there are other notes, *sol* and *ut* and *la*,
And that troublesome wretch men call *fa*:
Often it makes me ill and makes me full of woe;
I can never get it in tune when it is *ta*.'[20]

'And there is a held note with two long tails;
For it our master has often knocked down my skittles.
How little you know what sorrow ails me:
It is but child's play what you do with the psalms!'

'When one note leaps to another and causes riot,
That we call motion in high *ge-sol-re-ut*.'
You were better not born if a mistake you would;
For then our master says 'You're no good.'[21]

[20] A rule of *musica ficta* was that *ti* is sung like *fa* (*ta*, as our singer says), or B-natural becomes B-flat, when it is the top of a phrase.

[21] 'Choristers Training,' in our modern English from the original quoted in Celia and Kenneth Sisam, ed., *The Oxford Book of Medieval English Verse* (Oxford: Clarendon Press, 1970), 184ff.

All students of music, like these, have used solfege in their study process. The name 'solfege' comes from two of the syllables, 'sol' and 'fa.' The syllables together had their origin in the late middle ages, being devised by Guido d'Arezzo and taken from a hymn to St. John. The first six syllables were taken from the beginning of the lines of text, and the seventh, 'Si,' was taken from the first letters of the final two words.

Ut queant laxis **re**sonare fibris
Mira gestorum **fa**muli tuorum,
Solve polluti **la**bii reatum,
Sancte **I**oannes

It is not clear when these syllables became commonly used in music education. Another fourteenth-century reference to them is found in a treatise by Eustache Deschamps, *L'Art de Dictier*. The passage in question is one in which he is discussing 'two kinds of music,' meaning poetry and music.

> It must be understood that we have two kinds of music: one is *artificial* and the other is *natural*.
> *Artificial* music is ... called *artificial* as an art for by its six notes, which are called *us, re, my, fa, sol, la*, one may teach the most uncultivated man in the world to sing, make harmony and an octave, fifth and third, make a tenor, and descant by the form of notes, by clefs and by staves.[22]

[22] Quoted in Christopher Page, 'Machaut's "Pupil" Deschamps on the Performance of Music,' in *Early Music* 5 (1977), 489.

The complaint of the choral students above also reminds us of the great poet Francesco Petrarch's (1304–1374) warning that in music, 'much avails practice.' He sang his own poetry in public and in the following he attributes his success to practice.

> Saw too a race of melodious singers, all of them masters,
> Content to stand under its shade and fashion the rarest of garlands.
> And on that greensward I too have learned—for much avails practice
> Long and laborious—how to vary my notes, singing many
> Albeit modest songs, and have dared to crown my own temples
> Finally with that same leafage.[23]

[23] 'Remedies for Fortune Fair and Foul,' trans., Conrad Rawski (Bloomington: Indiana University Press, 1991), X, 366ff.

And those who did not practice, then as now, suffered in public. John Gower (1330–1408), complains that the priests themselves were no exception.

A priest of God rarely rises sober from the table or chaste from a bed. When exhilarated by taverns his voice sings on high, but in churches it is all too mute.[24]

[24] John Gower, *The Voice of One Crying*, trans., Eric Stockton in *The Major Latin Works of John Gower* (Seattle: University of Washington Press, 1962), III, xx.

There must have also been many people who educated themselves in music in the fourteenth century. A rather unusual example must have been the Squire in Chaucer's *Canterbury Tales*. He not only sang and played flute, but could also compose and notate his own music. Another we find especially attractive is Nicholas, the 'poor scholar' of Oxford. He sang only at night, in his room, for himself, sweetly singing to the accompaniment of his psaltery. But he sang a varied repertoire, some sacred songs and some secular ones, such as 'The King's Note.'

> And al above ther lay a gay sautrie,
> On which he made a-nyghtes melodie
> So swetely that all the cyhambre rong;
> And *Angelus ad virginem* he song;
> And after that he song the kynges noote.[25]

[25] 'The Miller's Tale,' 3213.

In closing we must mention that the *scolae ministrallorum* (Minstrel Schools) were still meeting during the fourteenth century. These were informal gatherings of wandering minstrels, held during Lent, for the purpose of learning new repertoire and exchanging instruments. Often they gathered by the hundreds in agreed upon small villages and the only contemporary description of any kind is found in Chaucer's 'The House of Fame.' This was self-education and entirely aural and it must have been something to witness, for Chaucer says there were more musicians 'than there be stars in heaven.' He also mentions the educational aspect in a passage where he records seeing famous shawm players from The Netherlands.

> Ther saugh I famous, olde and yonge,
> Pipers of the Duche tonge,
> To lerne love-daunces, sprynges,
> Reyes, and these strange thynges.

10 *Music Education in the Fifteenth Century*

THE RAPIDLY SPREADING IDEALS OF HUMANISM in music, based on the rediscovery of the books of the ancient Greek philosophers, together with the general spirit of the Renaissance itself, were creating a new understanding of music. Music was gradually becoming to be understood as a voice of emotions and of one's personal experience. Fewer and fewer people were still buying into the Church's old contention that music was a branch of mathematics, although, of course, there were some who could not free their minds of the old dogma.

One of the most conspicuous of these persons was Johannes Tinctoris (1435–1511), the best known music theorist of the fifteenth century. One of his books, *Proportionate Musices*, was so old-fashioned and so indebted to the Church teaching regarding mathematics that Tinctoris himself tells us that a singer who was so appalled by this book threatened to make Tinctoris eat it! When he writes that only musicians can judge sounds correctly, he means that only someone educated to understand the mathematical aspects of the vibrations, etc.

> Although the Spartans may have said that they could judge without learning about good and bad harmonies, this position has not been completely defended, for as the universal opinion of all philosophers holds, a sense of hearing is too often lacking. If the truth is to be confessed I have known and put to the test many people, not deaf, but experts in the art of music, who, not admiring the size or beauty of the voice, prefer calflike bellowings to moderate rationalities and, as I say, to angelic songs. I think these people worthy to have their human faces with their stupid ears changed by divine intervention into those of an ass ...
> Only musicians judge sounds correctly.[1]

In another place, Tinctoris specifies the performer in this regard, paraphrasing an old idea first advanced by the Church philosopher, Guido d'Arezzo.

> A musician is one who takes up the metier of singing, having observed its principles by means of study. Hence, someone has set down the difference between a musician and a singer in the following jingle:

[1] *Concerning the Nature and Propriety of Tones*, trans., Albert Seay (Colorado Springs, 1976), 5.

> There is a big difference between musicians and singers.
> These know, those talk about, what music is.
> And he who doesn't know what he talks about is considered an animal.[2]

In his book on proportional music he gives musical examples of such extraordinary mathematical difficulty that it is impossible to believe that any student could have ever sung them. Even the conservative Gustav Reese agrees:

> We find him here a musical mathematician, at times explaining proportions that can have had little to do with actual practice, though they may have been studied for purposes of exercise.[3]

And it is on the basis of his mathematics-governed theory that he criticizes some of his contemporaries whom we regard today as having been great composers. He does this, he says, not from arrogance, but for the purpose of fighting for truth.[4] He criticizes 'the inexcusable error of Okeghem'[5] and a 'bad use' by Dufay.[6] In one place his admiration for Dufay sneaks in when he says the composer has 'most wonderfully erred.'[7]

But, we must give Tinctoris credit for two views which departed dramatically from the old Church dogma about the nature of music. First, he is beginning to understand that the ear must be the judge in music, not the eye; experience is replacing mathematics. In his *Dictionary*, for example, he defines dissonance as 'a combination of different sounds which by nature is displeasing to the ears.'[8] Not only this, but in another place he adds emotion to the definition, something for which the Church might have imprisoned him in the sixth century. Now Tinctoris calls a dissonance that which is

> a mixture of two pitches naturally offending the ears. And it is called discord metaphorically from 'dis' and 'corde,' for, just as the bitterness of enmity arises from the separation of two hearts from a mutual uniformity of sentiment, so the harshness of a discord is produced from two pitches not agreeing with each other.[9]

---

[2] *Dictionary of Musical Terms*, trans., Carl Parrish (New York: Free Press of Glencoe, 1963), 45.

[3] Gustave Reese, *Music in the Renaissance* (New York: Norton, 1959), 146.

[4] *Proportionale Musices*, trans., Albert Seay in *Journal of Music Theory* (1957), Prologue.

[5] ibid., I, iii.

[6] ibid.

[7] ibid., III, vi.

[8] *Dictionary of Musical Terms*, op. cit., 25.

[9] *The Art of Counterpoint*, trans., Albert Seay (American Institute of Musicology, 1961), 85.

The second view he states which is a dramatic departure from one thousand years of Church philosophy, yet very characteristic of humanism and the Renaissance, is when he finds the essence of music not in the old 'speculative' definition, but in performance, or as the Church used to say, 'practical' music.

> Music is that skill consisting of performance in singing and playing.[10]

[10] *Dictionary of Musical Terms*, op. cit., 43.

A particularly old-fashioned Scholastic philosopher who commented on the liberal arts, including music, was the German, Nicholas of Cusa (1401–1464). Reflecting only the rational side of man, he declares,

> No one can ignore that the truth is attained in mathematics more certainly than in all other liberal arts.[11]

[11] Nicholas of Cusa, 'Theological Complement,' II, trans., William Wertz, Jr., in *Toward a New Council of Florence* (Washington DC: Schiller Institute, 1993), 274. He returns to the subject of the importance of mathematics in mind function in his treatise, 'On Actualized-possibility,' 43.

One of his rather strange thoughts was that God used the liberal arts to create the world. The only way he could fit music into this discussion, given his perspective, was to speak of proportional music, an old-fashioned theory of composition which was virtually dead by the time of his writing.

> In creating the world, God used arithmetic, geometry, music, and likewise astronomy. (We ourselves also use these arts when we investigate the comparative relationships of objects, of elements, and of motions.) For through arithmetic God united things. Through geometry He shaped them, in order that they would thereby attain firmness, stability, and mobility in accordance with their conditions. Through music He proportioned things in such a way that there is not more earth in earth than water in water, air in air, and fire in fire, so that no one element is altogether reducible to another. As a result, it happens that the world-machine cannot perish …
>
> And so, God, who created all things in number, weight, and measure, arranged the elements in an admirable order. (Number pertains to arithmetic, weight to music, measure to geometry.)[12]

[12] Nicholas of Cusa, 'A defense of Learned Ignorance,' trans., Jasper Hopkins in *Nicholas of Cusa's Debate with John Wenck* (Minneapolis: Banning Press, 1981), II, xiii, 175. Nicholas does not explain the reference of weight to music.

Nicholas of Cusa would by no means be the last philosopher to attempt to force music into the world of mathematics, but fortunately there would be few whose minds traveled the paths of Cusa.

> All harmony therefore rests in these numbers 1, 2, 3, 4 and their combinations. The cause of every harmony arises therefore from the necessity of this rational progression. However, the fact that the precision of [the] semi-tone remains hidden to rationality, is because one cannot attain it without the coincidence of the even and the odd. You see that sensible combinations are unfoldings so to speak of rational unity, whence the harmonic rational unity; when it is closely contracted in the combination of sensible things, rationality takes delight in it just as though in its own work or in its close similitude.
>
> ...
>
> If you wish to assemble a more detailed treatment by means of these aforementioned principles of conjecture, then refer back to the figure of the universe, and take the maximum circle as rationality, and elicit from it the most lucid, more brilliant and more abstract rational art; the lowest more adumbral; and the median rational arts. If you inquire into mathematics, do the same, so that you constitute one as it were intellectual, another as it were sensible, and a median as it were rational; likewise with music. If you wish to know more about music itself, then take the circle of the universe as the rational nature of music; and you will intuit a music as it were more intellectually abstract, another as it were sensible, and a third as it were rational. You can effect the miraculous in all these things, if you devote yourself to them with diligent meditation.[13]

[13] Nicholas of Cusa, 'On Conjectures,' XIII, trans., William Wertz, Jr., in *Toward a New Council of Florence* (Washington DC: Schiller Institute, 1993), 96ff.

The other principal source of lingering medieval dogma about music was the universities. The University at Salamanca, along with those of Paris, Bologna and Oxford, was one of the important centers for the study of music and the first in Europe to have an endowed chair in music (1254), although the associated records reveal that the music professor received the lowest pay of the faculty.[14] By the fifteenth century the treatises on music produced in this university tended to remain in the old Church mold, in which music was firmly rooted in the larger field of mathematics. The *Musica practica* (1482) by Ramos de Pareja was one of the few to put forward original ideas, although this treatise is also heavily grounded in mathematics. One of his innovations was the replacement of the solemnization syllables based on Guido with a new set of his invention based on the octave. This brought upon him great controversy, which was due in part, according to Reese, to the establishment of a chair in music at the University of Bologna in 1450—the mathematical faculty demanding that music belonged to its

[14] Enrique Esperabe y Arteaga, *Historia pragmatica e interna de la Universidad de Salamanca* (Salamanca, 1914–1917), I, 22.

field.[15] The treatise *Lux bella* (1492) by Domingo Duran is also heavily weighted with mathematics (based on Boethius), but also includes a section on the uses and effects of music.[16]

During the fifteenth century university statutes in Vienna and Heidelberg clearly specify the study of music as part of the lectures of the arts faculty.[17] In addition, the University of Vienna began to present plays with musical chorus and solos, written by humanists such as Celtes and Wimpheling.

In the works by Christine de Pizan, of France, it sometimes curiously seems as if she deliberately omits music. For example, in one of her books, she describes, in a vision, visiting 'a noble university.' She finds there 'each separate branch of knowledge,' including grammar, dialectic, arithmetic, geometry, astrology, theology, philosophy, 'and so on with the other forbidden and liberal arts.' Music is conspicuously missing.[18]

In another book, she quotes a story of Cyrus, King of Persia (ca. 550 BC), one often retold in early literature, which told of his concern over a conquered people and his decision to have the people instructed in music so that they might become effeminate and thus be unlikely to cause trouble. It is interesting that when Christine de Pizan tells this story, she omits 'music' and substitutes for it 'gambling and accustoming themselves to merchandise.'[19]

It was during the fifteenth century that the first of the lay organizations for men, known as academies, was founded by Marsilio Ficino. Ficino, founder of the Florentine Academy, was a philosopher who was an active musician in his leisure, playing the lyre for his own relaxation, but also in concerts in the Medici palace.[20] His combined interests in music and philosophy resulted in some very interesting conclusions on the virtues of music. In a view which would have never been approved by the Church, he believed that music served man's 'spirit' in the same way medicine serves the body and theology the soul. The music one hears provokes a memory in the soul of the divine music found in the mind of God and in the music of the spheres. Through affecting the spirit, music also affects the body and soul. He says he personally found music valuable for ridding the body of disturbances and lifting his mind to a higher level of intellect.

[15] Gustave Reese, *Music in the Renaissance* (New York: Norton, 1959), 587.

[16] Nan Cooke Carpenter, *Music in the Medieval and Renaissance Universities* (Norman: University of Oklahoma Press, 1958), 218.

[17] ibid., 224, 230.

[18] Christine de Pizan, *Christine's Vision*, trans., Glenda McLeod (New York: Garland Publishing, 1993), II, ii.

[19] Christine de Pizan, *The Book of the Body Politic*, trans., Kate Forhan (Cambridge: Cambridge University Press), I, xxviii.

[20] Paul Kristeller, 'Music and Learning in the Early Italian Renaissance,' in *The Journal of Renaissance and Baroque Music* (1947), I, Nr. 4, 269ff.

Some of the most important ideas of the fifteenth century that departed from one thousand years of Church dogma about music were not so much new ideas as very ancient ideas. That is, they are part of the humanism movement in music which began with the rediscovery of the books of the ancient Greek philosophers. In terms of music education, one fifteenth-century treatise which clearly reflects the ancient Greek ideas is the *Practica musicae* (1496) by Franchino Gaffurio (1451–1518). He begins his book, which was intended as a counter-balance to the centuries of treatises on 'speculative music' (meaning theory), by praising the effects on society of ancient music education.

> It is readily apparent, illustrious Prince, how much influence the profession of the art of music had and with what veneration it was held among the ancients. We know this both from the example of the greatest philosophers, who, when they were very old, devoted themselves to this discipline as if in it they put the finishing touch to their studies, and from the practice of the strictest governments, which with the utmost diligence saw to it that whatever was harmful to public morals should be eliminated. Not only did these states not banish the art of music; they cultivated it with the utmost zeal as the mother and nurse of morals. In a word, the position of music is firmly established by the unanimous and steadfast conviction of all people and all nations who have held this art in greater honor than any other.
>
> What other discipline has ever been accepted with so much approval? What other discipline has ever been accepted with so much unanimity by people of every age or sex, so that no one, in any condition of life, has yet been found who was not eager to soothe his cares with music.[21]

[21] Irwin Young, trans., *The Practica musicae of Franchinus Gafurius* (Madison: University of Wisconsin Press, 1969), 3.

Now he writes specifically of the wide benefits of music education and it is interesting here that he is very conscious of the *quality* of music used in music education.

Portrait of musician Franchino Gaffurio, Milan, by Leonardo da Vinci, ca. 1490

> Now music is not, like the other learned disciplines, merely a speculative pursuit: it reaches out into practice, and as was said previously, is connected with morality. I would not have fulfilled my duty if I had remained in the field of research only, serving a few without toiling diligently for the public good also.
>
> Thus this field of music theory is valuable not only because of the knowledge it gives music itself, but also because its roots extend very far; it aids other disciplines. This has been verified by the testimony of very influential men who have acknowledged that they learned

literature from music above all else. Fabius Quintilian declares, on the authority of Timagenes, that this art 'is the most ancient of all studies in liberal education.'

Now when I talk about music, I do not mean that theatrical and effeminate music which destroys rather than forms public morals, but rather that moderate, manly music celebrated by the ancient heroes, that music which was presented at the tables of kings and festive banquets when the guests, vying with one anther as the cithara circulated among them, sang of famous deeds of famous men, which was certainly a great inducement to kindle their eagerness for brave deeds. Truly this music rose even higher: she penetrates the heavens, and according to the testimony of the most celebrated bards, tells of the labors of the sun and the wandering moon and the titan stars, and as if not content to have filled the spaces of earth with merit, she invades the skies and takes her place among the mysteries of things divine.[22]

[22] ibid., 5ff.

The association with the divine, which he describes in the last sentence, was something frequently mentioned by the ancient writers. It was encouraged, we suppose, due to the fact that music is the only art you cannot see. This unique quality of music also sets it apart from the other senses, a fact that continued to be mentioned in the fifteenth century. Christine de Pizan, for example, points out that this very characteristic of music sets it apart from generalizations on rational truth.

Whatever we cannot see with our eyes, as the fools say, we cannot know, except what is given to us to hear.[23]

[23] Christine de Pizan, *The Epistle of the Prison of Human Life*, trans., Josette Wisman (New York: Garland Publishing, 1984), 49.

Leonardo da Vinci (1452–1519) also mentioned this unique aspect of music.

The poet ranks far below the painter in the representation of visible things, and far below the musician in that of invisible things.[24]

[24] Jean Paul Richter, ed., *The Literary Works of Leonardo da Vinci* (London: Phaidon, 1970), I, 80.

Even though Gaffurio had dedicated his treatise to 'practical' music, as opposed to 'speculative music,' meaning music theory, he seems somewhat surprised that he has noticed that musicians on the street have learned about chords without studying the 'speculative' books.

Even though the majority of scholars have pursued the science of harmony, while neglecting its practical application, far more extensively than those who have studied the practical application of the science—after all, the science of harmony is the domain of the theoretician—nevertheless, it is incredible that musicians could have attained the practical skill in harmony which they did attain without any study of theory.[25]

The answer is, of course, that musicians learn to perform on an experiential level, not on a rational level. Gaffurio, in fact, seemed to understand this, as he observed:

> It is true that these sounds are assembled in vain by theory and science unless they are expressed in practice. Hence one must become thoroughly conversant with the highness, lowness, and the combinations of these sounds not only through one's mind and reason but also through the habit of listening to and [performing] them.[26]

This recognition of the legitimate value of experience is also a new manifestation of humanism. The old Church had refused to assign any value to personal experience because to do so opens the door to individual thinking, instead of following the Church's thinking. One who frequently argued the educational importance of experience was Leonardo da Vinci. Even when it comes to writing, itself considered a rational exercise, Leonardo finds personal experience indispensable.

> They will say that I, having no literary skill, cannot properly express that which I desire to treat of; but they do not know that my subjects are to be dealt with by experience rather than by words; and experience has been the mistress of those who wrote well. And so, as mistress, I will cite her in all cases.[27]

Even when it comes to core science, Leonardo finds experience critical.

> They say that knowledge born of experience is mechanical, but that knowledge born and consummated in the mind is scientific, while knowledge born of science and culminating in manual work is semi-mechanical. But to me it seems that all sciences are vain and full or errors that are not born of experience, mother of all certainty, and that are not tested by experience, that is to say, that do not at their origin, middle or end pass through any of the five senses. (For if we are doubtful about the certainty of things that pass through the senses how much more should we question the many things against which these senses rebel, such as the nature of God and the soul and the like, about which there are endless disputes and controversies. And truly it so happens

[25] Young, op. cit., 11.

[26] ibid., 12.

Self-portrait of Leonardo da Vinci, Turin, Royal Library, ca. 1510-1515

[27] Richter, op. cit., I, 116. Da Vinci, by the way, wrote at least two books on music, one on the voice and one on instruments, which are lost.

that where reason is not, its place is taken by clamor. This never occurs when things are certain. Therefore, where there are quarrels, there true science is not; because truth can only end one way—wherever it is known, controversy is silenced for all time, and should controversy nevertheless again arise, then our conclusions must have been uncertain and confused and not truth which is reborn.) All true sciences are the result of experience which has passed through our senses, thus silencing the tongues of litigants.[28]

[28] ibid., I, 33ff.

Leonardo addressed the importance of the role of experience through numerous observations, as the following will illustrate:

Experience, the interpreter between formative nature and the human race, teaches how that nature acts among mortals; and being constrained by necessity cannot act otherwise than as reason, which is its helm, requires it to act.

...

Experience does not err; only your judgments err by expecting from her what is not in her power. Men wrongly complain of Experience; with great abuse they accuse her of leading them astray. Let experience alone, and turn your complaints against your ignorance, which causes you to be carried away by vain and foolish desires as to expect from it things that are not in her power; saying that she is fallacious.

...

Wisdom is the daughter of experience.[29]

[29] ibid., II, 240.

The skill, or craft, of the artist, in Leonardo's view, was first based on experience, and as anyone knows who has seen the meticulous notes and drawings of Leonardo's sketchbooks, his concept of experience included the most precise discipline of observation. From experience comes the knowledge and rules of the craft.

Good judgment is born of clear understanding, and a clear understanding comes of reasons derived from sound rules, and sound rules are the product of sound experience—the common mother of all the sciences and arts.[30]

[30] ibid., I, 119.

...

Those who devote themselves to practice without science are like sailors who put to sea without rudder or compass and who can never be certain where they are going. Practice must always be founded on sound theory.[31]

[31] Quoted in Anthony Blunt, *Artistic Theory in Italy, 1450–1600* (Oxford: Clarendon Press, 1959), 28.

Leonardo da Vinci, in his private writings, also made some interesting observations about education in general. Leonardo regarded knowledge as so fundamental to man that he several times spoke of it as a kind of food.

> The knowledge of past times and of the places on the earth is both ornament and nutriment to the human mind.[32]
>
> ...
>
> Acquire learning in youth which restores the damage of old age; and if you understand that old age has wisdom for its food, you will so conduct yourself in youth that your old age will not lack sustenance.

[32] Richter, op. cit., II, 243.

He continued this analogy in recommending that education should seek to make the acquisition of knowledge palatable.

> Just as food eaten without caring for it is turned into loathsome nourishment, so study without a taste for it spoils memory, causing it to retain nothing which it has taken in.[33]

[33] ibid., II, 244.

Among the virtues of knowledge, Leonardo often points to their moral contribution.

> The acquisition of any knowledge is always of use to the intellect, because it may thus drive out useless things and retain the good.[34]

[34] ibid., II, 244.

Similarly, in the first of two reflections on culture in general, Leonardo found those who had not obtained knowledge to be little above animals.

> It seems to me that men of coarse and clumsy habits and of small knowledge do not deserve such fine instruments or so great a variety of natural mechanism as men of speculation and of great knowledge ... for it seems to me they have nothing about them of the human species but the voice and the figure, and for all the rest are much below beasts.[35]

[35] ibid., II, 235.

But, in this regard, the knowledge must be personally understood and absorbed, and not merely data which is employed in quotation.

Any one who in discussion relies upon authority uses, not his understanding, but rather his memory. Good culture is born of a good disposition; and since the cause is more to be praised than the effect, you will rather praise a good disposition without culture, than good culture without the disposition.[36]

With regard to traditional education, Leonardo had one great chip on his shoulder. He mentions in several places that he could not understand why painting had not been admitted as one of the liberal arts, in particular why music was admitted as a member of the Liberal Arts, while painting was not.

After giving a place to Music among the Liberal Arts you must place Painting there, too, or else withdraw Music.[37]

Finally, we should mention that Leonardo makes a passing reference to the difficulty in re-educating the mind of an artist who makes mistakes. This reflection follows Leonardo's acknowledgment that mistakes, so easily painted over in painting, in sculpture cannot be corrected. This apparent demand for perfection, however, cannot be taken as meaning sculpture is a higher art. The postscript he adds to this thought appears to be a very personal confession.

It is a poor argument to try to prove that a work is nobler because oversights are irremediable; I should rather say that it will be more difficult to mend the mind of a master who commits such errors than to mend the work he has spoiled.[38]

One writer who made specific recommendations regarding music education was Christine de Pizan of France. She favored the reinstitution of the ancient Greek educational use of sung epic poetry. Christine de Pizan thought children should hear 'songs of great deeds' as part of their education.[39] We might also mention that a Ballade by Charles of Orleans mentions in passing that young ladies were expected to have been educated with some level of musical culture.[40]

There were others in the fifteenth century who were interested in the ancient Greek belief in the use of music education to form character in students. Vittorino da Feltre (1396–1415), who established a humanistic school in the court of Gianfrancesco Gonzaga in Mantua, was a strong believer in

[36] ibid., II, 241.

[37] ibid., I, 79.

[38] ibid., I, 95.

[39] Christine de Pizan, *The Book of the Body Politic*, trans., Kate Forhan (Cambridge: Cambridge University Press), I, xxxiii.

[40] 'Ballade IX,' quoted in Robert Steele, *The English Poems of Charles of Orleans* (London: Oxford University Press, 1941), 16.

the Greek ideals of music having a beneficial effect on character, and for this purpose he introduced music at meal times for his students.[41]

[41] Carpenter, op. cit., 44.

Another who believed in the use of music during meals for educational purposes was Paolo Cortese. In a treatise on the organization of the household of a cardinal, *De cardinalatu libri tres*, he observes,

> The same must be said about the kind of all other passions, against which an adverse position must be taken always by the [cardinal] at other times, but more than ever at this time of recreation, lest his body be prevented from digesting the food by some intervening discomfort of his soul. Wherefore, since at this time those things must be sought after by which a cheerful mood is usually aroused, it may well be inquired whether the pleasure of music should be put to use particularly at this point, inasmuch as many, estranged from the natural disposition of the normal sense, not only reject it because of some sad perversion of their nature, but even think it to be hurtful for the reason that it is somehow an invitation to idle pleasure, and above all, that its merriment usually arouses the evil of lust. On the opposite side, however, many agree to resort to it as to a certain discipline that is engaged in the knowledge of concordance and modes.
>
> Indeed, we are convinced that music should be put to use at this time for the sake not only of merriment, but also of knowledge and morals ...
>
> It must be said that music must be sought after for the sake of morals, inasmuch as the habit of passing judgment on what is similar to morals in its rational basis cannot be considered to be different from the habit of passing judgment on the rational basis of morals themselves, and of becoming expert in this latter judgment through imitation. Also, since the melodious modes of music appear to imitate all the habits of morals and all the motions of passions, there is no doubt that to be entertained by a temperate combination of modes would also mean to get in the habit of passing judgment on the rational basis of morals. This can also be proved, inasmuch as it is evident that all the habits and motions of the soul are found in the nature of the modes, in which nature the similarity to fortitude, or temperance, or anger, or mildness is exhibited, and it can easily be observed and judged that the minds of men are usually brought to those motions just as they are excited by the action of the modes.[42]

[42] Cortese, quoted in Nino Pirrotta, in *Music and Culture in Italy from the Middle Ages to the Baroque* (Cambridge: Harvard University Press, 1984), 102.

Carlo Valgulio, a secretary to the papal treasurer (1481–1485), and later to cardinal Cesare Borgia, believed that the performance of music was in a general state of decay. In the preface to his translation of Plutarch's *De musica*, dedicated to the singer Titus Pyrrhinus, he urges the latter to raise the level of performance and its ethical efficacy to that of the ancients.⁴³ He found that musicians have little regard for these effects, 'filling their books with mere play of notes.' He recommends to this singer his interpretation of Aristotle's division of songs into three classes: edifying, purgative and recreational.

⁴³ Quoted in Claude V. Palisca, *Humanism in Italian Renaissance Musical Thought* (New Haven: Yale University Press, 1985), 88ff.

> Some songs were moral, others suitable for imbuing the soul with divine spirit, and still others active. The first category is suited to customs that are consistent with the most gentle virtue. The second class, songs which induce ecstasy, has the capacity to purge men who are disturbed by entering into subjects that are arousing and soft and by opening the affections to the purgation of fear and pity, which depress and afflict men's souls. Such melodies fill souls with a beneficial contentment.⁴⁴

⁴⁴ ibid., 100.

Franchino Gaffurio, in his *Theorica musice*, also stresses the ethical potential of music.

> Socrates and Plato and also the Pythagoreans, attributing a moral resource to music, ordered by a common law that adolescents and youth, and young women too, be educated in music, not for inciting to desire, through which this discipline becomes cheapened, but for moderating the movements of the soul through rule and reason. Just as not every note is valid for a melody of sounds but only that which makes a good consonance, so also not all motions of the soul but only those that are suited to reason belong to the correct harmony of life.⁴⁵

⁴⁵ ibid., 193.

A fifteenth-century English poem by John Lydgate contends that the ancients civilized the common people through music education and the resultant concord made possible both philosophy and the building of cities. Music, he suggests, contributes to peace and prudent policies.

> Philisophres of the goldene ages
> And poetes that [found] out fressh [songs],
> As kyng Amphioun with his fair langages
> And with his harpyng made folk of [low] degrees,
> As laborers, tenhabite first cities;—
> And so bi musik and philosophie
> Gan first of comouns noble policie.
>
> The cheeff of musik is mellodie & accord;
> Welle of philosophie sprang out of prudence,
> Bi which too menys gan unite & concord

With politik vertu to have ther assistence:
Wise men to regne, subiectis do reuerence.
And bi this ground, in stories men may see,
Wer bilt the wallis of Thebes the cite.

Accord in musik causith the mellodie;
Wher is discord, ther is dyuersite,
And wher is [peace] is prudent policie
In ech kyngdam and euery gret [country].[46]

The one area of music performance which was most frequently mentioned as having been deficient in education was clerical singing. Craig Wright has found among the documents for even a large cathedral such as that of Cambrai evidence of the employment of adult singers who could not read music.[47] Perhaps another clue to the education of these singers may be inferred from documents which refer to disciplinary actions taken against them for various offenses committed during the actual church service. The most surprising of these is one of 1493 when the singers were admonished for

> throwing meat and bones from one side of the choir to the other during the divine service.[48]

An important fifteenth-century treatise on singing, *De modo bene cantandi* (1474) by Conrad von Zabern is quite critical of the education of church singers.[49] He begins with basic vocal production such as singing through the nose and adding an 'h' before vowel sounds. The latter he says reminds him of the sounds butchers make in driving sheep to pasture.

> This is not elegant singing, and we can say without fear of contradiction that it is very coarse.

In this regard he stresses the importance of correct Latin, in the syllables and vowels. Some clerics, he has observed, sound as if they had food in their mouths.

> Indeed, from Frankfurt to Koblenz and as far as Trier I have noticed this very often, especially in students. They all distort the chant, inclined as they are to pronounce the vowels e and i poorly and without

[46] John Lydgate, *Fall of Princes*, ed., Henry Bergen (London: Oxford University Press, 1967), VI, 337ff. This work is ostensibly a translation of Giovanni Boccaccio's *De Casibus Virorum Illustrium*, although Lydgate freely engages in his own commentary and philosophy.

[47] Craig Wright, 'Performance Practices at the Cathedral of Cambrai 1475–1550,' in *The Musical Quarterly* (1978), LXIV, Nr. 3, 313.

[48] ibid., 297.

[49] This discussion is based on Joseph Dyer, trans., 'Singing with Proper Refinement,' in *Early Music* (April, 1978), 207ff.

sufficient differentiation—a situation which has not infrequently caused me much displeasure. Their masters ought to restrain them from this error forthwith, lest they perpetuate it into old age.

He criticizes inaccurate intonation, especially in ascending and descending pitches. This may have been caused in part by his next objection, forcing the voice.

Truly I know people better instructed than others in chant who nevertheless render all their singing unworthy of praise by this very defect. Though it appears to them that they are singing well, this is just because no one has suggested to them how offensive this fault really is, and how much to be avoided.

And we recall Queen Isabella of Spain (1474–1504) is reported as personally assuming the role of teacher and correcting such errors by the singers of her court.

If anyone of those who were saying or singing the psalms, or other things of the church, made any slip in diction or in the placing of a syllable, she heard and noted it, and afterwards—as teacher to pupil—she emended and corrected it for them.[50]

[50] L. Marineus Siculus, *De las cosas memorables de Espana* (1539), 182v.

Finally, there are two more things which we begin to see in the fifteenth century which cannot be separated from education. First, after centuries of being valued for its functional use, there are increasing hints that music is now something to be valued for contemplation for its own sake. The humanist philosopher, Paolo Cortese, mentions this in a discussion of pleasure and pain. He emphasizes that the mere stopping of pain results in pleasure, but an ideal form of pleasure is one which also holds the potential for learning. Here he points to music as an example.

We can easily establish that the stopping of anything from which sadness arises must be considered joyous by its own nature. Thus, if a discipline—which is a certain function of understanding something with the guidance of reason—is recognized to have a way of seeking not only a profit but also becoming pleasure, it is proper that whatever must be sought after for the sake of understanding and results by its own nature is a pleasure, this same should be sought after for the sake of both diversion and learning. Also, nobody who accords to music the faculty of contemplation, while its own nature is cheerful, should hesitate to confess that it must be rightly sought after for the sake of both pleasure and learning.[51]

[51] Paolo Cortese, 'De cardinalatu libri tres,' quoted in Nino Pirrotta, op. cit., 102.

Second, century by century, there is a growing sense of personal involvement in music. We can see a nice example of this personal enthusiasm on the part of Carlo Valgulio, a late fifteenth-century writer who was drawn to music scholarship because of 'an incredible love for music and musicians.' He wrote of the importance of music in his preface to his translation of Plutarch's *De musica*.

Since melos [also] signifies what someone cares about, and almost nothing ought to be of greater concern to a man than song and music, as it moves men and gods so much, they called song melos. Nor did they call absolutely any song thus but only that consisting of harmony.[52]

[52] Quoted in Palisca, op. cit., 88, 94.

11 *Music Education in Sixteenth-Century Italy*

IT IS IN SIXTEENTH-CENTURY ITALY that one first sees the full intensity of the climax in debate between the long Church dominated intellectual atmosphere and the full arrival of the new humanist movement, a debate that would resonate until our own time. Consequently, sixteenth-century philosophic commentary on music tends to fall into two schools. First, as Carpenter clearly documents, in the Italian universities music remained bound in its old Church-influenced association with mathematics. Thus when, for example, Ludovico Ferrari wished to defend Cardano against Niccolo Tartaglia, he offered to debate the latter 'on any mathematical discipline, including music.'[1] These universities, therefore, continued to grind out music treatises in the old Church mathematics-based perspective, a typical example being Stephano Venneo's *Recanetum* (1533).

The second school of thought was that of the humanists, whose great achievement was the restoration to music of its most fundamental purpose, the expression of feelings. They arrived at this purpose from their study of the ancient Greek treatises which discussed music. Vincenzo Galilei (1533–1591) in his *Dialog on Ancient and Modern Music* recalled the disappearance of the Greek ideals in music during the Dark Ages, a period which he characterizes 'as if all men had been overcome by a heavy lethargy of ignorance, they lived without any desire for learning and took as little notice of music as of the western Indies.'[2] Although this treatise is largely an attack on the ideas of Zarlino, Galilei credits him, together with Glarean and Gafurius, as being responsible for the renewal of Greek ideals. He found they did not completely succeed, which 'may have been owing to the rudeness of the times, the difficulty of the subject, and the scarcity of good interpreters.' When Galilei speaks of the 'renewal of Greek ideals,' everything he meant by this was related to feelings.

We have one first-person account of study at an actual sixteenth-century Italian music school. Vincenzo Giustiniani tells us that his father sent him to a music school, where he studied

[1] Nan Cooke Carpenter, *Music in the Medieval and Renaissance Universities* (Norman: University of Oklahoma Press, 1958), 129.

[2] Vincenzo Galilei, 'Dialogo della musica antica e della moderna,' in Oliver Strunk, *Source Readings in Music History* (New York: Norton, 1950), 303.

Vincenzo Giustiniani by Nicolas Regner, ca. 1630

the works of Arcadelt, Orlando Lassus, Striggio, Cipriano de Rore and Filippo di Monte, whom he considered the best composers of their time. There he also studied secular music with 'a certain Pitio, excellent musician and jongleur.'[3]

The late medieval Church separation of the study of music into the 'speculative' (music theory, etc.) and the 'practical' (performance) has influenced music education until the present day. The philosophical debates among music theorists of the sixteenth century are very important, therefore, because they document the beginning of a slow moving away from the old Church Scholastic theories of music being a branch of mathematics toward a more modern understanding that music is of the province of the expression of feelings. In his book on lute intabulation, Galilei raises the fundamental question of whether the practice of music is derived from the ear or from mathematics.

[3] Vicenzo Giustiniani, *Discorso sopra la Musica* (ca. 1628), trans., Carol MacClintock (American Institute of Musicology, 1962), 67.

> Tell me, please, if lute intabulation consists solely in the practice of the lute, playing the consonances according to the judgment of the ear, or is it in art founded on rules, with solid and true principles?[4]

[4] Vincenzo Galilei, *Fronimo* (1584), trans., Carol MacClintock (Neuhasen-Stuttgart: Hänssler-Verlag, 1985), 36.

Hedging his bets, Galilei has an answer provided by another character which covers all possibilities.

> The intabulation of music for instruments is understood in different ways by different people. Nevertheless, I hold it to be an art calling for the greatest judgment ... in addition to which one tries not only to be a good singer, and sound contrapuntist, but to be also a sound musician, or theorist, as we like to say.

Later, in a courageous step for an Italian of the sixteenth century, Galilei finally contends that it is the ear, and not the numbers, which define music. In discussing Pythagoras and his reputed discovery of the mathematical relationships in the lower part of the overtone series while listening to a blacksmith, we find for the very first time, in reference to this often repeated tale, the thought that perhaps it is the *sound*, and not the mathematics, which we hear.

> FRONIMO. So, because the consonance was contained in certain numbers and not in others, don't you think that in the sound itself was the real reason that one pleased him more than another, because of the proportion and the enjoyment that he perceived more or less by his hearing?
>
> GALILEI. Truly one should believe thus, since the judgment of sounds was made by the senses long before he was aware of what proportions were and the numbers containing them.[5]

[5] ibid., 146.

Even the conservative music theorist, Zarlino, seemed to be aware of the necessity of formulating a new kind of analysis which recognized the ear and live performance.

> For music, being a science that deals with sounds and tones—particular objects of the sense of hearing—is concerned only with the sonority that springs from pitches and tones, and with nothing else. Therefore it seems to me that all musical speculations not directed toward this end are vain and useless. Since music was really discovered for the purpose of pleasing and edifying, nothing beyond this end is important.[6]

[6] Gioseffo Zarlino, *The Art of Counterpoint*, trans., Guy Marco and Claude Palisca (New Haven: Yale University Press, 1968), 264.

Giovanni Benedetti took a stronger position. In a letter to the composer, de Rore, he maintained that it was wrong to say one could understand the theory of music without experiencing music with the senses, nor can one understand without actually practicing music.[7] Whereas writers such as Zarlino sought scientific reasons to explain the nature of music, Benedetti correctly realized that the actual practice of music is simply not a science.[8]

But such a viewpoint was still rare in sixteenth-century Italy. Gioseffo Zarlino, in Part Four of his *Le Istitutioni Harmoniche* (1558) follows the old Church Scholastic dogma that music must be judged by Reason and not merely the senses. In a chapter entitled, 'What Anyone Must Know Who Desires to Arrive at Some Perfection in Music,' he writes,

[7] Quoted in Claude V. Palisca, *Humanism in Italian Renaissance Musical Thought* (New Haven: Yale University Press, 1985), 261.

[8] ibid., 265.

[9] Gioseffo Zarlino, *On the Modes*, trans., Vered Cohen (New Haven: Yale University Press, 1983), 102ff.

> We should not surrender judgment of musical matters to the senses alone, for they are fallible, but rather we should accompany the senses with reason. Whenever these two parts are joined together in concordance, there is no doubt that no error can be committed, and perfect judgment will be made.[9]

Gioseffo Zarlino

This view goes hand in hand with his complete acceptance of the medieval concept of the liberal arts, in which music was considered a branch of mathematics. 'It should be known,' says Zarlino, 'that music is a science subordinate to arithmetic.' Curiously making the study of music even more left-brained, he also made brief arguments for the importance of the study of geometry, grammar, dialectics, rhetoric, natural science and natural philosophy for the well-educated musician.

He recommends, further, the study of the harpsichord and monochord, primarily as an aid to understanding the mathematical side of music ('investigate the effects of the sonorous numbers'), as well as singing, counterpoint and composition. Only with all this 'speculative' knowledge will the musician be prepared to perform.

> For bringing things of music to life is really nothing other than leading them to their ultimate end, or perfection, as also happens in others arts and sciences (such as medicine) which [also] contain both speculative and practical aspects.

Gioseffo Zarlino's monochord for 2/7-comma meantone temperament, 'Le istitutioni harmoniche', 1558, p. 130

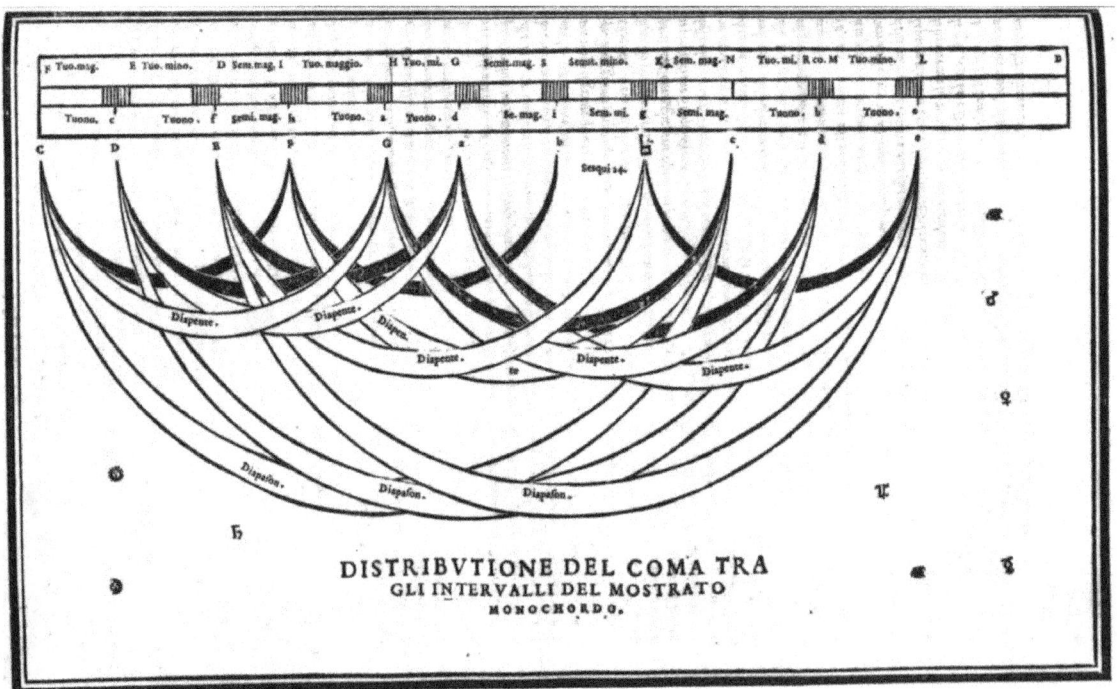

Later he summarized these arguments as follows:

> In order to have perfect knowledge concerning music, it does not suffice to appeal to the sense of hearing, even if it is most keen, but rather one should seek to investigate and know the whole, so that reason is not discordant with sense, nor sense with reason; and then everything will be well.
>
> But just as it is necessary that sense and reason concur in order to make judgment in things of music, so it is necessary that he who wants to judge anything pertaining to art have two capabilities: first, that he be expert in things of science, that is, of speculation; and second, that he be expert in things of art, which consists of practice ...
>
> Accordingly, just as it would be insane to rely on a physician who does not have the knowledge of both practice and theory, so it would be really foolish and imprudent to rely on the judgment of [a musician] who was solely practical or had done work only in theory.[10]

In Part Three of this book, Zarlino discusses this question again, now leaning a bit more in the favor of performance.

> Theory without practice is of small value, since music does not consist only of theory and is imperfect without practice. This is obvious enough. Yet some theorists, treating of certain musical matters without having a good command of the actual practice, have spoken much nonsense and committed a thousand errors. On the other hand, some who have relied only on practice without knowing the reasons behind it have unwittingly perpetrated thousands upon thousands of idiocies in their compositions.[11]

Bottrigari also takes the view that practice cannot be respected without theory. After a discussion of the complexities of tuning based on the old tetrachord system, the character Desiderio asks,

> I was thinking about asking you if it is necessary for all musicians, such as those of today who compose madrigals and motets, to know these things, and if they do know them, or if simple practice suffices.[12]

Benelli answers, yes, every musician *should* know these things, but it is also possible to succeed without knowing or understanding the theoretical explanations.

[10] ibid., 106.

[11] Gioseffo Zarlino, *The Art of Counterpoint*, trans., Guy Marco and Claude Palisca (New Haven: Yale University Press, 1968), 226ff.

[12] Hercole Bottrigari, *Il Desiderio*, trans., Carol MacClintock (American Institute of Musicology, 1962), 35.

> If, then, simple practice is sufficient to such composers to compose madrigals or motets or other kinds of *cantilene*, I will answer 'yes'; since I see and feel that most of them succeed with great applause, and in a short time even youths nowadays do marvelous miracles. But I will add also that it does not seem to me to be a great honor to accomplish things and not to be able to give the reasons for them.[13]

[13] ibid., 36.

In general, however, during the sixteenth century the deck was still stacked in favor of the 'speculative' teaching of music. We can see a definite prejudice in favor of the speculative studies, as opposed to those who are performers, and this prejudice is still very much present in many academic institutions today. We can see an example of this thinking in Girolamo Mei (1519–1594) in a letter he wrote to Galilei.

> You ask me in yours of 17 August how it happens that the practitioner does not follow at all the designs of the theorist, as he should, since the theorist gives the reason why. My answer to you is that considering and understanding are one thing and putting into operation another. The former belongs to the intellect and the latter to the sense. However, the sense of hearing is not as perfect as the judgment of the intellect because of the material and other circumstances that always necessarily accompany the former. Thus the practitioner, having simply to satisfy the sense, does not need as much refinement and punctiliousness, so to speak, as the theorist requires. He does not esteem reason as much as the theorist and is content whenever his art succeeds in satisfying the sense without going any further, his end being none other than this.[14]

[14] Quoted in Claude Palisca, *Letters on Ancient and Modern Music* (American Institute of Musicology, 1960), 66.

There is an important observation made at this time which should be acknowledged. Gianfrancesco Pico della Mirandola (1470–1533), was one of several important philosophers who, as a response to the Reformation, attempted to reconcile the ideas of the humanists with the Church. He was a late medieval Scholastic, but in the dress of the new 'Parisian style,' the Aristotelian School of the University of Paris. Without any knowledge of today's clinical discoveries of our separate hemispheres of the brain, he correctly deduces that the left hemisphere does not recognize the existence of the right hemisphere. This is the primary reason why we feel the need to conceptualize things which are of the domain of the right hemisphere, such as the experience of music. Pico describes this taking over, this conceptualization, as follows:

Pico della Mirandola, ca. 1400s, original artist unknown

The intellect does not permit any lower faculty to function in collaboration with it. Rather, whenever anything comes near the intellect and arouses it, the intellect, like a roaring fire, burns it up, and converts it into itself.[15]

Another philosopher whom we associate with the spirit of the Catholic counter-revolution is Giordano Bruno. Born in Nola, near Naples, in 1548, he entered the Order of Dominic at age fifteen, became a priest at age twenty-four and traveled in university circles in a number of countries, including England and Germany. From our perspective, his philosophic views were very conservative, indeed some call him the last medieval philosopher, but ironically the Church considered him a freethinker and the Inquisition had him put in prison and then burned. In one place he mentions music with respect to the learning process and he concludes that the learning facet, or as we would say today the conceptual facet, cannot be associated with the highest results.

> Aristotle demonstrates this by the example of a perfect writer or lutanist. Here, while nature does not reason and reflect, he doesn't wish the conclusion to be drawn that she works without intellect and final intention, because profound writers and musicians pay less attention to what they create, and yet do not go astray like the more inexpert and clumsy, who, though giving more thought and attention, produce a less perfect result and show no lack of faults.[16]

Vincenzo Giustiniani, whose writings reflect the end of the sixteenth century, argued for a balance between knowledge and practice.

> And to succeed in this task the inclination given to many by nature will not be sufficient; there is required also study and application of mind and body. For possessing the rules and the just proportions of numbers, joined with those of the voice or of sound and the knowledge of the effects which are caused by these in the souls of men, not only in general but in particular corresponding to the individual inclinations of everyone and to the taste which prevails in different periods, one may be able to apply skill and experience to his own times, to human inclinations in general, and to the particular tastes of each person.[17]

[15] Giovanni Pico della Mirandola, *Commentary on a Canzone of Benivieni*, Sears Jayne, trans. (New York: Peter Lang, 1984), 148.

Giordano Phillipo Bruno from 'Livre du recteur', 1578

[16] Giordano Bruno, *Cause, Principle and Unity*, trans., Jack Lindsay (New York: International Publishers, 1962), 85.

[17] Vicenzo Giustiniani, *Discorso sopra la Musica* (ca. 1628), trans., Carol MacClintock (American Institute of Musicology, 1962), 67ff.

Giovanni Giraldi, also known as Cinthio, wrote an important treatise, *Discorso intorno al comporre dei romanzi* (1549), which discusses the current state of the ancient epic and heroic poetic forms. He notes that one still hears the heroic poets singing their works but regrets that this tradition is being taken over by popular singers, those in the public piazzas who 'sing their idle nonsense to earn their bread.' He does mention that the serious artists of this form regularly improvise preludes before they begin to sing.

With regard to the epic poem, which was also sung, and which in ancient times had a specific educational purpose, he now writes of the continued educational purpose but only refers to it as being read.

> The function, then, of our poet, as regards the inducing of mores, is to praise virtuous actions and censure the vicious; and by means of the terrible and the miserable to make the vicious actions odious to him who reads.[18]

[18] Giraldi Cinthio, *Discorso intorno al comporre dei romanzi*, in Henry Snuggs, *Giraldi Cinthio On Romances* (Lexington: University of Kentucky Press, 1968), 52.

Two writers in sixteenth-century Italy mention catharsis, the educational process using emotions in music. Tasso mentions this, but only after the manner of the ancient Greek philosophers who emphasized the kind of music appropriate. Unfortunately there is so much lost information from the ancient period of Greek philosophy that no one today knows what they really meant by Phrygian, Lydian and Dorian styles, other than their origin being in individual societies of people.

> The Phrygian and Lydian modes, and the one formed by combining them [Mixolydian] are much more desirable in tragedy and the canzone as in these they can move the mind and, so to speak, draw it out of itself. But they are not suitable for instruction …
>
> Since music was invented not merely to entertain idleness or as a medicine and catharsis for the mind but for instruction as well … A solemn and steady music like the Doric will serve the heroic poem better than any other.[19]

[19] Torquato Tasso, *Discourses on the Heroic Poem*, trans., Mariella Cavalchini (Oxford: Clarendon Press, 1973), 199.

Cardano also mentions the employment of catharsis in music but unfortunately his discussion is so general that one can gain little from it.

> [Music's] usefulness is divided into three parts, for it pertains to instruction and study, or to the cleansing of the spirit, or to spending time pleasurably in leisure, tranquility, and freedom from the pressure of more serious matters. It is often said that emotions in music reflect weakened and enervated morals, but I believe such emotions consist of gentle virtues, and correspond to those more appropriate to action and also to those most divine virtues suitable for intellectual endeavor. Accordingly music celebrates those moral virtues which are especially appropriate to that useful quality which pertains to learning. Teachers and disciplinarians have agreed on the expiative and purgative force of strong emotions. When these emotions subside they may become excessively reversed and softened by giving way especially to emotions of misery and pity, causing dejection and depression. Music also proposes to fill such moods with a certain innocuous pleasure.[20]

[20] Clement Miller, *Hieronymus Cardanus, Writings on Music* (American Institute of Musicology, 1973), 105.

It seems curious that there is so little discussion of the character of the teacher in this literature. Baldassare Castiglione (1478–1529), in his famous book on the courtier, *Il Cortigiano*, recommends that old men should confine themselves to being music teachers. While he speaks of their being able to share their greater experience, etc., he seems equally concerned that they are too old to perform well.

> Then if the courtier should be so old that it is unbecoming to him to indulge in music, merrymaking, games, arms and similar recreations, even so one cannot say that it is impossible for him to win his prince's favor in this way. For even if he is too old to take part in these things himself, he can still understand them; and, given that he has practiced them when young, seeing that years and experience bring with them so much more knowledge of everything, age does not prevent his having a more perfect judgment, and a more perfect understanding of how to teach them to his prince.[21]

[21] Baldassare Castiglione, *The Courtier,* trans., George Bull (New York: Penguin Books, 1967)

Cardano also writes of the music teacher, but with a warning of their bad character as people. Indeed he admits that by having them in his home, 'I corrupted the morals of my own children.' But then he goes on and lists the principal educational advantages available to children who study music. He concludes by recommending a kind of music appreciation, rather than actual performance. And then, seemingly assuming that this will be ignored, he recommends against the use of some instruments in particular.

> If we do it at home the singers will be maintained at great expense and they will corrupt the characters of our young boys and adolescents, for most of them are drunkards and gluttons, also wanton, fickle, impatient, coarse, indolent, and tainted with every kind of unlawful desire. The best of them are fools.
>
> Does this mean then that music must be expelled from the home and the education of children? Not at all. Music has three attributes: sound, rhythm, and cognition arising from perception. Cognition is useful in all activities, in recognizing men of talent, in deriving pleasure from listening to singers, and in pursuing music yourself, although I will say later how you do this. It is also worthwhile to grasp the rhythm for the sake of the poetry and for the pleasure, understanding, and practice of the music. But sound must be employed to the degree that it can be applied to musical instruments, not to singing polyphonically. Such instruments are the lute, lira, pipe organ, and other string instruments. These instruments are complete in themselves and need only one person to play them, so that one can practice by himself and receive pleasure. In this kind of music one can satisfy the three conditions that Aristotle proposed, namely, the confirmation or change of morals, moods, or actions. These conditions also apply to the present times, both in the morals of children and adolescents and in the organization of life.
>
> Yet the rich can learn polyphonic music thoroughly and can form a group of singers from chosen men; although this is difficult it still can be done. But for the poor, or children, or youths, or those who want to teach their children at home, social music is not practical. Understanding it is more beneficial than participation, also having a knowledge of the complete instruments, but not of the kind of instrument in which the cheeks are puffed up; among such instruments I detest mostly the playing of horns, because their use is neither distinguished nor noble nor beneficial to the brain, lungs, or abdomen, for it causes hernias.[22]

[22] Miller, op. cit., 197ff.

There was considerable interest during the sixteenth century regarding the education needed by the well-bred young man, the 'Renaissance man' if you will. Only Castiglione goes into further detail regarding the specific music education needed by the ideal young courtier. It would be an ideal society indeed if music education could give every young man an understanding of music, the ability to sight-read and ability on several instruments. Castiglione adds a further enticement: it helps one be popular with the ladies!

> Gentlemen, I must tell you that I am not satisfied with our courtier unless he is also a musician and unless as well as understanding and being able to read music he can play several instruments. For, when we think of it, during our leisure time we can find nothing more worthy or commendable to help our bodies relax and our spirits recuperate, especially at Court where, besides the way in which music helps everyone to forget his troubles, many things are done to please the ladies, whose tender and gentle souls are very susceptible to harmony and sweetness. So it is no wonder that both in ancient times and today they have always been extremely fond of musicians and have welcomed music as true refreshment for the spirit.[23]

[23] *The Courtier*, op. cit., I, 94ff.

Castiglione displays his disdain for the man who will not listen to music, and thus has no place in court, in the following anecdote about a courtier whom a lady had asked to dance,

> and who not only refused but would not listen to music or take part in the many other entertainments offered, protesting all the while that such frivolities were not his business. And when at length the lady asked what his business was, he answered with a scowl: 'Fighting ... '
> 'Well then,' the lady retorted, 'I should think that since you aren't at war at the moment and you are not engaged in fighting, it would be a good thing if you were to have yourself well greased and stowed away in a cupboard with all your fighting equipment, so that you avoid getting rustier than you are already.'
> And of course everyone burst out laughing at the way she showed her contempt for his stupid presumption.[24]

[24] ibid., I, 58.

Castiglione also brought up the question of how much music education the well-bred young lady should have. For him, their very femininity placed limits on what was appropriate.

> For example, when she is dancing I should not wish to see her use movements that are too forceful and energetic, nor, when she is singing or playing a musical instrument, to use those abrupt and frequent *diminuendos* that are ingenious but not beautiful. And I suggest that she should choose instruments suited to her purpose. Imagine what an ungainly sight it would be to have a woman playing drums, fifes, trumpets or other instruments of that sort; and this is simply because their stridency buries and destroys the sweet gentleness which embellished everything a woman does.[25]

[25] ibid., III, 215.

We also have an enlightening and very informative firsthand discussion of a music student in the famous *Autobiography* of Benvenuto Cellini. Early in his book he mentions that his father was a proficient musician and was, in fact, a member of the civic wind band of Florence.[26] Cellini speaks often of his father's fervent desire that his son devote himself to music, and just as often of his own preference not to do so. In a typical passage, Cellini clearly suggests that some considered the career of musician was somewhat less than honorable.

> I used to play treble in concert with the musicians of the palace before the Signory, following my notes ... The Gonfalonier, that is, Soderini, ... was wont to say to my father: 'Maestro Giovanni, beside music, teach the boy those other arts which do you so much honor.' To which my father answered: 'I do not wish him to practice any art but playing and composing; for in this profession I hope to make him the greatest man of the world, if God prolongs his life.' To these words one of the old counselors made answer: 'Ah! Maestro Giovanni, do what the Gonfalonier tells you! for why should he never become anything more than a good musician?'[27]

Despite his claim that he found no satisfaction in music, which he concentrated on until age fifteen, he often reveals how much his playing meant to his father.

> I did not, however, neglect to gratify my good father from time to time by playing on the [shawm] or cornett. Each time he heard me, I used to make his tears fall accompanied with deep-drawn sighs of satisfaction. My filial piety often made me give him that contentment, and induced me to pretend that I enjoyed the music too.[28]

In another place, his father pleas,

> My dear son, I too in my time was a good draughtsman; but for recreation, after such stupendous labors, and for the love of me who am your father, who begat you and brought you up and implanted so many honorable talents in you, for the sake of recreation, I say, will not you promise sometimes to take in hand your [shawm] and that seductive cornett, and to play upon them to your heart's content, inviting the delight of music?[29]

Taking his book as a whole, one finds a universal circumstance. When one is forced to study music, he often hates it. But when he studies on his own, his attitude is quite different. In the following two passages, for example, his distaste for his studies in music is quite evident.

[26] John Addington Symonds, trans., *The Life of Benvenuto Cellini* (New York: Scribner's, 1914),, I, v. He suggests that most of these musicians had other professions, primarily in the silk and wool trades.

[27] ibid., I, vi.

[28] ibid., I, vii.

[29] ibid., I, ix.

> A certain pupil of my father's, moved by his own bad nature, suggested to the Cardinal that he ought to send me to Bologna, in order to learn to play well from a great master there. The name of his master was Antonio, and he was in truth a worthy man in the musician's art. The Cardinal said to my father that, if he sent me there, he would give me letters of recommendation and support. My father, dying with joy at such an opportunity, sent me off; and I being eager to see the world, went with good grace.
>
> When I reached Bologna, I put myself under a certain Maestro Ercole del Piffero, and began to earn something by my trade. In the meantime I used to go every day to take my music-lesson, and in a few weeks made considerable progress in that accursed art.[30]
>
> ...
>
> My father, in the meanwhile, kept writing piteous entreaties that I should return to him; and in every letter bade me not to lose the music he had taught me with such trouble. On this, I suddenly gave up all wish to go back to him; so much did I hate that accursed music; and I felt as though of a truth I were in paradise the whole year I stayed at Pisa, where I never played the [shawm].[31]

On the other hand, when Cellini was older, and removed from his father's demands that he study music, his attitude toward music was quite different. Now he praises its virtues, as we see first in a passage describing his infatuation with a young boy.

> Paulino was the best-mannered, the most honest, and the most beautiful boy I ever saw in my whole life. His modest ways and actions, together with his superlative beauty and his devotion to myself, bred in me as great an affection for him as a man's breast can hold. This passionate love led me oftentimes to delight the lad with music; for I observed that his marvelous features, which by complexion wore a tone of modest melancholy, brightened up, and when I took my cornett, broke into a smile so lovely and so sweet, that I do not marvel at the silly stories which the Greeks have written about the deities of heaven.[32]

Similar comments can be found throughout his discussion of his later life.

> I took much pleasure in music.[33]
>
> ...
>
> ... my charming art of music ...[34]

[30] ibid., I, ix.

[31] ibid., I, xi.

[32] ibid., I, xxiii.

[33] ibid., I, xxxiv.

[34] ibid., I, xxxvii.

We suspect that the following discussion by Cardano of the frustrations of studying music is also in part autobiographical, certainly the first portion in which he speaks of the difficulty of finding colleagues to sing polyphonic music.

> In our time a person may seek to study music, and when he has barely mastered it after much effort he finds that there is a lack of fellow singers. And even if he meets with them they often make mistakes, causing laughter among the listeners, so that he gets contempt in place of praise and sorrow in place of pleasure. When they do sing well one wants to be more prominent than another, a circumstance which creates tension.
>
> If the instruction has been satisfactory another concern may come to mind, [should] you learn to play the lute or recorder. How much labor and tedium is there in this effort? After an entire year of work, if the study is as successful as you had wished, you will be pleased with a few things, but not without great effort. Meanwhile one thing or other will be lacking, and even if everything has turned out well you find that your efforts are disdained more than they are praised. Your incentive disappears, and cares of the family and business interfere. One becomes a servant of fellow musicians, and must put up with all their faults and troublesome natures.
>
> So you can see how hostile these things are to tranquility; nor is the source of this impediment to be found anywhere but in ourselves. But you say: 'I enjoy music a great deal and have studied since childhood.' In that case there is no instrument more perfect than a lira, none more unlimited, none more pleasant, none more comfortable. Yet it causes a great deal of inconvenience when strings are tightened, loosened, changed or restrung. When they are tuned they break from humidity and rain or from dryness and wind.[35]

[35] Miller, op. cit., 200.

12 *Music Education in Sixteenth-Century France*

As in the rest of Europe, exciting new intellectual and musical ideas were transforming the musical life of France. But these ideas were not coming from the Church or from the universities. The University of Paris, for all its importance, was still locked into the medieval misconception of music being a branch of mathematics. Carpenter documents this extensively and lists numerous sixteenth-century treatises that link music and mathematics.[1] It seems odd to the modern reader that a professor such as Oronce Fine, professor of mathematics in the College de France and himself an outstanding performer on the lute, did not perceive that to speak of mathematics is to miss the point of music. However out of touch the universities were, their influence was still present. Thus, Anthoine de Bertrand (b. 1545), when publishing some of his music in 1587, felt the necessity to add the plea that 'music should appeal to the senses and not be bound by mathematical subtleties.'[2]

Neither did the aristocratic part of society provide innovative ideas in music and music education. With the court of Louis XII (1498–1515) the century began with only the most necessary ceremonial music, the king observing 'I had rather make courtiers laugh by my stinginess, than make my people weep by my extravagance.'[3] Under Francois I (1515–1547), however, it was a different story. This king,[4] who devoted so much attention to poetry, language, art and music, established an administrative basis for music which would influence all aristocratic music until the end of the eighteenth century. Among his innovations was the creation, in 1543, of his *schola cantorum*, consisting of two undermasters, six children, two cornett players, twenty-six singers, twelve clerics and two grammar teachers for the children.[5] It was the only organized music education in the court.

The sixteenth century saw much new creative energy related to the academies, the male meetings devoted to serious discussion and concerts. In Paris these developed into an active program of adult education, including music. One of the earliest of these, a group of poets known as the Pleiade, was led by

[1] Nan Cooke Carpenter, *Music in the Medieval and Renaissance Universities* (Norman: University of Oklahoma Press, 1958), 140ff.

[2] Quoted in Gustave Reese, *Music in the Renaissance* (New York: Norton, 1959), 389.

[3] Fr. Guizot, *History of France* (London: 1872), II, 627. Louis was discerning enough to hire Josquin, who wrote the well-known 'Vive Le Roy' and the famous vocal work in which the part for Louis to sing which has but one pitch throughout.

[4] History concentrates mostly on the battles of Francois against the Emperor, Charles V. After his famous meeting in 1520, 'The Field of Cloth of Gold,' with Henry VIII of England, Henry himself described Francois as,
> stately of countenance, mery of cheer, roune coloured, great iyes, high nosed, bigge lipped, faire brested and shoulders, small legges, and long fete. [Edward Hall, *The Triumphant Reigne of Kyng Henry VIII* (London, 1542), I, 200]

[5] *Recueil des Choses Notables qui ont este faites a Boyonne ...* (Paris, 1566), 7.

the most famous French poet of the sixteenth century, Pierre de Ronsard. In Ronsard's dedication to Francois II of his *Livre des melanges* (1560), he writes of the profound influence music has on man.

> He that hearing a sweet accord of instruments or the sweetness of the natural voice feels no joy and no agitation and is not thrilled from head to foot, as being delightfully rapt and somehow carried out of himself—it is the sign of one whose soul is tortuous, vicious, and depraved, and of whom one should beware, as not fortunately born. For how could one be in accord with a man who by nature hates accord? He is unworthy to behold the sweet light of the sun who does not honor music as being a small part of that which, as Plato says, so harmoniously animates the whole great universe. On the contrary, he who does honor and reverence to music is commonly a man of worth, sound of soul, by nature loving things lofty, philosophy, the conduct of affairs of state, the tasks of war, and in brief, in all the honorable offices he ever shows the sparks of his virtue.[6]

Portrait of Pierre de Ronsard by François-Séraphin Delpech

[6] Quoted in Oliver Strunk, *Source Readings in Music History* (New York: Norton, 1950), 287.

The official beginning of the most important of the French academies, Baif's Academy, is documented by the Letters Patent issued by Charles IX in 1570. The principal objective given in this document is to re-establish 'both the kind of poetry and the measure and rule of music anciently used by the Greeks and Romans.'[7] The document indicates that work and discussion along these lines had been in progress for three years, resulting in some progress in 'attempts at measured verses set to measured music.'

The Academy was to consist of members in two categories: 'composers, singers and players' and listeners. The following statutes are very similar to, and unquestionably derived from, constitutions of the musician guilds of Paris and elsewhere. In particular, the musicians are to meet at specified times to rehearse together and separately, there is provision for sick members, a medallion is to be worn by the members (to be returned by his heirs upon his death) and finally, restrictions against quarrels and fighting amongst members—within one hundred feet of the meeting place.

Some of the most interesting language in this document begins to shape the aesthetic environment for concerts as we know them today. When performances are underway, in particular singing, the listeners must not speak, whisper, nor

King Charles IX of France by François Clouet

[7] Quoted in Frances Yates, *The French Academies of the Sixteenth Century* (London: University of London, 1947; Nendeln: Kraus Reprint, 1968), 21.

make any noise. No one can enter during a song, but must await its conclusion. Interestingly enough, the listeners were not to approach the musicians in the private place where they prepared before the performances.

In a broader sense, Charles IX notes, in this same document, that his grandfather was a strong supporter of the arts and that in following suit he is acknowledging their importance to society. It is particularly interesting that he refers to the use of music education to shape character and to the relationship of music education and society.

> It is of great importance for the morals of the citizens of a town that the music current and used in the country should be retained under certain laws, for the minds of most men are formed and their behavior influenced by its character, so that where music is disordered, there morals are also depraved, and where it is well ordered, there men are well disciplined morally.[8]

[8] Quoted in ibid., 23.

We find additional valuable information regarding the curriculum of Baif's Academy in the form of a document discovered by Yates, written early in the seventeenth century by the famous Marin Mersenne. It is apparently based on personal information given Mersenne by an older man who had been a member of the Academy. Once again there is strong evidence in the belief that music education was important for shaping character.

Marin Mersenne, artist unknown

> [The Academicians] did not wish to bring in a new kind of music, unless you call that new when something is restored to wholeness, but wished to recover those effects which, as we read, were once produced by the Greeks, by joining Gallic verses to our carefully cultivated music. For they hoped to exhilarate the depressed spirit, to reduce the over-elated spirit to modesty, and to stir themselves to other feelings by their own music ...
>
> When Jean Antoine de Baif and Joachim Thibault de Courville labored together to drive barbarism from Gaul, they considered that nothing would be of more potency for forming the manners of youth to everything honorable than if they were to recover the effects of ancient music and compose all their songs on the models of the fixed rules of the Greeks.
>
> Wherefore they wished so to provide that nothing should be lacking in the Academy which should make it suitable for the perfecting of a man, both in mind and body. Therefore they appointed to this Academy men most skilled in every kind of natural sciences, and instituted

a prefect of it who should be called the Head Teacher. I leave out the other masters, of sciences, of tongues especially, of music, of poetry, of geography, of the various parts of mathematics, and of painting, who promoted the good of the mind, and the military prefects who taught all those things which are useful for military discipline and for the good of the body.[9]

[9] Quoted in ibid., 24.

The purpose of the Academy was to recreate the aim of Greek music in acquiring direct educational effects. As Yates observes,

> These artistic labors were undertaken, not for art's sake alone, but for certain effects which are expected of them. These melodies in the antique manner are believed to have the power of refining and purifying the minds of the auditors, and, through this purification, of initiating them into higher states of knowledge.[10]

[10] ibid., 36.

A similar discussion is found in an important Spanish work by Vives, entitled, *On Education*. He shares the goal of reaching back to the ancient Greeks for using music to form the character of students. His description of the educational end is remarkably similar to Aristotle's theory of catharsis. It is curious he could believe so strongly in the power of emotion in music, while his basic definition of music is the old Church nonsense about music being part of mathematics. 'Music,' he writes, is 'arithmetic applied to sounds.'

> In music we have deteriorated much from the older masters, on account of the dullness of the ear which has utterly lost all discrimination of subtle sounds, so that now we no longer distinguish even the long and short sounds in common speech; and for this reason we have lost some kinds of meters, and that primitive harmony of tones, the effects of which the ancient writers testify were vast and marvelous. Young men should receive theoretical instruction in music, and should also have some practical ability. Only let the pupil practice pure and good music which, after the Pythagorean mode, soothes, recreates, and restores to itself the wearied mind of the student; then let it lead back to tranquility and tractability all the wild and fierce parts of the student's nature, as it is related in the ancient world, under the guise of stories, that rocks were moved and wild beasts allured by it.[11]

[11] Foster Watson, trans., *Vives: On Education* (Cambridge: University Press, 1913), IV, v.

Returning to the French Academy, we conclude by noting that the faculty of the University of Paris was jealous and concerned that their role was being usurped. Growing efforts to eliminate the Academy were eventually silenced by the king himself and interestingly enough this ultimatum was addressed to the Faculty of Medicine.[12]

The civic music guild of Paris, the *La confrerie Saint-Julien*, was continuing to prosper during the sixteenth century. It now had some one hundred 'masters,' in addition to some lower members known as Compagnons. We also have a little more information for their music educational apprenticeship requirements of this period. The average apprentice was from ten to sixteen years of age and was expected to sign, with his parents, a legal document regarding the conditions of his service. The duration of the apprenticeship was officially six years, but if one were the son of a 'master' it was usually less. The master was expected to treat the apprentice humanely and to provide for his welfare.

The famous Puritan, John Calvin, arrived in Strasbourg, France, in 1538 to begin work on his own Psalter to reflect these views. When published, in 1543, it included a clear exposition of his views of the aesthetics of church music. Because of the power of music to communicate to a listener, he says, the character of the music used in church becomes an important consideration.

> We know by experience that song has great force and vigor to move and inflame the hearts of men to invoke and praise God with a more vehement and ardent zeal. It must always be looked to that the song be not light and frivolous but have weight and majesty.[13]

His final thought, after calling attention to the just concern of the early Church fathers, is quite interesting as it is a rare negative endorsement of the power which music has on character. One can imagine him saying that music was too dangerous to be used in education. While the Church had always emphasized that it was the words, and not the music, that was important in church music, Calvin found the danger in the music greater than the value of the words.

[12] The reader is reminded that Apollo was the god of both music and medicine.

John Calvin by Georg Osterwald

[13] Jean Calvin, *Geneva Psalter*, quoted in Strunk, op. cit., 346ff.

For this reason the early doctors of the Church often complain that the people of their times are addicted to dishonest and shameless songs, which not without reason they call mortal and Satanic poison for the corruption of the world. Now in speaking of music I understand two parts, namely, the letter, or subject and matter, and the song, or melody. It is true that, as Saint Paul says, every evil word corrupts good manners, but when it has the melody with it, it pierces the heart much more strongly and enters within; as wine is poured into the cask with a funnel, so venom and corruption are distilled to the very depths of the heart by melody.

Some of the French poetry of the sixteenth century comments on education in the liberal arts. But as music was gradually losing its definition as a science, it appears that the French view was that it was therefore losing its place among the liberal arts. A poem by Joachim du Bellay, for example, describes the importance of philosophy and mathematics in education, but assigns music only the role of a recreation.

> I will master the secrets of philosophy,
> Of mathematics and of medicine as well,
> Become a legal expert and—who can tell?—
> Perhaps even aspire to theology:
> For recreation painting and playing the lute …[14]

[14] Joachim du Bellay, *The Regrets*, trans., C. H. Sisson (Manchester: Carcanet Press, 1984), Nr. 32. Bellay (b. 1525), was a friend to most of the sixteenth-century French poets, including Ronsard, with whom he taught at the college of Coqueret in Paris.

A similar poem by Marguerite de Navarre speaks of the difficulty and rewards of the study of the liberal arts, in particular philosophy and mathematics, but does not mention music at all.

> Along one side I set Philosophy
> Where reason challenges dull ignorance
> And makes man prize himself above his worth.
> Those books are hard to force or break; close sealed,
> They cannot be laid open to the eye
> Without a struggle that no words can tell;
> And when at last the battle has been won
> And something of that hidden lore laid bare,
> A man can never rest, he must press on,
> Intent on knowing all the learned know …

Portrait of Marguerite de Navarre by Jean Clouet, ca. 1530

> Then next I put together those fine books,
> So full of strange delights, where you can read
> of Mathematics. Study them with zeal
> And you will give up all the body craves,
> For they hold lore so subtle and so rare
> A man's whole self must work to master it;
> The way is barred by thorns, and hard it is
> To bend those briars and make a passage through;
> But he who, once that tedious task is done,
> Can freely roam about the verdant plain,
> The fruitful garden of those liberal arts,
> Would not exchange the joy they give to him
> For all the treasures of the Caesars, nor
> For all their pomp and mad delight in fame.[15]

[15] Marguerite de Navarre, *The Prisons*, trans., Hilda Dale (Reading: Whiteknight's Press, 1989), III, 37ff., 85ff. Marguerite (1496–1549) was a sister to King Francois I, and mother to an extraordinary woman, Jeanne d'Albret, mother to Henri IV.

The greatest French writer of the sixteenth century was unquestionably Michel Montaigne (1533–1592). After an education in law at Toulouse, he became in turn a soldier, courtier, traveler and mayor of Bordeaux. We can see in Montaigne the clear influence of humanism in music as he contends that music education must be a matter of direct experience in performance, not in conceptual theory.

> Take Palvel and Pompeo, those excellent dancing masters when I was young: I would like to have seen them teaching us our steps just by watching them without budging from our seats, like those teachers who seek to give instruction to our understanding without making it dance—or to have seen other teach us how to manage a horse, a pike or a lute, or to sing without practice.[16]

[16] Michel de Montaigne, *Essays*, trans., M. A. Screech (London: Penguin, 1993), I, xxvi, 171.

Montaigne strongly believed in the necessity of other kinds of learning than books and literature. The boy needs sports and social graces, among which he includes 'music-making.' After all, he observes, 'we are not bringing up a body: we are bringing up a man.' He mentions music in education again when addressing the general climate of the learning experience. His description of the sixteenth-century classroom environment will strike the reader as quite remarkable.

> Go there during lesson time: you will hear nothing but the screaming of tortured children and of masters drunk with rage. What a way to awaken a taste for learning in those tender timorous souls, driving

them to it with terrifying scowls and fists armed with canes! An iniquitous and pernicious system. And besides such imperious authority can lead to dreadful consequences—especially given our form of flogging.

How much more appropriate to strew their classrooms with leaf and flower than with blood-stained birch-rods. I would have portraits of Happiness there and Joy, with Flora and the Graces ...

When they have something to gain, make it enjoyable. Healthy-giving foods should be sweetened for a child: harmful ones made to taste nasty.

It is amazing how concerned Plato is in his Laws with the amusements and pastimes of the youths of his city and how he dwells on their races, sports, singing, capering and dancing ... He spends little time over book-learning; the only thing he seems specifically to recommend poetry for is the music.[17]

[17] ibid., I, xxvi, 186.

13 Music Education in Sixteenth-Century Germany

As with France and Italy, it was not to the universities of the German-speaking countries that one could look for new ideas in music. Here also they remained locked in the old medieval Church Scholastic notion that music was a branch of mathematics. Thus, in 1505, the University of Leipzig appointed Sebastianus Muchelon as '*lector musicae et aritmetice*,'[1] a document of the University of Köln in 1515 specifies the teaching of 'the books on mathematics, that is geometry, arithmetic, music and astronomy' and in 1558 the University of Heidelberg employed a lecturer in mathematics who was expected to include music in his teaching.

Of course, at the beginning of the sixteenth century the universities had close ties with the Church and so even the exciting discussions of the humanists appear to have had little influence. A rare exception was the University of Vienna, where Maximilian I, in 1501, added to the arts faculty a '*Collegium poetarum et mathematicorum*,' bringing poetry and oratory into the curriculum.[2]

We can see the old relationship between mathematics and music again in the works of the German philosopher, Henry Agrippa (1486–1536). In one of his books, *Of the Vanitie and Uncertaintie of Arts and Sciences*, Agrippa does give music a separate chapter. However, this chapter follows one on 'Arithmetic,' which Agrippa concludes by ridiculing those mathematicians who count themselves among the divine, because they work with numbers. He quickly adds, 'Musicians hardly grant them his prerogative, as they are more willing to give this honor to their Harmonie.'[3] Agrippa does refer to ancient and medieval writings, which associate music with a variety topics, from the soul to mathematics, and admits, therefore, that one cannot treat the subject of music apart from all other disciplines. Nevertheless, he writes that his intent is to discuss music as an art unto itself.

> But I speak of that which consists of pleasant tunes, which is in agreement with strings or voices, according to their tune and meter, without offending the ears.[4]

[1] Nan Cooke Carpenter, *Music in the Medieval and Renaissance Universities* (Norman: University of Oklahoma Press, 1958), 251. Carpenter documents the association with mathematics extensively.

[2] ibid., 228.

[3] Henry Cornelius Agrippa, *Of the Vanitie and Uncertaintie of Arts and Sciences*, ed., Catherine Dunn (Northridge: California State University, Northridge Press, 1974), 63. Agrippa was born near Köln and graduated from the university there in 1499.

[4] ibid., 64ff.

He makes an interesting observation, which we have not seen in earlier literature, that music, unlike other disciplines of the Liberal Arts, has no terminal point of completion, but must be a lifelong study.

> They say, moreover, that music is an endless art, and that it cannot be thoroughly learned with any wit: but that daily according to the capacity of every man, it gives fresh melody.[5]

[5] ibid., 68.

While most members of the Germany aristocracy at this time were devoted to drinking and hunting, there was one notable exception of a man who seems to have been touched by the humanities. He was Moritz, Landgraf of Hesse-Cassel, whose interest in music is documented by his personal instrument collection of 44 strings, 10 keyboards and 142 wind instruments.[6] According to Henry Peacham, a contemporary, Moritz was also a composer.

Moritz Landgraf von Hessen-Kassel by Matthaeus Merian, 1662

> But above others who carrieth away the palm for excellency, not only in music, but in whatsoever is to be wished in a brave prince, is the yet-living Maurice, Landgrave of Hesse, of whose own composition I have seen eight or ten several sets of motets and solemn music set purposely for his own chapel, where, for the great honor of some festival, and many times for his recreation only, he is his own organist. Besides, he readily speaketh ten or twelve several languages. He is so universal a scholar that, coming, as he doth often, to his University of Marburg, what questions soever he meeteth with set up, as the manner is in the German and our universities, he will extempore dispute an hour or two, even in boots and spurs, upon them with their best professors. I pass over his rare skill in chirurgery, he being generally accounted the best bonesetter in the country.[7]

[6] Anthony Baines, 'Two Cassel Inventories,' in *The Galpin Society Journal* (1951), 32ff.

[7] Henry Peacham, *The Complete Gentleman*, ed., Virgil Heltzel (Ithaca: Cornell University Press, 1962), 111ff.

Another visiting Englishman describes him in much the same fashion.

> His education prince-like, generally known in all things, and excellent in many, seasoning his grave and more important studies for ability in judgment, with studies of pastime for retiring, as in poetrie, musike, and the mathemitikes; and for ornament in discourse in the languages, French, Italian and English.[8]

[8] Edward Monings, quoted in Nichols, *The Progresses and Public Processions of Queen Elizabeth* (London, 1805), III.

In a separate chapter we will present some of the comments from several music education treatises designed for the instruction of choir boys. Apart from these, there is a particularly interesting document which deals with music education, the *School Ordinance ... for the Town of Brunswick* of 1528 by Johann Bugenhagen.[9] He identifies the first purpose of school as being to teach

[9] See Frederick Eby, *Early Protestant Educators* (New York: McGraw-Hill, 1931), 193ff. Bugenhagen (1485–1558) worked in the northern part of Germany and had considerable influence on the schools.

> the ten commandments, the creed, the Lord's prayer, the Christian sacraments ... also to sing the psalms ... In addition they are to study the humanities from which one learns to understand such matters.

One purpose in the teaching of singing to children was to help provide music for the Sunday services. Therefore, Johannes Bugenhagen notes that 'the children shall attend the choir on the sacred evening and sacred days in that congregation to which their parents belong.'

Interesting also is his insistence that the music teacher and his children are not to be used as a form of free music for extra services.

> Moreover when some people during the funeral procession would have the pupils with one of the assistants sing before the coffin German psalms or other sacred songs not to help the dead but to admonish the living, also the Te Deum laudamus or any other song when the bride is led into the church, let the assistants divide the money among themselves. They are not to sing without pay.

Regarding the basic curriculum, he recommends the plan by Philipp Melanchthon, *Book of Visitation School Plan*, which was based on a similar plan by Luther. In one place he describes the musical education in more detail.

> The two choristers in the two schools shall perform their labors like the other assistants according to the command and will of their respective rectors. Furthermore it is the particular duty to teach all children, large and small, learned and ignorant, to sing ... common songs in German and Latin.
>
> ...
>
> Therefore he shall select three or four good boys who can hold the song for him with strong voices, but all the other boys in the parish shall accompany them. Some have poor voices which can be well controlled so that they shall sing low and listen to the others. In this way all children and youth shall learn to sing in the schools.

Philipp Melanchthon by Lucas Cranach, ca. 1537

Sternfeld provides extensive information on the music used in school dramatic performances as well as singing for the community in the street, for banquets, weddings and funerals.[10] He finds the curriculum in German schools at all levels always included reading, music and Latin. Ability in singing was examined as part of the entrance requirements of many higher schools. Sternfeld mentions the Neckar School in Heidelberg which examined prospective students both by the rector in the arts and by the cantor in music.[11]

Documents from the reorganization of the Neckar School in 1587 are more specific in the use of music. Now there was two hours of instruction in singing each week by the cantor, which included singing in four-parts, in addition to the singing of a composition from part-books before and after meals.[12]

Finally, Michael Praetorius, in his *Syntagma Musicum*, Book III, includes an interesting discussion on the education of choir singers, or as he calls it, 'The Method of Teaching Choir Boys who Love and Enjoy Singing, According to the new Italian Style.'[13] Praetorius begins this discussion by presenting his primary aesthetic purpose in music. As the orator must, through his style of speaking, arouse the emotions of the listeners, so

> similarly a musician must not only sing, but he must sing artfully and expressively in order to move the hearts of the listeners, to arouse their emotions and to allow the music to accomplish its ultimate purpose.

In order to accomplish this, Praetorius says the singer must have a naturally fine voice, a good mind and a thorough knowledge of music. But he must also understand what makes good taste in music, in particular the art of improvisation.

> He must know ... where to introduce runs or coloraturas (called *passaggi* by the Italians), that is, not anywhere in a composition, but appropriately, at the right time and in a certain way, in order that the listener may not only be aware of the loveliness of the voice, but also be able to enjoy the art of singing.

[10] Frederick Sternfeld, 'Music in the Schools of the Reformation,' in *Musica Disciplina* (1948), 106ff. Gustave Reese, *Music in the Renaissance* (New York: Norton, 1959), 647, 691, identifies a work by Isaac apparently intended for school use, as well as motets by Lassus intended as exercises for the students of the Bavarian chapel. Nan Cooke Carpenter, in *Music in the Medieval and Renaissance Universities* (Norman: University of Oklahoma Press, 1954), 224ff., gives numerous references to music used in the universities of the German-speaking countries.

[11] Sternfeld, ibid., 112.

[12] Carpenter, op. cit., 235.

[13] A facsimile of the original German publication has been printed by Barenreiter Kassel, 1958. The page numbers we cite, therefore, are from the original print, in this case, 229ff.

Michael Praetorius by Michael Schönitzer, 1606

The singer who has been gifted with a fine voice, but does not know how to do these things correctly will 'provide little joy for the listeners, particularly those who have some knowledge of the art; on the contrary, it makes them sullen and sleepy.'

Learning the art of beautiful singing, says Praetorius, as in all the other arts, is a matter of Nature, Doctrine and Practice. Regarding Nature, Praetorius says again that the singer must have a beautiful, pleasantly vibrating voice ('not, however, in the manner to which some singers in schools are accustomed, but with moderation'), a smooth round throat (which apparently was thought to aid improvisation), be able to sustain a long tone and find some range in which he can produce a full sound without falsetto. The undesirable qualities in a voice are taking too many breaths, singing through one's nose and keeping the voice in the throat and singing with the teeth closed.

Praetorius mentions two specific sixteenth-century vocal techniques which are quite interesting. The first, *Intonatio*,

Page from Michael Praetorius' 'Syntagma Musicum'

> refers to the manner in which a vocal piece is started. Opinions vary about this, some wanting to start the tone on the proper written pitch, some a second below, but in a way that the pitch is gradually raised. Some prefer to begin on the third, some on the fourth, some with a delicate and soft voice. All these methods, for the most part, are designated by the term *accentus*.

The second vocal technique, *Exclamatio*,

> is the proper means of moving the emotions and must be achieved by increasing the voice. It can be employed with all dotted minims and semiminims in descending motion. Especially the following note which moves somewhat fast, arouses the emotions more than the semibreve, which is more frequently used and more effective with a raising and lowering of the voice, and without *exclamatio*.

By Doctrine, Praetorius seems to mean the proper art of embellishment and improvisation. He provides considerable discussion, including musical examples, but we shall only quote his basic definitions. He begins with diminution.

> One speaks of diminution when a longer note is broken up into many other faster and smaller notes. There are different kinds of them [including] accent, tremulo, groppi and tirata.

His examples of 'accent' appear to be single and multiple passing tones, in a variety of rhythmic configurations.

Tremulo 'is nothing but a quiver of the voice over one note; organists call it a mordent.'

Gruppi 'are used in cadences and have to be executed more sharply than the tremuli.' His examples appear as main-note trills.

Tirate 'are long, fast, diatonic runs up or down the keyboard.' The examples, in each case, fill an octave diatonically.

Trills, although he provides numerous configurations in which a trill may be found, he finds more difficult to explain.

> These can only be learned through live demonstration and the efforts of a teacher. Then one may learn from the other just as one bird learns by watching another.

Passaggi 'are fast runs which are employed over longer notes, both diatonically and in skips of any size, ascending as well as descending,' in other words, improvisation.

Regarding the third essential, Practice, Praetorius says it would take too long to discuss—better to just study everything he has provided in his volume!

14 *Music Education Treatises of Sixteenth-Century Germany*

THE TREATISES ON MUSIC written during the sixteenth century in Germany remain focused on mathematics, although ironically they are ostensibly intended for music education, for the education of choir boys. In the previous chapter we have given a brief overview of the emphasis of music education in sixteenth-century German life. Here we will take a closer look at those portions of contemporary music treatises which are concerned with music education.

Johannes Cochlaeus, who would be only a footnote but for the fact that he was the teacher of the more famous Glarean, was *Magister Artium* at the University of Köln. Later he studied theology at Ferrara and eventually became rector at St. Lorenz school, in Nurnberg. It was for the students of this school that he wrote his treatise, *Tetrachordum Musices*, in 1511.

Johannes Cochlaeus, artist unknown

> Everyone who delights in the arts of the muses, and who has concern for harmonious song, is supported by nature, guided by discernment, and rewarded by honor. Just as in former times poets and wise men were musicians, so also today they rejoice in churches with sweet sounding melody. Therefore, dear youth, accept these books with cheerful countenance, books written with labor and published with loving care.[1]

[1] Johannes Cochlaeus, *Tetrachordum Musices*, trans., Clement Miller (American Institute of Musicology, 1970), 90.

The few insights we have to music eduction in this treatise are found in a letter of dedication to the prior of the school. Cochlaeus reveals that he was hired with three areas of responsibility, the first being 'the education of our youth in literature and morals' (which also included grammar) and the second was 'ecclesiastical song.'[2] The third is quite interesting. Cochlaeus was to see that 'polyphonic music (which is very pleasing to our people) should not be neglected entirely.' 'Our people,' meant the Church officials while the phrase that polyphony should not be 'neglected entirely' reflects, quite contrary to the impression given by modern music history texts, that polyphony had long been considered by many people actually living

[2] ibid., 17.

in the Renaissance as archaic and irrelevant. Cochlaeus adds a comment on the importance of this instruction in music for these boys,

> so that they do not continue on to the priesthood without knowledge of music, always singing like laboring oxen, and, being ignorant of the rules of music, deriving no profit or enjoyment from such poor singing.

Andreas Ornithoparchus was associated with several universities, in particular Leipzig and Tubingen. His treatise, *Musice active micrologus* of 1517, was widely used as an educational text in sixteenth-century Germany, republished in several editions and even translated and published in English in 1609.[3] This treatise is unique among early sixteenth-century German treatises in two regards. First, it is almost a source book of quotations from ancient and medieval treatises, indeed he admits 'whatever flowers the volumes of other men had in them, like a bee I sucked them out.'[4] Ornithoparchus typically cites earlier authors before making his own observations and, if nothing else, it marks him as being well read and very industrious. He recalls that this effort

> made me travel to many countries, not without financial loss, to search out the Art; these made me often become wearied, when I might have [remained home] at rest; filled with grief, when I might have solaced myself; disgraced, when I might have lived in good reputation; impoverished, when I might have lived in plenty.[5]

Second, this treatise, more than any other of its time, concentrates on the ethical values of music education. The very purpose of his book, he announces, is to provide the youth of all of Germany with a book which would introduce them to good fashions, the honest delights of music and 'little by little stir them to virtuous actions.'[6] He continues,

> Among those things by which the mind of man is wont to be delighted, I can find nothing that is more great, that appeals to any age or sex … There is no breast so savage and cruel, which is not moved with the touch of this delight. For it drives away cares, persuades men to gentleness, represses anger, nourishes arts, promotes concord, inflames heroic

[3] By John Dowland, whose work we quote here, in modernized English.

[4] Ornithoparchus, *Musicae active mirologus* and Dowland, *Introduction: Containing the Art of Singing* (New York: Dover, 1973), 157.

[5] ibid., 117.

[6] ibid.

minds to gallant deeds, cures vice, breeds virtues and nourishes them when they are born and introduces men to good fashion … Therefore this Art is of a holy, sweet, heavenly, divine, fair and blessed nature.

Ornithoparchus next turns to the virtues of speculative versus practical music, or theory versus performance. He admits that speculative understanding of music judges not by the ears, but by 'wit and reason.' In defense of the importance of speculative, or theoretical, knowledge of music, Ornithoparchus concludes,

> It is therefore no small praise, no little profit and labor which should not be lightly esteemed, which makes the Artist both a judge of those songs which have been composed, a corrector of those which are false and an inventor of new [ones].[7]

[7] ibid., 123.

This leads him to establish three categories of musician: performers, poets and critics (those who judge music only by 'speculation and reason'). It is the first category which he discusses at length, following the old Church prejudices against musicians who are 'merely' performers. The basic argument here is that the performer is merely a kind of craftsman who engages in performance while understanding nothing he does. One would like to think that this is the last time we shall confront this relic of the worst of medieval Church Scholastic values, but alas this attitude is still found in some universities today. Here is Ornithoparchus on the performing musician:

> The first category deals with instruments, such as harpists, organists and all others who prove their skill by instruments. They are removed from the intellectual part of music, being as servants, and using no Reason, void of all speculation and following their sense only. Now though they may seem to do things with learning and skill, yet it is plain that they have no knowledge, because they do not comprehend what they profess. Therefore we deny that they have Music, which is the Science of making melody. One can have knowledge without practicing and this is a greater end than being an excellent practitioner. We do not associate nimbleness of fingers with Science, which resides in the soul, but rather to practice. If it were otherwise the more one knew about the Art, the more he would automatically become swift in his fingerings.[8]

[8] ibid.

Ornithoparchus includes singers among instrumentalists, which is to say performers, and again he says their performance means nothing if it is without 'the rules of Reason.' Thus, as regards the speculative versus the practical musician (theoretical versus performance), Ornithoparchus accepts the old Church dogma that it is more honorable to know than to do. Supposing the reader may wonder about the musical performers in the Old Testament, Ornithoparchus quickly adds that, well, they were also prophets and wise men!

Given this very limited definition of what a true musician is, one can understand Ornithoparchus' concern that the art was dying out.

> Hence it is, that excepting those which are, or have been in the chapels of princes, there are none, or very few true musicians. Whereupon the Art itself doth grow into contempt, being hidden like a candle under a bushel, the praising of the almighty Creator of all things decreases and the number of those which seek the overthrow of this Art increases daily throughout Germany.

We have no doubt that he was aware of the attacks of the humanists on the old contrapuntal Church style and that he saw the harbingers of the Reformation.

Ornithoparchus returns to the subject of the importance of musicianship based on theoretical learning in his discussion of mensural music. Now it is the composer who is the object of his attention and he lashes out at those who compose without 'following the rules.' In mid-stream he suddenly recalls having heard some effective music by composers not trained in theoretical knowledge, which is something he cannot quite explain. We know today that theory is left hemisphere of the brain and that the experience and emotional qualities of music are in the right hemisphere. It was the lack of this knowledge, together with the fact that the left hemisphere tends to deny the very existence of the right, which helps explain much of the early attacks on 'practical' musicians by 'speculative' musicians. But these prejudices against performance were rapidly fading due to the increasingly valuable music of the Renaissance. Indeed, our author seems, in the following, to be rather on the defensive.

I cannot but scorn certain composers (for so they will be called, though indeed they are Monsters of Music), who, though they know not so much as the first elements of the art, yet proclaim themselves 'the musicians' musician,' being ignorant in all things, yet bragging of all things and do ... disgrace, corrupt and debase this art, which was in many ages before honored and used by many most learned, most wise men. They use any signs at their pleasure, neither reckoning of value, nor measure, seeking rather to please the ears of the foolish with the sweetness of the melody ... I know such a man, who has been hired to be the organist at the castle in Prague, who though he know not (and I conceal his greater faults) how to distinguish a perfect time from an imperfect, yet maintains publicly that he is writing from the very depth of music ... Many more have violently inundated the art of music, as those which are not compounders of harmonies, but rather corruptors, children of the furies rather than the Muses, not worthy of the least grace I may do them. For their songs are ridiculous, not grounded on the principles of the art, though perhaps true enough. For the artist does not grace the art, but the art graces the artist. Therefore a composer does not grace music, but the contrary. There are some who make true songs not by art, but by custom, as having happily lived among singers all their life, yet do not understand what they have made, knowing that such a thing is, but not what it is.[9]

[9] ibid., 169.

Among his comments focusing on education, Ornithoparchus mentions some 'forbidden intervals,' such as the tritone, 'very rare and forbidden to young beginners.' His implication is that only the most experienced composers can use these. He also praises the use of the monochord, 'a rude master which makes learned scholars.' The value of this instrument, apart from ear training is to 'show hair-brained false musicians their errors.'

Most of his precepts for the education of the choir boys stress the importance of the singer knowing the theoretical rules of music. One of these, for illustration, is the necessity of keeping the beat, 'for to sing without law and measure is an offense to God himself.'

Whole Vigils are performed with such confusion, haste and mockery ... that neither one voice can be distinguished from another, nor one syllable from another, nor one verse sometimes throughout a whole Psalm from another. An impious fashion to be punished with the severest correction. Think you that God is pleased with such howling, such noise, such mumbling, in which there is no devotion, no expressing of words, no articulating of syllables?

Nicolaus Listenius (ca. 1500–1550) matriculated at Wittenberg in 1529, when both Luther and Melancthon were teaching there. As a theorist, his most important work was his *Musica*, of 1537, which was largely a revision of a *Rudimenta musicae* of 1533. This work was one of the two most popular music education books in Germany during the sixteenth century, and was reissued in numerous editions.

Listenius begins his book with one of the old medieval definitions, 'Music is the science of singing correctly and well.' However, in his next sentence he clearly dates himself in the Renaissance and makes one of the most important contributions to this body of sixteenth-century music education treatises when he states that the knowledge of music consists of three kinds: theoretical, practical and *poetic*. The theoretical is concerned only with understanding the subject. Hence, he says, the 'theoretical musician' is content in this knowledge and 'presents no example of his work in performance.'

His definition of practical music, which he divides into Choral and Figured, or Mensural, goes considerably beyond the usual definitions given in the university circles in France, England, and Italy, where the term is given to mean little more than simply performance itself. Listenius speaks of something beyond skill and says the performer teaches the listener something more than mere appreciation.

> Practical, whose goal is doing, is that which delights not only in the intricacies of skill, but extends into performance itself, leaving out no part of the act of performance. Hence the practical musician, who teaches others something more than the recognition of art, trains himself in it for the goal of any performance.[10]

His third kind of knowledge is an aesthetic definition quite new to the Renaissance. Here he is thinking of the meaning left with the listener when the performance is concluded. This he calls '*total* performance.' It is most important and enlightening that he observed that the practical and the poetic always include the theoretical, 'but the reverse is not true.'

> Poetic is that which is not content with just the understanding of the thing nor with only its practice, but which leaves something more after the labor of performance, as when music or a song of musicians is composed by someone whose goal is total performance and accom-

[10] Nicolaus Listenius, *Musica*, trans., Albert Seay (Colorado Springs: Colorado College Music Press, 1975), 3.

plishment. It consists of making or putting together more in this work which afterwards leaves the work perfect and absolute, which otherwise is artificially like the dead.[11]

[11] ibid.

The best known of these sixteenth-century German music education treatises is the *Dodecachordon* of 1547 by Heinrich Glarean (1488–1563) of Switzerland. He did his higher education at the University of Köln where one of his teachers was Cochlaeus. Glarean was a man of many talents as is testified to in numerous letters by Erasmus, who gives the impression that he was unusually proficient in all the Liberal Arts. In letters of recommendation, Erasmus calls Glarean a mathematician, meaning four branches of the Liberal Arts. It was from this perspective that Glarean was interested in music[12] and our guess is that he probably did not think of himself as a performing musician, in spite of the fact that on one occasion he so impressed Maximilian I in his singing of a poem that he was made poet laureate. Such a widely talented man is never universally popular and in the fictitious, satirical 'Letters of Obscure Men,' of 1515, by Crotus Rubeanus and Ulrich von Hutten, Glarean is described as

[12] Glarean does say, in his prefatory letter to Cardinal von Waldburg, that he had spent twenty years thinking about the musical problems presented in his book. See Glarean, *Dodecachordon*, trans., Clement Miller (American Institute of Musicology, 1965), I, 39.

> a very headstrong man ... A terrible man, a choleric, for ever threatening fights—and he must be possessed of a devil[13]

[13] Letter of 'Demetrius Phalerius to Ortwin Gratius,' in Francis Stokes, trans., *On the Eve of the Reformation* (New York: Harper & Row, 1909), 183.

In any case, Glarean was the author of one of the most extensive music treatises of the sixteenth century, a work he had apparently finished writing by 1539. Ironically, the real heart of the treatise is the most extensive exposition on the church modal system, although by the time the book was published the modal system was rapidly being replaced by the major–minor system. Beyond this, it is a treatise which treats all elements of music theory in very great detail. Glarean, fully aware of this, and perhaps reflecting on his experience in the university, observes at one point,

> Perhaps we have treated this in more detail than is necessary But it had to be done for the state of mind of the masses, to whom nothing is explained sufficiently.[14]

[14] Glarean, op. cit., I, 79.

In another place, however, he seems to suggest the difficulty lay with the professors as much as the minds of the masses.

> If by chance this has seemed insufficiently clear to anyone, I beg him to remember how uneducated and unpolished our present age is, that among the highly learned, even among those teaching mathematics, not one in twenty has a clear conception of this matter.[15]

In any case, it is clear that Glarean's purpose was one of education and early in the treatise he cautions the student regarding the broad knowledge necessary to master music.

> I appeal to every earnest youth, I exhort and admonish you, if you desire to be initiated into the secrets of this science and want to become a priest truly worthy of this discipline, you will make use of three principal points without which this study cannot be fully mastered, however much you may speculate, and even may surpass Prometheus himself in observation. The first is that you have the precepts of arithmetic clearly in mind and also those of theory and practice. Then it follows that you cannot be entirely ignorant of the Greek language. For a great many of the terms of this study are Greek. The third is that you have some instrument at hand on which you can measure all sounds by ear.[16]

[16] ibid., I, 82ff.

This last sentence is very important and represents one of the distinguishing hallmarks of this treatise. Many earlier treatises were written from the perspective that music was something to be understood intellectually. For Glarean, no matter how extensively he explains the cerebral definitions, in the end it was a matter of the ear. For this reason he also treats the practicing musician with more respect than earlier treatises. In a typical passage, Glarean writes,

> Modes are also changed from one into another but not with equal success. For in some cases the change is scarcely clear even to a perceptive ear, indeed, often with great pleasure to the listener, a fact which we have frequently declared is very common today in changing from the Lydian to the Ionian. Those who play instruments and who know how to sing readily the verses of poets according to a musical play, understand this. Indeed, in this way they are frequently worthy of praise if they do it skillfully, especially if they change the Ionian into Dorian. But in other cases the changing seems rough, and scarcely ever without a grave offense to the ears, as changing from the Dorian to the Phry-

gian. And so whenever present day organists encounter this difficulty in changing church songs in such a way, if they are not well trained and quick, they often incur the derision of experienced listeners.[17]

[17] ibid., I, 129.

It is also from this perspective that Glarean begins his treatise by reminding the reader that music, as something heard by the ear, came before theory. After stating that music consists of theory and practice, the separation of the speculative and the practical so long favored by early theorists, he observes,

> Since truly all learning consists in demonstration and neither facts themselves can be computed nor tones be written musicians have invented symbols of the tones partly through figures which they now call notes partly through the naming of syllables.[18]

[18] ibid., I, 41

This recognition of the importance of the ear, with respect to music, while obvious to us today, was new in the sixteenth century and was the harbinger of the death of the old speculative and practical division of music. Another step in this direction by Glarean comes when he begins to understand that real talent in composition is not learned by theory at all, but is perhaps genetic. He addresses this by asking which is more important, the ability to compose a beautiful melody or the craft of counterpoint.

> As we were hastening to the end of this very toilsome book, this not entirely inconsequential thought came to our mind about a matter which I say has been considered in doubt a long time now among men of our times, that is, which is more deserving of praise, the invention of a theme or the addition of several voices; namely, so that the uninitiated may also understand, whether it is of more value if one can invent a natural tenor, which affects all minds, which takes hold of a man's heart, in short, which so clings to our memory that it often steals upon us without our even thinking, and into which we break as if awakened from sleep, as we commonly see concerning many tenors; or if one adds three or more voices to the tenor invented in the aforementioned way, which voices, so to speak, embellish it with imitations, canons, changes of modus, tempus, and prolatio …
>
>   Here is an example of this matter, so that one may comprehend so much the better what we say. Whoever first invented the [melody] *Te Deum laudamus* or any other as *Pange lingua*, may he not be preferred in talent to one who afterwards composed a complete Mass according to it? First, indeed, to say as a preface, we cannot deny that this happens to each through the power of his talent, and through a certain natural and native capacity rather than through art. The reason for this seems to be

that very frequently those who are untrained in music are also surprisingly proficient in inventing tenors in our vernacular, whether Celtic or German, and further, that many who are proficient in adding voices likewise have learned music badly, to say nothing of other disciplines. Therefore, it is clear that neither talent is really possible for a man unless he is born to it, and, as it is commonly said, unless he received it from his mother. This is likewise true of painters, also of sculptors, and preachers ... , in short, of all works dedicated to Minerva.[19]

[19] ibid.., I, 205ff.

We should like to conclude with a passage in which Glarean again makes the point that when it comes to music, it is the ear, not theory, which must judge. Here he makes a reference to the old Church polyphony and suggests that even the highly educated cannot *really* understand these works, but only praise these works for fear they will be criticized. He follows this by pointing to Church composers who are still promoting works based on theory, rather than on feeling. This, he says, is stupid. It is also, in a way, a testimonial to the full arrival of humanism in Germany.

> Moreover, since music is the mother of pleasure, I consider much more useful that which pertains to the pleasure of many than what pertains to the pleasure of a few. And when a monophonic [melody], noble, distinguished, and having suitable words, has been brought forth among men, it is pleasing to many, educated as well as uneducated. For how many are there, even among the very highly educated, who truly understand a composition of four or more voices? Indeed, all praise it when they hear it, lest one may be considered less educated if he would disparage it ...
>
> But those who do not understand the nature of modes, as singers in general in our time, and who do not judge the import of a song except through the consonances, since they have disregarded its moods and neglected its true beauty, disparage what they do not understand. I will spare the names here. For I could name some, more uncouth than any ass, who have rejected what has been successful, and in its place have instituted so much that is absurd, so much that is stupid, that they have shown themselves to be completely insensate. But such are the customs of this age.

With the treatise, *Compendium Musices* of 1552, by Adrian Coclico we finally, after one thousand years, come to a music treatise written by a true musician and not a mathematician. Coclico was engaged as a music teacher at the university in Wittenberg in 1545. Although he remained only a brief time,

Adrianus Petit Coclico, 1552

due to lack of funds, he was popular not only with students but with Melanchthon. Coclico has left a very important treatise from this period, in so far as it documents the shift away from the old Scholastic complexities of speculative music to the more modern emphasis on expressive, practical musicianship.[20] In this work, written for the training of boys, he constantly warns against merely following the rules. Indeed, in his 'Preface to Nordic Youth' he suggests that traditional books on music do not even treat what he calls the 'art' of music, 'which is seen more in practice than in rules.'[21]

Coclico begins by stating his purpose is teaching 'correct, smooth and elegant singing.'

> I see today German youth not only ignorant of the traditions of music, of which many praises will be expounded elsewhere, but also ruined and kept back from the true force and reason of singing. As long as they [held back in] the memorizing of precepts, for them to learn to sing rapidly and correctly cannot be done.[22]

He quickly adds a significant qualification to the last sentence, noting,

> I would say that whoever keeps his students too long on precepts and theory lacks judgment and evidently is ignorant of the goal of music.

Coclico, no doubt from experience, is quite specific regarding the qualities which the student must bring to his study. He again stresses that it is performance, not speculative music, which produces a musician.

> First, adolescents or better, boys, ... should bring to their teacher a great zeal and desire for learning music, together with their natural enthusiasm, so that they may listen as eagerly and attentively as possible to whoever teaches and guides. For, if anyone by his nature is perhaps more estranged from the love of music or he may not have wanted to learn what he should, I cannot sensibly promise great things for him. He, however, who is possessed by a certain single-minded zeal for learning and does not have forces of nature repelling him from music, if they have molded him skillfully and carefully, this person I hold myself committed that he will be an excellent musician. In a Greek proverb it is beautifully stated: Love teaches music. Then, if the boy has this proposed goal for himself, so that he will become a better performer than theorist, I would not want to load him down with many precepts

[20] In Adrian Coclico, *Musical Compendium*, trans., Albert Seay (Colorado Springs: Colorado College Music Press, 1973), 30, Seay writes, 'Music by 1550 was less and less of a liberal art and more and more a fine art, while theory had begun to lose most of its speculative character in favor of the purely practical.'

[21] ibid., 1.

[22] Coclico, op. cit., 5.

and almost overwhelm him. He who wishes first to explore all the reasonings of speculative music and turns himself to this rather than to singing; he will, in my opinion, only arrive at the hoped for and preset goal much later on.[23]

[23] ibid., 5ff.

Later he adds an observation which might be found in any era.

But I do not know how it happens that our youth not only despises work and does not submit well to good recommendations, but even grows angry.[24]

[24] ibid., 7.

Coclico promises his book will give the necessary rules and knowledge which the student needs, but he seems eager to get beyond this to the purpose of the study. It is particularly important that he defines this purpose here as being to give pleasure and to exhilarate the listener, as well as stressing that it is the *ear* which must judge.

When he has learned these things clearly and rapidly, he will then begin to sing, not only as [the music] is written but also with embellishments, and to pronounce skillfully, smoothly and meaningfully, to intone correctly and to place any syllable in its proper place under the right notes.

As a singer, he will study especially how to please the ears of men and how to inspire pleasure in them, as well as admiration and favor for himself. He will also be continually guided by the judgment of his ears. The ears easily understand what is done correctly or badly and are truly the masters of the art of singing. What difference is there, I ask, between a dog's barking and he who does not hear or does not notice what and how he sings?

To be avoided are the vices of certain nations, which, if they stay in us, must be corrected by zeal and industry. Insane clamor and huge roaring and that noise like the voice of certain ignorant men, lacks grace. While they weep, scream or bark, they please no one, they take away all pleasure from their hearers and deprive themselves of praise. A smooth song truly seeks this end, which the musician looks and hunts for, namely, to delight and to exhilarate.[25]

[25] ibid., 6.

Almost as an afterthought, Coclico provides his credentials. His own study was with that 'most noble musician, Josquin,' from whom he learned 'incidentally, from no book.'

Now Coclico sets the framework for the 'rules' portion of his book by explaining that he divides musicians into four categories. We read his discussion as a virtual history of music, with a clear emphasis on the values of the sixteenth century. The first were the original musicians who discovered music, including Greek mythical figures, figures from the Old Testament and medieval theorists. These, he says, 'were only theorists.'[26]

[26] ibid., 8.

The second type he calls mathematicians, and seems to have in mind the polyphonic Church composers of the fifteenth century. Everyone knows their compositions, he admits,

> but these men did not pursue the goal of music. Even if they understand the force of this art and also compose, they do not honor the smoothness and sweetness of song. What is worse, when they hope to spread their invented art widely and make it more outstanding, they rather defile and obscene it. In teaching precepts and speculation they have specialized excessively and, in accumulating a multitude of symbols and other things, they have introduced many difficulties. Disputing much a long time, they never arrived at the true rationality of singing.

The third type are the most outstanding musicians, who 'join theory and practice in the best and learned way.' These men, among whom he lists numerous sixteenth-century composers, understand 'how to embellish melodies, to express in them all the emotions of all kinds.'

The fourth type he calls poets, but he means those artistic singers who compose, improvise and sing 'smoothly, ornately and artfully for the delight of men.' He adds that he finds such singers particularly in France and Belgium and, once more, stresses that such ability rests more upon the practical than the theoretical.

Coclico now begins the theoretical portion of his book, but he repeatedly renews his criticism of rules-based learning. No sooner has he begun writing of scales, than he stops and observes that this can only be understood in performance.

> I have wished to train this boyish industry in music through but few words and precepts on that account, so that no youth running to the books of musician-mathematicians will waste his life in reading them and never arrive at the goal of singing well.[27]

[27] ibid., 10.

Similarly, he barely introduces his discussion of mensural rules, when he promises to leave out 'a mass of definitions, lest boys staying for a longer time on precepts arrive too late at the purpose of singing well.'

> For this reason I do not cease to dissuade [students] from remaining tied to the prolix writings of musician-mathematicians who have drawn up so many types of signs of augmentation and diminution, from which no fruit, but rather controversy and discord arises.[28]

[28] ibid., 16.

Having made this digression, he continues with some fascinating first-hand observations. Of great importance here is his emphasis on learning through performance itself, rather than through the conceptualization of music, in an extremely valuable insight into the teaching of the great Josquin.

In Belgian cities, where prizes are given to singers and, because of the prizes to be gained, no procedure or labor is undertaken unless it pertains to the goal of singing well, no music is written down or prescribed by precept.

> My teacher, Josquin des Pres, never rehearsed or wrote out any musical procedures, yet in a short time made perfect musicians, since he did not hold his students back in long and frivolous precepts, but taught precepts in a few words at the same time as singing through exercise and practice ...
>
> Josquin did not judge everyone capable of the demands of composition. He felt that it should be taught only to those who were driven by an unusual force of their nature to this most beautiful art.[29]

[29] ibid., 16.

Once again, after giving his subject as the rules of prolations, he is able to produce only two sentences before returning to his chief concern.

> I have wanted something here planned for adolescents so that they will not stick to the books of musician-mathematicians, who have contrived an infinite number of other signs and have turned away the souls of adolescents from the true use of music, making something clear in itself obscure, as when they write so many things about proportions of minor inequality, or sesquitertia.[30]

[30] ibid., 18.

Coclico again interrupts his presentation of the rules of composition, this time to comment on the qualities of the fine singer. He first recommends that the student choose a teacher who sings beautifully and smoothly, who sings by

> special natural instinct and makes Music joyful by the ornaments of [improvisation], at the same time omitting throat clearings, shouting and other absurdities, leading most noble Music into the hatred of men.[31]

He again points to Belgium and France as the most likely source for fine singing and observes that in Germany the knowledge of such singing is rarely found. He cautions that the singing must come from the throat and that the student will not be able to do this unless he 'sweats and works a great deal.'

When discussing counterpoint, Coclico implies that in Germany polyphonic music had become unpopular among many musicians.

> If anyone makes mention of counterpoint and demands it in a perfect musician, they destroy it with a more than snarling distaste, impudently asserting it as truth that many improper and corrupt types [of intervals] occur in counterpoint, ones that offend the ears and have no place in compositions.

Coclico admits the basic contention, but finds the reason for their views in their improper understanding of the style.

> I agree that counterpoint offends their ears, for theirs are like those of asses, to whom nothing is agreeable except that which they produce as braying or makes a sound like braying. If it has offended the ears of men, why not more those of Josquin, Pierre de la Rue and their successors, whose ears were most delicate? ...
>
> But knowledge has no enemy except the ignorant and, since the despisers of this art are ignorant of the practice of music, their foolishness easily adds many allies.
>
> A boy should curse the perverse judgment of these men as utter nonsense, and, as with the prince-singers, should hold as true that he will never become a perfect musician without the knowledge and use of counterpoint.[32]

Later he mentions that Josquin compared those inferior in counterpoint to trying to fly without wings.

[31] ibid., 20.

[32] ibid., 21.

After a brief discussion of intervals, Coclico briefly mentions improvisation, which he recommends should first be studied in note to note practice of the intervals, followed by more 'florid counterpoint.'[33] This art, he advises, requires constant practice. Later, he gives ability in improvisation even more weight.

[33] ibid., 23.

> The first requirement of a good singer is that he should know how to sing counterpoint by improvisation. Without this he will be nothing.[34]

[34] ibid., 24.

Perhaps because of the rules he has been presenting, Coclico now pauses to make the point that the urge to compose must be an inspired compulsion, not simply the next step after learning the necessary rules.

> [The Student] should be led to composing by a great desire, and by a certain natural impulse he will be driven to composition, so that he will not taste food nor drink until his piece is finished, for, since this natural impulse so drives him, he accomplishes more in one hour than others in a whole month. Composers to whom these unusual motivations are absent are useless.[35]

[35] ibid.

Returning to the art of singing, Coclico mentions the difficulties in singing multi-part polyphony. One must learn how to do this by study with a practical musician, otherwise 'he will leave in shame and be laughed at.' And, he adds, 'even if [the student] reads books for ten years, he will not advance at all without use and practice.'

15 Martin Luther on Music Education

TEN YEARS BEFORE LUTHER posted his famous ninety-five theses on the door of the Castle Church in Wittenberg he was a model Catholic priest preparing, at age twenty-four, to conduct his first mass. In a letter inviting a friend to attend, Luther describes himself in these words:

> God, who is glorious and holy in all his works, has deigned to exalt me magnificently—a miserable and totally unworthy sinner—by calling me into his supreme ministry, solely on the basis of his bounteous mercy.[1]

By 1517, LUTHER was serving as a lecturer at the university in Wittenberg, in addition to his duties as a priest. Now age thirty-four, nothing remarkable had happened in his life when one day a papal representative appeared selling indulgences to help raise money for the rebuilding of St. Peter's in Rome. When members of Luther's flock showed him the documents they had purchased which, among other things, obtained the entry into Heaven for their long dead ancestors who were never even believers, Luther refused to play the game. His 'Theses' were in effect statements in opposition which he offered to discuss or debate with whomsoever. This was the last chance the Church had either to deal with him rationally or, as Erasmus volunteered, to burn him at the stake. The story of Luther from this point is the transformation of the humble priest illustrated by the letter above to a man who, in 1541, could call the pope, a 'stupid ass.'[2]

Apart from his historic role in the Reformation, Luther also played an important role in the reformation of German schools. Perhaps from his own experience, Luther developed very critical views on the German universities. For example, on one occasion he offered this view of university professors:

> We have taken upon ourselves the support of a host of doctors, preaching friars, masters, priests, and monks; that is to say, great, coarse, fat asses decked out in red and brown birettas, looking like a sow bedecked with a gold chain and jewels. They taught us nothing good, but only

Opposite page: Martin Luther by Wenzel Hollar

[1] Letter to John Braun [1507], in *Luther's Works* (St. Louis: Concordia, 1961), XLVIII, 3.

[2] 'Against Hanswurst' [1541], in ibid., XLI, 221.

made us all the more blind and stupid. In return, they devoured all our goods and filled every monastery, indeed every nook and cranny, with the filth and dung of their foul and poisonous books, until it is appalling to think of it.³

3 'To the Councilmen of All Cities in Germany That They Establish and Maintain Christian Schools' [1524], in ibid., XLV, 351, 375.

First, let us consider his views lower school education.

In 1524 Luther became very interested in promoting the idea of general public education. He published a treatise on this subject, pointing to the positive impact on society and cites the ancient Roman example in which young men studied languages and the liberal arts, which of course included music.

A city's best and greatest welfare, safety, and strength consist rather in its having many able, learned, wise, honorable, and well-educated citizens …

So it was done in ancient Rome. There boys were so taught that by the time they reached their fifteenth, eighteenth, or twentieth year they were well versed in Latin, Greek, and all the liberal arts, and then immediately entered upon a political or military career. Their system produced intelligent, wise, and competent men, so skilled in every art and rich in experience that if all the bishops, priests, and monks in the whole of Germany today were rolled into one, you would not have the equal of a single Roman soldier.⁴

4 ibid., XLV, 356.

Of more recent experience, he remarks that he is thankful that schools were not as they were, with 'flogging, trembling, anguish, and misery.' Then he presents the basic curriculum he would establish and we find music a central subject, although it is still in the context of the universities' dogma about its being a branch of mathematics.

I would have them study not only languages and history, but also singing and music together with the whole of mathematics.⁵

5 ibid., 369.

Interestingly enough, he projects all of this would require only two hours of school per day! His closing remarks include a reference to the Dark Ages and the rediscovery of ancient literature during the Renaissance.

This situation lasted until, as we have experienced and observed, the languages and the arts were laboriously recovered—although imperfectly—from bits and fragments of old books hidden among dust and worms. Men are still painfully searching for them every day, just as people poke through the ashes of a ruined city seeking the treasures and jewels.[6]

[6] ibid., 374.

In a treatise of 1525, Luther again turns to education, saying 'The preachers are to exhort the people to send their children to school so that persons are educated for competent service both in church and state.'[7] He now presents more specific details on how this public education should be organized and again music is a core subject. First, instruction should be done in Latin, and only Latin, as including German, Greek or Hebrew for children is 'not only useless but even injurious.' Second, the students should not be burdened with too many books. And finally, he proposes dividing the children into three age groups.

[7] 'Instructions for the Visitors of Parish Pastors in Electoral Saxony' [1525], in ibid., XL, 314ff.

The First Division, are children just beginning to read. These children are to learn Latin a phrase or two at a time and are to be taught to write.

> These children shall also be taught music and shall sing with the others.

The Second Division includes those children able to read and now ready for grammar, which he says should only be taught in the hours before noon.

> Where the schoolmaster shuns [teaching grammar], as is often the case, he should be dismissed and another teacher found for the children, who will take on this work of holding the children to grammar. For no greater harm can be done to all the arts than where the children are not well trained in grammar.

While discussing this group Luther specifies,

> All the children, large and small, should practice music daily, in the first hour in the afternoon.

The Third Division, consisting of children well trained in grammar, are now given substantial literature, including Virgil, Ovid and Cicero. And once again,

> along with the others these shall rehearse music the hour after noon.

No doubt one of the advantages of this school program which Luther had in mind was the availability of the students to sing in church. In one place, while discussing the ceremonies of the old Church, he says in passing,

> When the pupils kneel and fold their hands as the schoolmaster beats time with his baton during the singing of 'And was made man ... '[8]

[8] 'On the Councils and the Church' [1539], in ibid., XLI, 137.

Finally, when the time came for Luther to send his own son to school, the boy's musical education was clearly on his mind.

> I am sending my son John to you so that you may add him to the boys who are to be drilled in grammar and music ...
> Tell John Walter that I pray for his well-being, and that I commend my son to him for learning music. For I, of course, produce theologians, but I also would like to produce grammarians and musicians.[9]

[9] Letter to Marcus Crodel [1542], in ibid., L, 231ff.

In several places, Luther also comments on the purpose of music so often mentioned by the ancient Greeks: the power of music to affect the character of the listener. Because of his personal observation of this powerful connection between music and character he could not help making a further association with religion. In a letter to the famous German composer, Ludwig Senfl in 1530, Luther observes,

> There is no doubt that there are many seeds of good qualities in the minds of those who are moved by music. Those, however, who are not moved by music I believe are definitely like stumps and blocks of stone. For we know that music, too, is odious and unbearable to the demons. Indeed I plainly judge, and do not hesitate to affirm, that except for theology there is no art that could be put on the same level with music, since except for theology, music alone produces what otherwise only theology can do, namely, a calm and joyful disposition ... This is the reason why the prophets did not make use of any art except music; when setting forth their theology they did it not as geometry, not as arithmetic, not as astronomy, but as music, so that they held theology and music most tightly connected, and proclaimed truth through Psalms and songs.[10]

[10] Letter to Ludwig Senfl [1530], in ibid., XLIX, 427ff.

In a conversation with Anthony Lauterbach, Luther was thinking along the same lines.

> Excellent was the arrangement of the ancients that required men to exercise, lest they fall into debauchery, drunkenness, and gambling. I especially admire these two noble exercises, music and gymnastics. The first of these pertains to the spirit and serves to drive away care, while the second pertains to the body.[11]

[11] In a conversation of 1536 reported by Anthony Lauterbach, in ibid., LIV, 206.

He seems to have noticed this first in the quality of people he knew who were also musicians. We may presume that it was his recognition of this purpose of music which fostered his frequent recommendation that music be part of the school curriculum.

> I have always loved music. Those who have mastered this art are made of good stuff, they are fit for any task. It is necessary indeed that music be taught in the schools. A teacher must be able to sing; otherwise I will not as much as look at him. Also, we should not ordain young men into the ministry unless they have become well acquainted with music in the schools.
>
> Music is a beautiful and glorious gift of God and close to theology. I would not give up what little I know about music for something else which I might have in greater abundance. We should always make it a point to habituate youth to enjoy the art of music, for it produces fine and skillful people.[12]

[12] Quoted in Walter Buszin, 'Luther on Music,' in *The Musical Quarterly* (January, 1946), 85.

In 1524 Luther returned to this idea when he wrote the preface to his and Walter's *Geistliches Gesangbuchlein*.

> That it is good and God pleasing to sing hymns is, I think, known to every Christian; for everyone is aware not only of the example of the prophets and kings in the Old Testament who praised God with song and sound, with poetry and psaltery, but also of the common and ancient custom of the Christian church to sing Psalms ...
>
> And these songs were arranged in four parts to give the young—who should at any rate be trained in music and other fine arts—something to wean them away from love ballads and carnal songs and to teach them something of value in their place, thus combining the good with the pleasing, as is proper for youth. Nor am I of the opinion that the gospel should destroy and blight all the arts, as some of the pseudo-religious claim. But I would like to see all the arts, especially music, used in the service of Him who gave and made them ... As it is, the world is too lax and indifferent about teaching and training the young for us to abet this trend.[13]

[13] *Luther's Works*, op. cit., LIII, 315ff.

Luther is reported to have mentioned this purpose in another dinner conversation.

> Music is a semi-discipline and taskmistress, which makes people milder and more gentle, more civil and more sensible. The wicked gut-scrapers and fiddlers serve the purpose of enabling us to see and hear what a fine and wholesome art music really is; for white is more clearly recognized when it is contrasted with black.[14]

[14] Quoted in Buszin, op. cit., 92.

Given Luther's appreciation of the positive purposes of music, it follows that he was concerned that it might be misused. He mentions some specific examples of the misuse of music in the preface he wrote for a collection of part-songs published in 1538.

> Take special care to shun perverted minds who prostitute this lovely gift of nature and of art with their erotic rantings; and be quite assured that none but the devil goads them on to defy their very nature which would and should praise God its Maker with this gift, so that these bastards purloin the gift of God and use it to worship the foe of God, the enemy of nature and of this lovely art.[15]

[15] *Luther's Works*, op. cit., LIII, 324.

In another place he seems to have had this same thought in mind, although he does not quite complete the analogy.

> Wine inflames to many evils, but especially to thirst and more drinking. What would the prophet have said to the Germans for whom natural capacity is insufficient to drain so much drink? Theirs are not feasts of joy but feasts of pigs. It is all right to eat and to drink, but to cultivate drunkenness is evil. So also music is a gift of God. Elisha says (2 Kings 3:15) 'Bring me a minstrel, etc.' Amos 6:5 says: 'Like David they invent for themselves instruments of music.' Certainly if you make use of music as David did, you will not sin.[16]

[16] 'Lectures on Isaiah,' in ibid., XVI, 62.

Since Luther's primary interest in music was centered in singing, his few remarks on performance practice are concerned with the proper spirit of the singer. In his preface to the Babst *Hymnal* of 1545, Luther writes of the proper manner of religious singing.

As the prophet Malachi asks in the first chapter, 'Who is there even among you that would shut the doors for nought or kindle a light on my altar for nothing?' Now with a heart as lazy and unwilling as this, nothing or nothing good can be sung. Heart and mind must be cheerful and willing if one is to sing ...

Thus there is now in the New Testament a better service of God, of which the Psalm [96] here says: 'Sing to the Lord a new song ... ' For God has cheered our hearts and minds through his dear Son, whom he gave for us to redeem us from sin, death, and the devil. He who believes this earnestly cannot be quiet about it. But he must gladly and willingly sing and speak about it so that others also may come and hear it. And whoever does not want to sing and speak of it shows that he does not believe and that he does not belong under the new and joyful testament, but under the old, lazy, and tedious testament.[17]

[17] ibid., LIII, 332ff.

Heydenreich reports hearing Luther make the observation during a dinner conversation, that music must be performed with a certain seriousness of purpose.

Music doesn't sound right when there is laughter in connection with it, for music is intended to cheer the spirit. The mouth gets no pleasure from it. If one sings diligently, the soul, which is located in the body, plays and derives special pleasure from it.[18]

[18] In a conversation of 1542 reported by Caspar Heydenreich, in ibid., LIV, 420.

Luther also makes one reference to the listener, drawing on an analogy often mentioned by ancient philosophers regarding the ass and the lyre, by which is meant the ass can hear music but not listen to it.

No matter how much is said about this, the others neither understand nor heed it any more than a sow appreciates music played on the harp.[19]

[19] 'Sermon on the Fourteenth Chapter of St. John,' in ibid., XXIV, 89

Finally, we should mention that in a publication of 1526 dealing with the new order of the service, Luther mentions the possibility of doing the church service in varying languages to aid in the education of children in languages.

For in no wise would I want to discontinue the service in the Latin language, because the young are my chief concern. And if I could bring it to pass, and Greek and Hebrew were as familiar to us as the Latin and had as many fine melodies and songs, we would hold mass, sing, and read on successive Sundays in all four languages, German, Latin, Greek, and Hebrew. I do not at all agree with those who cling to one language and despise all others.[20]

[20] 'The German Mass and Order of Service' [1526], in ibid., LIII, 63.

16 Music Education in Sixteenth-Century England

WITH RESPECT TO THE AESTHETIC AND SOCIAL RECOGNITION given music and music education in the English-speaking world, the late sixteenth century must in retrospect be viewed as an unfortunate turning point. There were several significant reasons for this change in attitude.

One contributing influence was the fact that many of the musicians were foreign born. Many of these had come on their own to England for religious reasons, but some have suggested that there was a shortage of skilled musicians in England as a consequence of Henry VIII closing the monasteries and Church schools. This is one of the observations Nichols makes, writing in 1788:

> This Matthew Gwin was a Fellow of St. John's College, studied physic, poetry, chemistry, etc., and made a great figure in almost every part of learning. He was chosen Music Professor of Oxford University in 1582, though he understood not a title either of the theory or practice of that science ... The greatest wound, which music ever received in England, was from the suppression of the monasteries; after which the Puritans often made it their business to run it down as a relic of popery. For both these reasons, very few Englishmen regarded it in Queen Elizabeth's time. Her own band of musicians were many of them foreigners (Venetians).[1]

In spite of these many foreign musicians present in England, a growth in intellectual self-confidence, so apparent in the development of sixteenth-century literature, led to a certain insular isolation.[2] We will let an anonymous poem of 1600 represent many contemporary references to the general problem.

> A Painter lately with his pencil drew
> The picture of a Frenchman and Italian,
> With whom he placed the Spaniard, Turk, and Jew;
> But by himself he sat the Englishman.[3]

This self-imposed isolation is especially evident in the frequent ridicule of English students going to Italy for further study, for whom there was a commonly used term of con-

---

[1] Quoted in John Nichols, *The Progresses and Public Processions of Queen Elizabeth* (London, 1788, 1805), II [these volumes carry no page numbers].

[2] Gustave Reese, in *Music in the Renaissance* (New York: Norton, 1959), 763, dates this isolation in music even earlier, to the latter part of the fifteenth century. That this was widely recognized, Reese points to Tinctoris' observation regarding the 'wretched poverty of invention' in English music.

[3] Anonymous, 'Tom Tel-Troths Message,' (1600) in F. Furnivall, ed., *Miscellaneous*, Series VI, Shakespere's England, Nr. 2 (Vaduz: Kraus Reprint, 1965), 122. We have modernized the English of most of these sixteenth-century texts.

tempt, the 'Italianate Englishmen.' Unfortunately this attitude blinded English high society to the most important insights of humanism. What was sensitive in Italy was called effeminate in England and thus the active interest demonstrated by Italian nobles in promoting high quality music represents an attitude rarely found in England.

Finally, in spite of the extraordinary example set by both Henry VIII and Elizabeth I, as members of the highest class who were active musicians, the view that nobles should be performing musicians was clearly changing. This was largely the result of the influence of the growing religious right movement known as the Puritans.

All of this seems to have created in some a perceived danger in extended study and, indeed, Roger Ascham specifically points to the ill effects of the extended study of music.

Portrait of Henry VIII, ca. 1560–80, after Hans Holbein the Younger

> Some wits, moderate enough by nature, be many times marred by overmuch study and use of some sciences, namely, music, arithmetic and geometry. These sciences, as they sharpen men's wits overmuch, so they change men's manners oversore, if they be not moderately mingled and wisely applied to some good use of life. Notice all mathematical heads which be only and wholly bent to those sciences, how solitary they be themselves, how unfit to live with others, and how unapt to serve in the world.

He quotes the early medical writer, Galen (second century AD), as saying 'Much music marreth men's manners,' and then concludes that 'overmuch quickness of wit,' whether by nature or by study, does not result in the 'greatest learning, best manners, or happiest life.'

In another book, a treatise on long bow shooting called *Toxophilus*, Ascham elaborates on the dangers of music. In this dialog, Toxophilus has been explaining the many virtues of shooting, when Philologus introduces the subject of music by observing that it is a common recreation for scholars. Toxophilus answers,

> I cannot deny that some music is fit for learning, and I trust you cannot choose but grant that shooting is also fit … But as concerning which of them is most fit for learning and scholars to use, you may say what you will for your pleasure; [but] this I am sure, that Plato and Aristotle … do mention music and all kinds of it; wherein they both agree, that music used amongst the Lydians is very ill for young men which

be students for virtue and learning, for a certain nice, soft, and smooth sweetness of it, which would rather entice them to naughtiness than stir them to honesty.

Another kind of music, invented by the Dorians, they both wonderfully praise, allowing it to be very fit for the study of virtue and learning, because of a manly, rough, and stout sound in it, which should encourage young stomachs to attempt manly matters. Now whether [today's] ballads and rounds, these galliards, pavanes, and dances, so nicely fingered, so sweetly tuned, be more like the music of the Lydians or the Dorians, you may judge for yourself.[4]

Toxophilus then quotes the same Galen comment above, that 'Much music marreth men's manners,' and elaborates on its meaning.

Although some men will say that it is not so, but rather recreateth and maketh quick a man's mind; yet, methink, by reason it doth as honey doth to a man's stomach, which at the first receiveth it well, but afterward it maketh it unfit to abide any good strong nourishing meat, or else any wholesome sharp and quick drink. And even so in a manner these instruments make a man's wit so soft and smooth, so tender and queasy, that they be less able to brook strong and tough study. Wits be not sharpened, but rather dulled and made blunt, with such sweet softness, even as good edges be blunter which men whet upon soft chalk stones.

Toxophilus then quotes an often repeated anecdote which maintains that Cyrus, after conquering the Lydians and desiring to keep them peaceful, arranged for

every one of them should have a harp or a lute, and learn to play and sing. Which thing if you do ... you shall see them quickly of men made women. And thus luting and singing take away a manly stomach, which should enter and pierce deep and hard study.

Toxophilus concludes by questioning whether Aristotle and Plato knew what they were talking about.

Therefore either Aristotle and Plato know not what was good and evil for learning and virtue, and the example of wise histories be vainly set before us, or else the minstrelsy of lutes, pipes, harps, and all other that standeth by such nice, fine, minikin fingering (such as the most part of scholars whom I know use, if they use any), is far more fit, for the womanishness of it, to dwell in the Court among ladies, than for any great thing in it, which should help good and sad study, to abide in the University among scholars.

[4] *Toxophilus*, in Rev. Giles, ed., *The Whole Works of Roger Ascham* (London: John Russell Smith, 1864), II, 25ff. Ascham explains at length why shooting is the ideal exercise for the student—such things as tennis and bowling being too 'vehement.'

Now Philologus agrees 'to say the truth, I never thought myself these kinds of music fit for learning.' Nevertheless he attempts to come to the defense of music, although his arguments, while interesting, are all of secondary values.

> That milk is no fitter or more natural for the bringing up of children than music is, both Galen proveth by authority, and daily use teacheth by experience. For even the little babes lacking the use of reason, are scarce so well stilled in sucking their mother's pap, as in hearing their mother sing. Again, how fit youth is made by learning to sing, for grammar and other sciences, both we daily do see ... The godly use of praising God, by singing in the church, needeth not my praise, seeing it is so praised through all the scripture ...
> Beside all these commodities, truly two degrees of men, which have the highest offices under the King in all this realm, shall greatly lack the use of singing, preachers and lawyers, because they shall not, without this, be able to rule their breasts for every purpose. For where is no distinction in telling glad things and fearful things, gentleness and cruelness, softness and vehementness, and such-like matters, there can be no great persuasion ... But when a man is always in one tune, like a humble bee, or else now in the top of the church, now down, that no man knoweth where to have him; or piping like a reed, or roaring like a bull, as some lawyers do, which thing they do best when they cry loudest, these shall never greatly move, as I have known many well-trained have done, because their voice was not stayed afore with learning to sing. For all voices, great and small, base and shrill, weak or soft, may be helped and brought to a good point by learning to sing.
> Whether this be true or not, they that stand most in need can tell best; whereof some I have known, which, because they learned not to sing when they were boys, were fain to take pain in it when they were men ...
> TOXOPHILUS. It were pity truly, Philologus, that the thing should be neglected; But I trust it is not as you say.
> PHILOLOGUS. The thing is too true; for of them that come daily to the University, where one hath learned to sing, six hath not.

Because of these negative attitudes toward music, specific comments on music education in sixteenth-century England are rather rare. Regarding higher education, the headmaster of the Merchant Tailors School, Mulcaster, required extensive musical exercises by all students, although this was almost certainly an exception.[5]

[5] Frederick Sternfeld, 'Music in the Schools of the Reformation,' in *Musica Disciplina* (Rome: American Institute of Musicology in Rome, 1948), 121.

Sir Philip Sidney saw the end of education to be the understanding of the grand harmony of all creation, sounding very much like the ancient Greeks for a modern Christian![6] He briefly epitomizes the importance of Grammar, Rhetoric and Logic and then turns to the mathematical sciences. Like the old Scholastics, it is here that he includes Music, and like them he can describe its essence only in theoretical terms.

> Arithmetic proceeds from unity, Geometry from a prick; and Music from agreement of sounds; and the end of them is to reduce things to one common reason, to one proportion, and to one harmony, all of which are kinds of unity, and their branches are branches of the same.

Henry Peacham (1576–1643), in his *The Complete Gentleman*, discusses the education of the noble and includes music as an important subject for study.[7] He begins, curiously enough, with a little attack on the Italians which runs contrary to virtually everything written in the sixteenth century. After quoting a current proverb, 'Whom God loves not, that man loves not music,' he observes,

> But I am verily persuaded that they are by nature very ill-disposed and of such brutish stupidity that scarce anything else that is good and favorable to virtue is to be found in them.[8]

Peacham recommends the composers he regards as most worthy of study, beginning with William Byrd, 'whom in that kind I know not whether any may equal.' Byrd is followed by Victoria, Lassus, Marenzio and Ferrabosco, the father, among many others.[9]

We also find in the poetry of this period some interesting reflections of where music stood with respect to the other liberal arts. Fulke Greville, in his 'A Treatie of Human Learning,' in two places questions various branches of the liberal arts, and other disciplines. Within his rather pessimistic discussions we discover the relatively low value he assigns to music. First, he questions Reason:

> Reason we make an art, yet none agree
> What this true reason is, nor yet have powers
> To level other's reason unto ours.[10]

---

[6] Sir Philip Sidney, 'On the Trueness of Christian Religion,' in *The Prose Works of Sir Philip Sidney*, op. cit., III, 222. Later [ibid., 305] he was careful to clarify his position.
  The Aristotelians have no voice here, because they stand all in commenting upon Aristotle, who gave himself more to the liberal Arts and the searching of Nature, than to looking up to God the maker of all things.

[7] Henry Peacham, *The Complete Gentleman*, ed., Virgil Heltzel (Ithaca: Cornell University Press, 1962), 108ff. Although this work was not published until 1622, we regard it as a reflection of the end of the sixteenth century. Peacham (1576–1643) was born to a literary family and graduated from Cambridge. He thought of himself as a scholar, but he was apparently also a musician, painter and mathematician.

[8] Of the French, he says,
  They delight for the most part in horsemanship, fencing, hunting, dancing, and little esteem of learning and gifts of the mind. [ibid., 163]

[9] ibid., 112ff.

[10] Fulke Greville, 'A Treatie of Human Learning,' XXVI, in Robert Bender, ed., *Five Courtier Poets of the English Renaissance* (New York: Washington Square Press, 1967), 568ff. Greville (1554–1628) was active in the Elizabethan court and amassed a large fortune. He began writing poetry in the 1570s.

We are, he adds, no more successful with Nature.

> Nature we draw to art, which then forsakes
> To be herself when she with art combines.

Then he discounts the value of Astrology, Philosophy ('nothing but books of poetry in prose,' meaning fables) and Physicians ('they never helpeth the disease'). Music, he says, teaches the different modes, but, he wonders, why can't she teach me to control my emotions?

> Music instructs me which be lyric moods;
> Let her instruct me rather how to show
> No weeping voice for loss of fortune's goods.

Regarding all of the above 'arts,' he summarizes,

> Then, if our arts want power to make us better,
> What fool will think they can us wiser make;
> Life is the wisdom, art is but the letter
> Or shell which oft men for the kernel take.

His comments on the value of music are more revealing when he returns to this subject later. Now he ranks the intellectual disciplines in order of their importance, after a discussion of divine wisdom, which, of course, is the highest.[11] Following this, in order of importance, come Physics, Philosophy, Grammar, Logic and Rhetoric. In reference to the latter, curiously, he unwittingly provides the most important definition of music.

[11] ibid., XCVIff.

> Because no language in the earth affords
> Sufficient characters to express all things.

Next come Poetry and Music, both of which are of value only for recreation, for idle men. They can move us temporarily, even affect our emotional state, but not really enrich the intellect, which is more important. They are the sauce for the food of life.

> Poesy and music, arts of recreation,
> Succeed, esteemed as idle men's profession,
> Because their scope, being merely contentation,
> Can move but not remove or make impression
> Really, either to enrich the wit,
> Or, which is less, to mend our states by it.
>
> This makes the solid judgments give them place
> Only as pleasing sauce to dainty food,
> Fine foils for jewels, or enamel's grave,
> Cast upon things which in themselves are good,
> Since, if the matter be in nature vile,
> How can it be made precious by a style?

He admits that music has a value in church in helping to 'move thoughts' to God, but he says again Poetry and Music are not really important. Indeed, he finds too much study of Music leads to 'disease of mind.'

> Let therefore human wisdom use both these,
> As things not precious in their proper kind,
> The one a harmony to move, and please,
> If studied for itself, disease of mind,
> The next [poetry], like nature, doth ideas raise,
> Teaches, and makes, but hath no power to bind,
> Both, ornaments to life and other arts,
> Whiles they do serve and not possess our hearts.

It is interesting that he has separated Music from the next three 'mathematical arts,' to which it had been joined for a thousand years: Arithmetic, Geometry, and Astronomy. Finally, in view of the doubts we have seen him express toward books above, it is not surprising that he stipulates that all these arts must be learned from practice, not from books.

> Again, the active, necessary arts
> Ought to be brief in books, in practice long …
>   …
> For sciences from nature should be drawn,
> As arts from practice, never out of books.[12]

[12] ibid., LXVIII, LXXV.

Sir Walter Raleigh seems to have had a similar general disrespect for the liberal arts.

> Tell arts they have no soundness,
> But vary by esteeming;
> Tell schools they want profoundness,
> And stand too much on seeming.
> If arts and schools reply,
> Give arts and schools the lie.[13]

Samuel Daniel, in his Romance 'Musophilus,' also senses a decline in the appreciation of music. He finds late sixteenth-century England more interested in making money. The [singing] poet, he says, can no longer be subtle.

> Now when this busy world cannot attend
> Th'untimely music of neglected [songs].
> Other delights than these, other desires,
> This wiser profit-seeking age requires ...
> Besides, so many so confusedly sing,
> As diverse discords have the music marred,
> And in contempt that mystery doth bring,
> That he must sing aloud that will be heard.[14]

As we have mentioned, the attacks on society by those representing the religious right had a very negative influence on society's views on music and music education. For a thousand years universities had stressed the so-called 'speculative' form of music, the theoretical, with very little reference to the 'practical,' or performance. Only in the sixteenth century did most universities in other countries begin giving performance more respectability. But the religious right returned to fundamentalist views and therefore argued for the theoretical, or speculative, form of music education. Thus, in the following, Gosson's point is that the student must forget performance and return to the study of 'speculative' music and to the concept of Harmony used by the Greeks to represent the order of the world. First, he quotes Pythagoras, in something the philosopher surely never said, as 'condemning as fools, anyone who judges Music by sound and by ear.' Then, to the point he wishes to make,

Sir Walter Raleigh by 'H' monogrammist

[13] Sir Walter Raleigh, 'The Lie,' in ibid., 622. Ralegh (1552–1618) was a major figure in the court, due to his personal closeness to Elizabeth. After a romantic indiscretion with one of her maids of honor he fell into disfavor. He and his family spent some years in the Tower, but he was released and sent to capture Guiana from Spain, as a means of restoring himself to favor. When this effort failed, he was beheaded to appease Spain.

Frontispiece of 'The Civile Wares' with portrait of Samuel Daniel, 1609

[14] Samuel Daniel (ca. 1563–1619), 'Musophilus,' in Emrys Jones, ed., *The New Oxford Book of Sixteenth Century Verse* (Oxford: Oxford University Press, 1991), 519ff.

If you wish to be good Scholars, and to profit from the Art of Music, shut your fiddle cases, and look up to heaven: the order of the Spheres, the infallible motion of the Planets, the just course of the year, and variety of seasons, the concord of the elements and their qualities, Fire, Water, Air, Earth, Heat, Cold, Moisture and Drought concurring together to the constitution of earthly bodies and sustenance of every creature.[15]

Due to the influence of English theories on religion and education on America, there remain many in America today who argue this same philosophy: 'shut your fiddle cases' and get out the books to study music.

Finally, we must not forget to mention the views on music education by the greatest writer of the English sixteenth century, Shakespeare. To begin with it seems clear that he was aware of the old Church Scholastic misunderstanding, by which music was taught as a branch of mathematics. He leaves this clue in *The Taming of the Shrew*, when Hortensio presents himself in the disguise of a music teacher, Shakespeare has him introduced as a man 'Cunning in music and the mathematics.'[16]

One reference to music education in the plays of Shakespeare is an observation on children's performance. In *A Midsummer Night's Dream*, after the prologue of a play within a play, Hippolyta observes,

> Indeed he hath played on his prologue like a child on a recorder; a sound, but not in government.[17]

There are several comic situations in his plays through which Shakespeare makes several observations on music education. Hamlet uses the playing of a recorder as metaphor for the courtier's manipulation of others. He says, 'O, the recorders! Let me see one,' and proceeds to give the courtier, Guildenstern, a lesson.

> HAMLET. It is as easy as lying. Govern these ventages with your fingers and thumb, give it breath with your mouth, and it will discourse most eloquent music. Look you, these are the stops.
> GUILDENSTERN. But these cannot I command to any utterance of harmony. I have not the skill.
> HAMLET. Why, look you now, how unworthy a thing you make of me. You would play upon me; you would seem to know my stops; you would pluck out the heart of my mystery; you would sound me

[15] Stephen Gosson, *The Schoole of Abuse* (1579), ed., Edward Arber (London, 1868), 26

[16] *The Taming of the Shrew*, act 2, scene 1, line 57.

[17] *A Midsummer Night's Dream*, act 5, scene 1, line 123ff.

from my lowest note to the top of my compass. And there is much music, excellent voice, in this little organ, yet cannot you make it speak. 'Sblood, do you think I am easier to be played on than a pipe? Call me what instrument you will, though you can fret me, yet you cannot play upon me.[18]

[18] *Hamlet*, act 3, scene 2, line 345ff.

In a reference to a frequently given purpose of music, to refresh the mind, we find in *The Taming of the Shrew*, when Lucentio, in criticizing a pretended music teacher, he observes,

> Preposterous ass, that never read so far
> To know the cause why music was ordained!
> Was it not to refresh the mind of man
> After his studies or his usual pain?[19]

[19] *The Taming of the Shrew*, act 3, scene 1, line 9ff.

We get an extensive portrait of a private music lesson in the comedy, *The Taming of the Shrew*. The nobleman, Baptista, observing that his daughter, Bianca, loves music and poetry, decides to hire a 'schoolmaster' in those subjects to come to the palace to instruct both his daughters. Hortensio, desiring to woo Bianca, disguises himself as a music teacher and is hired, but he first must give a music lesson to the older sister, the 'shrew' Kate. After this ill-fated lesson, he reports to the father that Kate hit him over the head with his lute and called him a 'fiddler,' an intended derogatory reference to an instrument still associated with peasants.

> BAPTISTA. How now, my friend! why dost thou look so pale?
> HORTENSIO. For fear, I promise you, if I look pale.
> BAPTISTA. What, will my daughter prove a good musician?
> HORTENSIO. I think she'll sooner prove a soldier.
>   Iron may hold with her but never lutes.
> BAPTISTA. Why, then thou canst not break her to the lute?
> HORTENSIO. Why, no; for she hath broke the lute to me.
>   I did but tell her she mistook her frets
>   And bowed her hand to reach her fingering;
>   When, with a most impatient devilish spirit,
>   'Frets, call you these?' quoth she; 'I'll fume with them';
>   And, with that word, she stroke me on the head,
>   And through the instrument my pate made way.
>   And there I stood amazed for a while.
>   As on a pillory, looking through the lute,
>   While she did call me rascal, fiddler.[20]

[20] *The Taming of the Shrew*, act 2, scene 1, line 145ff.

When Hortensio arrives to give a music lesson to Bianca,[21] he finds her having a Latin lesson with another gentleman, Lucentio, who also wishes to woo her. When he tries to interrupt, Bianca tells him to go tune his instrument while she finishes with Lucentio. Hortensio interrupts again,

> HORTENSIO. Madam, my instrument's in tune.
> BIANCA. Let's hear.—O fie! the treble jars.
> LUCENTIO. Spit in the hole, man, and tune again.

When it is finally his turn, Hortensio tells Lucentio to leave. Lucentio, correctly guessing that Hortensio is another suitor, decides to stay and listen.

> HORTENSIO. You may go walk and give me leave a while;
>   My lessons make no music in three parts.
> LUCENTIO. Are you so formal, sir? [Aside] Well, I must wait
>   And watch withal; for, but I be deceived,
>   Our fine musician groweth amorous.
> HORTENSIO. Madam, before you touch the instrument
>   To learn the order of my fingering,
>   I must begin with rudiments of art
>   To teach you gamouth in a briefer sort,
>   More pleasant, pithy, and effectual,
>   Than hath been taught by any of my trade;
>   And there it is in writing, fairly drawn.
> BIANCA. Why, I am past my gamouth long ago.
> HORTENSIO. Yet read the gamouth of Hortensio.
> BIANCA.
>   'Gamouth' I am, the ground of all accord,
>   'A re,' to plead Hortensio's passion;
>   'B mi,' Bianca, take him for thy lord,
>   'C fa ut,' that loves with all affection;
>   'D sol re,' one clef, two notes have I;
>   'E la me,' show pity or I die.
>   Call you this gamouth? tut, I like it not.
>   Old fashions please me best; I am not so nice
>   To change true rules for odd inventions.

[21] *The Taming of the Shrew*, act 3, scene 1.

Music is a science of the phenomena of love in [its] application to harmony and rhythm.[1]

Plato (427–347 BC)

What strange, what sweet and bitter harmonies the wounded heart must learn at Cupid's school![2]

Giambattista Marino (1569–1625)

17 On Music Education in Baroque Italy

TOMMASO CAMPANELLA (1568–1626), a member of the Dominican order at age fourteen, suffered from an intellectual curiosity which brought him into constant conflict with the Inquisition, resulting in years of imprisonment and unspeakable torture. In 1602 he wrote, no doubt to the displeasure of the Church, a poetical dialogue called *The City of the Sun*, which describes his view of a fictional, utopian society. Among the officials who watched over this society were those who held offices called 'Magnanimity, Chastity, Fortitude, Zeal, Truth, Beneficence, Gratitude and Mercy.'[3] These were positions elected from candidates who had demonstrated these various qualities.

Education for both sexes began at age three, with language. At age seven they are exposed to the workshops of the various crafts, needle-workers, goldsmiths and painters. The purpose of this was to create respect for honest work, and the Genoese sailor who narrates this tale (having visited this mythical land) observes,

> Thus they laugh at us because we consider craftsmen ignoble and assign nobility to those who are ignorant of every craft and live in idleness.[4]

At the age of seven, also, study of the natural sciences begin and at age ten, mathematics, medicine and the other sciences. Regarding study of the arts, Campanella observes,

> If a woman has skill in painting, she is not forbidden to pursue it. Music, except for the playing of trumpets and drums, is reserved to women and children since they give most pleasure by it.[5]

This being a utopian society, perhaps Campanella's emphasis on reserving the pursuit of music to woman may have been to balance somewhat an Italian society in which men enjoyed a vigorous adult education outlet in the well-known acad-

Tommaso Campanella by Nicolas de Larmassin, from Isaac Bullart's Académie des Sciences et des Arts, livre II, 1682

[1] *Symposium*, 187b.

[2] Giambattista Marino, *L'Adone* (1623), trans., Harold Priest (Ithaca: Cornell University Press, 1967), VII, 57.

[3] Tommaso Campanella, *La Citta del Sole*, trans., Daniel Donno (Berkeley: University of California Press, 1981), 41.

[4] ibid., 43.

[5] ibid., 49.

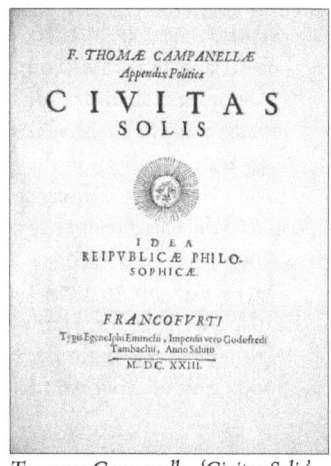

Tommaso Campanella, 'Civitas Solis' (The City of the Sun), 1623

emies. The academies were gatherings of noble and upper class persons interested in intellectual discussion, as a contemporary treatise explains,

> an assembly of free and virtuous intellects, ready to look for knowledge with honest and friendly emulation; who under prescribed laws and statutes exert themselves in different honorable studies, now learning, now teaching, in order to become each day more virtuous and more wise.[6]

[6] Scipione Bargagli, *Della lodi dell' accademie* ... (Florence, 1569), 13.

A contemporary poet, Antonio Abbatini, has left a poem which documents the fact that these academies were also very active in discussing and performing music. In this case, we find them studying older music, which at the time was a very rare activity, and then later actually performing themselves. Perhaps most interesting is the implication that they performed not to show off their skill, but to demonstrate their true virtue. It is as if music could do this, in the event the prior discussions had left some doubt.

> First, the now-lost madrigals of once upon a time
>   are, at table, sung with great delight:
>   the reason, for respect, I will not tell.
> There follows my address: I spread my wings
>   to raise myself to the harmonious skies;
>   but they are just like those of Icarus.
> Every liberty the virtuosi are allowed
>   to contradict whatever I have said,
>   though this role with reluctance do they play.
> Kircher has, however, always argued,
>   as, too, Orlandi, general of the Carmelites,
>   Dal Pane has his doubts, beloved Lelio too.
> Discussion over, as, by grace of God,
>   invariably occurs without ill-will,
>   due praise is then accorded he who most deserves.
> Here the unveiled truth is seen,
>   since almost all are in the fore-front row
>   and everything is discerned minutely.
> Then to the harpsichord the company transfers,
>   and each man takes upon himself to show, with song
>   and sound, his virtue, which binds the heart and soul.
> In all are set aside three hours of time,
>   from nine o'clock for the remainder of the day,
>   and never without wonder do those present go away.[7]

[7] Quoted in Lorenzo Bianconi, *Music in the Seventeenth Century*, trans., David Bryant (Cambridge: Cambridge University Press, 1989), 290ff.

Aside from these academies, there was a great deal of performance in seventeenth-century Italy and most of it was available to the public, something not found generally this early in other countries. We might assume that this wide availability in performance was one of the attractions for the numerous young Englishmen who saw traveling to Italy after their formal education as a kind of cultural finishing school. One of the venues for performance for which we can specifically document visitors from other lands was the performances at the *ospedali*, educational institutions for orphans, which in the case of those in Naples and Venice began to develop into early conservatories. We are fortunate to have eyewitness accounts by visitors of several of the individual *ospedali* in Venice. In 1698 the Russian, Petr Tolstago, wrote from Venice regarding the *Incurabili*:

> In Venice there are convents where the women play the organ and other instruments and sing so wonderfully that nowhere else in the world could one find such sweet and harmonious song. Therefore people come to Venice from all parts with the wish to refresh themselves with these angelic songs, above all those of the Convent of the Incurables.[8]

[8] Quoted in W. Kolneder, *Antonio Vivaldi, his life and work* (London, 1756), 10ff.

A rather extraordinary account of another of these *ospedali*, that of the *Mendicanti*, is found in the *Confessions* of Jean-Jacques Rousseau, dating from two years after the death of Vivaldi.

> A kind of music to my mind far superior to that of the operas, and which has not its like in Italy is that of the *scuole* ... Every Sunday at the Church of each of these schools one has during Vespers motets for full choir and orchestra composed and directed by the greatest masters in Italy, performed in balconies with grilles, entirely by girls of whom the oldest is not twenty. I can imagine nothing so voluptuous, so touching as this music ... The church [the *Mendicanti*] was always full of those who liked this sort of music; even the actors from the Opera would come and conform themselves to the true taste in singing on these excellent models. What grieved me were those accursed grilles, which only allowed the sound to pass, and hid from me the angels of beauty of which the sound was worthy. I only talked of that. One day when I was talking about it to Monsieur le Blond:
>
> 'If you are so curious,' he said to me, 'to see these little girls, it is easy to satisfy you. I am one of the administrators of the house; I want to give you tea there with them.'

Jean-Jacques Rousseau (1712–1778) by Maurice Quentin de La Tour

I did not let him rest until he had kept his word to me. As we entered the salon which enclosed these such coveted beauties, I felt a shiver of love that I had never felt before. Monsieur le Blond introduced one after another to me of these famous singers whose voices and names were all known to me. 'Come, Sophia ... ' she was horrible. 'Come, Cattina ... ' she was blind in one eye. 'Come, Bettina ... ' smallpox had disfigured her. There was hardly one that did not have some notable defect. The executioner laughed at my cruel surprise ... I was grieved.[9]

Naturally we are most interested today in the *Seminario musicale dell' Ospitale della Pieta*, for it was there that the great Vivaldi was employed between 1704 and 1740. An account from early in Vivaldi's tenure records a visit by Frederick IV, king of Denmark and Norway:

Il Pio Ospedale della Pietà in Venice

[9] J. J. Rousseau, *Confessions*, II, vii.

[10] Quoted in Remo Giazotto, *Antonio Vivaldi* (Turin, 1973), 105.

His Majesty made an appearance at the Pieta at eleven o'clock in the morning after hearing the embassy from the lords of Savoy, and the girls sang with the instruments of the maestro [Vivaldi] who occupies the podium in the absence of Gasparini. Great was the applause for the *Credo* and *Agnus Dei* that were performed with the instruments, and then there was a concerto in great taste, as was appropriate.[10]

There is a curious reference to this *Ospitale*, and its musical activities, by a traveling Englishman in 1720. We can only speculate that it was for the benefit of the English reader that he characterizes Vivaldi as a eunuch and the general environment more like a Turkish harem!

There are in Venice four of these female hospitals ... the Incurabili, the Pieta, Ospitaletto and the Mendicanti ...
Every Sunday and holiday there is a performance of music in the chapels of these hospitals, vocal and instrumental, performed by the young women of the place; who are set in a gallery above and are hid from any distinct view of those below by a lattice of iron-work. The organ parts, as well as those of the other instruments, are all performed by the young women. They have an eunuch for their master and he composes their music. Their performance is surprisingly good; and many excellent voices are among them.[11]

[11] Quoted in Marc Pincherle, 'Vivaldi and the Ospitali of Venice,' in *The Musical Quarterly*, XXIV (July, 1938), 301.

Another interesting account, because it hints at the amorous activities for which the Italian Catholic institutions were known, is by K. L. von Poellnitz, who visited in 1729.

> I am in some doubt whether I should reckon the music of the Venetian churches in the number of its pleasures; but on the whole, I think I should, because certainly their churches are frequented more to please the ear, than for real devotion. The church of La Pieta which belongs to the nuns who know no other father but love, is most frequented. These nuns are entered very young, and are taught music, and to play on all sorts of instruments, in which some of them are excellent performers. Apollonia actually passes for the finest singer, and Anna-Maria for the first violin in Italy. The concourse of people to this church on Sundays and holidays is extraordinary. It is the rendezvous of all the coquettes in Venice, and such as are fond of intrigues have here both their hands and hearts full. Not many days after my arrival in this city I was at this very church, where was a vast audience, and the finest of music.[12]

[12] K. L. von Poellnitz, *Memoirs* (London, 1737), I, 414.

In 1739, just before Vivaldi retired from this service, another visitor recalled,

> The most transcendent music here is that provided by the Ospitali. There are four of these, all of them for girls—illegitimate, orphans, or those whose relatives are not able to care for them. They are being brought up at the expense of the state and are being trained most especially to excel in music. In addition they sing like angels, they play the violin, the flute, the organ, the clarinet, the violoncello, and the bassoon. In short, there is no instrument so large as to give them pause ... They are the sole performers at each concert, and some forty of them take part. I swear there is nothing more pleasing to be seen than one of these pretty young sisters in her white dress with a cluster of pomegranate blossoms over one ear, conducting an orchestra and beating time with all the grace and precision imaginable.[13]

Antonio Vivaldi by François Morellon de la Cave, 1725

[13] Quoted in Denis Arnold, 'Music at the Scuola de San Rocco,' in *Music and Letters* (July, 1959), 301ff.

In this same year Charles de Brosses also mentions the quality of the orchestral performances.

> The one of the four *ospedali* I visit most often, and where I enjoy myself most, is the Ospedale della Pieta; it is also the first for the perfection of the symphonies. What strictness of execution! It is only there that one hears the first attack of the bow, so falsely vaunted at the Paris Opera.[14]

[14] Charles de Brosses, *Lettres familieres sur l'Italie* (Paris, 1931), I, 238ff.

It is generally understood that a great deal of Vivaldi's music, in particular the concerti, was composed for these students, as is clearly suggested in the duties outlined in his contract of 1735.

> The same maestro will have to provide for our girls concertos and other compositions for all sorts of instruments, and he will have to come with the assiduousness necessary for instructing the girls and making them well able to perform them.[15]

[15] Archivio di Stato, Venice, Ospitali, busta 692, Notatorio Q, fol. 113r.

Regular Church schools also sponsored public concerts, the best known of which were held in the Scuole San Rocco in Venice. The English visitor, Thomas Coryat, describes a performance there on 16 August 1608, which included among its participants none other than Giovanni Gabrieli. Of particular interest is the description of a countertenor, whom the writer could hardly believe was not a castrato.

> This feast consisted principally of Musicke, which was both vocall and instrumental, so good, and delectable, so rare, so admirable, so super-excellent, that it did even ravish and stupifie all those strangers that never heard the like. But how others were affected with it I know not; for mine own part I can say this, that I was for the time even rapt up with Saint Paul into the third heaven. Sometimes there sung sixteen or twenty men together, having their master or moderator to keepe them in order; and when they sang, the instrumentall musitians played also. Sometimes sixteene played together upon their instruments, ten Sagbuts, foure Cornetts, and two Viol-de-gambaes of a extraordinary greatness; sometimes tenne, six Sagbuts and foure Cornets; sometimes two, a Cornet and a treble violl. Of these treble viols I heard three severall there, whereof each was so good, especially one that I observed above the rest, that I never heard the like before. Those that played upon the treble viols, sung and played together, and sometimes two singular fellowes yeelded admirable sweet musicke, but so still that they could scarce be heard but by those that were very neare them. These two Theorbists concluded that nights musicke, which continued three whole hours at the least. For they beganne about five of the clocke, and ended not before eight. Also it continued as long in the morning: at every time that every severall musicke played, the Organs, whereof there are seven faire paire in that room, standing all in a rowe together, plaied with them. Of the singers there were three or foure so excellent that I think few or none in Christendome do excell them, especially one, who had such a peerless and (as I may in a manner say) such a supernaturall voice for such a privilege for the sweetness of his voice as sweetness, that I think there was never a better singer in all the world,

insomuch that he did not onely give the most pleasant contentment that could be imagined, to all the hearers, but also did as it were astonish and amaze them. I alwaies thought that he was a Eunuch, which if he had beene, it had taken away some part of my admiration, because they do most commonly sing passing well; but he was not, therefore it was much the more admirable. Againe it was the more worthy of admiration, because he was a middle-aged man, as about forty yeares old. For nature doth more commonly bestowe such singularitie of voice upon boyes and striplings, than upon men of such yeares. Besides it was farre the more excellent, because it was nothing forced, strained or affected, but came from him with the greatest facilitie that ever I heard. Truely, I thinke that had a Nightingale beene in the same roome, and contended with him for the superioritie, something perhaps he might excell him, because God hath granted that little birdie such a privilege for the sweetness of his voice, as to none other: but I thinke he could not much. To conclude, I attribute so much to this rare fellow for his singing, that I thinke the country where he was borne, may be proude for breeding so singular a person as Smyrna was of her Homer, Verona of her Catullus, or Mantua of Virgil. But exceeding happy may the Citie or towne, or person bee that possesseth this miracle of nature.[16]

[16] Quoted in Arnold, op. cit., XL, 236ff.

The jurist, Grazioso Uberti, in a book of 1630, also mentions that concerts could be heard in schools, in addition to 'private houses where concerts are given, palaces of princes, churches, oratories, open-air settings and the homes of composers.'[17] Many distinguished composers associated with churches were also teachers of music and other subjects in attached Church schools, the best-known of which was Bach who taught music and Latin. One choir member complains about the teaching of the man in charge of church music at the cathedral, S. Petronio, in Bologna in 1657:

[17] *Contrasto musico*, quoted in Bianconi, op. cit., 71.

> He teaches neither singing nor playing nor counterpoint, and never goes to the school, as is his duty, so that my son finds a way of life and a moral code which is totally unacceptable in this city;
>
> ...
>
> He does not know how to teach the sopranos, who are necessary for the service of the church—which it is his duty to do—and concerning this, he has never crossed the threshold of the school to go and teach them.[18]

[18] Ursula Brett, *Music and Ideas in Seventeenth Century Italy* (New York: Garland Publishing, 1989).

Because of the birth and rapid growth of opera in Italy it is no surprise that it is from her that we have our first accounts of specialized schools for singing. We have a valuable first-hand account of the curriculum of one of these schools, written by a famous castrato, Giovanni Bontempi. His recollections are of vocal study in Rome during the 1640s.

> The schools of Rome obliged their pupils to dedicate a total of one hour per day to the singing of difficult things; this served for the acquisition of experience. One hour on the trill, another on *passaggi*, a third on the study of letters, a fourth on training and other exercises—in the presence of the master and/or in front of the mirror—with the purpose of eliminating all unseemly movement of body, face, brows and mouth. These were the morning activities.
>
> After noon, pupils underwent half an hour of theoretical training, half an hour of counterpoint above a cantus firmus, an hour of instruction and practice in counterpoint in open score and a further hour in the study of letters; the remainder of the day was spent at the harpsichord or in the composition of some psalm, motet, canzonetta or other form of song, in accordance with individual flair and ability. These were the normal exercises for days on which pupils remained indoors.
>
> Outdoor exercises consisted of frequent trips to sing and listen to the echo outside Porta Angelica, with the aim of increasing self-criticism of the scholar's tone of voice; participation in almost all the music of the various churches of Rome; observation of the manners of performance of the many illustrious singers who flourished under Urban VIII; later, at home, practice in these manners of singing and description thereof of the maestro: who himself, in his efforts to impress them more firmly upon the minds of the pupils, added all necessary warnings and other remarks. These exercises and general training in the art of music are those given us in Rome by Virgilio Mazzocchi, illustrious professor and maestro di capella of St. Peter's.[19]

[19] From *Historia musica* (Perugia, 1695), quoted in ibid., 61.

From the Italian Baroque we have a famous treatise on vocal teaching by P. F. Tosi. Within this treatise are a few specific references to teachers and teaching which we should like to quote here. One passage warns the students regarding their personal associations with teachers of bad reputation.

> Let the singer shun low and disreputable company, but, above all, such as abandon themselves to scandalous liberties. [Avoid teachers, who] though excellent in this art, whose behavior is vulgar.[20]

[20] *Observations on the Florid Song* (London: Wilcox, 1743), IX, viiiff.

In another place he singles out diction as the element of singing most poorly taught.

> This defect, although one of the greatest, is today more than common, to the greatest disgrace of the teachers and the profession; and yet they ought to know, that it is only the words which give preference to a singer above an instrumental performer, assuming they were equal in judgment and knowledge.[21]

[21] ibid., IV, xx.

On the other hand, Tosi points out that when it comes to improvisation in arias, the singer's success was a matter of experience and taste, not conceptual study alone.

> A singer is under the greatest obligation to the study of the arias; for by them he gains or loses his reputation. To the acquiring this valuable art a few verbal lessons cannot suffice; nor would it be of any great profit to the student, to have a great number of arias, in which a thousand of the most exquisite passages of different sorts were written down: For they would not serve for all purposes, and there would always be wanting that spirit which accompanies extempore performances, and is preferable to all servile imitations.[22]

[22] ibid., VII, iii.

Later he returns to this topic for the purpose of emphasizing the relationship between the student and the teacher's instruction.

> A singer should not copy ... to copy is the part of a scholar, that of a master [performer] is to invent.[23]
> ...
> The most admired graces of a professor ought only to be imitated and not copied; on condition also, that it does not bear even so much as a shadow of resemblance of the original; otherwise, instead of a beautiful imitation, it will become a despicable copy.[24]

[23] ibid., IX, xxxii.

[24] ibid., IX, xxxviii.

Tosi gives the impression that most vocal teachers he knew were more interested in money than in producing fine artists. Very few teachers will refuse a student, he observes, so long as they are paid and 'little do they care if their greediness ruins the profession.'[25] Beware, Tosi warns the teacher, you will be held responsible for any omissions in your teaching and

[25] ibid., I, iv.

for any errors you did not correct.[26] Regarding the teacher's demeanor in making such corrections, Tosi offers the following observation:

[26] ibid., I, viiiff.

> Let him be moderately severe, making himself feared, but not hated. I know it is not easy to find the mean between severity and mildness, but I know also that both extremes are bad: too great severity creates stubbornness, and too great mildness creates contempt.

Tosi also has much sound advice for the student, beginning with a comment on a question much discussed in earlier centuries, but rarely mentioned today—Can we expect the quality of the music to be unaffected by the quality of the *character* of the musician?

> After a strict care of his morals, he should give the rest of his attention to the study of singing in perfection, that by this means he may be so happy as to join the most noble qualities of the soul to the excellencies of his art.[27]

[27] ibid., VI, ii.

Beyond this, since music is an experiential art, in the end one must teach oneself. 'Till a singer pleases himself,' writes Tosi, 'it is certain he cannot please others.'[28]

[28] ibid., VI, xvii.

> Let the student hear as much as he can the most celebrated singers, and likewise the most excellent instrumental performers; because, from the attention in hearing them, one reaps more advantage than from any instruction whatsoever.
> Let him endeavor to copy from both, that he may insensibly by the study of others, get a good taste.[29]

[29] ibid., VI, xiiiff.

Here he means copy the style, not copy the actual material.

> Whoever accustoms himself to have things put in his mouth, will have no invention, and becomes a slave to his memory.[30]

[30] ibid., VI, xxv.

Finally, the student must learn from his mistakes.

> Abhor the example of those who hate correction; for like lighting to those who walk in the dark, though it frightens them, it gives them light.
> Learn from the errors of others: O great Lesson! it costs little and instructs much. Of everyone something is to be learned, and the most ignorant is sometimes the greatest master.[31]

[31] ibid., X, xxxviff.

Finally, there is a passage we like from a treatise by Francesco Gasparini. He is aware that in the Renaissance the ability to perform was considered a mark of culture in the aristocrat, but during the Baroque the noble generally became only the employer of musicians. Gasparini takes it for granted that the noble no longer has time for music. He makes this observation while reflecting that most experts consider three things necessary for the making of a musician: resolve, application and a good teacher. But even more important than these, he says, is a natural disposition. This, he says, is a gift of God and nature and cannot be otherwise obtained at any price.[32]

> There are an infinite number of nobles, gentlemen, ladies, and princes, who feel an inclination toward music, but should they start in, it is certain that, because of their customary preoccupation with studies of literature or other gentlemanly exercises, a generation, so to speak, would not suffice them to arrive at the playing of four notes.[33]

[32] Francesco Gasparini, *The Practical Harmonist at the Harpsichord* [1708], ed., Franks S. Stillings (New Haven: Yale School of Music, 1963), 9.

[33] ibid., 10.

18 On the Philosphical Roots of German Music Education

Even before the revolutionary results we have all come to know from clinical research in the hemispheres of the brain, research which has earned a Nobel Prize in Medicine, contemplative persons for many centuries have understood that man has two sides: a rational side and an experiential side. This understanding was at the root of the division of music in the early universities into two branches, the speculative (theory) and the practical (performance). The early universities took the position that only the first could be taught, and therefore performance to this very day has not quite been accepted in the university environment as something important.

By the Baroque in Germany, this division between theory and performance had evolved into the question, 'Should music be judged by the rules or by the ear?' A particularly relevant introduction to this debate in Germany is found in *Das Neu-Eroffnete Orchestre*, the first important book by the most comprehensive observer of German musical life during the Baroque, Johann Mattheson (1681–1764). This book begins with a startling chapter title: 'The Fall of Music and its Cause.' It was his view in 1713 that

Portrait of Johann Mattheson, from an engraving by Johann Jacob Haid after a painting by J. S. Wahl, 1746

> through misuse and ignorance the noble art of music, contrary to its very purpose, causes, alas!, more ill-humor than pleasure among many.[1]

The first reason Mattheson gives for this decline must be seen in context with his belief expressed in later writings, that the true essence of music was something very close to Nature. But, the rational side of man, the product of traditional education (then as now), is compelled to think that the Truth of a thing can be evident only if it can be expressed in rational thought. The academic world therefore tends to turn music, which by nature is associated with the non-rational, into a series of concepts understandable by only the rational part of our brain. The student, and unfortunately especially the

[1] *Das Neu-Eroffnete Orchestre*, quoted in Beekman Cannon, *Johann Mattheson, Spectator in Music* (Archon Books, 1968), 1. We cite the original page numbers, but the English translation is by Cannon.

layman, is therefore led to believe that he knows nothing of music unless he knows the conceptual form of it. Mattheson expressed it in this way:

> For they are persuaded that this beautiful and perfect creation, which a beneficent God has given us men for our pleasure, and likewise as a model of the eternal, harmonious Splendor, depends solely upon deep learning and laborious knowledge. To prove this, they dispense their philosophical rules and scholarly vagaries, not only with great authority, but likewise with such obscurity that one has a rightful aversion for the stuff, and would rather remain in permanent ignorance than to go through such *horrenda*.[2]

But Mattheson, having been a performer, knew that rational concepts cannot well describe the experience of music. Thus he advises the pursuit of performance, after the necessary foundation, as a means of finding a 'healthy idea of music, purified of all unnecessary school-dust.'

Mattheson himself could not entirely escape the Germanic need to conceptualize music, as can be seen in his attempt to explain melody through the rules of rhetoric.[3] And so another reason he gives for the decline of music, not quite the reverse of the first one, was that there are too many composers who just write lots of notes without knowing what they are doing. His third cause for the decline of music is also educationally oriented: the ancient guild system, through which music was learned as a trade rather than as an art.

Two additional negative circumstances, Mattheson finds, the artist must simply accept as being the way things are. These are the ignorance and poor taste of the general public and the fact that good musicians are not well paid.

In the Foreword to his *Der vollkommene Capellmeister*,[4] Mattheson continues his somewhat pessimistic view of the relationship of music and society. He finds many noble and educated persons who know nothing about music, either because they lack the time to study it or fail to understand the 'dignity and great benefit' which derives from music. On the other hand, most of those who practice music are rarely scholarly. They merely take pleasure from music, turning it into

> a menial trade, an item to market, a means to obtain food, indeed even into a society of flagellants, and nothing more.

[2] ibid., 2ff.

[3] See Johann Mattheson, *Der vollkommene Capellmeister* (1739), trans., Ernest Harriss (Ann Arbor: UMI Research Press, 1981), II, iv, 62.

[4] ibid., Foreword, II.

'Der vollkommene Capellmeister' by Johann Mattheson, 1739

At the same time, he finds some who merely collect beautiful musical instruments (and are called 'true connoisseurs') and others who think music exists merely to please and to pass the time. All of the above, he says, are on the wrong path.

Another important writer of the German Baroque, Johann David Heinichen (1683–1729), was also aware that German composers had to come to grips with this philosophical choice. Heinichen was thinking of this when he wrote,

> One need not even think of *Musica didactica, poetica, modulatoria* and other *Capita suprema & subalterna* common to music to realize that music has boundaries as wide as all the other sciences, arts, and advanced studies. Music is just as *theoretica & practica* as theology and jurisprudence; music is as *thetic & polemica* as other advanced disciplines, this being particularly evident in our century as one tries hard to separate oneself both in music, theory and practical music from many principles and preconceived opinions of the past.[5]

[5] Johann David Heinichen, *General-Bass Treatise* [1711], quoted in George Buelow, *Thorough-Bass Accompaniment according to Johann David Heinichen* (Ann Arbor: UMI Research Press, 1986), 310ff.

It is our personal view that the main reason that so much beautiful music came to life during the German Baroque was because those composers had the courage to follow their hearts and write what they felt, rather than feeling duty bound to ancient rules of composition, the heritage of which, of course, lay in ancient Church dogma. As we have mentioned above, the old division of speculative versus practical music had become by the German Baroque a debate over whether composition should be controlled by rules or the ear. No one attacked the old theory-based philosophy with more fervor than Heinichen himself.

> If a composer, who is more concerned with sensitivity, good taste, and brilliance in music than with paper nonsense, writes with reason one little note contrary to their antiquated, platonic rules, they want to turn him over to the Inquisition to discover whether or not he can be classed among composers. Only it is remarkable how such musical pedants, though they involve themselves so willingly in harmful, authoritative prejudices, do not notice, however, that already in our time not only native but also the most famous foreign composers have begun to neglect the unnecessary eccentricities in composition and to seek a freer way in music by refining many of the old rules …
>
> If we examine more closely the motives causing famous composers to deviate frequently from the artificial accuracies of pure theorists, then in my judgment they might be: first, they are ashamed in general of pedantry and forced school book rules … Second, they have sound

practical judgment and know when and where to depart with good reason from theoretical rules. Third, they will not be slaves to the many poorly founded rules from the past, but they would rather agree with the rule, founded on reason itself, though otherwise juristic: *Cessante ratione prohibition is, cessat ipsa prohibitio*—whenever the cause for the prohibition on which a rule is based becomes null and void, the prohibition of the given rule itself becomes null and void. And this judicious practice is ten times more difficult than the frequently prescribed, dry theory. Indeed, for this very reason the unskilled theorists remain so willingly with their dull, antiquated rules, because their judgment is inadequate to allow deviation from them with reason …

All arts and sciences have rules and must be learned through rules, if we do not wish to remain simple naturalists, ie., half-ignorant. But we must not err excessively on the side of rules; furthermore, we should not accept so crudely the equivocal word: Rule, as if we would serve as high sounding rule makers, prescribing laws even to Nature, according to which she must limit herself to *auctoritate nostra*. No! All of our useful rules must be derived from Nature; and we must investigate on all levels the will, preference, and character of this mistress and learn from her *cum submissione*.[6]

[6] ibid., 315ff.

Heinichen returns to the subject of 'the old rules,' the older polyphonic style, again with even more vigor. There are some church composers, he finds, who 'have learned something besides counterpoint' and have good taste whose music delights the ear. However, those who continue to compose only in the old polyphonic style,

those who are not endowed with good taste and who stick to a common repertory of notes are pursued by the natural punishment, resembling the original sin: their music is not liked by a single living soul. It would be better, therefore, to burn immediately their all too artificial compositions before they cool down, and to scatter the ashes into their eyes. Then at least one of the senses would gain something from it, for otherwise neither the eye nor the ear profits from such a paper art.[7]

[7] ibid., 326.

He concludes, somewhat sarcastically, that he has known some old theater composers, who due to old age had lost all their 'creative fire and invention.' These men, he notes became for the first time good church composers.

In a more general sense, Heinichen writes that the essential abilities needed for successful composition include natural aptitude and diligence, as well, of course, as knowledge of the basic conceptual information on writing music. However, as he quotes Andreas Werkmeister, rules alone do not suffice.

If one has no musical aptitude 1,000 rules could be illustrated with 10,000 examples and still the purpose would not be achieved.[8]

[8] Andreas Werckmeister, *Nothwendigsten Anmerckungen*, 40ff.

In one of Heinichen's most valuable passages, one which demonstrates brilliant deductions regarding the physiology of music aesthetics, he addresses the fundamental distinction between Baroque music and earlier music. The old music, he says, was for the eye (Reason and conceptual understanding), but modern music is for the ear.

> The old musicians side more with Reason, but the new with the Ear; and since both parties do not agree on the first fundamental, it is evident that the conclusions and consequences made from two contrary fundamental principles should breed just as many controversies of inferior rank and thousands of diametrically opposed hypotheses. Musicians of the past, we know, chose two judges in music: Reason and the Ear. The choice would be correct since both are indispensable to music; yet, because of the use of these two concomitants, the present cannot reconcile itself with the past, and in this the past is blamed for two errors. First, it wrongly classed the two judges and placed the Ear, the sovereign of music, below the rank of Reason or would divide its commanding authority with the latter. Whereupon the blameless Ear must immediately cede half of its monarchical domain. In addition, unfortunately, the composers of the past poorly explained the word ratio. In those innocent times (in which one knew nothing of present day good taste and brilliance in music, and every simple harmony seemed beautiful), they thought Reason could be put to no better use than the creation of supposedly learned and speculative artificialities of note writing. Therefore, they began on the one hand to measure out theoretically innocent notes according to mathematical scales and with the help of the proportioned yardstick, and on the other hand, to place these notes in musical practice on the staves (almost as if they were on a rack) and to pull and stretch them (or in the language of counterpoint, to augment them), to turn them upside down, to repeat and to change their positions, until finally from the latter resulted a practice with an overwhelming number of unnecessary instances of contrapuntal eye-music and from the former resulted a theory with amassed metaphysical contemplations of emotion and reason. Thus, one no longer had cause to ask if music sounded well or pleased the listener, but rather if it looked good on paper. In this way, the Visual perceptibly gained the most in music and used the authority of the imprudent Reason only to cover its own lust for power. Consequently, the suppressed Ear was tyrannized so long that finally it hid behind table and chairs to await from the distance the condescending, merciful glance of its *usurpatores regni* (*ratio & visus*). This grave injustice to the musical sovereign, the Ear, has been reprehended more by present-day musicians than by those of

the past. They have begun vigorously to understand the many absurd and preposterous principles of the past and to form completely new ideas about the noble art of music unlike those of the learned ignoramuses. Above all, they return to the oppressed Ear the sovereignty of its realm; they displace Reason from its judicial duties and give it [Reason] to the Ear, not as Domino or co-regent, but as an intelligent minister and counselor with the absolute mandate to warn its master (the occasionally deceived Ear, if indeed 'deceived' can be spoken of) of every false step; but otherwise, Reason differs in opinion, it must serve the Ear with the complete obedience and employ all of its skill, not for the visual appearance on paper, but to give the Ear the satisfaction of an absolute ruler. Really! What has the visual to do with music? Could anything more absurd be stated? The art of painting is for the eye, music, however, for the ear. Similarly, food is for the sense of taste and flowers for the sense of smell. Would it not be ridiculous to say the dinner was especially good because it smelled good, even though it was disagreeable to the taste and stomach? It is just as absurd if one should say along with pedants: this is outstanding music because it looks so fine (I mean pedantic) on paper, even though it does not please the ear, for which music is solely made ... As we must now admit unanimously that our *Finis musices* is to stir the affections and to delight the ear, the true *Objectum musices*, it follows that we must establish all our musical rules according to the Ear.[9]

[9] Johann David Heinichen, op. cit., 278.

In another place, Heinichen, in 1711, returns to this philosophical tension between the rules and the ear and now approaches the problem from the perspective of Taste. This passage is particularly interesting in his contrast with the musical practice of Germany with other European countries, in particular France and Italy. The reader might enjoy deducing which countries he is referring to.

Experience teaches that ... paper music receives more credit in one nation than in another. One nation is industrious in all endeavors; another laughs over useless school work and tends to believe skeptically that the 'Northerners' work like a team of draft horses. One nation believes art is only that which is difficult to compose; another nation, however, seeks a lighter style and correctly states that it is difficult to compose light music ... One nation seeks its greatest art in nothing but intricate musical 'tiff-taff' and elaborate artificialities of note writing. The other nation applies itself more to good taste, and in this way it takes away the former's universal applause; the paper artists, on the contrary, with all their witchcraft remain in obscurity and, in addition, are proclaimed barbarians, even though they could imitate the other nations blindfolded if they applied themselves more to good taste and brilliance of music than to fruitless artificialities. An eminent foreign composer once gave his frank opinion ... regarding the differences in music of two nations.

> Our nation, he said, ... is more inclined to *dolcezza* in music, so much so that it must take care not to fall into a kind of indolence. Most 'Northerners,' on the other hand, are almost too inclined to liveliness in music, so that they fall too easily into barbarisms. If they would take pains over adapting our *tendresse* and would mix it together with their usual *vivacite*, then a third style would result that could not fail to please the whole world.

I will not repeat the comments I made at that time, but will say only that this discourse first brought to my mind the thought that a felicitous melange of Italian and French taste would affect the ear most forcefully and must succeed over all other tastes of the world ... Nevertheless, the Germans have the reputation abroad that if they would apply themselves industriously they could usually surpass other nations in learning. From this principle I hope that some day our composers will try in general ... to surpass other nations in matters of musical taste as well as they have succeeded long ago in artful counterpoint and theoretical accuracies.[10]

[10] Johann David Heinichen, op. cit., 281ff.

And in yet another place, Heinichen now equates personal experience with good taste. His attempt here appears to have been to explain that experience is the basis of the rules.

> If experience is necessary in any art or science, it is certainly necessary in music. In this *Scientia practica*, first of all, we must gain experience ... either at home, provided opportunities are sufficient, or through traveling. But what is it that one believes one must seek in the experience? I will give a single word ... *Gout*. Through diligence, talent, and experience, a composer must achieve above all else an exquisite sense of good taste in music ... The definition of *Gout*, *Gusto* or *guter Geschmack* is unnecessary for the experienced musician; and it is as difficult to describe in its essentials as the true essence of the soul. One could say that good taste was in itself the soul of music, which so to speak it doubly enlivens and brings pleasure to the senses. The *Proprium 4ti modi* of a composer with good taste is contained solely in the skill with which he makes his music pleasing to and beloved by the general, educated public, or which in the same way pleases our ear by experienced artifices and moves the senses ... In general, this can be brought about through a good well-cultivated, and natural invention or through the beautiful expression of words. In particular, through an ever dominating *cantabile*, through suitable and affecting accompaniments, through a change of harmonies recommended for the sake of the ears, and through other methods gained from experience and frequently looking poor on paper, which in our times we only label with the obscure name of 'rules of experience ... ' An exceptional sense of good taste is so to say the

musical *Lapis philisophorum* and the principal key to musical mysteries through which human souls are unlocked and moved and by which the senses are won over ... For even the natural gift or talent endowed with most invention resembles only crude gold and silver dross that must be purified first by the fire of experience before it can be shaped into a solid mass—I mean into a finely cultivated and steadfast sense of good taste.[11]

[11] Johann David Heinichen, op. cit., 285ff.

As troubling to the free thinking Baroque Germans as the old tradition of thinking of music being based on rules rather than on the ear was, an ancient dogma of the Roman Church was even more strongly attacked, and rightly so. This was the sixth-century invention by the Church, created for the purpose of justifying the inclusion of music in the curriculum of Church schools, that music was a branch of mathematics. In his *Neu-Eroffnete Orchestre* Mattheson attacks this old notion of mathematics-based theory in music by going directly to the elements upon which the older theorists had based their reasoning, in particular the nature of the intervals. In his discussion of whether the interval of the fourth should regarded as a consonance or dissonance, Mattheson concludes it is not a matter of mathematics, but rather a matter of the ear, that is how the fourth is used. The reader should particularly notice, as a hallmark of the Baroque's movement away from music based on concepts to music based on feeling, that Mattheson specifies here that music communicates with 'the inner soul.'

Numbers in music do not govern but merely instruct. The Hearing is the only channel through which their force is communicated to the inner soul of the attentive listener ... The true aim of music is not its appeal to the eye, nor yet altogether to the so-called 'Reason,' but only to the Hearing, which communicates pleasure, as it is experienced, to the Soul and the 'Reason.' Hence, if the testimony of the ear is followed, it will be discovered that in its relation to the surrounding sounds and harmony, the fourth will be either consonant or dissonant.[12]

[12] Johann Mattheson, *Das Neu-Eroffnete Orchestre*, op. cit., 126ff. Mattheson also writes at length in opposition to the old dogma that mathematics is the basis of music in his book, *Das Forschende Orchestre* of 1721.

Such views, which would seem obvious to most modern readers, were nevertheless a direct attack on the old mathematics-based theories of music and resulted in letters and books attacking Mattheson for his views. Johann Buttstedt, an organist in Erfurt, attacked Mattheson in a book, *Ut, Mi, Sol, Re, Fa, La, Tota Musica et harmonia Aeterna ... entgegen gesetzt Dem neu-*

eroffneten Orchestre ... , in which he contends that since German music is now practiced only by craftsmen [*Spielmanns-Wesen*] the current musicians are not even educated in the older rules.

> How many musicians will one find today who have real knowledge? Most of them do not even know how many styles and modes there are and what music is suitable for ecclesiastical or motet styles. The knowledge of such styles is almost entirely lost ... Why? [Modern music] is hard to understand and not well paid for. And so, instead of correct knowledge mere *Galanterie* suffices, just as the finery of ladies once consisted of pearls and golden chains but now of mere ribbons and laces.[13]

To defend himself, Mattheson published a new book, *Das Beschutzte Orchestre*, in which he appealed to a number of distinguished German musicians to join in the debate over mathematics versus feelings. One who responded was the most old-fashioned of all, Fux, author of the monument to the former style, *Gradus ad Parnassum*. He was particularly angered by an attack, in this latest book by Mattheson, on the medieval theorist, Guido d'Arezzo, to whom Fux believed all subsequent music was indebted.

> I am not at all a blind worshiper of superstitious antiquity; but until something better has been invented, I shall venerate in every way what through so many centuries the noblest masters have held to be good and proper.[14]

Some distinguished musicians, however, came to the defense of Mattheson. Handel wrote Mattheson at this time, taking a very practical approach to the debate.

> The question seems to me to reduce itself to this: whether one should prefer an easy & most perfect Method to another that is accompanied by great difficulties capable not only of disgusting pupils with Music, but also making them waste much precious time that could better be employed in plunging deeper into this art & in the cultivation of one's genius?[15]

Johann Heinichen, in language much stronger than Mattheson's, ridiculed the old-fashioned theorists as having wasted their entire life in pursuit of *rudera antiquitatis*.

[13] Quoted in Cannon, op. cit., 135ff.

Portrait of Johann Joseph Fux

[14] ibid.,140.

[15] George Friedrich Handel, letter to Johann Mattheson, February 24, 1719, quoted in Piero Weiss, *Letters of Composers Through Six Centuries* (Philadelphia: Chilton, 1967), 63.

> All will be sheer Greek to those steeped in prejudices when nowadays they hear that a moving music composed for the ears requires even more subtle and skillful rules—to say nothing of lengthy practice—than the heavily oppressive music composed for the eyes which the cantors of even the tiniest towns maltreat on innocent paper according to all the venerable rules of counterpoint ... And we Germans alone are such fools as to jog on in the old groove and, absurdly and ridiculously, to make the appearance of the composition on paper, rather than the hearing of it, the aim of music.[16]

[16] Quoted in Cannon, op. cit., 141ff.

Johann Kuhnau also was strong in his support of Mattheson.

> As regards the great controversy that the gentleman of Erfurt has brought upon you, I do not believe that, save for him, anyone will disapprove of your *Orchestre*. This is especially true of your point of view in matters of the solmisation and the old ecclesiastical modes; for you wrote your *Orchestre* for a *galant-homme* who, being no professional musician, has not the least interest in amusing himself with innumerable old freaks which are usually outmoded at best and worth—virtually nothing.[17]

[17] Quoted in ibid.,142.

In his *Der vollkommene Capellmeister* of 1739 Mattheson returns to this question.[18] Here he begins with the basic point that mathematics is an aid to music, as it is to most disciplines. However, 'they are wrong who believe or want to teach others that mathematics is the heart and soul of music' or that it is responsible for changes in emotion in the music. He begins his argument with the concept of proportions in general, which he finds in natural, moral, rhetorical and mathematical relationships. For the first three of these, natural, moral and rhetorical relationships, Mattheson maintains no precise mathematical measure is possible. One cannot, for example measure the distance from the earth to the sun precisely because the flames leaping out from the sun render no fixed edge. His comment regarding precision in language is quite perceptive. Everyone would agree, he supposes, that 'life' is a positive, happy word. But if one says 'life is denied,' the meaning is changed. Thus, 'the heart's emotion no longer has its basis in mere sounds and words.'

[18] Johann Mattheson, *Der vollkommene Capellmeister*, op. cit., Foreword, VI.

Turning to music, he proposes two rhetorical questions:
1. If someone wants to be a sound musician, must he not attain this through mathematics?
2. Cannot one become an admirable composer and musician without thorough knowledge of the arts of measuring?

> Now if someone says yes to the first question, and no to the second, then he contradicts ancient and modern experience, indeed, his own eyes, ears, hands, the combined senses of all mankind, and shuts the only door through which his intelligence gives him what he has. Whereas if he answers no to the first question and yes to the second, then mathematics cannot possibly be the heart and soul of music.

From this he concludes mathematics can measure, but not determine the essence of a thing. 'Everything that goes on in music is based on mathematical relationships of intervals just about as much as seamanship is based on anchors and cables.'

> However one defines the mathematical relationships of sounds and their quantities, no real connection with the passions of the soul can ever be drawn from this alone.

Mathematics is only the 'science, theory and scholarship' of music. To introduce what exists beyond this he quotes Andreas Papius.

> The mere *cognition of the ratio* of a step, a half step, a comma, the consonances, etc., will bring the name virtuoso or artistic prince to no one, but rather the minute examination *according to the laws of nature* of the various works which are produced by great artists: from this we can understand the composer's *soul*, in regard to how and to what extent, in his particular work, one thing more than another masters the *human mind and emotions*, which is the *highest pinnacle of the discipline of music*.

Again, his point here is that mathematics can measure the elements of music, but not how these elements are used. It is the latter, not the former, which concern feelings in music.

> A perfect understanding of the human emotions, which certainly are not to be measured by the mathematical yardstick, is of much greater importance to melody and its composition than the understanding of tones ... This is certain: it is not so much good *proportion*, but rather

the apt *usage* of the intervals and keys, which establishes the beautiful, moving and natural quality in melody and harmony. Sounds, in themselves, are neither good nor bad; but they become good and bad according to the way in which they are used. No measuring or calculating art teaches this.

How then does one describe the role mathematics plays in music, together with its other elements? Mattheson offers the following metaphor:

> The human mind is the paper. Mathematics is the pen. Sounds are the ink; but Nature must be the writer. Why have a silver trumpet if a competent trumpeter is not available?

Mattheson points out that sculptors know and can measure the proportions of the human body, but 'heart and soul ... and beauty is not on this account to be found in such mathematical measuring; but only in that force which God put in Nature.' Similarly, in painting, when 'mathematics ceases entirely, true beauty really first begins.' And so with music,

> A composer can succeed quite well without special mathematical skills. Many who virtually climbed to the pinnacle of music can hardly name or interpret all parts of mathematics; not to mention anything more ... However, the best mathematician, as such, if he were to want to compose something, could not possibly achieve this with mere logic.
> Let it be said once in fact for all: Good mathematical proportions cannot constitute everything: this is an old, stubborn misconception.

The point, he says, is this: 'music draws its water from the spring of Nature; and not from the puddles of arithmetic.' The composer expresses something understood from Nature. Only then can this be mathematically expressed, but not the other way around. When Mattheson speaks here of Nature, he is also thinking of God.

> Mathematics is a human skill; nature, however, is a divine force ...
> Now the goal of music is to praise God in the highest, with word and deed, through singing and playing. All other arts besides theology and its daughter, music, are only mute priests. They do not move hearts and minds nearly so strongly, nor in so many ways ...
> Music is *above*, not in *opposition* to mathematics.

In conclusion, Mattheson cannot resist taking a shot at those remaining exponents of the old mathematics-based polyphony.

> I have occupied myself with music, practical as well as theoretical, with great earnestness and ardor for over half a century already: I have also met many very learned *Mathematici* in this not insubstantial time who thought they made new musical wonders out of their old, logical writings; but they have, God knows! always failed miserably. On the other hand, I have quite certainly and very often experienced that not a single famous actor, musician, nor composer, not only in my time but as far as I can remember having read or heard about, has been able to construct even a simple melody which was of any value on the feeble foundations of mathematics or geometry … What will happen in the future is yet to be seen.

In another place, Mattheson makes this point again.

> The entire art of harmonic calculating and measuring, even if we also were to include algebra, cannot alone produce a single skilled Capellmeister; whereas our very best composers have scarcely ever taken a ruler in hand for the sake of their beautiful work.[19]

We should add here that in his book, *Ehrenpforte* (Hamburg, 1740), Mattheson mentions a contemporary composer who argued for making 'music a scientific or scholarly pursuit' and associated himself with Bach in this regard. Mattheson quickly adds that Bach certainly did not teach this man 'the supposed mathematical basis of composition.' 'This,' Mattheson testifies, 'I can guarantee.'[20]

Ironically, while all this criticism of every form of the 'older rules' was taking place, there were some who were exploring the idea of creating an entire new species of rules expressing what we now call the Doctrine of Affections. After several centuries of the efforts of humanism to reintroduce feeling into music, an obvious question followed. How, exactly, does music create the communication of emotion (with a notational system which has no symbols for emotions)? There were some who wanted to discover new rules upon which a composer could draw in seeking to write music which expressed a specific emotion. But (thank God!) the better German composers, having freed themselves from the old Church rules, were in no mood to worry about new ones. As Heinichen observed, no one was interested.

[19] ibid., I, vii, 11.

[20] Quoted in Hans T. David and Arthur Mendel, *The Bach Reader* (New York: Norton, 1966), 440.

What a bottomless ocean we still have before us merely in the expression of words and the affections in music. And how delighted is the ear, if we perceive in a refined church composition or other music how a skilled virtuoso has attempted here and there to move the feelings of an audience through his *galanterie* and other devices that express the text, and in this way to find successfully the true purpose of music. Nevertheless, no one wants to search deeper into this beautiful musical *Rhetorica* and to invent good rules. What could one not write about musical taste, invention, accompaniment, and their nature, differences, and effects? But no one wants to investigate the matters aiming at this lofty practice or to give even the slightest introduction to it.[21]

It was these philosophical debates which set the stage for German music education, which was and is today performance oriented.

America has gone the opposite direction, seeking to conceptualize music education. The failure of this philosophy is clear to any objective observer.

[21] Johann David Heinichen, op. cit., 326. In a footnote, Heinichen observes that some attempts at expressing emotions in music sound mannered and make people laugh. Thus, he says, 'a mighty chasm stretches between knowledge and ability.'

19 *The Music Education Scene in Baroque Germany*

DURING NEARLY HALF OF THE BAROQUE PERIOD in Germany the country suffered from the effects of the Thirty Years War and music education was not immune. At the beginning of the seventeenth century music education was still considered a branch of the liberal arts and we can see in the testimony of the great Heinrich Schutz that these studies were suffering. In 1636 Schutz portrays a general decline:

> Everyone can see how, as the result of the still continuing, dangerous vicissitudes of war in our dear fatherland of German nationality, the laudable art of music, among the other liberal arts, has not only greatly declined but at some places has even been completely abandoned, succumbing to the general ruination and disorder which unhappy war is wont to bring in its train.[1]

In this same year Schutz's pupil, Martin Knabe, wrote of the effects of war in the dedication of his *Lamentation on the Protracted War: When at Last Will My Grief be Ended?*:

> It is unnecessary to speak at length concerning this long-protracted, wearisome war. Suffice is to say that its destructive fire is still burning at all corners of the Roman Empire. It is enough to observe how daily, yes, hourly, so many countless sighs are emitted with broken words by many thousands of souls: Oh, if there were only peace! Oh, if only the war would come to an end! Not to mention the collapse of studies which bloodthirsty Mars occasions in all the branches of the university and among the other liberal arts, and only to recall with a few words the state of music, how this noble art, even before the other arts, has sunk to the lowest level.[2]

We might also add that Schutz, much like the tradition of English young men traveling to Italy to 'finish' their education, made two such trips himself to Italy, as did Michael Praetorius before him. Years later he would refer to Italy as 'the true university of music.'[3]

Heinrich Schütz by Christoph Spetner, Leipzig, ca. 1650–1660

[1] Henrich Schutz, *Kleine geistliche Concerte*, Preface.

[2] Quoted in Hans Moser, *Heinrich Schutz* (St. Louis: Concordia, 1936), 162.

[3] *Geistliche Chormusik* (1648).

The most perceptive comments regarding the need for improvement in music education following the effects of the war are found in Johann David Heinichen (1683–1729).

> Work of reform in composition and music would be as useful as it would be necessary (even the critics would not deny this). And it seems to me that this important, but surmountable, and certainly useful effort would not be ill-spent if a well-schooled, unprejudiced composer would take composition in hand and separate the chaff from the grain by abolishing all musical quackery, metaphysical contemplations, barbaric nomenclatures, ridiculous classifications, antiquated, abolished rules, and similar fruitless nonsense, while choosing only the useful rules truly applicable to the real practice. By bringing these rules into a correct and accurate classification, a well-founded, orderly, and useful method could finally be chosen to determine how and in what manner similar excellent principles could be given to a naturally-talented student and how to put them into practice. In this way, the innocent art of composition would be cleansed of all sophistry, prejudice, and especially of the blind faith with which many rules were held for good and true up to now, only because the ancient musical Christian church had held them for true.[4]

[4] Johann David Heinichen, *General-Bass Treatise* [1711], quoted in George Buelow, *Thorough-Bass Accompaniment according to Johann David Heinichen* (Ann Arbor: UMI Research Press, 1986), 376.

Heinichen also makes an interesting observation on the progress of modern education in general as it finally began to abandon the old Church-dominated, theory-oriented Scholastic university traditions.

> Formerly one studied only philosophy until one was twenty-four or twenty-five before advancing to higher studies. Today they leave the university at twenty with more knowledge. Formerly it took five years to finish the law course, and even then one did not know how in practice to dispute in order to regain a stolen egg from a farmer. Today three years is sufficient to complete the entire philosophical and law courses. What is the reason for such great changes in the times? Answer: The changing of old, pedantic methods, since today one usually studies all things more completely, more briefly, and with greater vigor, for which a good order or a good, applicable method is absolutely necessary.[5]

[5] ibid., 377.

Finally, Heinichen also includes a comment on the quality of the teaching.

> Many years ago I had the opportunity to recognize by my own experience that the greatest hindrance to the ambitious student in this knowledge lies purely in the confused leadership of the teacher.[6]

[6] ibid.

We get a view of quite a different kind of music teacher in Friedrich Erhardt Niedt (d. 1717), who published a satire, *Musikalische Handleitung*, in 1700, which portrays music practice in Germany during the late seventeenth century. That this is satire, and not fiction, and thus reflects experience known to him, may be seen in his story of a musician who was invited to consider a position in the town of 'Dantzfurt,' where an organist had just died. Upon his arrival there the musician found he was expected, as part of the contract, to marry 'my lady's chambermaid.' As fictional as this may seem, such circumstances actually occurred. In one notable instance, Johann Mattheson was invited to Lubeck, in 1703, as a candidate for a position succeeding Buxtehude but found that he was expected to marry Buxtehude's daughter!

We are particularly interested in Niedt's account of the experience of a private keyboard student, for the insights it may reflect on both pedagogy and discipline. His teacher began with simple popular songs, progressing to dance music such as '*sarabandes*, a *courante simple*, and a *ballo*.'[7] The next level of difficulty was the 'dreadful long *praeludia*, *toccate*, *ciaconne*, *fughe*, and more such zoological marvels.' These his teacher demanded he learn from memory, as a prerequisite to the final goal: the study of thorough bass.

[7] Quoted in Oliver Strunk, *Source Readings in Music History* (New York: Norton, 1950), 459ff.

> I worked hard, and many a time, over those splendid pieces of writing, my master roughly boxed my ears, slapped my face, rapped me on the nose, pinched my ears, and pulled my hair; at other times I was treated to live coals, the strap, and more such delicacies. Willy-nilly, he was determined to beat music into my head. But, for all his good intentions, this would not do; the more he abused me, the more stupid I became; indeed, be it said in all modesty that, though I had to work for at least half a year over a single *toccata* or *praeludium* and *fuga*, when I came to play it—just when things were going splendidly and at the best—I stuck fast all of a sudden and could recall neither beginning nor end. At this, from my master's kindly fists there rained down on my ears some three score blows; meanwhile he consoled me with words like these: 'May you be this, that, and the other, you bloodhound! Even the sparrows on the roof will learn before you do!' In this manner I had spent seven years with my master before I could play five *praeludia* and the chorale, or German psalm, in two parts.

Finally, the student was ready to be taught the art of thorough bass.

> From the first I was in terror, thinking 'Now you will really begin to catch it!' I had noticed that whenever he and the cantor tried anything over together they often came to blows over the thorough bass; I could only conclude that my own head would still more often be the target. In instructing me, my master's procedure was as follows. He showed me neither rules nor figures—even to him the numerals standing above the bass were no better than towns in Bohemia; he simply played the bass through for me once or twice, saying: 'You must play it thus and so—that's the way I learned it.'[8] But if I was not getting on, you would have been entertained to see the admirable means my master found to teach me the art after his own fashion. The *sexta* was situated behind my right ear, the *quarta* behind my left, the *septima* on my cheeks, the *nona* in my hair, the false *quinta* on my nose, the *secunda* on my back, the *tertia minor* across my knuckles, the *tertia major* and *quinta* on my shins; the *decima* and *undecima* were special sorts of boxes on the ear. Thus, from the whereabouts of the blow or kick, I was supposed to know what to play; the best part of it was that continual kicking in the shins made my feet active on the pedals, the use of which I was also beginning to learn at this time ... Once he hit upon an extraordinary measure; since with no foundation none of his teaching could drive the thorough bass through my head, he actually decided to kick it into me. Seizing my hair, he pulled me down from the organ bench on which I was sitting before the keyboard, threw me to the ground, lifted me up by the hair so that, when I fell back, my head struck sharply against the floor, and then trampled all over me, stamping on me for some time.

[8] The present writer once had the educational experience of hearing the most famous conducting teacher in Europe play non-stop through *Figaro* on the piano, as a lesson in how to conduct it. At the final chord, the teacher stood and exclaimed, 'Das ist *Figaro*,' and left the room.

At length, Niedt assures us, the student was thrown down a set of stairs.

We get a view of the expectations of the more conservative teacher in the list of demands which Bach was given as part of his contract when he was hired at St. Thomas church in Leipzig. Included in his oath, were the following:

> I shall set the boys a shining example of an honest, retiring manner of life, serve the school industriously, and instruct the boys conscientiously;
>
> Not take any boys into the school who have not already laid a foundation in music, or are not at least suited to being instructed therein;
>
> [I will] faithfully instruct the boys not only in vocal but also in instrumental music;
>
> Treat the boys in a friendly manner and with caution, but, in case they do not wish to obey, chastise them with moderation or report them to the proper place.[9]

[9] Quoted in Hans T. David and Arthur Mendel, *The Bach Reader* (New York: Norton, 1966), 91ff.

Bach's son, K. P. E. Bach, confirms that in his private teaching Bach would refuse to take a student in composition until he had seen evidence of their talent.[10] The son also provides an overview of Bach's pedagogy. Bach, we are told, omitted 'all the dry species of counterpoint that are given in Fux and others,' beginning instead with studies in four-part part-writing. After this came the study of adding individual parts to the Chorale, followed by thorough bass study and finally original counterpoint. And we have another interesting document relative to the teaching of Bach in the form of a comment by one of his students on the importance of adding emotion to the performance of the chorales.

[10] ibid., 279.

> As concerns the playing of chorales, I was instructed by my teacher Kapellmeister Bach, who is still living, not to play the songs merely offhand but according to the emotion [*Affect*] of the words.[11]

[11] Johann Ziegler (1746), quoted in Ibid, 237.

One philosophical idea which was not discussed by the best-known German writers of the Baroque Period is the ancient Greek concept that the study of music affects the shaping of the character of the student. Johann Mattheson briefly mentions this in passing and one gets the feeling that he wanted to believe this but, as he points out, no one knows anymore what the ancient Greeks were talking about.

> Plato thought men's habits change with music, namely when it is changed; Cicero maintained however if habits were to change, then music would change. Both can serve our purpose, and neither is wrong. Music and customs should be altered together, so that the former does not damage the latter, nor the latter the former. It is the same with the political ...
>
> Besides it is quite regrettable that none of us now knows what constitutes *Musica moralis*. If ethical, or moral philosophy, which concerns the inner man, were only well cultivated; then morals, or ethics which concern the extrinsic, would function better.[12]

[12] Johann Mattheson, *Der vollkommene Capellmeister* (1739), trans., Ernest Harriss (Ann Arbor: UMI Research Press, 1981), I, v, 33ff.

This topic is discussed today by some in Germany who believe that the character of the German people was shaped to a considerable degree by the spiritual music they heard being played by civic bands from towers throughout the day. It is interesting, in this regard, that a letter of recommendation by a father for his son who had applied for a civic band position in the town of Stettin in 1607, mentions in addition to the astonishing number of instruments the young man can play, and the large number he owns, his good deportment.

> My son has arrived at a point in his art where he has studied and learned diligently all the musical instruments. First, he is a good trumpeter and secondly a good cornett player and plays well the discant violin, Querpfeife, dulcian, quart-, tenor- and alto-trombone. In summary: all perfect instruments, although without proclaiming his fame—for as one says, 'Self praise stinks.' But he can prove himself where it matters, in what the ear hears and the eye sees. To cover the subject, he doesn't quarrel or criticize, and can use the instruments I have given him in praise of God: trombones, cornetts, a good quart-trombone; a dulcian consort; a large and small bombard consort; a large cornett consort; a crumhorn consort; a Querpfeiffen consort; a flute consort; and a violin consort. He can play all parts and use the fifth, sixth, or eighth voices [ie., read the various clefs], comes from a good home ... and is 26 years old.

The civic band movement in Germany also produced some of the earliest etude books for music education. A well-known example is a publication by Daniel Speer, who served during the late seventeenth century in Breslau. Speer, who was also highly educated, has left an education treatise, *Musicalisches Kleeblatt*, which contains ensemble music with his own comments on instrumental technique. In this work, for example, he finds five indispensable qualities for good trumpet playing: good health, good breath control, a fast moving tongue, willingness for constant practice and good, long trills made with the chin. He discusses the embouchure in detail, concluding with,

> Above all, an incipient shall accustom himself to draw in his cheeks, not blow them out, for this is not only unseemly, but hinders the breath from having its due outlet and causes a man pains at the temples, so that true teachers are accustomed to box the ears of their pupils to cure them of this bad habit.

We also have some interesting insights into the education of those who would become an aristocratic trumpet player. In 1653 a new edict by the Emperor Ferdinand III was issued, due to 'various difficulties, errors and abuses' relative to the edict of 1623 by his father. The new edict deals at length with the

Emperor Ferdinand III (1608–1657) by Frans Luycx, ca. 1637–1638

apprentice system, after first stipulating that a prospective student must first present information relative to his 'honorable ancestry and birth.'[13] In this regard the aristocratic trumpeter is warned that if he 'behaves dishonorably toward a widow or an honest man's daughter and makes her pregnant,' even though he acknowledges the child, he may not instruct him in trumpet playing. The student must study with the noble trumpeter for two years, after which a final exam is given.

[13] Antonium Fabrum, *Europaischer Staats-Kantzley* (Leipzig, 1700), IV, 848ff.

> Each master shall instruct his apprentice very diligently in his art, and shall not send him into the field until he knows his Feldstucke perfectly. In order to test this, the apprentice must present himself beforehand to the highest and oldest trumpeter and play his test piece for him. If this is not done, then as a bungler he will not be allowed to go into the field.[14]

[14] in Don Smithers, *The Music and History of the Baroque Trumpet* (London: Dent), 115.

It is also interesting that the edict places strict limitations on how many students one trumpeter could teach, and how often, which was an attempt to guard against overcrowding the profession.

There are two subjects dealing with music education about which we wish we had more information. The first falls in the period of Friedrich I (1688–1713), when the true Hautboisten band, consisting of modern oboes and bassoons, can be documented as appearing in Germany and Austria. During the first generation of Hautboisten the players were no doubt struggling with the new French oboes. Friedrich I arranged for his Hautboisten to study for two years under Johann Theile (1646–1724).[15]

[15] *Die Musik in Geschichte und Gegenwart* (Kassel, 1949–1968), XIII, 278.

The other is the first military music school, established by Frederick William I in 1724. The school was housed in the Military Orphans Home in Potsdam and its original purpose seems to have been to create Hautboisten musicians from the orphans. The first director of the school was Gottfried Pepush and he appears to have been in charge of about twenty students by 1750.[16]

[16] Panoff, *Militarmusik* (Berlin, 1944), 109, where there is also included a drawing of the building.

Finally, Johann Mattheson wrote on several aspects of music education necessary to the preparation of a court director of music. It is interesting from the perspective of the breadth of studies he considers fundamental if one is to be taught the 'essence of music.'[17] The list includes all the elements of what

[17] Johann Mattheson, *Der vollkommene Capellmeister*, op. cit., I, i, 9ff.

we would call theory and composition today, plus organ building. Included as well are acoustics, music history,[18] a study of how music functions in society and the training of the voice as well as various instruments.[19] Interesting specific topics include,

> The special qualities of a conductor.
> Expression in singing.
> The difference between vocal and instrumental melodies.
> How to direct, produce and execute music.

In another place,[20] Mattheson focuses specifically on the education and skills needed by the Kapellmeister and composer. Without education, he says, a musician can exercise his trade, but he cannot be an artist. This education need not be found at a university, but can be gained at home under 'clever leadership.'

The specific requirements of this education begin with languages: Greek, Latin, French and Italian, the language of the theater. Without these languages, how can the Kapellmeister ever be a *galant homme*? He must also have considerable knowledge in poetry and, in an emergency, be able to write good verse himself.

Mattheson considered music to be a 'substantial part of erudition and one of the disciplines which is closest to theology.' Perhaps this explains his following statement that 'whoever advances in music and goes backwards in morals walks like a crab and misses the proper goal.'

For the composer, in addition to the usual studies in the Klavier, counterpoint and harmony, Mattheson gives the highest priority to being able to sing, which he clearly believed was an essential key to understanding the emotions in a composition.

> If the stirring of the affections and passions of the soul depends on something quite different, namely upon the skillful composition of an intelligible, clear, and expressive melody; then no one who is not well experienced in the art of singing can reach this goal.[21]

But, for composition, not everything can be learned, in particular 'a good natural ability or innate instinct and spirit.' To find if he has this, Mattheson recommends his looking into his own heart to see

> whether he would be satisfied with mere patchwork and pieces from diverse sources, which were toilsomely collected by begging?

---

[18] ibid., I, iv, 6ff, divides the field of music history into Chronology, Biography and the study of instruments. He divides the history of music into three eras: the beginning of time until the sixth century AD (a total of four thousand years!), the sixth century until 1600 and 1600 until the present (1739). This last period, he says, contains so much material that the first two periods seem only trifling by comparison.

[19] ibid., III, xxiv, discusses the need for someone to write an up-to-date treatise on instruments. He mentions the fine work by Praetorius [of 1619], but points out that 'all musical instruments have changed a great deal since then.'

[20] ibid., II, iiff.

[21] ibid., II, ii, 40, 44.

It is not necessary, when one composes a dirge or lamentation, to begin to cry, 'yet it is absolutely necessary that he open his mind and heart to the affection at hand.' For how, Mattheson asks, will he be able to excite a passion in other people's feelings if he has not experienced it himself?[22] Here Mattheson, remarkably, adds a precise comment on the nature of the communication of emotions in music, that they are both universal and personal at the same time.

[22] ibid., II, ii, 64ff.

> He must also study the affective disposition of his listeners as much as possible. For although it is true: Each head has its own mind; still a certain propensity, a certain taste, usually predominates with wise and attentive listeners.[23]

[23] ibid., II, ii, 66.

Mattheson would have probably acknowledged that composers are 'born, not made,' for he found that in some cases Nature has left the requisite qualities incomplete.

> One sometimes encounters fine minds without true desire and love for it; thus one encounters nothing more seldom than the required diligence and necessary, untiring industry, joined together with these two things, natural ability and real desire: because commonly not a little laziness and idleness, lasciviousness, comfortableness, and the like, tend to go side by side with innate gifts and inclinations.
>
> A so-called natural disposition without ambition or love is like a buried treasure ... Desire and diligence without natural ability is really the worst of all.[24]

[24] ibid., II, ii, 59ff.

This role which Nature plays, led Mattheson, in another place, to comment on the treatment of students.

> Natural stupidity or innate simplicity is among the failures of the intellect which no one can rightfully punish, though it can be deplored or at best ridiculed. Desiring to make youngsters intelligent with thrashing is not only futile, but godless. Many examples verify that beatings make heads ten times more dumb than they were previously. This is and remains abysmally characteristic of education in almost every guild and apprenticeship.[25]

[25] ibid., II, ii, 30. Mattheson specifically was thinking, in the last statement, of civic band guilds.

Additional education is required for the conductor and Mattheson mentions the ability to sing, to play the clavier, knowledge of tuning, knowledge of principles of seating plans and 'the greatest difficulty' of all: having the discernment required to succeed in divining the sense and meaning of another composer's thoughts.

20 *On the Philosophical Roots of French Music Education*

IT MIGHT BE APPROPRIATE to begin with a brief summary of the development of theories of aesthetics during the seventeenth century. The *Academie Francaise* had been founded in 1635 and was originally dedicated 'to the giving of certain rules to our language, to rendering it pure, eloquent, and capable of treating the arts and sciences,' a function it claims even today. But it was the founding, in 1648, of the *Academie Royale de Peinture et de Sculpture* which would lead to serious discussions regarding aesthetics in the arts. Its pronouncements were doomed to failure for two reasons. Not only did its 'rules' set a standard too high to encompass many artists, but 'rules' in aesthetics can never contain the breadth of artistic talent. As a result, during the seventeenth century there was a debate on aesthetics in the arts which far surpassed similar discussions in other countries. While these debates, at least within the Academy, were centered in painting, the general principles discussed clearly framed similar discussions which included music.

One of the important accomplishments of the Baroque in music was the freeing of music from the old Church Scholastic understanding that music was a branch of mathematics. It was this fact which made the question of taste immediately important, for in the past 'good taste' was tied to 'following the rules.' Therefore, when Jean Rousseau (not to be confused with Jean-Jacques Rousseau) considered this question in 1687, it was the proper role of the rules which had to be addressed.

> But genius and fine taste are gifts of nature, which cannot be learnt by rules, and it is with the help of these that the rules should be applied, and that liberties may be taken so fittingly as always to give pleasure, for to give pleasure means to have genius and fine taste.[1]

Similarly, when Couperin, in 1717, mentions the 'old' style, it was the rules-dominated polyphonic style he was thinking of.

> Let the style of playing be directed by the good taste [bon-gout] of today, which is incomparably purer than the old.[2]

---

[1] Jean Rousseau, *Traite de la Viole* (Paris, 1687), quoted in Robert Donnington, *The Interpretation of Early Music* (New York, 1964), 425.

[2] Francois Couperin, *L'Art de toucher* (Paris, 1717, reprinted Wiesbaden: Breitkopf & Härtel, 1933), 33.

Rameau, writing in 1726, makes the same point.

> It is often by seeing and hearing musical works (operas and other good musical compositions), rather than by rules, that taste is formed.³

The following year Rameau views the question in a more practical perspective. Perhaps more significant is the fact that he does not include the theorists, the 'learned,' among those with 'good taste.'

> You will then see that I am not a novice in the art and that it is not obvious that I make a great display of learning in my compositions, where I seek to hide art by very art; for I consider only people of taste and not at all the learned, since there are many of the former and hardly any of the latter.⁴

In another place however, Rameau questions the results of possible alternatives to 'playing by the rules.'

> A learned musician is generally understood to be a man who understands everything about the various combinations of sounds. At the same time, however, he is so engrossed in these combinations that he sacrifices everything: good sense, feeling, imagination, and reason. Such a musician is an academician, of a school that is concerned with notes alone and nothing further. We are right to prefer to him a musician who prides himself less on learning than taste.
>
> The latter, however, whose taste is limited by the range of his sensations alone, can excel only in certain types of music that are natural to his character. If he is naturally tender, he will express tenderness. If his temperament is witty, lively, playful, his music will correspond accordingly. Moreover, since he draws on his imagination for everything, without the assistance of art, by this means of expression he soon burns himself out. In his first fire he was all brilliance, but this fire consumes itself as he tries to rekindle it, and nothing remains but banality and repetitions.⁵

For Rameau, as he points out in 1726, a greater concern for the composer was to find a deeper meaning of feeling in the musical materials.

> We may note that the semi-skilled generally use a chord because it is familiar to them or pleases them, but the expert uses it only to the extent that he feels its power.⁶

Jean-Philippe Rameau (1683–1764) by Jacques Aved

³ Rameau, *Le Nouveau Systeme de musique theorique* (1726), quoted in Sam Morgenstern, *Composers on Music* (New York: Pantheon, 1956), 43.

⁴ Letter of Rameau to La Motte (1727), quoted in Julie Anne Sadie, 'Paris and Versailles,' in *The Late Baroque Era* (Englewood Cliffs: Prentice Hall, 1994), 182.

⁵ Letter to Houdart de la Motte, October 25, 1727, quoted in Gertrude Norman and Miriam Shrifte, *Letters of Composers* (New York, Knopf, 1946), 18ff.

⁶ Rameau, *Le Nouveau Systeme de musique theorique*, op. cit., 42.

For Rameau, the 'rules' now take second place.

> While composing music is not the time to recall the rules which might hold our genius in bondage. We must have recourse to the rules only when our genius and our ear seem to deny what we are seeking.[7]

[7] ibid., 41.

The following year he observed that it is Nature which, for him, precedes rules.

> Nature has not completely deprived me of her gifts and I have not surrendered myself to mere combinations of notes so far as to forget their intimate relationship with that beautiful Nature which by itself suffices to give pleasure.[8]

[8] Letter to Houdart de la Motte, October 25, 1727, quoted in Gertrude Norman and Miriam Shrifte, op. cit., 19.

It seems clear that all of Couperin's contemporaries would have at least agreed with him when he observed,

> Just as there is a difference between grammar and declamation, so there is an infinitely greater one between musical theory and the art of fine playing.[9]

[9] Francois Couperin, *L'Art de toucher*, op. cit., Preface.

These famous composers also stress that in listening to music one should not listen to the 'rules,' or the conceptual aspects of music—although, of course, that is all we teach in school. Rameau writes in 1726: don't think, don't put academic rules first, just let yourself be carried away.

> To enjoy the effects of music fully, we must completely lose ourselves in it; to judge it, we must relate it to the source through which we are affected by it. This source is nature. Nature endows us with the feeling that moves us in all our musical experiences; we might call her gift *instinct*. Let us allow instinct to inform our judgments, let us see what mysteries it unfolds to us before we pronounce our verdicts, and if there are still men sufficiently self-assured to dare make judgments on their own authority, there is reason to hope that none will be found weak enough to listen to them.[10]

[10] Jean Philippe Rameau, *Le Nouveau Systeme de musique theorique*, op. cit., 43.

In a remarkable passage eight years later, which represents a dramatic departure from the contentions of the sixteenth-century French philosophers who placed all meaning in the words, Rameau makes the same point even with regard to listening to music with words. He says find your meaning in the music, don't force your impressions of the music to fit the accepted meaning of the words. He might as well say, listen with the right brain, not the left. He concludes here with a reference to the dawn of the Enlightenment.

> Often we think we hear in music only what exists in the words, or in the interpretation we wish to give them. We try to subject music to forced inflections, but that is not the way to be able to judge it. On the contrary, we must not think but let ourselves be carried away by the feeling which the music inspires; without our thinking at all, this feeling will become the basis of our judgment. As for reason, everybody possesses it nowadays; we have just discovered it in the bosom of nature itself. We have even proved that instinct constantly recalls it to us, both in our actions and in our speech. When reason and instinct are reconciled, there will be no higher appeal.[11]

[11] Jean Philippe Rameau, *Observations sur notre instinct pour la musique et sur son principe*, 1734, 44.

Titlepage of Charles Batteux's 'Les beaux-arts réduits à un même principe', 1746

It is surprising that so few early philosophers concerned themselves with the nature of the perception of music, for it is here that music is so different from the other arts. By this we mean that while the other arts are only a representation of something, music is the real thing, a direct communication between composer and listener. Batteux, the only one of these French writers to discuss musical perception at all, does not refer to this distinction, but he does touch on a very valid and important point: we do not understand music, as listeners, in anything remotely near the conceptual aspects of it we study in school.

> If I were to say that I could derive no pleasure from a lecture that I did not understand, my confession would in no way seem strange. But if I ventured to say the same of a piece of music, people would ask whether I considered myself enough of a connoisseur to appreciate the merits of so carefully constructed and fine a composition. I would dare to reply yes, for it is a matter of feeling [and not conceptual knowledge]. I do not [while listening to music] pretend in any way to calculate the sounds, their interrelationships or their connection with the ear. I am speaking here neither of oscillations, string vibrations, nor mathematical proportions. I leave such speculations to learned theorists; these are akin to the grammar and dialectic of a lecture which I can appreciate without going into such details. Music speaks to me in tones: this language is natural to me. If I do not understand it, art has corrupted nature rather than perfected her.[12]

[12] Charles Batteux (1713–1780), *Les beaux-arts reduits a un meme principe* [Paris, 1746], quoted in Peter le Huray and James Day, *Music and Aesthetics in the Eighteenth and Early-Nineteenth Centuries* (Cambridge: Cambridge University Press, 1981), 48ff.

This is perfectly correct, but as he continues, returning to the error of including music and painting in the same category, he seems to lose touch with the importance of what he has just written.

> A musical composition must be judged in the same way as a picture. In the picture I find shapes and colors that I can comprehend; it charms and touches me. What would we think of a painter who was content to throw on the canvas bold shapes and masses of the liveliest color without reference to any known object? The same argument can be applied to music. There is no disparity here, and if there were it would strengthen my argument. The ear is said to be much finer than the eye.[13] I am therefore much more capable of judging a musical composition than a painting.

At the end of the seventeenth century, Charpentier concludes his book on the rules of composition by admitting,

> Practice teaches more about this than all the rules.

During the seventeenth century and the first half of the eighteenth century in France, we believe it is safe to say that most musicians and philosophers thought of music with respect to its relationship with the communication of emotions. This, being a dramatic evolution from the old mathematics-based concepts of music of earlier Church Scholastic philosophies, is, after all, the very hallmark of the Baroque in music. Nevertheless, since the French philosophers of this period were much engaged in creating aesthetic definitions for the other arts, there were some philosophers who attempted to discover aesthetics principles in music. The central aim of this activity seems to have been to determine the 'rules' by which music could be judged. For example, Jean-Baptiste Du Bos, writing in 1719, attempts to equate music with other arts. He makes a fundamental mistake here, for music is not an imitation like the other arts. Music is the real emotion, not an imitation of an emotion.

> The basic principles that govern music are thus similar to those that govern poetry and painting. Like poetry and painting, music is an imitation. Music cannot be good unless it conforms to the general rules that apply to the other arts on such matters as choice of subject and exactness of representation.[14]

[13] All ancient and medieval philosophers argued just the reverse.

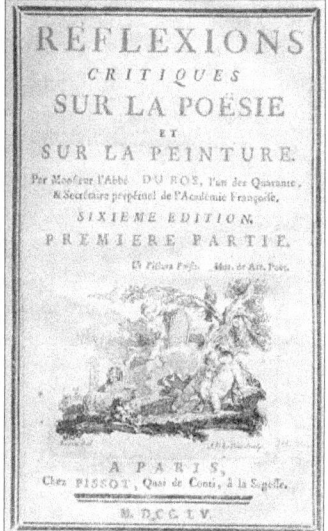

'Réflexions critiques sur la poésie et la peinture' (Critical Reflections on Poetry and Literature) by Jean-Baptiste Dubos, 1755

[14] Jean-Baptiste Du Bos (1670–1742), *Reflexions critiques sur la po'sie et la peinture* [Paris, 1719], quoted in Peter le Huray and James Day, *Music and Aesthetics in the Eighteenth and Early-Nineteenth Centuries* (Cambridge: Cambridge University Press, 1981), 21. Du Bos served in the Foreign Affairs department of the government and later served as secretary of the Academie francaise.

Ironically then, although the French composers argued against the primary significance of the rules of theory, in the seventeenth century there was a temptation, due to the general increased intellectual activity, to create new rules. Andre, for example, attempts a detailed analysis of Beauty specifically in music. His purpose appears to have been to attempt to counter the influence of the humanists, with their emphasis on the emotions, by returning to the old focus on Reason. He begins by reflecting on the great reputation of music among the ancient Greeks, but observes that the opinion of some moderns is much more reserved.

> I am aware that some philosophers do not have such an exalted respect for music. Some even hold opinions that are quite to the contrary, claiming that feeling is the sole judge of harmony and that the pleasure of the ear is the only beauty that music affords. They argue moreover, that this pleasure is far too dependent on opinion, prejudice, convention and acquired habit to be the object of firm rules. And, they ask, is not the proof of this obvious enough? Are there any two nations whose musical tastes are the same? Europeans and Orientals, French, Italians, Germans, Spaniards and Englishmen, Turks and Tartars even, has not each race its own particular music which it unquestioningly values above all others? Since each nation is evidently charmed and satisfied by its own music, what more is to be said? Nothing indeed, so far as those peoples are concerned who only conduct their lives and their thoughts in a haphazard way. But for thinking people—for men—something more is needed, namely that in all pleasures reason must at least be on an equal footing with the senses.[15]

[15] Yves Marie Andre (1675–1764), *L'Essai sur le beau* [1741], quoted in Peter le Huray and James Day, *Music and Aesthetics in the Eighteenth and Early-Nineteenth Centuries* (Cambridge: Cambridge University Press, 1981), 28. Andre was a professor of mathematics at Caen. The present Essay followed three earlier ones on the topics of artistic and moral beauty.

Andre proposes to 'place reason on an equal footing with the senses' by proposing that beauty in music exists on three levels, which he lists as,

1. There is an essential musical beauty that is absolute, wholly independent of human institutions and even divine,
2. There is a natural beauty which comes from the Creator and is not connected to human taste or opinion,
3. There is an artificial musical beauty that is to some degree arbitrary but which none the less is dependent on the eternal laws of harmony.[16]

[16] ibid.

To attempt to explain the first of these, Andre imagines a conversation with a person who has just left a concert, while still filled with the impressions of the music. Andre asks the listener what exactly pleased him in the concert. In the end all the listener can put into words is that he listened to the ordering of the sounds, the propriety of the progressions, the regularity of the flow of time, the tempo, the balance of the ensemble, etc. We would regard this answer as a 'left-brained' one, for the listener only mentions conceptual aspects of the performance. But for Andre it was apparently not conceptual enough, for he proposes there must be

> a purer pleasure than the sweetness of the actual sounds, and a beauty that does not have its roots in the senses, a particular beauty that charms the mind and which the mind alone perceives and judges.[17]

[17] ibid., 29ff.

What this purer pleasure is, in Andre's view, is a connection between the music and some innate form of rational understanding within the listener.

> In other words, sir, during the time that this large ensemble of sonorous instruments was impressing your ear with pleasurable sounds, you experienced deep down within you a master of music who beat time, if I may put it thus, to show how right the music was, and who revealed its principles by means of a light that was superior to that of the senses. These principles are grounded in order, in the structural beauty of the piece, in harmonic numbers, in the rule of proportion and harmonious progression, and in the idea of propriety, a sacred law that allots each part its position, its conclusion and the right path by which to reach its end. Thus while all those who took part in the concert were reading their individual parts, you were also reading yours, written in eternal and ineffaceable notes from the great book of reason which is open to all receptive minds.

By the second form of beauty, that which comes from the Creator, Andre means natural things, beginning with the physics of music, in particular the overtone series. But also he has in mind the body of the listener, which has a kind of receptive harmony: the nerves stretched over bones like strings of an instrument, arteries which beat time and especially the physical components of the ear, throat and mouth. Thus he finds a natural sympathy between the vibrations of music and the body, although he cannot explain how it works. Further, he regards this relationship as the key to understanding emotions in music.

> There is a natural sympathy between certain sounds and the emotions of the soul. There is no question here of explaining how this comes about; all that we need to know is this indubitable fact. There are sounds which have a secret understanding with the heart, and this we cannot deny. Lively sounds inspire courage, languishing sounds appease, laughing sounds cheer, mournful sounds sadden, majestic sounds uplift the soul, harsh sounds irritate, gentle sounds soften.[18]

[18] ibid., 31.

The third kind of beauty in music, Andre finds, is that which belongs to the human contribution, including the conventions of art and taste in composition and performance.

An important publication which attempted to define taste in music was by Jean Laurent le Cerf de La Vieville (1647–1710), a French aristocrat who was a strong supporter of Lully and who published a response to Raguenet's *Parallele des Italiens et des Francais* in 1704, called *Comparaison de la musique italienne et de la musique francaise*. The second part of this publication is an interesting discussion on 'Good Taste in Music,' set in the form of an imaginary discussion between two anonymous noble ladies and the author, whom is called a Chevalier. First, the 'Countess du B' asks if the Chevalier will teach her the rules of 'how to distinguish perfectly the beauties of music.' The answer is, unwittingly, a reference to the rational and experiential parts of the brain, for he weighs the merits of judging by feeling versus 'rules.'

> There are two great ways of knowing good and bad things: by our inward feeling and by the rules. We know the good and the bad only by these means. What we see and what we hear pleases us or displeases us. If one listens only to the inward feeling, one will say, 'It seems to me that that is good, or that it is not.' On the other hand, the masters, the skilled, following the observations they have made, have established precepts in every craft. These comprised whatever had seemed to them to be the best and the surest. The established precepts are the rules, and if one consults them regarding what one sees and what one hears, one will say that this is good or is not good, according to such and such a rule, or for such and such a reason. These masters were men; were they incapable of being deceived? The authority of the rules is considerable, but after all it is not a law. Inward feeling is still less sure, because each should distrust his own, should distrust that it is what it should be. Who will dare flatter himself that he has a fortunate nature, endowed with sure and clear ideas of the good, the beautiful, the true? We have all brought into the world the foundation of these ideas, more or less clear and certain, but since our birth we have received, and this it is sad

and painful to correct, a thousand false impressions, a thousand dangerous prejudices, which have weakened and stifled within us the voice of uncorrupted nature.

I think that in this uncertainty and confusion the remedy is to lend to the inward feeling the support of the rules, that our policy should be correct and strengthen the one by the other, and that it is this union of the rules and the feeling which forms good taste. To listen attentively to the inward feeling, to disentangle it, and then to purify it by the application of the rules; there is the art of judging with certainty, and therefore I am persuaded that good taste is the most natural feeling, corrected or confirmed by the best rules.[19]

[19] Le Cerf de la Vieville, 'Traite du bon gout en musique,' in Oliver Strunk, *Source Readings in Music History* (New York: Norton, 1950), 491ff.

The Countess now begs the Chevalier to please teach her the rules for judging music.

There are little rules and great rules, Madame, and we have touched upon both sorts in our conversation. The little rules are those of composition, on which twenty treatises have been written, of which I do not cite a single one, because I am waiting for somebody to write a twenty-first one that will be good.[20]

[20] ibid., 492.

The Chevalier gives, as an example of a 'little' rule, the formula that low or high notes should accompany low or lofty concepts. As for the great rules,

A piece of music should be natural, expressive, harmonious. In the first place, natural, or rather, simple, for simplicity is the first part, the first sign of the natural, which is almost equally an ingredient in these three qualities. In the second place, expressive. In the third place, harmonious, melodious, pleasing—take your choice. These are the three great, the three important rules which one must apply to the airs that the inward feeling has approved, and it is they which in the last resort decide.[21]

[21] ibid., 493.

As an after thought the Chevalier adds another rule, 'always to abhor excess. Let us make it a habit and a merit to have contempt, distaste, and aversion without quarter for all that contains anything superfluous.'

The Countess, still not satisfied, wants a simple rule to test whether her judgments were correct. She says, for example,

Am I not justified in saying that my heart, my ear, and all the rules agree in persuading me that 'Bois Epais' is a charming melody. And it is by Lully, a new pledge of the correctness of my taste. This other melody does not flatter my ear, nor does it touch me; it has neither sweetness nor expression. And it is by Charpentier. Yes, I am judging it rightly; it is bad. Would that be bad reasoning, Chevalier?[22]

[22] ibid., 495.

The Chevalier cautions the Countess on the dangers of judging on the basis of the composer's name or reputation and, finally, offers her a practical means of judging music.

You will need to carry in your head two melodies representing the two qualities, one good and one bad; that is, good and bad by almost unanimous consent, and two symphonies, one good and one bad, and you must have all their beauties and all their faults at the tip of your fingers. You must have the knowledge of the least of the beauties and faults of these two melodies and these two symphonies ever at command and thoroughly familiar, and compare with these models the melodies and symphonies you hear.

[23] ibid., 495ff.

These latter you will esteem in proportion to their resemblance to the others, and the idea of this resemblance alone, accordingly as it strikes you more or less forcibly, will cause you to say, with greater or less force, 'I like that melody; that symphony does not please me.' I am convinced that the ablest connoisseur should not neglect to combine with the judgments based on reasoning these judgments by comparison, from which will be derived an additional clearness, well adapted to confirm our feelings.[23]

The Countess says that if she understands correctly, 'the more perfectly a melody complies with the rules the better it is, and the further it departs from them the worse.' In his response, the Chevalier touches on the important aesthetic principle of universality. To put it in the form of a question, can one trust the judgment of the masses?

There are precepts with regard to this matter. First, infringements of the little rules are as nothing in comparison with violations of the great ones. Listen to a lesson of Holy Week which begins with a sixth, but go out when one begins with a roulade. In the second place, the pleasures of the heart being, by the principles we have established, superior to those of the ear, a melody which offends against the laws that are directed toward touching the heart offends more than one which disregards merely those which aim to satisfy the ear. Let us forgive two similar cadences which are too near to each other, or a poor thorough bass, but let us never forgive a melody which is cold and forced …

In the third place, the most beautiful thing is that which is equally admired by the people and by the learned or by all the connoisseurs. Then, after this, I should admire more that which is generally admired by all the people. Finally, that which is admired by all the learned. The learned are the masters of music, the musicians by profession, stubborn about rules. The people is the multitude, the great mass, which has not risen to special knowledge and has only its natural feeling as its guide and as the warrant for its judgments. The connoisseurs are those who are neither altogether of the people nor altogether learned, half the one and half the other, a shade less learned than of the people, that is to say, crediting the rules a shade less than natural feeling …

As to the half-learned, they are in music what they are in any art, in anything whatever, the most contemptible and the most insupportable of all men.[24]

[24] ibid., 496ff.

The other noble lady present, the 'Marquis des E,' contributes an interesting observation on universality, as measured by the response of the public, and the recommendation of a system for using that judgment.

That characterization of the people, the connoisseurs, and the learned makes me realize that we must listen to the reasoning of the learned, defer to the feeling of the connoisseurs, and study how the people are moved by theatrical representations can infinitely clarify and facilitate our judgments and help us to make them true. At the first three representations of an opera, let us concern ourselves only with ourselves; it will keep us sufficiently occupied … But at the fourth and later performances let us apply ourselves to studying in what manner and how greatly the people are touched. The value and the degree of value of pieces will certainly be revealed by the impression which they make on the heart of the people and by the vivacity of that impression. When Armida works herself up to stab Rinaldo in the last scene of the second act, I have twenty times seen everybody seized by terror, holding his breath, motionless, all the soul in the ears and eyes, until the melody of the violin which ends the scene gave leave to breathe, than at that point breathing again with a murmur of delight and admiration. I had no need to reason. That unanimous response of the people told me with certainty that the scene was of overpowering beauty.[25]

[25] ibid., 499.

When the noble lady suggests that perhaps one should form one's taste after that of the highest nobles, the Chevalier makes a comment which clearly reflects the beginning of the Enlightenment and the coming Revolution.

In the matter of taste, mademoiselle, great nobles are only men like ourselves, whose name proves little. Each has his voice and the voices are equal, or at least it is not their quality which will determine their weight.[26]

[26] ibid., 505.

Another issue which arises in this discussion is whether good taste demands that one give praise where praise is due the performer. The Chevalier adds,

> That is not enough; the degree of praise must correspond to the degree of value of the work. To praise more or less than this is bad taste, and I am persuaded that here is the reef on which the greatest number of people are wrecked. He who can praise with reason and in due proportion will be of a perfect connoisseur.[27]

[27] ibid., 504.

Practice teaches more about this than all the rules.
Marc-Antoine Charpentier (1643–1704)

21 *The Music Education Scene in Baroque France*

MICHEL DE SAINT-LAMBERT in his treatise of 1702 discusses music education, which he specifies should begin at five or six.[1] He also observed that regardless of the aptitude of the student, his final achievement was often made possible, or prevented, by the quality of his teacher. He then provides the most remarkable portrait of a good music teacher to be found in early literature.

[1] Michel de Saint-Lambert, quoted in Robert Donnington, *The Interpretation of Early Music* (New York, 1964), 213.

> A teacher to be good must have two qualities: *knowledge* and *probity*; because to make a good pupil the master must absolutely have two rules: *he can* and *he will*.
>
> By the 'knowledge' of a teacher is not meant simply that he is a very expert player on the clavecin and an excellent composer of music; it must be demonstrated that he joins to those two advantages the talent of expounding clearly, which is a quality completely apart from that of being a celebrated musician.
>
> A good teacher knows to the bottom the abilities of those who put themselves in his hands, and accommodating himself to the range and capacity of each of them, he teaches each in the way that suits their talent. He devises as many methods as he has different talents to bring along. He speaks childishly to children, reasonably to reasonable persons: to both he speaks intelligently and tersely. He expounds his principles in an orderly way and always presents them as simple and separate ideas. He does not embarrass the memory of those he is teaching with useless fine distinctions. He teaches a general rule as if it had no exceptions, waiting for the time when this exception arises to talk about it, because he knows that it is better understood at this point, and he knows that if he had talked about it earlier it would have confused the general rule. He gives his first rule as if it were the only one he would ever have to talk about, and when he passes to the second he never mentions those which are about to follow.
>
> Passing from theory to practice, the good teacher is able to choose for each pupil the pieces best suited to the abilities of their hands. He even composes some expressly for those who may need them. But after having given some easy piece to his pupils to assure them at the beginning, he then gives them some that are directly opposed to the abilities of their hands in order to correct the faults.
>
> The good teacher brings far along the road to perfection the student who has much facility in this practice and even further the one who has more facility. He causes the male and female students who may have more talent than he has to play better than he does. And because he

knows that one cannot profit unless one really likes playing, he has a special secret to cause his pupils to like learning. This talent is the most necessary when he has children to teach, for the natural fickleness of young children often, after having desired ardently to play the clavecin, makes them take a distaste for it after the third or fourth lesson because of the difficulty they have found; and their distaste goes so far at times that an exercise which is really a game, and should really be learned as a game, becomes for them a cause for sadness and tears. So it is up to the teacher to relieve his young pupils of the difficulties that annoy them and to act so that they give themselves over to their exercises, if not with pleasure at least with courage and perseverance.[2]

In another place, Saint-Lambert, in his *Les Principes du Clavecin* of 1702, makes a remarkable deduction, one which has only recently been confirmed in clinical research, that is that we carry genetically into birth specific information of a musical nature. We are, in fact, born musicians and Saint-Lambert's insight is quite remarkable. After briefly mentioning some of the abilities needed in performance, he says,

> Though this at first sight may appear a large order, it is nevertheless sure that this extreme accuracy in intonation and rhythm is a gift given to almost all men, like sight and speech. There are very few who do not sing and dance naturally; if it is not with the delicacy and correctness that Art has sought, it is at least with the correctness which Art dictates and which Art itself has derived from Nature. It is already a great asset for those who want to learn music or to play some instrument that they know they have discernment of the ear by nature, that is, the first and most important of these aptitudes.[3]

We also have a number of interesting observations on music education by Francois Couperin. First, he specifies that the proper age at which children should begin is from six to seven years.[4] Then, regarding the actual pedagogy,

> During the first lessons given to children, it is better not to advise them to practice in the absence of the person who is teaching them; little people are too easily distracted ... For myself, when giving children their first lessons, as a precaution I take away the key of the instrument on which I have been giving them instruction, so that, during my absence, they cannot spoil in one instant all that I have most careful taught them in three quarters of an hour.[5]

...

[2] ibid., 213ff.

[3] Michel de Saint-Lambert, *Les Principes du Clavecin* (1702), quoted in Carol MacClintock, *Readings in the History of Music in Performance* (Bloomington: Indiana University Press, 1979), 212.

[4] Francois Couperin, *L'Art de toucher* (Paris, 1717, reprinted Wiesbaden: Breitkopf & Härtel, 1933), 10.

[5] ibid., 12.

François Couperin, etching by Jean-Jacques Flipart, after a painting by André Boüys, 1735

> One should not begin teaching the tablature, or musical notation to children until after they have a certain number of pieces in the fingers [from memory]. It is almost impossible for them while looking at their book, not to let their fingers get out of proper position, and not to make contortions with them; and even the *agremens* themselves might be spoilt by it; moreover, the memory improves greatly in learning by heart.[6]

[6] ibid., 13.

> ...
>
> Those who instruct young people would do well to instill into them gradually a knowledge of the intervals, of the modes; of their cadences, both perfect and imperfect; of chords, of chords by supposition. This develops in them a sort of 'local memory,' which makes them surer, and helps them to put themselves right again, with understanding, when they have broken down.[7]

[7] ibid., 22.

> ...
>
> It would be well if parents, or those who have the care of children, showed less impatience, and more confidence in the teacher: (being sure of having made a good choice) and if the able Master, on his side, showed less condescension.[8]

[8] ibid., 18.

And regarding the physical problems of older students:

> People who begin late, or who have been badly taught must be careful; for as the sinews may have become hardened, or they may have got into bad habits, they should make their fingers flexible, or get someone else to do it for them ... that is to say, they should pull, or get someone to pull their fingers in all directions; that, moreover, will stir up their minds, and they will have a feeling of greater freedom.[9]

[9] ibid., 12.

> ...
>
> Men, who wish to attain a certain degree of perfection, should never do any rough work with their hands. Women's hands, on the contrary, are generally better ... A man's left hand, which he uses less in this work, is usually the more supple at the harpsichord.[10]

[10] ibid., 13.

Finally, Rameau, in 1744, gives advice for a young composer on the developmental stages of composing.

> It would be necessary, before undertaking so great a work, to have written small compositions, cantatas, divertissements, and a thousand trifles of the kind that nourish the spirit, fire its imagination, and make one imperceptibly capable of greater things. I have followed the theater since the age of twelve; I did not work for the Opera before I was fifty years old, even then doubting my capacity to do so.[11]

[11] Jean-Philippe Rameau, letter to Mongeot, 1744, quoted in Piero Weiss, *Letters of Composers Through Six Centuries* (Philadelphia: Chilton, 1967), 81.

In his discussion of French and Italian music, Raguenet makes a brief reference to the musical education of children in 1702.

> [It is no wonder the Italians excel in music] when we consider that they learn music as we do to read; they have schools among them where their children are taught to sing as soon as our learn their A B C's; they are sent thither whilst they are very young and continue there for nine or ten years, so that by the time our children are able to read true and without hesitation, theirs have been taught to sing with the same judgment and facility. To sing at sight with them is no more than to read so with us. The Italians study music once for all and attain it to the greatest perfection; the French learn it by halves, and so making themselves never masters of it, they are bound always to be scholars.[12]

[12] Francois Raguenet, 'Parallele des Italiens et des Francais,' (1702), quoted in Oliver Strunk, *Source Readings in Music History* (New York: Norton, 1950), 484.

Unfortunately, we have little information about the music education taught in the Versailles palace under Louis XIV. It was found under the administrative division, *Musique de la Chambre*, one of the superintendents of which was the famous Jean-Baptiste Lully. The actual music education of the children in the palace was conducted by Michael Lambert (1610–1696).

Lully, 'who has given, and continues to give, daily—and pleasurable—proof of his abilities,' also obtained a valuable patent from the king to establish a Royal Academy of Music for the establishment of 'public performance of theatrical dramas in the manner of Italy, Germany and England.' Lully was appointed for life to this position which put him virtually solely in charge of large musical production in Paris. His instructions from the king in 1672 included an order to create civic music schools,

> who shall also be empowered to establish private schools of music in Our city of Paris and wherever else he deems necessary for the good and well-being of the aforesaid *Academie royale*.[13]

We also have a valuable actual teaching contract belonging to a member of the court. The musicians of another division of the court organization, the Ecurie, enjoyed high prestige, having the right of *commensaux* (meal companions of the king), exemption from many taxes and obligations to church-wardens and civic officials. They received gifts of food, clothing and financial bonuses and they were allowed to live and do

Portrait of Louis XIV by Pierre Mignard

Jean-Baptiste Lully by Jean-Claude Chabert

[13] Quoted in Lorenzo Bianconi, *Music in the Seventeenth Century*, trans., David Bryant (Cambridge: Cambridge University Press, 1989), 240.

extra work in Paris. At this time the members appear to have been hired more on the basis of recommendation, than by audition. It follows that study with a current member was the most promising route to success for a young musician. The importance of such teacher–pupil relationships can be seen in a typical contract drawn up between Jean Baptiste Desjardins, a member of the *Les Grands Hautbois*, and a student named Francois Gillotot. The modern teacher might feel reluctant to assume some of the responsibilities expected of the seventeenth-century teacher.

> Today it has appeared in front of the notary of Paris that the undersigned Jean B. Desjardins ... is obligated to Francois Gillotot, a servant of M. the Abbey Bouchart ... to show him how to play the oboe, flute and instrumental music which this entails. Gillotot may be free to obtain this goal and do his profession without being obligated. Mr. Desjardins will furnish him with instruments. This contract entails the sum of 185 livres ... [The final payment] is made when Mr. Desjardins succeeds in placing Gillotot in a quality position as an oboist. Desjardins must try to place Gillotot ... Gillotot must go precisely all the days to take his lessons with Desjardins.[14]

[14] Dated October 3, 1701, quoted in 'Documents du Minutier Central,' in *Recherches sur la Musique francaise classique* (Paris, 1968), 245.

Regarding the music education of the gentlemen of the rising commercial middle class, we have in Moliere's *Le Bourgeois Gentilhomme* an extended view of the household music in the home of a socially aspiring businessman, named Mr. Jourdain. Act One begins with a music master, a dancing master, three singers, two violinists and four dancers on stage. The music master mentions that he has had his student compose a melody while they all are waiting on the gentleman to wake up. The initial dialogue is concerned with describing what it is like for artists who work in such an environment.

Moliere, 1905

> MUSIC MASTER. We have found the very man we both wanted. He brings us in a comfortable little income, with his notions of gentility and gallantry which he has taken into his head; and it would be well for your dancing and my music if everybody were like him.
> DANCING MASTER. No; not altogether. I wish, for his sake, that he would appreciate better than he does the things we give him.
> MUSIC MASTER. He certainly understands them but little; but he pays well, and that is nowadays what our arts require above all things.

DANCING MASTER. I must confess, for my part, that I rather hunger after glory. Applause finds a very ready answer in my heart, and I think it mortifying enough that in the fine arts we should have to exhibit ourselves before fools, and submit our compositions to the vulgar taste of an ass. No! say what you will, there is a real pleasure in working for people who are able to appreciate the refinements of an art; who know how to yield a kind recognition to the beauties of a work, and who, by felicitous approbations, reward you for your labor ...

MUSIC MASTER. I grant it; and I relish them as much as you do. There is certainly nothing more refreshing than the applause you speak of; still we cannot live on this flattering acknowledgment of our talent. Undiluted praise does not give competence to a man; we must have something more solid to fall back on, and the best praise is the praise of the pocket. Our man, it is true, is a man of very limited capacity, who speaks at random upon all things, and only gives applause in the wrong place; but his money makes up for the errors of his judgment. He keeps his discernment in his purse, and his praises are golden. This ignorant, commonplace citizen is, as you see, better to us than that clever nobleman who introduced us here.

DANCING MASTER. There is some truth in what you say; still I think that you set a little too much value on money, and that it is in itself something so base that he who respects himself should never make a display of his love for it.

MUSIC MASTER. Yet you receive readily enough the money our man gives you.

The businessman, Mr. Jourdain, finally appears and, after soliciting compliments on the new dressing gown he has had made, he asks to see what 'little drollery' the music and dancing masters have prepared.

MUSIC MASTER. I should like, first of all, for you to hear a melody which [my student] has just composed for the serenade you asked of me. He is one of my pupils, who has an admirable talent for this kind of thing.

MR. JOURDAIN. Yes; but you should not have had it done by a pupil; you were not too good for the business yourself.

MUSIC MASTER. You must not be deceived, Sir, by the name of pupil. These kinds of pupils know sometimes as much as the greatest masters; and the melody is as beautiful as possible. Only just listen to it.

MR. JOURDAIN. (to his servants) Hand me my dressing gown, so that I may hear better ...

THE PUPIL (sings)
All night and day I languish on; the sick man none can save
Since those bright eyes have laid him low, to your stern laws a slave ...

Mr. Jourdain. This song seems to me rather dismal; it sends one to sleep; could you not enliven it a bit here and there?
Music Master. We must, Sir, suit the music to the words.

This performance has reminded the businessman of a song which he now sings. At its conclusion, he asks 'Now, isn't it pretty?'

Music Master. The prettiest thing in the world.
Dancing Master. And you sing it very well.
Mr. Jourdain. Do I? I have never learned music.
Music Master. You ought to learn it, Sir, as you do dancing. These are two arts which are closely bound together.
Dancing Master. And which open the human mind to the beauty of things.
Mr. Jourdain. Do people of rank learn music also?
Music Master. Yes, Sir.

Upon hearing this, the businessman decides to study music. On second thought, he remembers he has also engaged a fencing teacher and a professor of philosophy and therefore fears he may not have time. The music and dancing masters, in response, begin to speak of the purposes and virtues of their arts.

Music Master. Philosophy is something, no doubt; but music, Sir, music ...
Dancing Master. Music and dancing, Sir; in music and dancing we have all that we need.
Music Master. There is nothing so useful in a state as music ... Without music no kingdom can exist ... All the disorders, all the wars that happen in the world, are caused by nothing but the lack of music ...
Mr. Jourdain. How is that [possible]?
Music Master. Does not war arise from a lack of concord between them?
Mr. Jourdain. True.
Music Master. And if all men learned music, would not this be the means of keeping them in better harmony, and of seeing universal peace reign in the world?

Mr. Jourdain accepts this idea and now the music master proposes that the businessman see the musical composition which the student has composed. A female and two male singers, dressed as shepherds, now prepare to sing the music, which the music master promises will 'represent the different passions which can be expressed by music.' Jourdain asks why such Intermezzi always involve shepherds. The interesting answer is one which was occasionally given as an objection to opera itself, that 'normal' people do not discuss their affairs in singing.

> When we make people speak to music, we must, for the sake of probability, adopt the pastoral. Singing has always been affected by shepherds, and it is not very likely that our princes or citizens would sing their passions in dialogue.

During Act Two this dialogue between the music and dancing masters and the businessman continues, now focusing on music of a concert nature as the Music Master recommends that Mr. Jourdain establish his own salon.

> MUSIC MASTER. But, Sir, this is not enough; a gentleman magnificent in all his ideas like you, and who has taste for doing things handsomely, should have a concert at his house every Wednesday or Thursday.
> MR. JOURDAIN. But why should I? Do people of quality have concerts?
> MUSIC MASTER. Yes, Sir.
> MR. JOURDAIN. Oh! very well! Then I too must have some. It'll be fine?
> MUSIC MASTER. Very. You must have three voices: a treble, a countertenor, and a bass; which must be accompanied by a bass-voil, a theorbo lute, and a harpsichord for the thorough-basses, with two violins to play the harmony.[15]

Mr. Jourdain requests that singers for the dinner table not be forgotten.

A fencing master comes on the scene and a brief argument ensues over the relative value of each of their arts. Now a professor of philosophy is introduced and speaks with disdain for the arguments at hand.

> Is there anything more base and more shameful than the passion which changes a man into a savage beast, and ought not reason to govern all our actions?

[15] In act 3, scene 3, Jourdain's wife complains there was a 'regular din of violins and singers, that are a positive nuisance to all the neighborhood.'

Shortly the philosopher equates music and dancing with 'the trades of prize-fighter, street-singer, and mountebank,' which brings insults upon him from the music, dancing and fencing masters.

We might also mention that there is extant a by-law of 1606 for a civic musicians guild in Strasbourg which includes two regulations related to the apprentices, or student musicians:

5. To be admitted a player in the city, a minstrel must have served two years apprenticeship.
6. The right to join as an apprentice, or to resign an apprenticeship, costs 12 Strasbourg *schellings*.

Finally, we cannot omit from a discussion of seventeenth-century France the great encyclopedia author, Marin Mersenne (1588–1648), who studied mathematics, physics, the classics and metaphysics at the Jesuit College of Le Mans and later at the college at La Fleche, where one of his classmates, and life-long friend, was Rene Descartes. After becoming a Jesuit priest, and a member of the Minorite friars, Mersenne began teaching Hebrew, philosophy and theology at the Sorbonne in Paris in 1619. His residence became a required stopping place for every intellectual visiting Paris, which, together with his correspondence with persons throughout Europe, including Galilei, Huygens and Descartes, made him a virtual one-man academy.

His studies and experimentation in music resulted in his *Harmonie universelle* (1636), a work in five treatises. They are,

I. *Traite de la nature des sons, et des mouvements de toutes sortes de corps.*
II. *Traite de mechanique.*
III. *Traite de la voix, et des chants.*
IV. *Traite des consonances, des dissonances, des genres, des modes, et de la composition.*
V. *Traite des instruments.*

It is a disappointment that this great thinker was so grounded in the old Church Scholastic mathematics-based explanations of music to have been unable to apply his great mind to the new humanistic movement sweeping Europe. It is curious to read Mersenne's extensive attempts to base explanations of music on mathematics in his *Traite de mechanique*. In great mathematical detail, he attempts to relate consonance and dissonance to solid geometry, physics and mechanics. For Mersenne, this mathematical knowledge was central to the 'theory' of music and like a medieval academic this, in turn, was central to the definition of 'musician.' Here he argues for the need for music education:

> Those who know only singing and the manner of composing, as well as singers and those who play instruments, do not merit the name of musician, just as bricklayers do not deserve to be called architects, since the former do not know the ratio of the harmonics which they make or in which they assist, as the latter do not know why palaces and other edifices have one figure rather than another. Thus the practice of music is like a body without a soul if one does not know the theory, which surpasses practice as much as the spirit surpasses the body and the heavens surpass the Earth.[16]

[16] Marin Mersenne, *Harmonie Universelle*, II, ii. The English translation is taken from John Egan (Bloomington: Indiana University, unpublished dissertation, 1962). [All translations from the Second Treatise are taken from this source]

In his fourth treatise, Mersenne seems to suggest that goodness in a composition is a matter of mathematics. Can we find here the birth of the rationale for modern analysis?

> Since the goodness of composition consists in the natural order of the consonances, in their succession, and in the harmony which they make, we can say that the examination of this order is the idea of all the examinations which can be made of all the other kinds of compositions.[17]

[17] Marin Mersenne: *Fourth Treatise of the Harmonie Universelle*, ed., Robert Williams (Rochester: Eastman School of Music, unpublished dissertation, 1972), IV, iv, 24. As hereafter, these numbers represent: Treatise, Book, and Proposition. [All translations from the Fourth Treatise are taken from this source].

Mersenne did recognize that math and science cannot account for everything and that to some degree taste is an individual matter. This has more than ordinary significance, for in a series of treatises so highly dependent on mathematics, it is an admission that mathematics and science can not account for everything in music.

> Since the rules have been formulated only upon the different observations of the mixture of sounds, some of which have been more agreeable to those who formulated the rules than others were, it is free to those who are as capable, or more so, than they, to observe that which pleases them, since their ear is as good and as well trained, and since that which is offensive to some can be pleasing to others. For the rules of harmony are not like those of geometry, which force the mind of all those who have common sense to adopt them. They depend upon the ear and upon custom.[18]

[18] IV, iv, 21.

But a Church philosopher cannot long leave Reason behind. Judgment of the good is partly Reason, not just the ear, Mersenne maintains. Speaking of the interval of the fourth, he observes,

> If perchance someone finds it a little harsh in certain places, he will judge it quite good when his ear is accustomed to it. The same thing will happen to him as to the disciples of Pythagoras who did not wish to approve of thirds and sixths until time and their use, based upon Reason, made them understand the excellence of these consonances, so that he will judge that the fourth is an excellent chord.[19]

[19] IV, v, 5.

Mersenne does make one very important point: one can only learn to judge music by hearing it. He reminds us that before the advent of recordings, persons heard much less music than we hear today. Perhaps more than anything else this helps explain the emphasis on theory over practice in earlier periods, for they had to work from imagination rather than from direct, live experience.

> If we wished to have all the pleasure which can result from music, it would be necessary to have all the ways of singing and make them appear one after the other, in order to judge how one surpassed the other. For example, it would be necessary to have one or two madrigals or other Italian melodies sung by a dozen fine Italian voices, as well as sarabandes by the Spanish, and courantes and melodies by French; and then to have the best pieces of music written for instruments played by each of them … Since, however, no book can furnish the practice of this music, and since it is not easy to encounter it, it is sufficient to show what our France has invented, or what it has added to music, or at least its attempts, which can only be praiseworthy, even though they have not attained perfection.[20]

[20] IV, vi, 24.

However, in a letter to Huygens, he privately confessed great doubt whether music can in fact have significant influence on the actions of man.

> Now to begin this examination, it is first necessary to assume that music, and consequently melodies are made particularly and principally to charm the mind and ear and to make us pass our lives with a little sweetness among the bitter things encountered in it. For to think that music serves to persuade us of the intention of the musician as perfectly as could a good orator, and that it has as much power to conduct us to virtue and to make us hate vice as much as the voice of a good preacher,

even though the same things are sung as he recites in the pulpit, and to believe that singing can be used as easily for instruction as can speaking and lecturing, it is this that it is difficult for us to accept.[21]

Mersenne also wished that an academy like Baif's might be re-established. The kind of academy he envisioned was one that studied ancient music, as we can see in his comments in the preface to his *Quaestiones in Genesim* (1623). He begs the archbishop to found an academy, bringing together men from throughout Europe, to restore 'ancient music,' which will have the goal, among others, of restoring virtue and refuting deists and atheists. His discussion here indicates he was, like the Greeks, still thinking of music as a branch of mathematics. Nothing came of this and thirteen years later he bemoaned that there was still

> no academy for the theoretical study of music, although it is well known that good music of the Dorian mode is so necessary for the good of the state and the good of religion.[22]

Mersenne makes one further observation on the nature of musical study, or as he calls it, the 'science' of learning an instrument. He points out that all the arts and sciences are governed by three conditions for acquiring perfection. These are *Nature*,

> which must be understood to be the inclination and the natural disposition that we have toward certain sciences, and toward the particular arts, as happens when some are attracted to painting or sculpture, and others to architecture, to geometry, etc.[23]

The second condition is *Discipline*, which refers to study with 'good masters,' and the third is *Exercise*, which means practice.

[21] Letter to Constantin Huygens [November 14, 1640], quoted in 'Embellissement des chants,' according to David Duncan, 'Persuading the Affections: Rhetorical Theory and Mersenne's Advice to Harmonic Orators,' in *French Musical Thought, 1600–1800* (Ann arbor: UMI Research Press, 1989).

[22] I, 'Preface au Lecteur.'

[23] V, ii, 91.

As for children, I think easier ways might be found than the soured and mysterious Gamut, which they must rehearse antrorsum & retrorsum, *without the least proffer to them of an explanation of it.*[1]

Roger North (1653–1734)

22 The Music Education Scene in Jacobean England

ROGER NORTH (1653–1734), an amateur musician born to a well-to-do family and educated in law, brought to his writing a breadth of knowledge not enjoyed by his contemporaries who wrote on music and who were primarily working musicians. Of all the English Baroque writers on music before Avison, North is the only one who might be also called a philosopher.

Roger North seemed to understand through deduction and observation that the mind of man is clearly divided into rational and experiential forms of understanding. In the following passage he attempts to explain the distinction between rational learning and music. After so many centuries during which higher education in music emphasized so-called 'speculative,' or as we would say today, theoretical, music, it is of significance that North attempts here to separate real musical learning from conceptual studies. In the final sentence, which we have quoted above, he hints at the lesson we still have not learned, that conceptual teaching is foreign to what children instinctively love in music.

> The teaching of music and languages are very different, although the masters of the former affect the methods used by them of the other; that is, a sort of grammar to be [learned] by heart, whether it be or be not understood. The difference lies in this, that languages are mere memory, and come from the arbitrary use of nations, and may be as well one way or another; and this use grammarians endeavor to reduce to rule, which must be learnt and remembered. But music is taken from nature itself, and depends on body in a physical sense, even as the mathematical sciences do, and takes place finally in our imagination and fancy; and therefore should be taught by explaining it to the understanding as well as by giving the rules to which the practice of it is reduced. And for this reason it is that in the musical science the rules are very few, and those but introductory as it were to show what the subject matter is, that the learner might not have the trouble of being an original inventor of the whole science ... And yet the real knowledge that belongs to music is dilated enough, and it is through that, that a man must learn the skill of a musician, whether he be showed it, or gathers it of himself by observation, as generally is done ... As for children, I think easier ways might be found than the soured and mysterious Gamut, which they must rehearse *antrorsum & retrorsum*, without the least proffer to them of an explanation of it.[2]

[1] Quoted in John Wilson, *Roger North on Music* (London: Novello, 1959), 59.

Roger North (1653–1734) by Peter Lely

[2] ibid., 59.

For North, the central purpose and meaning of music was its ability to communicate feeling. We understand today that it *is* the most important virtue of music, but, before the humanists began to think in these terms during the sixteenth century, this had been a concept opposed for one thousand years by the Church, and therefore for the entire early history of modern university study in music. While North is indebted to the earlier humanists, none of them expressed so clearly the dimension of this role of music.

> My thoughts are first in general that music is a true pantomime or resemblance of Humanity in all its states, actions, passions and emotions. And in every musical attempt reasonably designed, Humane Nature is the subject ... so that an hearer shall put himself into the same condition, as if the state represented were his own ... So the melody should be referred to [man's] thoughts and emotions. And an artist is to consider what manner of expression men would use on certain occasions, and let his melody, as near as may be, resemble that.[3]

It is also worthy of notice that it is in the subject of the emotions in music that North finds the distinction between serious music and entertainment music.

> Lord! how at the wagging of an elbow the whole theater claps, though no single note is heard: just like a circle of fools laughing at the wagging of a feather, such power hath ignorance and partiality. I would go to such music and pay my scott as I do to the posture man, or a rope dancer, to see somewhat done which I scarce thought possible. But if I went for the sake of the music in earnest, it should be to feel my spirits moved, and together with the delightful sounds, enjoy the gentle enlivenings of passions, which ... may justly be accounted the best of human life.[4]

He also points to the human characteristics of the familiar Italian tempo markings, concepts we have long forgotten.

> The *Adagios* are designed for pure and simple harmony, for which reason measure of time is so little regarded in them. The *Grave* comes nearer a sober conversation, and the *Allegro* light and chirping. The *Tremolo* is fear and suspicion, the *Andante* is a walking about full of concern, the *Ricercata* is a searching about for somewhat out of the way; the *Affectuoso* is expostulating, or *amour*; and so every other manner, as masters are pleased to title them, are but so many states of humane life, as they have a fancy to represent or imitate.

[3] ibid., 110ff.

[4] ibid., 129.

North writes in several places on the subject of music education, a subject which he seems to have given more thought to than most of his contemporaries.[5] His first recommendation is that the teacher should be older, rather than a young man. The older man has more experience and is more likely to have reasons for what he teaches, as opposed to mere intuition. Also the younger teacher is much more likely to seduce the children, especially the daughters, whereas the older man who has a family of his own will be more prudent.

[5] ibid., 16ff.

One should teach music the way one teaches the beginner in manufacture, he suggests, beginning with the fundamentals and proceeding step by step. North stresses that the beginning point in music is tone, the development of a clear plain sound with no ornaments. Next he recommends the development of a crescendo of this tone, 'the louder and harsher the better.' This is how one learns to develop body in the sound, 'which else will be faint and weak.'

> Then next I would have them learn to fill, and soften a sound, as shades in needlework, by imperceptible steps, so as to be alike a gust of wind which begins with a soft air, and fills by degrees to a strength as makes all bend, and then softens away again ... and so vanish.

North recommends careful teaching of ornaments, especially trills, which disturb the basic pitch. He also advises the introduction of lessons in harmony at an early stage in teaching. This is all so complicated and difficult that the child is unlikely to want to pursue music for pleasure. Therefore the parent must insist.

> But parents have authority, and do exert it in these cases, to oblige their children to endure the fatigue of learning many things, which they would altogether decline if left to themselves. Therefore if there be not either compulsion, or an extraordinary inclination and perseverance, it is in vain for a master to pursue teaching; and the one supposed, the other must be granted.

Since the study of fundamentals is so tedious, North recommends getting the student into an ensemble, 'which is the greatest perfection and pleasure music can afford to performers.'

North returns to the tedious nature of the study of fundamentals with some advice which might well be considered by modern music education. There is, North reminds us, more to music than meets the eye.

> It were to be wished that a talent of unfolding secrets in music, so making them familiar to the understanding of beginners, went always along with the profession of teaching.[6]

[6] ibid., 60.

He concludes by lamenting the opportunities for music education then available in England.

> And as to the learning of music in general, I must out of my experience say, that of those persons who are so happy to acquire it, more teach themselves, than are taught. And all that advantage is from society: for all arts are more effectually learned under a social than under a solitary discipline, and none more eminently so than music ... It is an unhappiness in England that there are not music schools for young people to be taught, [as there are] reading and writing schools.[7]

[7] ibid., 238.

Another important English Baroque writer, Thomas Mace, also emphasizes the importance of training children in music. Not only does he have in mind the improvement of church music, but he reminds the reader of the social advantages associated with music education.

[8] Thomas Mace, *Musick's Monument* [1676] (Paris: Editions du Centre National de la Recherche Scientifique, 1966), 14ff. Mace (1613–1709) was a 'clerk' at Trinity College, Cambridge.

> It will adorn your children much more than ten times the cost can be worth, which you shall bestow upon them in the gaining of it.
> Besides, it will make them acceptable to all ingenious people, and valued amongst the best.
> They will be more capable of preferment in the world, in case of any necessity.[8]

George Frideric Handel by Balthasar Denner

He recommends that all children in grammar school should have one hour of music taught them every day. The cost of finding a music teacher would be minimal, or as he calls it a 'little-poor-trifle' or 'pitiful inconsiderable.'

Handel as a music teacher, was remembered by Charles Burney, who was nineteen at the time (1745) he describes.

> He was a blunt and peremptory disciplinarian on these occasions, but had a humor and wit in delivering his instructions, and even in chiding and finding fault, that was peculiar to himself, and extremely diverting to all but those on whom his lash was laid.[9]

[9] Charles Burney, *A General History of the Science and Practice of Music* (London, 1789), IV, 666.

Judging by an extant letter of Handel to Johann Mattheson, however strict the former may have been in his discipline, he was at least not a teacher who blindly followed former dogma. When Mattheson had questioned the value of continuing to study the old Scholastic, math-based rules of composing in the style of earlier polyphony, Handel indicates he generally agrees with this viewpoint, adding,

> The question seems to me to reduce itself to this: whether one should prefer an easy & most perfect Method to another that is accompanied by great difficulties capable not only of disgusting pupils with Music, but also making them waste much precious time that could better be employed in plunging deeper into this art & in the cultivation of one's genius?[10]

[10] George Friedrich Handel, letter to Johann Mattheson, February 24, 1719, quoted in Piero Weiss, *Letters of Composers Through Six Centuries* (Philadelphia: Chilton, 1967), 63.

Charles Avison, one of the most important English writers of this period, makes a number of suggestions for educating would be composers. He recommends it would be helpful if someone would publish a history of important composers, explaining their 'characteristic taste and manner.'[11] He seemed to feel support and direction was necessary to prevent young talents from turning their attention 'to instant profit, rather than to future fame.'

[11] Charles Avison, *An Essay on Musical Expression* [London, 1753] (New York: Broude Reprint, 1967), 98. Avison (1709–1770) was an organist and composer.

Since the period of the Elizabethan theater one of the objects of the English stage was to portray life as it really is. It is in the Jacobean stage repertoire, therefore, that we have the closest extant portrayal of actual music education. In Dekker's *The Roaring Girl* (act 4, scene 1), we find a reflection of the small value placed on music education by the upper class at this time. Here we have Moll, disguised in the dress of a man.

> ALEXANDER. Now sir I understand you professe musique.
> MOLL. I am a poore servant to that liberal science sir.
> ALEXANDER. Where is it you teach?
> MOLL. Right against Cliffords Inne.
> ALEXANDER. Hum that's a fit place for it: you have many schollers.
> MOLL. And some of worth, whom I may call my masters.
> ALEXANDER. Aye true, a company of whoremasters; you teach to sing too?
> MOLL. Marry do I sir.
> ALEXANDER. I think you'll find an apt scholler of my son, especially for pricke-song.
> MOLL. I have much hope of him.
> ALEXANDER. I am sorry for it, I have the less for that.

In Middleton's *More Dissemblers Besides Women* there is a character, Crotchet, who is a singing teacher. Act 5 begins with an extended attempt by Crotchet to give a singing lesson to a Page, who is one of the principal female characters in disguise. The Page is an unwilling student who begins by observing that she has 'a great longing to bite a piece of the musician's nose off.' As the lesson begins,

> CROTCHET. Rehearse your gamut, boy.
> PAGE. Who'd be thus toiled for love, and want the joy?
> CROTCHET. Why, when! begin, sir: I must stay your leisure?
> PAGE. Gamut *[sings]* a, re, b, me, etc.
> CROTCHET. *[sings] Ee la*: aloft! above the clouds, my boy!
> PAGE. It must be a better note than *ela*, sir,
>   That brings musicians thither; they're too hasty,
>   The most part of 'em, to take such a journey,
>   And must needs fall by the way.
> CROTCHET. How many clefs are there?
> PAGE. One clef, sir.
> CROTCHET. O intolerable heretic
>   To voice and music! do you know but one clef?
> PAGE. No more, indeed, I, sir;—and at this time I know too much
>   of that.
> CROTCHET. How many notes be there?
> PAGE. Eight, sir.—I fear me I shall find nine shortly,
>   To my great shame and sorrow. O my stomach!
> CROTCHET. Will you repeat your notes then? I must *sol fa* you;
>   Why, when, sir?
> PAGE. A large, a long, a breve, a semibreve,
>   A minim, a crotchet, a quaver, a semiquaver.

Now Crotchet and the Page sing a 'prick-song,' after which Crotchet asks the waiting-lady,

>   How like you this, modonna?
> CELIA. Pretty;
>   He will do well in time, being kept under.
> CROTCHET. I'll make his ears sore and his knuckles ache else.
> CELIA. And that's the way to bring a boy to goodness, sir.

We find another brief, actual lute lesson—all as a double-entendre of another activity—in Cyril Tourneur's, *The Atheist's Tragedy* (act 4, scene 1).

> CATAPLASMA. Lirie, your lute and book.
> SEBASTIAN. Well said. A lesson o'the lute to entertain the time with till she comes.
> CATAPLASMA. Sol, fa, mi, la ... mi, mi, mi ... Precious! Dost not see 'mi' between the two crotchets? Strike me full there ... So ... forward ... This is a sweet strain and thou finger'st it beastly. 'Mi' is a large there and the prick that stands before 'mi' a long; always halve your note ... Now ... Run your division pleasingly with those quavers. Observe all your graces I'the touch ... Here's a sweet close ... strike it full—it setts off your music delicately.

In terms of the philosophical background of music education in Baroque England, it seems clear that the old problems created by the early Church remained the objects of discussion. First, there remained some in England who still accepted the old Church dogma that music was a branch of mathematics. We see this for example in a passage where Christopher Simpson is discussing the use of music in religion.

> In this divine use and application, music may challenge a preeminence above all the other mathematical sciences as being immediately employed in the highest and noblest office that can be performed by men or angels.[12]

[12] Christopher Simpson, *A Compendium of Practical Music*, Second Edition of 1667 (Oxford: Blackwell, 1970), 76. Simpson (d. 1669) was a composer of string music, especially for the viola da gamba.

We would guess that most intelligent Englishmen were beginning to understand that music was not an expression of mathematics or even, as Avison points out, of the realm of Reason.

> After all that has been, or can be said, the energy and grace of musical expression is of too delicate a nature to be fixed by words: it is a matter of taste, rather than of reasoning, and is, therefore, much better understood by example than by precept.[13]

[13] Charles Avison, op. cit., 81.

By learning by example, he means, of course, by experience. This point was also made by King James I when he advised his son, 'Art is better learned by practice than speculation.'[14]

[14] James I, *Basilicon Doron* (1599) (Menston: Scolar Press, 1969), 67.

The more discussed issue was how to deal with the old Church's division of music between the 'speculative' (theory) and the 'practical' (performance). One evidence of how familiar this discussion was is symbolized in the fact that Ben Jonson, in his play *Cynthia's Revels* (act 2, scene 3), presents a satire of this academic division by using it to discuss the courtier's practice of facial expressions.

> But now, to come to your face of faces, or courtier's face, 'tis of three sorts, according to our subdivision of a courtier, elementary, practic, and theoric. Your courtier theoric is he that hath arrived to his farthest, and doth now know the court rather by speculation than practice; and this is his face: a fastidious and oblique face, that looks as it went with a vice, and were screwed thus. Your courtier practic is he that is yet in his path, his course, his way, and hath not touched the punctilio, or point of his hopes; his face is here: a most promising, open, smooth, and overflowing face, that seems as it would run and pour itself into you. Somewhat a northerly face. Your courtier elementary is one but newly entered, or as it were in the alphabet, or *ut–re–mi–fa–sol–la* of courtship. Note well this face, for it is this you must practice.[15]

From the perspective of music education, the importance of performance is that it is the student's vehicle of exploring his emotional make-up. The way this works is very much like the process mentioned above, and which we repeat, by North.

> My thoughts are first in general that music is a true pantomime or resemblance of Humanity in all its states, actions, passions and emotions. And in every musical attempt reasonably designed, Humane Nature is the subject ... so that an hearer shall put himself into the same condition, as if the state represented were his own.

This was, of course, what the ancient Greek philosophers wrote about in arguing for the inclusion of music in education. They spoke of this process as affecting the character of the student and we find English writers of the Baroque making the same arguments. Charles Butler, in 1636, expresses this idea in language similar to that used by nearly all early writers.

> Music ... having a great power over the affections of the mind, by its various Modes produces in the hearers various affects.[16]

[15] In Jonson's comedy *The Silent Woman* (act 5, scene 2) Centaur observes of a court lady, 'she is a perfect courtier, and loves nobody, but for her uses: and for her uses, she loves all.'

[16] Charles Butler, *The Principles of Musik in Singing and Setting* [1636] (New York: Da Capo Press, 1970), 112. Butler (d. 1647) was a music theorist attached to Oxford whose interests extended to agriculture and grammar.

John Playford, in 1674, is much more specific.

> Nor doth music [not] only delight the mind of man, and beast, and birds, but also conduceth much to bodily health by the exercise of the voice in song, which doth clear and strengthen the lungs, and if to be also joined the exercise the limbs, none need fear asthma or consumption; the want of which exercise is often the death of many students: Also much benefit hath been found thereby, by such as have been troubled with defects in speech, as stammering and bad utterance. It gently breathes and vents the Mourners grief, and heightens the joy of them that are cheerful: it abates spleen and hatred, the valiant soldier in fight is animated when he hears the sound of the trumpet, the fife and drum: All mechanical artists do find it cheers them in their weary labors. Scaliger (Exercet. 302) gives a reason of these effects, because the spirits about the heart taking in that trembling and dancing air into the body, are moved together, and stirred up with it; or that the mind, harmonically composed, is roused up at the tunes of music. And farther, we see even young babes are charmed asleep by their singing nurses, nay the poor laboring beasts at plow and cart are cheered by the sound of music, though it be but their master's whistle.[17]

Thomas Mace made fervent testimonials to the power of music. He begins in a passage where he is lamenting the music of former times, specifically the consort music of the early seventeenth century.

> We had for our grave music, Fancies of 2, 3, 5, and 6 parts to the organ; interposed (now and then) with some pavans, allmaines, solemn, and sweet delightful ayres; all of which (as it were) so many Pathetical Stories, Rhetorical and sublime discourses; subtle, and acute argumentations, so suitable, and agreeing to the inward, secret, and intellectual faculties of the soul and mind; that so set them forth according to their true praise, there are no words sufficient in language; yet what I can best speak of them, shall be only to say, that they have been to myself (and many others), as divine raptures, powerfully captivating all our unruly faculties, and affections (for the time) and disposing us to Solidity, Gravity, and Good Temper, making us capable of Heavenly, and Divine influences.
>
> It is a great pity few believe thus much; but far greater, that so few know it.[18]

English music publisher John Playford by David Loggan

[17] John Playford, op. cit., preface. Playford also relates,
> Myself, as I traveled some years since near Royston, met a herd of stags, about twenty, upon the road following a bagpipe and a violin, which while the music played they went forward, when it ceased they all stood still.

[18] Thomas Mace, op. cit., 234. One of the interesting things Mace presents in his book is his design for the ideal performance hall.

The fashion today, he laments, has replaced these things with an emphasis on the virtuoso performer, 'the Great Idol,' and music

> which is rather fit to make a man's ears glow, and fill his brains full of frisks, etc., than to season, and sober his mind, or elevate his affection to Goodness.

During his discussion of country church music, Mace's heartfelt testimonial to the moral virtues of music becomes more personal.

> For if [children] be once truly principled in the grounds of piety and music when they are young, they will be like well-seasoned vessels, fit to receive all other good things to be put into them. And I am not only subject to believe, but am very confident, that the vast jarrings, the dischording-untunableness, over-spreading the face of the whole earth, might be much rectified, and put into tune sooner this way, than by any other way that can be thought upon.
>
> This I speak from an experience in my own soul, who am a man subject to the passions and imperfections of the worst of men. Yet by this virtue, this sublime elixir of musical and harmonical divinity, have found as much (in a comparative way) as this comes to, upon my own soul and violent passions.
>
> It cannot be too often repeated, how the evil spirit departed from Saul, when David played upon his harp. True music being a certain Divine-Magical-Spell, against all diabolical operations in the souls of men. But how little this is taken notice of, believed, or regarded by most, is grievous and lamentable to be thought upon.[19]

One even finds this subject mentioned by the Jacobean poet, George Wither. In one poem, which he disseminated by passing it out a loophole in the Tower of London where he was imprisoned, he decided it 'would better stir up the hearts of some, by being sung, than read.' In this complaint on the manners of London, the stern Puritan poet implores London to turn to music to help improve the behavior of the citizens.

> Thou, London, whofoe're doth weep,
> Do, on thy viol, play and sing;
> Thy children, daily revel keep.[20]

[19] ibid., 12.

[20] *Works of George Wither* (New York: Franklin, 1967), Spenser Society, Nr. 18, 'A Warning-Piece to London,' 34. George Wither (1588–1667), one of the so-called Cavalier Poets was an officer in the Puritan army and most of his poetry is political in nature.

Before his 'Hymn for a Musician,' Wither writes a comment suggesting that some musicians have manners which might be improved by changing their repertoire.

> Many musicians are more out of order than their instruments: such as are so, may by singing this Ode, become reprovers of their own untunable affections. They who are better tempered, are hereby [reminded] what music is most acceptable to God, and most profitable to themselves.[21]

[21] ibid., Nr. 26–27, 'Halelviah,' Hymn XXXVIII.

We also find in John Milton's work references to the ancient Greek assertion that music can change one's character or manners. In the poem 'Arcades,' he attributes to music the ability to raise man above disturbing influences.

> Such sweet compulsion doth in musick lie,
> To lull the daughters of Necessity,
> And keep unsteady Nature to her law,
> And the low world in measured motion draw
> After the heavenly tune, which none can hear
> Of human mold with gross unpurged ear.[22]

[22] 'Arcades,' in Frank Patterson, ed., *The Works of John Milton* (New York: Columbia University Press, 1931–1938), I, 74.

In the poem, 'To Leonora, as She Sings at Rome,' music is referred to as a 'Third Intelligence' which comes from Heaven which enters the throat of the singer and 'graciously teaches mortal hearts the power to grow accustomed insensibly to sounds immortal.'[23]

[23] 'To Leonora, as She Sings at Rome,' in ibid., I, 229.

We should also mention that on two occasions Milton wrote of the use of music in education, although not meaning music education as such. In Milton's treatise, *On Education*, he recommends music for the student's periods of rest, for education in manners and to temper the passions.

> The interim of unsweating themselves regularly, and convenient rest before meat may both with profit and delight be taken up in recreating and composing their travailed spirits with the solemn and divine harmonies of Musick heard or learned; either while the skillful organist plies his grave and fancied descant, in lofty fugues, or the whole Symphony with artful and unimaginable touches adorn and grace the well studied chords of some choice Composer; sometimes the Lute, or soft Organ stop waiting on elegant Voices either to Religious, martial, or civil verses; which if wise men and Prophets be not extremely out, have a great power over the dispositions and manners, to smooth and make

them gentle from rustic harshness and distempered passions. The like also would not be unexpedient after Meat to assist and cherish Nature in her first concoction, and send their minds back to study in good tune and satisfaction.[24]

[24] 'On Education,' in ibid., IV, 288ff.

In another place, perhaps a hint of Milton's views of the music appropriate for education can be found in a passage in which he questions the advisability of civic censorship.

If we think to regulate Printing, thereby to rectify manners, we must regulate all recreations and pastimes, all that is delightful to man. No musick must be heard, no song be set or sung, but what is grave and *Dorick*. There must be licensing dancers, that no gesture, motion, or deportment be taught our youth but what by their allowance shall be thought honest … It will ask more than the work of twenty licensers to examine all the lutes, the violins, and the guitars in every house; they must not be suffered to prattle as they do, but must be licensed what they may say. And who shall silence all the melodies and madrigals, that whisper softness in chambers? … The villages also must have their visitors to enquire what lectures the bagpipe and the rebec reads even to the ballatry, and the gammuth of ever municipal fiddler, for these are the Countryman's Arcadia's and his Monte Mayors.[25]

[25] 'Areopagitica,' in ibid., IV, 317.

For Avison, the chief characteristic of the seventeenth century was that serious music had been transformed from a composer's medium to a performer's medium.

Thus the old music was often contrived to discover the composer's art, as the modern is general calculated to display the performer's dexterity.[26]

[26] Charles Avison, op. cit., 44.

He found the popularity of performance, with audience as well as with the players themselves, placed the spotlight on improvisation. It is no surprise that he concludes that people are more interested in studying performance than in studying composition.

Thus they strive, rather to surprise than to please the hearer: and, as it is easier to discern what is excellent in the *Performance*, than *Composition* of music; so we may account, why many have been more industrious to improve and distinguish themselves in the *Practice*, than the *Study* of this science.

In the case of singers, Mace found that church singers were so poorly paid, 'very low, inconsiderable, insufficient, unbecoming and uncomfortable,' that they could not afford to get proper educational help. As a consequence, he found the singers often were forced to take other jobs. Why should we be surprised, Mace asks, that when they sing in church they 'make sour faces, and cry, or roar out aloud.' He concludes,

> Now I say, these things considered how certainly true they are, first in reference to the [singers] pitiful-poor-wages, and likewise to the general dead-heartedness, or zeal-benumbed-frozen-emotions in these our time, toward the encouragement of such things; how can it be imagined that such [singers] should be fit and able performers in that duty, which necessarily depends upon education, breeding and skill in that quality of music, which is both a costly, careful and a laborious-attainment, not at all acquirable (in its excellency) by an inferior-low-capacitated men.[27]

[27] Mace, op. cit., 23ff.

Roger North agreed the singers were poorly trained, but he found a different reason. He complains that their education was in music theory, not in performance and hence they could not function as performing musicians.

> They do not understand the art of music that sing in public, but are scholars and taught [by those] not able to do anything themselves, and consequently cannot well distinguish when they do well and when ill. For this reason they will be horribly out of tune; and all this by a little understanding would correct itself in others as also in themselves. If it be said, some have no ears and cannot; I answer, send them to shops and trades, and let not the public be molested with their want of ears.

He also finds among singers, that 'women are fearful of the distortion of the face, which is their *sanctum sanctorum*, and therefore the sound is checked.'

The great English philosopher, John Donne, would have agreed with North that education from books has little to offer performance which learns from experience. In a letter of ca. 1600, he is speaking of the importance of not depending on books for one's education, but on personal observation and experience. Then, in analogy, he adds an extraordinary observation that everyone would rather hear improvised music than that which was notated.

For both listeners and players are more delighted with voluntary than with sett musicke.[28]

John Bunyan adds a comment very much related to the above. He maintains that unless a listener is educated in performance, he cannot be a good listener.

> He that can play well on an instrument,
> Will take the ear, and captivate the mind
> With mirth or sadness; for that it is bent
> Thereto, as music in it place doth find.
> But if one hears that has therein no skill,
> (As often music lights of such a chance)
> Of its brave notes they soon be weary will:
> And there are some can neither sing nor dance.[29]

We might mention in this regard that in one of the Jacobean plays, George Chapman's *All Fools* (act 2, scene 1) there is a scene with a courtier, Valerio, who is *self*-educated in music. As a comment on trying to teach one's self to perform, rather than obtaining the proper instruction, our courtier, when asked to play the Theorbo, makes many excuses and never does perform. He tries to substitute a song, but even he admits his vocal skills are also lacking.

CORNELIO. Prythee Val,
    Take thy Theorbo for my sake a little.
VALERIO. By heaven, this month I touched not a Theorbo.
CORNELIO. Touched a Theorbo? marke the very word. Sirra, go fetch.

Exit Page.

VALERIO. If you will have it, I must needs confess,
    I am no husband of my qualities.

While the page goes to get a Theorbo, Valerio dances and is complimented, but he is still requested to play.

CORNELIO. Come sweet Val, touch and sing.
DARIOTTO. Foote, will you hear
    The worst voice in Italy?
CORNELIO. O God, sir.

[Valerio] sings.

Courtiers, how like you this?

---

[28] John Donne, Letter [ca. 1600], quoted in John Donne, 'Paradoxes and Problems,' in *Selected Prose*, ed., Helen Gardner (Oxford: Clarendon Press, 1967), 109. John Donne (1573–1631) studied at both Oxford and Cambridge, but as a born Catholic was not permitted to receive a degree. After various attempts at professions brought him to poverty, he converted to the official Church, became famous for his sermons and eventually became dean of St. Paul's.

[29] 'Upon a Skillful Player on an Instrument,' in *A Book for Boys and Girls*, in. *The Works of John Bunyan*, ed., George Offor (London: Blackie and Son, 1853), III, 761. John Bunyan (1628–1688) is considered the greatest prose writer among the Puritans of the seventeenth century. Only the Bible was so widely read in English homes for the subsequent three centuries. Bunyan was also the epitome of the 'hell and brimstone' preacher.

DARIOTTO. Believe it excellent.
CORNELIO. Is it not natural?
VALERIO. If my father heard me,
  Foot, he'd renounce me for his natural son.
DARIOTTO. By heaven, Valerio, and I were thy father,
  And loved good qualities as I do my life,
  I'd disinherit thee: for I never heard
  Dog howl with worse grace.

Probably our courtier, Valerio, would have argued that he did not have time to keep up his skills on the Theorbo. Indeed, one often reads this in Jacobean literature which deals with the aristocracy and their involvement in personal performance. As an example, Robert Dowland, in his *Varietie of Lute-lessons* of 1610 points out,

> Perfection in any skill cannot be attained unto without the waste of many years, much cost, and excessive labor and industry.[30]

[30] Quoted in Robert Donnington, *The Interpretation of Early Music* (New York, 1964), 118.

But what does an aristocrat mean when he says he is too busy? A first-hand description of King Charles II in 1660 gives us, perhaps, a different perspective.

> His fiercest enemies are diligence and business. He worships comforts, pleasures, and practical jokes, hates implacably all sort of work, and loves with the greatest enthusiasm every kind of play and diversion.[31]

[31] Lorenzo Magalotti, *Relazione d'Inghilterra* (1668).

23 On Music Education in Restoration England

AMONG ALL THE PHILOSOPHERS of seventeenth-century England, the only one who wrote at any length on music education was William Wotton (1666–1727). Wotton, chaplain to the earl of Nottingham, published his *Reflections upon Ancient and Modern Learning* (1694) as a rebuttal to William Temple's essay, 'Of Ancient and Modern Learning,' which had suggested that little insight had been added to those of the ancient writers. Wotton observes that 'it may seem improper to speak of Musick here, which ought rather to have been ranked among those sciences wherein the Moderns have ... been found to have been outdone by the Ancients.'

Like Newton, for Wotton music was still a branch of mathematics and he complained that modern musicians were not studying ancient books. He found it most curious that while mathematicians were conversant with earlier writers, musicians were not.

> Whereas all modern mathematicians have paid a mighty deference to the ancients; and have not only used the names of *Archimedes*, *Apolonius* and *Diophantus*, and the other ancient mathematicians with great respect; but have also acknowledged, that what further advancements have since been made, are, in a manner, wholly owing to the first rudiments, formerly taught. Modern musicians have rarely made use of the writings of *Aristoxenus*, *Ptolemee*, and the rest of the ancient musicians; and, of those that have studied them, very few, unless their editors have confessed that they could understand them. Others have laid them so far aside, as useless for their purpose; that it is very probable, that many excellent composers have scarce ever heard of their names.

Nevertheless, he proposes that the essence of ancient music, insofar as its purpose, has not been entirely lost.

> Musick has still, and always will have very lasting charms. Wherefore, since the moderns have used their utmost diligence to improve whatever was improved in the writings of all sorts of ancient authors, upon other equally difficult and very often not so delightful subjects, one can hardly imagine but that the world would, long ere now, have heard something more demonstrably proved of the comparative perfection of ancient Musick, with large harangues in the commendation of the

respective inventors, if their memory had been preserved, than barely an account of the fabulous stories of *Orpheus* or *Amphion*, which either have no foundation at all, or, as Horace understood them, are allegorically to be interpreted of their reducing a wild and savage people to order and regularity. But this is not urged against Sir William Temple, who is not convinced of the extent of modern industry, sagacity and curiosity; but to other admirers of ancient Musick, who, upon hearsay, believe it to be more perfect than the modern.

The reason for this he gives in a brief, but interesting, suggestion that there are physical laws underlying music itself, which must create similarities between ancient and modern music.

Musick is a Physico-Mathematical Science, built upon fixed rules, and stated proportions; which, one would think, might have been as well improved upon the old foundations, as upon new ones, since the grounds of Musick have always been the same. And Guido's scale, as Dr. Wallis assures us, is the same for substance with the *Diagramma Veterum*.

Wotton makes a distinction between what he calls the skilled listener versus the common listener. The skilled listener understands music on a conceptual basis. It is a dogma which our modern music educators are told to worship. He begins by observing that on one level, all listeners appreciate certain basic qualities in music. These things he considers universal, regardless of the education of the listener.

It is very probably that the ancient Musick had all that which still most affects common hearers. Most men are moved with an excellent voice, are pleased when time is exactly kept, and love to hear an instrument played true to a fine voice, when the one does not so far drown the other, but that they can readily understand what is sung, and can, without previous skill, perceive that the one exactly answers the other throughout; and their passions will be effectually moved with sprightly or lamentable compositions. In all which things the ancients, probably, were very perfect.

He continues by distinguishing between the 'skilled' listener of music and the 'common' listener.[1] The skilled listener, according to Wotton, listens to the details, as left brain conceptual ideas, rather than on a more holistic level. Leaving no

[1] After the break-through in the medical understanding of left and right brain hemisphere function in the 1960s, this became a big topic in the field of music. 'Common' listeners, and musicians who do not concentrate on conceptual data, listen to music primarily with the left ear (right hemisphere). Musicians listening for conceptual parts of music, listen with the right ear (left hemisphere). From this follows the obvious conclusion that one of the chief accomplishments of music schools is to ruin persons as listeners.

doubt, he uses the analogy of looking at a painting. The expert, he says, looks at the detail, the technique and, for all we can tell, never sees the entire painting!

> To the [ancient] men, many of our modern compositions, where several parts are sung or played at the same time, would seem confused, intricate, and unpleasant: though in such compositions, the greater this seeming confusion, the more pleasure does the skillful hearer take in unraveling every several part, and in observing how artfully those seemingly disagreeing tones join, like true-cut Tallies, one within another, to make up that united concord, which very often gives little satisfaction to common ears; and yet it is in such sort of compositions, that the Excellency of Modern Musick chiefly consists. For, in making a judgment of Musick, it is much the same thing as it is of pictures. A great judge in Painting does not gaze upon an exquisite piece so much to raise his passions, as to inform his judgment, as to approve, or to find fault. His eye runs over every part, to find out every excellency; and his pleasure lies in the reflex act of his mind, when he knows that he can judiciously tell where every beauty lies, or where the defects are discernible: which an ordinary spectator would never find out.

The 'common' man, however, is interested in the theme or story of the painting and the emotions seen in it. Likewise in music, says Wotton, the common man has his 'passions raised,' without any contribution to his 'understanding.'

> The chief thing which the [common] man wants, is the story; and if that is lively represented, if the figures do not laugh when they should weep, or weep when they should appear pleased, he is satisfied. And this, perhaps, equally well, if the piece be drawn by Raphael, as by an ordinary master, who is just able to make things look like life.
> So likewise in Musick; He that hears a *numerous* Song, set to a very moving tune, exquisitely sung to a sweet instrument, will find his passions raised, while his understanding, possibly, may have little or no share in the business. He scarce knows, perhaps, the names of the notes, and so can be affected only with an Harmony, of which he can render no account. To this man, what is intricate, appears confused; and therefore he can make no judgment of the true excellency of those things, which seem *fiddling* to him only, for want of skill in *Musick*.

Again, for the 'skilled' listener of music, the satisfaction comes not simply from the emotions of the music, but from the combination of the emotions with intellectual understanding.

The skill or ignorance of the composer serve rather to entertain the understanding, rather than to gratify the passions of a skillful master; whose passions are then the most thoroughly raised, when his understanding received the greatest satisfaction.

Never did a writer so miss the point of music.

ONE ALSO FINDS A VERY INTERESTING OBSERVATION on music education in the English non-fiction literature. In an essay entitled, 'The Way to make London the Most Flourishing City of the Universe,' Defoe wonders why London has no university of its own. This eventually led him to propose the creation of an academy of music, 'to prevent the expensive importation of foreign musicians.' One cannot help but notice that this interesting discussion bears much in common with the principles advanced a few years later for the first European school of music, the national school of music in Paris formed during the French Revolution.

Daniel Defoe by Michael Van der Gucht

An academy, rightly understood, is a place for the propagation of science, by training up persons thereto from younger to riper years, under the instruction and inspection of proper artists; how can the Italian opera properly be called an academy, when none are admitted but such as are, at least are thought, or ought to be, adepts in music? If that be an academy, so are the theaters of Drury Lane, and Lincolns-inn Fields; nay, Punch's opera may pass for a lower kind of academy. Would it not be a glorious thing to have an opera of our own, in our own most noble tongue, in which the composer, singers, and orchestra should be of our own growth? Not that we ought to disclaim all obligations to Italy, the mother of music, the nurse of Corelli, Handel, Bononcini, Geminiani; but then we ought not to be so stupidly partial to imagine ourselves too brutal a part of mankind to make any progress in the science. By the same reason that we love it, we may excel in it; love begets application, and application perfection. We have already had a Purcell, and no doubt there are now many latent geniuses, who only lack proper instruction, application, and encouragement, to become great ornaments of the science, and make England emulate even Rome itself.

What a number of excellent performers on all instruments have sprung up in England within these few years? That this is owing to the opera I will not deny, and so far the opera is an academy, as it refines the taste and inspires emulation.

But though we are happy in instrumental performers, we frequently send to Italy for singers, and that at no small expense; to remedy which I humbly propose that the governors of Christ's Hospital will show their public spirit, by forming an academy of music on their foundation, after this or the like manner.

That out of their great number of children, thirty boys be selected of good ears and propensity to music.

That these boys be divided into three classes, viz., six for wind instruments, such as the hautboy, bassoon, and German flute.

That sixteen others be selected for string instruments, or at least the most useful, viz., the violin and bass violin.

That the remaining eight be particularly chosen for voice, and organ, or harpsichord. That all in due time be taught composition. The boys thus chosen, three masters should be elected, each most excellent in his way; that is to say, one for the wind instrument, another for the stringed, and a third for the voice and organ, etc.

Handsome salaries should be allowed these masters, to engage their constant attendance every day from eight till twelve in the morning ... The multiplicity of holidays should be abridged, and only a few kept; there cannot be too few, considering what a hindrance they are to juvenile studies. It is a vulgar error that has too long prevailed all over England to the great detriment of learning, and many boys have been made blockheads in complaisance to kings and saints dead for many ages past.

The morning employed in music, the boys should go in the afternoon, or so many hours, to the reading and writing school, and in the evening should practice, at least two hours before bed-time, and two before the master comes in the morning. This course held for seven or eight years, will make them fine proficients; but that they should not go too raw or young out of the academy, it is proper, that at the stated age of apprenticeship, they be bound to the hospital, to engage their greater application, and make them thorough masters, before they launch out into the world; for one great hindrance to many performers is, that they begin to teach too soon, and obstruct their genius.

What will not such a design produce in a few years? Will they not be able to perform a concert, choir, or opera, or all three, among themselves, and overpay the charge, as shall hereafter be specified?

For example, we will suppose such a design to be continued for ten years, we shall find an orchestra of forty hands, and a choir or opera of twenty voices, or admitting that of those twenty only five prove capital singers, it will answer the intent.

For the greater variety they may, if they think fit, take in two or more of their girls, where they find a promising genius, but this may be further considered of.

Now, when they are enabled to exhibit an opera, will they not gain considerably when their voices and hands cost them only a college subsistence? and it is but reasonable the profits accruing from operas, concerts, or otherwise, should go to the hospital, to make good all former and future expenses, and enable them to extend the design to a greater length and grandeur; so that instead of £1,500 per annum, the price of one Italian singer, we shall for £300 once in ten years, have sixty English musicians regularly educated, and enabled to live by their science.

There ought, moreover, to be annual probations, and proper prizes or premiums allotted, to excite emulation in the youths, and give life to their studies.

As an afterthought, on the subject of repaying the public for the cost of such an academy, Defoe suggests taking the students out to play spiritual music for the lower classes. Curiously, he values this as a form of entertainment and not for any ethical or cultural role in the music itself.

> That such an entertainment would be much preferable to drinking, gaming, or profane discourse, none can deny; and till it is proved to be prejudicial, I shall always imagine it necessary.

In the fictional literature one reads of the education of young ladies including the study of music. In Richardson's novel, *Clarissa Harlowe*, we are provided an interesting discussion of the *social* expectations of the young lady singing before private gatherings of society in early eighteenth-century England.[2] A Miss Howe first describes the singing of Miss Harlowe, after commenting on her melodious voice when she read poetry.

> But if her voice was melodious when she *read*, it was all harmony when she *sung*. And the delight she gave by that, and by her skill and great compass, was heightened by the ease and gracefulness of her air and manner, and by the alacrity with which she obliged. Nevertheless, she generally chose rather to hear others sing or play, than either to play or sing herself.

Miss Howe now recalls the advice given her by Miss Harlowe on the etiquette of being asked to sing.

> We form the truest judgment of persons by their behavior on the *most familiar* occasions. I will give an instance or two of the corrections she favored me with on such a one. When *very young*, I was guilty of the fault of those who want to be courted to sing. She cured me of it, at the first of our happy intimacy, by her own *example*; and by the following correctives, occasionally, yet privately enforced:

[2] Samuel Richardson, *Clarissa Harlowe* (New York: AMS Press Reprint, 1972), XII, 282ff. Samuel Richardson (1689–1761) was reared in the company of spinsters and his novels are considered to reflect unusual knowledge of female psychology.

Title page of Samuel Richardson's 'Clarissa', 1748

'Well, my dear, shall we take you at your word? Shall we suppose that you sing but indifferently? Is not, however, the *act of obliging* (the company so worthy!) preferable to the *talent of singing*? And shall not young ladies endeavor to make up for their defects in *one part* of education, by their excellence in *another*?'

Again, 'You must convince us, by attempting to sing, that you *cannot* sing; and then we will rid you, not only of *present* but of *future* importunity.' An indulgence, however, let me add, that but *tolerable* singers do not always wish to meet with.

Again, 'I know you will favor us by and by; and what do you by your excuses but raise our expectations, and enhance your own difficulties?'

At another time, 'Has not this accomplishment been a part of your *education*, my Nancy? How, then, for *your own* honor, can we allow of your excuses?'

And I once pleading a cold, the usual pretense of those who love to be entreated—'Sing, however, my dear, *as well as you can*. The greater the difficulty to you, the higher the compliment to the company. Do you think you are among those who know not how to make allowances? You *should* sing, my love, lest there should be anybody present who may think your excuses owing to affectation.'

At another time when I had truly observed that a young lady present sung better than I; and that therefore I chose not to sing before that lady – 'Fie, said she (drawing me on one side), is not this pride, my Nancy? Does it not look as if your principal motive to oblige was to obtain applause? A generous mind will not scruple to give advantage to a *person of merit*, though not always to *her own* advantage. And yet she will have a high merit in *doing that*. Supposing this excellent person absent, who, my dear, if your example spread, shall sing after you? You knew every one *else* must be but as a foil to you. Indeed I must have you as much superior to other ladies in these *smaller* points as you are in greater.'

Often, as the above suggests, when we read of the young lady singing in the private home, it appears that the etiquette was that she must first resist. In Richardson's novel, *Sir Charles Grandison*, however, one young lady is always eager to sing.

They, as we do, admire her voice and her playing. They ask her for a song, for a lesson on her harpsichord. She plays, she sings, at the very first word.[3]

[3] Samuel Richardson, *Sir Charles Grandison*, op. cit., XVII, 104.

In this same novel there is also a domestic music scene which touches on music education. A Miss Byron describes a scene with her cousin, James.

> You know and admire my grandmamma's cheerful compliances with the innocent diversions of youth. She made Lucy give us a lesson on the harpsichord, on purpose, I saw, to draw me in. We both obeyed.
> I was once a little out in an Italian song. In what a sweet manner did he put me in! touching the keys himself, for a minute or two. Every one wished him to proceed; but he gave up to me, in so polite a manner, that we all were satisfied with his excuses.[4]

[4] ibid., XVIII, 60.

In one very interesting discussion, Shenstone touches on the question of how music education affects the listener of music.

> I have heard it claimed by adepts in music, that the pleasure it imparts to a natural ear, which owes little or nothing to cultivation, is by no means to be compared to what they feel themselves from the most perfect composition—The state of the question may be best explained by a recourse to objects that are analogous—Is a country fellow less struck with beauty than a philosopher or an anatomist, who knows how that beauty is produced? Surely no. On the other hand, an attention to the cause may somewhat interfere with the attention to the effect—They may, indeed, feel a pleasure of another sort—The faculty of reason may obtain some kind of balance, for what the more sensible faculty of the imagination loses.[5]

[5] William Shenstone, *Men and Manners* (Boston: Houghton Mifflin, 1927), 96. William Shenstone (1714–1763) attended Oxford, but did not finish. He was one of the minor figures in English literature of the early eighteenth century, but was possessed of a perceptive intelligence.

Writing, and even publishing, diaries became a familiar characteristic of the higher class in seventeenth-century England. The author of the best-known of such diaries, Samuel Pepys (1633–1703), was a notable exception to the trend which began in sixteenth-century England, in which gentlemen disassociated themselves with the performance of music. His famous diary, covering the years 1660–1669, is a testimonial to his own love of music, his close attention to the musical scene and his private performance and attempts at composition. The diary is particularly valuable because it was never intended to be published, even being written in a private code, and therefore is much more candid than the publications of other gentleman at this time.

Painting of Samuel Pepys by John Hayls, 1666

He served as a kind of minister of the Navy under James II, during which time he introduced important economies into the Navy—and managed to improve his own economy immensely. Later he served in the House of Commons and was elected President of the Royal Society.

Pepys' most philosophical comments on music come in a letter of 5 November 1700, after the period covered by the famous diary. A correspondent had sent Pepys a proposal for a new method of teaching mathematics, written by Dr. David Gregory, the Savilian Professor of Astronomy at Oxford. It is evident that Pepys was still thinking of music as a branch of mathematics, for he wrote to the professor pointing out that his proposal had omitted music. In the course of his offering his views on the nature and purpose of music, we also see a reflection of his long experienced frustration that none of his composer friends would offer him a simple, effective set of rules for composition. It is quite nice to read that nothing has changed: the composers point to the official rules and then ignore them in the interest of art.

> I would now recommend to your giving the same regard to ... Musick, a science peculiarly productive of a pleasure that no state of life, public or private, secular or sacred; no difference of age or season; no temper of mind or condition of health exempt from present anguish; nor, lastly, distinction of quality, renders either improper, untimely, or unentertaining. Witness the universal gusto we see it followed with, wherever to be found, by all whose leisure and purse can bear it. While the same might to much better effect, both for variety and delight to themselves and friends, be ever to be had within their own walls, and of their own composures too as well as others, were the doctrine of it brought within the simplicity, perspicuity, and certainty common to all other parts of mathematical knowledge, and of which I take this to be equally capable with any of them, in lieu of that fruitless jargon of obsolete terms and other unnecessary perplexities and obscurities wherewith it has been ever hitherto delivered, and from which, as I know of nothing eminent, or even tolerable, left us by the Ancients, so neither have I met with one modern Master (foreign or domestic) owning the least obligation to it for any their now nobler compositions; but on the contrary charging all (and justly too) upon the happiness of their own genius only, joined with the drudgery of a long and unassisted practice. A condition not to be looked for from the more generous and elevated spirits of those we are here concerned for; and therefore most deserving, as well as most needing, the abilities and application of our present most learned Professor to remedy.[6]

[6] *Private Correspondence of Samuel Pepys*, ed., J. Tanner (London: Bell and Sons, 1926), II, 109.

Among the more interesting passages in his diary finds Pepys attempting to invent a new system of notation. It is this view which is reflected in an entry of December 1666. Here Pepys refers to a visit to the court organist, John Hingston,[7] to get him to either write, or rewrite, one of Pepys' songs.

[7] John Hingston (1612–1683) was also in charge of tuning and repairing the court keyboards.

> I took him to the Dogg tavern and got him to set me a bass to my 'It is decreed,' which I think will go well; but he commends the song, not knowing the words, but says the melody is good, and believes the words are plainly expressed. He is of my mind, against having [many] eighth-notes necessarily in composition. This did all please me mightily.[8]

[8] Pepys Diary, December 19, 1666.

On 10 December 1667 Pepys again mentions that he runs into Hingston and attempts to question him about composition, but is disappointed with the response.

> I do find that he can no more give an intelligible answer to a man that is not a great master in his art than another man—and this confirms me that it is only want of an ingenious man that is master in Musique, to bring music to a certainty and ease in composition.

Pepys becomes obsessed with discovering a simpler process of composition. In his diary he writes on 20 March 1668,

> At my chamber all the evening, writing down some things and trying some conclusions upon my viol, in order to the inventing a better theory of Musique than has yet been abroad; and I think verily I shall do it.

Three days later he writes he is thinking of acquiring a harpsichord,

> to confirm and help me in my music notions, which my head is nowadays full of, and I do believe will come to something that is very good.

On 29 March 1668 he reports that he had the opportunity to discuss composition with John Banister.[9]

[9] John Banister (1625–1679), born the son of a member of the London Waits, became proficient on numerous instruments. It was he who was displaced by the Frenchman, Grabu, as head of court music. He went on to organize concerts in the private sector.

> I had very good discourse with him about music, so confirming some of my new notions about music that it puts me upon a resolution to go on and make a Scheme and Theory of music, not yet ever made in the world.

Other than the fact that the surviving compositions of Pepys are in the nature of elementary songs, we are inclined, on the basis of the following, to think his new method of composition must also have been a simple one. He reports attempting to have a discussion with Hooke, who evidently brushed him off,

> so the reason of Concords and Discords in music—which they say is from the aequality of the vibrations; but I am not satisfied in it, but will at my leisure think of it more and see how far that does go to explain it.[10]

[10] Pepys Diary, April 2, 1668.

Journals and newspapers were not new to this period, but the extensive coverage of music and manners was. Richard Steele began the *Tatler* on 12 April 1709, writing primarily under the name Isaac Bickerstaff, as a paper designed for the conversation of the coffee house crowd. These journals are valuable in part for their presentation of this class, much of it middle-class, which is virtually absent in traditional political biographies and histories. Some have also pointed to these issues as the birthplace of modern short stories.

'The Tatler,' British magazine, 1709–1711, edited by Joseph Addison and Richard Steele

Steele and Joseph Addison created the *Spectator* with the issue of 1 March 1711. For the first year its actual circulation was small, rarely more than four thousand issues, but its influence became much larger as bound volumes were sold at the rate of nine thousand each year.

We have seen, in the novels of this period, testimony that music was considered a necessary part of the education of young ladies. A similar reflection is found in the *Tatler* for 23 May 1710, which compares the cultural education of a young lady and her brother.

'The Spectator' by Joseph Addison, 1711

> This state of her life is infinitely more delightful than that of her brother at the same age. While she is entertained with learning melodious melodies at her spinet, is led round a room in the most complaisant manner to a Fiddle, or is entertained with applauses of her beauty and perfection.

It is in this regard that a fictional letter to the editor of the *Tatler*, for 18 November 1710, carries the question by a father whether it is necessary to his daughter's education that he pay for lessons on the spinet, even though 'I know she has no ear.' This also carries an implication, of course, of how common this practice must have been.

The *Spectator* for 11 April 1711 carries a fictitious advertisement for a school for young women, promising among other things that 'those that have good voices may be taught to sing the newest opera melodies.' The *Tatler* for 8 October 1709 carries a fictional announcement of music instruction for gentlemen.

> This is to give notice to all ingenious Gentlemen in and about the Cities of London and Westminster, who have a mind to be instructed in the noble Sciences of Musick, Poetry, and Politicks, That they repair to the Smyrna Coffee-house in Pall-mall, betwixt the hours of eight and ten at night, where they may be instructed gratis, with elaborate Essays by word of mouth on all or any of the above mentioned Arts. The Disciples are to prepare their bodies with three dishes of Bohea, and purge their brains with two pinches of snuff.

Finally, the *Spectator* for 9 July 1711 mentions an 'itinerant Singing-Master' who apparently went from village to village teaching the melodies used for the Psalms.

24 Schumann on Music Education

THE GREAT COMPOSER, ROBERT SCHUMANN (1810–1856), obviously gave much thought to the subject of music education. He often framed his thoughts in the form of maxims and some of these are to be found in his diary, which dates from before 1833.[1]

[1] Those we quote are found in Fanny Raymond Ritter, trans., *Music and Musicians* (London: W. Reeves, 1877), 65ff.

> In every child there lies a wondrous depth.
>
> …
>
> [Teachers of theory] are not satisfied when a young student works out the old classic form, as a master, and according to his own understanding of it; he must do so according to theirs.
>
> …
>
> [To teachers of theory] If anyone, who owes nothing to your school, dares to write down anything that is not in your style, he is angrily abused. A time may come when that saying, already denounced by you as the saying of demagogues, 'That which sounds well is not wrong,' may become altered to 'All that does not sound well is wrong.'
>
> …
>
> Warn the youth who composes. Fruit that ripens too early, falls before its time. The young mind must often unlearn theory, before it can be put in practice.

Another rich source of such maxims is found under the title, 'Maxims for Young Musicians,' which were published in 1848 together with his *Album for Youth*, op. 68. As there is nothing else like them in music history, we will quote them at length.

> The cultivation of the ear is of the greatest importance. Endeavor, in good time, to distinguish tones and keys. The bell, the windowpane, the cuckoo—seek to discover what tones they produce.
>
> …
>
> You must practice scales and other finger exercises industriously. There are people, however, who think they may achieve great ends by doing this; up to an advanced age, for many hours daily, they practice mechanical exercises. That is as reasonable as trying to recite the alphabet faster and faster every day. Find a better use for your time.
>
> …

'Dumb keyboards' have been invented; practice on them for a while in order to see that they are worthless. Dumb people cannot teach us to speak.

...

Play in time! The playing of some virtuosos resembles the walk of a drunken man. Do not make these your models.

...

Learn the fundamental laws of harmony at an early age.

...

Do not be afraid of the words, 'theory,' 'thorough bass,' 'counterpoint,' etc.; they will meet you halfway if you do the same.

...

Never strum! Always play energetically and never fail to finish the piece you have begun.

...

Dragging and hurrying are equally great faults.

...

Try to play easy pieces well; it is better than to play difficult ones poorly.

...

See to it that your instrument is always in perfect tune.

...

It is not enough for your fingers to know your pieces; you should be able to hum them to yourself, away from the pianoforte. Sharpen your power of imagination so that you may be able to remember correctly not only the melody of a composition, but likewise its proper harmonies.

...

Try to sing at sight, without the help of an instrument, even if you have but little voice; your ear will thereby gain in refinement. If you possess a sonorous voice, however, do not lose a moment's time but cultivate it immediately, and look upon it as a most precious gift bestowed by Heaven.

...

You must reach the point where you can hear the music from the printed page.

...

When you play, do not concern yourself with who may be listening.

...

Always play as though a master were present.

...

Should anyone place an unknown composition before you, asking you to play it, first read it over.

...

If you have finished your daily musical work and feel tired, do not force yourself to labor further. It is better to rest than to practice without joy or freshness.

...

When you grow older, avoid playing what is merely fashionable. Time is precious. It would require a hundred lives merely to get acquainted with all the good music that exists.

...

No children can be brought to healthy manhood on candy and pastry. Spiritual like bodily nourishment must be simple and solid. The masters have provided it; cleave to them.

...

Virtuoso tricks change with the times; only where proficiency services higher purposes has it value.

...

You ought not help to spread bad compositions, but, on the contrary, help to suppress them with all your force.

...

Never play bad compositions and never listen to them when not absolutely obliged to do so.

...

Do not seek to attain mere technical proficiency—the so-called *bravura*. Try to produce with each composition the effect at which the composer aimed. No one should attempt more, anything further is mere caricature.

...

Question older artists concerning the choice of pieces for study; thus you will save much time.

...

You must gradually learn to know all the most important works of all the important masters.

...

Do not let yourself be led astray by the applause bestowed on great virtuosos. The applause of an artist ought to be dearer to you than that of the majority.

...

To play overmuch in society is more injurious than advantageous. Study your audience; yet never play anything of which in your own heart you feel ashamed.

...

Lose no opportunity for making music in company with others, in duos, trios, etc. This will render your playing more fluent and sweeping. Accompany singers often.

...

If all were determined to play the first violin, we should never have a complete orchestra. Therefore respect every musician in his proper field.

...

As you grow older, converse more frequently with scores than with virtuosos.

...

Industriously practice the fugues of good masters; above all, those of J. S. Bach. Let the *Well-Tempered Clavichord* be your daily meat. Then you will certainly become an able musician.

...

Seek out among your comrades those who know more than you do.

...

Rest from your musical studies by industriously reading the poets. Often take exercise out in the open.

...

Much is to be learned from singers male and female. But do not believe all they tell you.

...

The study of the history of music and the hearing of masterworks of different epochs will speediest of all cure you of vanity and self-adoration.

...

Lose no opportunity of practicing on the organ; there is no instrument which takes a swifter revenge on anything unclear or sloppy in composition and playing.

...

Regularly sing in choruses, especially the middle voices. This will make you musical.

...

What do we mean by being musical? You are not so when, with eyes painfully fixed on the notes, you struggle through a piece; you are not so when you stop short and find it impossible to proceed because someone has turned over two pages at once.

But you are musical when, in playing a new piece, you almost foresee what is coming; when you play an old one by heart; in short, when you have taken music not only into your fingers, but into your heart and head. How may one become musical in this sense? Dear student, the principal requisites, a fine ear and a swift power of comprehension, come, like all things, from above. But this foundation may and must be improved and enlarged. You cannot do this by shutting yourself up all day like a hermit, practicing mechanical exercises, but by a vital, many-sided musical activity; especially by familiarizing yourself with chorus and orchestral works.

...

Listen attentively to all folk songs. These are mines of the most beautiful melodies and will teach you the characteristics of the different nations.

...

Start early to observe the tone and character of the different instruments; try to impress the tone color peculiar to each upon your ear.

...

Never miss an opportunity of hearing a good opera.

...

Highly honor the old, but also meet the new with a warm heart.

...

Cherish no prejudice against unknown names.

...

Do not judge a composition on first hearing; that which pleases most at first is not always the best. Masters call for study. Many things will only become clear to you when you are old.

...

In judging compositions decide as to whether they belong in the realm of art, or merely in the domain of superficial entertainment. Stand for the first and do not let the other irritate you.

...

It is very nice indeed if you can pick out little melodies on the keyboard; but if such come spontaneously to you, and not at the pianoforte, rejoice even more, for it proves your inner sense of tone is awakening. Fingers must do what the head wills; not vice versa.

...

Acquire knowledge of conducting early; frequently observe good conductors; and nothing forbids you to conduct silently along with them. This will give you clarity.

...

Have an open eye for life as well as the other arts and sciences.

...

The laws of morality are also those of art.

...

You will steadily progress through industry and perseverance.

...

Nothing worthwhile can be accomplished in art without enthusiasm.

...

Only when the form is quite clear to you will the spirit become clear to you.

...

Possibly genius alone entirely understands genius.

...

Someone has declared that a perfect musician ought to be able to picture a piece which he is hearing for the first time, even the most complicated of orchestral pieces, as though he had the score before him. That is the limit of the imaginable.

...

There is no end to learning.

Finally, there are some interesting observations on the teaching of music which are found among Schumann's writing as a critic. First, a topic he was always sensitive about, teachers who limit the work of the student.

> Method, school mannerisms, advance improvement indeed, but narrowly, one-sidedly. Ah, teachers! How ye sin against yourselves! ... Like falconers, you pull out your pupils' feathers, lest they should fly too high! You should be guide-posts to point out the way, but not to run along the road yourselves also.[2]

[2] 'From the Criticisms of the Davidsbündler,' in *Neue Zeitschrift fur Musik*, 1834. Quoted in Ritter, Op. cit., 195ff.

We find an interesting note on repertoire:

> Do not give Beethoven to the children; strengthen them with Mozart, brimming with rich vitality. There are sometimes natures that seem to develop in opposition to the ordinary way, but there are natural laws which, if opposed, resemble the overturned torch, that consumes its bearer when it should have illuminated his path.[3]

[3] 'Theodore Stein,' 1834, in Ibid., 139.

And another perspective on repertoire:

> No one can become a master without previously becoming a scholar; even the master, indeed, is merely a superior kind of scholar, and Beethoven's *Sonata in Bb Major*, the uniquely great, was preceded by thirty-one other Beethovenian sonatas.[4]

[4] 'Sonatas for Pianoforte,' 1839, in Ibid., II, 270.

25 Chopin on Music Education

THE LETTERS OF CHOPIN reveal a very bored music teacher and if it were not necessary for financial reasons it seems clear he would have never given a lesson. His description of sitting through a lesson with a pedestrian student will recall similar feelings of some student in every teacher.

> I cannot bear to hear the doorbell; some person in whiskers, huge, tall, superb—comes in, sits down to the piano and improvises he doesn't know what, bangs and pounds without any meaning, throws himself about, crosses his hands, clatters on one key for five minutes with an enormous thumb that once belonged in the Ukraina, holding the reins or wielding a bailiff's cudgel. Here you have a portrait of Sowinsky … If ever I have seen a clear picture of charlatanism or stupidity in art, it is now … My ears burn; I could fling him out the doors; but I must spare his feelings.[1]

[1] Letter to Tytus Wojciechowski, Dec. 25, 1831.

On the other hand, he is somewhat more cheerful when speaking of better students. Nevertheless, he reminds his correspondent that he only teaches for money.

> The pupils of the Conservatoire, Moscheles' pupils, those of Herz and Kalkbrenner—in a word, finished artists, take lessons from me.
> …
> I have five lessons to give today; you think I am making a fortune? Carriages and white gloves cost more, and without them one would not be in good taste.[2]

[2] Letter to Dominik Dziewanowski, 1832.

Letters of the following years again suggest that teaching was boring and painful for Chopin. In the second excerpt which follows he reveals he was actually writing a letter while the student was playing.

> Why must it be twelve already? At twelve I have to give a lesson and to keep on till six.[3]
> …
> I must sit like a stone till five o'clock, giving lessons (just finishing the second one). God knows what will come of it.[4]
> …

[3] Letter to Teresa Wodzinska, Nov. 1, 1836.

[4] Letter to Wojciech Grzymala, undated.

It will soon be time to think of the treadmill, that is: the lessons.[5]

[5] Letter to his family, Oct. 11, 1846.

When Chopin had become very famous he had to accept a stream of wealthy ladies who wanted to say they had studied with him.

Yesterday I had to give seven lessons … Today I have to give a lesson to young Mme Rothschild, then to a lady from Marseilles, then to an Englishwoman, then to a Swedish one.[6]

[6] Letter to his family, April 19, 1847.

A similar letter continues at length with his complaints about teaching the ladies of society who really had little interest in the art of music.

Here and there I am beginning to get a reputation, but it needs time … But what are not so plentiful as they say, are guineas. There's a great deal of lying; directly they don't want anything, they have gone into the country. One lady pupil of mine has gone into the country without paying for nine lessons; and others, who are supposed to take two lessons a week, usually miss both; so there is more pretense than act. I'm not surprised, because they are trying to do too much all round. One pupil came here from Liverpool for a week! I gave her five lessons, as they don't play on Sunday, and she is satisfied. Lady Peel, for instance, wants me to give lessons to her daughter, who has a great deal of ability, but, as she has had a teacher who took half a guinea twice a week she wants me to give only one lesson a week, so that the effect on her purse shall be the same. This is to be able to say that she is having lessons from me; and she will probably leave town in two weeks.[7]

[7] Letter to Wojciech Grzymala, July 8–17, 1848.

If the truth were known, Chopin was probably not the first bored teacher who became that way in part from his own personal experience as a student. His own letters give us hints of the rather proficient, but uninspired teachers he had to suffer under in his youth.

I go to Elsner for strict counterpoint, six hours a week.[8]

…

No one here wants to take me as a pupil. Blahetka said nothing surprised him so much as my having learned all that in Warsaw. I answered that under Zywny and Elsner the greatest donkey could learn.[9]

[8] Letter to Jan Bialoblocki, Nov. 2, 1826.

[9] Letter to his family, Aug. 19, 1829.

It is clear that Jozef Elsner was a teacher he respected, as he mentions in a letter of 1830.

> The Official Bulletin says that if I had fallen into the hands of some pedant or Rossinist—which is a stupid term—I should not have been what I am. I am nothing, but he is right in saying that, if I had not been taught by Elsner, who imbued me with convictions, I should doubtless have accomplished still less than I now have.[10]

[10] Letter to Tytus Wojciechowski, April 10, 1830.

In one letter Chopin mentions Kalkbrenner, who was a respected composer and teacher, but he was, from Chopin's perspective, a teacher that moved too slowly.

> Kalkbrenner and I meet daily; either he comes to me or I go to him; and on closer acquaintance he has made me an offer; that I should study with him for three years, and he will make something really—really out of me. I answered that I know how much I lack; but that I cannot exploit him, and three years is too much.[11]

[11] Letter to Tytus Wojciechowski, Dec. 12, 1831.

In a long letter to his old teacher, Elsner, Chopin reflects on some of his experience studying in Paris.

> I know how much I lack and how far I have to go if I am to approach any standard of yours, I still made bold to think: 'At least I shall get a little nearer to him.'
>
> ...
>
> To be a great composer, one must have enormous knowledge, which, as you have taught me, demands not only listening to the work of others, but still more listening to one's own.
>
> ...
>
> Here and there in Germany I am known as a pianist; certain musical papers have spoken of my concerts, raising hopes that I shall shortly be seen taking rank among the first virtuosi of my instrument ... Today only one possibility offers for the fulfillment of this promise; why should I not seize it? In Germany I could not have learned the piano from anyone; for though there were persons who felt that I still lack something, no one knew what; and I also could not see the beam in my own eye which still prevents my looking higher. Three years of study with Kalkbrenner are a long time; too long; even Kalkbrenner admits that, now that he has examined more closely ... But I would be willing to stick to it for three years, if that will only enable me to take a big step forward in what I have undertaken. I understand enough not to become a copy of Kalkbrenner; nothing will interfere with my perhaps overbold but at least not ignoble desire to create a new world for myself; and if I work, it is in order to have a firmer standing.[12]

[12] Letter to Jozef Elsner, Dec. 14, 1831.

26 *Mendelssohn on Music Education*

THE EXTENSIVE CORRESPONDENCE of Felix Mendelssohn (1809–1847) reveals him to always be a very honest and perceptive observer. These characteristics are also representative of his comments on music education. An early letter shows him concerned about the availability of good teaching materials. This, of course, will always be a problem, for the part of the brain which writes books knows nothing about the experiential nature of music.

> Every day I give little Mademoiselle L. an hour's instruction in double counterpoint, and four-part composition, etc., which makes me realize more than ever the stupidity and confusion of most masters and books on the subject; for nothing can be clearer than the whole thing when properly explained.[1]

[1] Letter to his family, Oct. 6, 1831, quoted in G. Selden-Goth (ed.), *Felix Mendelssohn Letters* (New York: Kraus Reprint, 1969), 175.

A charming letter concerns a difficult and untalented student who had become frustrating for Mendelssohn. Mendelssohn's natural good humor is exhibited here as he portrays himself pontificating for the purpose of pontificating.

> A young musician has just been here with an atrocious fugue for me to look through; also another native genius who feels an impulse to write chorales, enough to make one turn yellow with impatience; and yet he has written chorales ever since I came here, the last always worse than the one before it; and as we go on being vexed with one another, there are some lively scenes, he not being able to understand that I still find his composition bad, and I that he has not improved them. I am, however, the very type of a good Cantor, and preach so much to the point that it is great fun to hear me.[2]

[2] Letter to Charlotte Moscheles, May 124, 1834, quoted in Felix Moscheles, *The Letters of Mendelssohn* (New York, Books for Libraries Press, Reprint, 1970), 110.

There is a particularly interesting letter of 1839 written to a father regarding the progress of his son's study under Mendelssohn. Of special interest is Mendelssohn's doubts of his own ability as a teacher, his recall of his own experience as a student and his remarks on the influence of the family.

> I am convinced, from repeated experience, that I am totally deficient in the talent requisite for a practical teacher, and for giving regular progressive instruction; whether it be that I take too little pleasure in tuition, or have not sufficient patience for it, I cannot tell, but, in short, I do not succeed in it. Occasionally, indeed, young people have stayed with me, but any improvement they have derived was solely from our studying music together, from unreserved intercourse, or casual conversation on various subjects, and also from discussions; and none of these things are compatible with actual teaching. Now the question is, whether in such early youth a consecutive, unremitting, strict course of discipline be not of more value than all the rest? It also appears to me that the estrangement of your son from the paternal roof just at his age forms a second, and not less important, objection. Where the rudiments of education are not wholly wanting … , then I consider that the vicinity of his parents, and the prosecution of the usual elements of study, the acquirement of languages, and the various branches of scholarship and science, are of more value to the boy than a one-sided, even though more perfect, cultivation of his genius. In any event such genius is sure to force its way to the light, and to shape its course accordingly, and in riper years will submit to no other permanent vocation, so that the early acquired treasures of interest, and the hours enjoyed in early youth under the roof of a parent, become doubly dear. I speak in this strain from my own experience, for I can well remember that in my fifteenth year there was a question as to my studying with Cherubini in Paris, and I know how grateful I was to my father at this time, and often since, that he at last gave up the idea, and kept me with himself.
>
> …
>
> I quite agree that it is most essential to cultivate pianoforte playing at present as much as possible, and not to fail in studying Cramer's exercises assiduously and steadily; but along with this daily training on the piano, two hours a week devoted to thorough-bass might be useful, as such a variety would be a pleasant change, rather than an interruption. The latter study indeed ought to be pursued in an easy and almost playful manner, and chiefly the practical part, that of deciphering and playing figured bass; these are the main points, and can be entirely mastered in a short time; but the sooner it is begun, the sooner is it got quit of, and this is always a relief with such dry things.[3]

[3] Letter to Professor Naumann, Sept. 19, 1839, quoted in Lady Wallace (trans.), *Letters of Felix Mendelssohn Bartholdy, from 1833 to 1847* (New York: Books for Libraries Press, Reprint, 1970), 168.

In the last decade of the eighteenth century the national military school of music in Paris was founded and by the early years of the ninteenth century it had become what is today the Paris Conservatoire. This model of an organized institution of musical instruction, teaching all the branches of music, was the envy of other countries. In a letter of 1840, Mendelssohn argues for the establishment of a similar national school of music. Of most interest to us are the values he presents for the need of such a school.

For a long time, music has been indigenous to this country, and just that trend which must lie nearest the heart of every ardent and thoughtful friend of art, namely the feeling for what is true and genuine, has always been able to strike roots in this soil. Such universal sympathy is certainly neither accidental nor has it been without important results for general education. Music has thus become an important factor—not a mere fleeting pleasure, but a spiritual and intellectual necessity. Whoever has a sincere interest in this art must eagerly desire to see its future in this land established on the most solid foundations possible. But the positive, and technically materialistic tendencies of the present day render the preservation of a genuine sense of art, and its further development, a doubly important, but also a doubly difficult task. It seems that this can be achieved only by working from the ground up; and as the expansion of sound instruction is the best mode of preserving every species of intellectual development, so it certainly is with music, too. If we had a good Music Academy which embraced all the various branches of this art, and taught them from one sole point of view, merely as the means to a higher end, and guided all its students as far as possible toward this goal, then this practical, materialistic tendency which, alas! can number, even among our artists, many influential followers, might yet be effectually checked. Mere private instruction, which once bore much good fruit, also for life in general, now, for many reasons, no longer suffices. Formerly, music students who learned to play various instruments were to be found in every class of society, whereas now the number of amateurs has become more and more reduced and those that are left confine themselves preferably to one instrument, the piano. The students who desire further instruction are almost invariably those who intend to devote themselves to this profession but who lack the means to pay for good private lessons. It is true that the best talents are often to be found amongst them, but, on the other hand, teachers are seldom placed in such fortunate circumstances as to be able to devote their time, without remuneration, to the training of even the greatest talents; thus both sides suffer; the former are deprived of the longed-for instruction, and the latter of the chance to impart their knowledge and keep its influence alive. A public institution would, therefore, just now be important to teachers as well as to pupils. These latter would be given the means of cultivating abilities which otherwise would often be wasted. But for the teachers of music it would be equally important; for to work in a group which has a common point of view and a common goal is the best means of preventing indifference and isolation, whose unfruitfulness these days can become genuinely harmful all too quickly.[4]

[4] Letter to the Kreisdirektor von Falkenstein, April 8, 1840, quoted in Selden-Goth, op. cit., 291.

Once ministers of government and pure academics, rather than artists, began to submit ideas regarding the foundation of a national school of music, Mendelssohn was shocked at the direction the idea was taking. In a letter to his brother he confides,

> Remarkable, very remarkable, these statutes of the Berlin Academy are, especially those of the school for composition. Imagine! Out of eleven different branches of instruction which they have instituted, seven are positively useless, and indeed preposterous. What do you think of the following, among others? Nr. 8: 'The relation Music bears to the other arts, especially to the *plastic* and to the stage' and also Nr. 11: 'A guide to the spiritual and worldly Drama.' I formerly read these things in the Government paper, and laughed at them; but when a grave minister or official actually sends such stuff, it is pitiable.[5]

[5] Letter to his Brother, Paul, Feb. 13, 1841, quoted in Wallace, op. cit., 217.

It appears that the more Mendelssohn thought about the nature of a national school of music, and the more he disagreed with the proposals he was hearing, the more concerned he became. At length he wrote a formal memo on the question, entitled 'Memorandum on the Music Academy to be Established in Berlin.' The most interesting to the reader today is Mendelssohn's view of an appropriate curriculum.

> It is proposed to establish a German Music Academy in Berlin, to concentrate in one common focus the now isolated efforts in the sphere of instruction in art, in order to guide rising artists in a solid and earnest direction, thus imparting to the musical sense of the nation a new and more energetic impetus; for this purpose, on one side, the already existing institutes and their members must be concentrated, and on the other, the aid of new ones must be called in.
>
> Among the former may be reckoned the various Royal Academies for musical instruction, which must be united with this Musical Academy, and carried on as branches of the same, with greater or less modifications, in *one* sense and in *one* direction. In these are included, for example, the Institute for Students of the Royal Orchestra; the Organ Institute; that of the Theater for instruction in singing, declamation, etc. Further, the members of the Royal Kapelle must be required to give instruction on their various instruments. A suitable locality can no doubt be found among the royal buildings, and also a library, with the requisite old and new musical works, scores and books.

The new appointments to consist of:

[1] A head teacher of composition; the best that can be found in Germany, to give regular instructions in theory, thorough-bass, counterpoint and fugues.

[2] A head teacher of solo singing; also the best to be had in Germany.

[3] A head teacher of choral singing, who should strive to acquire personal influence over the scholars under his care, by good pianoforte playing and steady direction.

[4] A head teacher of pianoforte playing, for which office a man of the most unquestionable talent and reputation must alone be selected.

The other teachers for these departments could be found in Berlin itself; nor would there be any difficulty in procuring teachers of Aesthetics, the history of music, etc.

The complete course to last three years; the scholars, after previous examination, to be instructed gratis; no prize works to be admitted but at stated periods; all the works of the scholars, from the time of their admission, to be collected and criticized in connection with each other, and subsequently a prize (probably consisting of a sum sufficient for a long journey through Germany, Italy, France and England) is to be adjudged accordingly. Every winter a certain number of concerts to take place, in which all the teachers (including the above-named members of the royal Kapelle) must co-operate, and by which, through the selection of the music, as well as by its execution, direct influence may be gained over the majority of the public.

The following principle must serve as a basis for the whole Institute: that every sphere of art can only elevate itself above a mere handicraft, by being devoted to the expression of lofty thought, along with the utmost possible technical finish, and a pure and intellectual aim; that also solidity, precision, and strict discipline in teaching and learning should be considered the first law, thus not falling short in this respect of any handicraft; that in every department, all teaching and learning should be exclusively devoted to the thoughts intended to be expressed, and to that more elevated mood, to which technical perfection in art must ever be subordinate.[6]

[6] Quoted in Wallace, op. cit., 233.

Mendelssohn adds another thought in a letter to his former teacher, Moscheles.

The pupils all want to compose and to theorize, whilst I believe that the principal thing that can and ought to be taught is sound practical work,—sound playing and keeping time, sound knowledge of sound music, etc. Out of that, all other knowledge grows of itself; and what is beyond is not a matter of teaching, but must come as a gift from above.[7]

[7] Letter to Ignaz Moscheles, April 30, 1843, quoted in Moscheles, op. cit., 242.

We wish to pass on another letter, this one dealing with private instruction in piano. In regard to his quotation that Clara Schumann asked for two thalers per lesson, we can help put that in perspective by noting that he mentions that the annual rent of a seven or eight room apartment was three hundred and fifty thalers per year, a good cook at forty thalers per year and a housemaid at thirty-two.

> It is difficult to fix the terms for your teaching piano lessons, even approximately, for there is no precedent in Leipzig to go by. Madame Schumann-Wieck asked 2 thalers, but at that price found but few pupils, and those mostly among foreigners spending a short time here.[8]

[8] Letter to Ignaz Moscheles, Jan. 17, 1846, quoted in Selden-Goth, op. cit., 348.

27   *Liszt on Music Education*

FRANZ LISZT WAS BY ANY MEASURE one of the great musicians and personalities of the nineteenth century. For the modern musician the span of time he represented is perhaps not so impressive in the actual length in years, 1811–1886, as in the fact that he knew *in person* both Beethoven and Debussy! As a music teacher, again the impressive thing is not so much his long service as a teacher as in the fact that pianists even today still speak of their relationship to him as a teacher. One will hear them say, for instance, 'I studied with a teacher, who studied with a teacher who was Liszt's pupil.' My own mother, Nevada Whitwell, studied piano with a student of Liszt who claimed that Liszt gave each of his students a different composition of his, which he coached in great detail and which became their personal responsibility to pass on to future generations. This man was assigned the *Liebestraume*, in which he then instructed his students, including my mother, in the personal style of Liszt. My mother continued to perform this work from memory for seventy years, often telling her audiences that this was how Liszt performed the work. Few teachers have had such direct and specific influence on future generations.

Liszt's personal remarks on teaching are varied and interesting. In this case we organize them by chronology and let them speak for themselves.

1829

I am so full of lessons that each day, from half-past eight in the morning till ten at night, I have scarcely breathing time … I don't write you a longer letter, for there is a pupil who has been waiting for me for an hour.[1]

[1] Letter to M. de Mancy, Dec. 23, 1829, quoted in La Mara, *Letters of Franz Liszt* (New York: Scribners, 1894), I, 5.

1831

I have my pupils go into the selections in depth, so that often one lesson is spent studying two pages.

…

Give all that you feel and do not encumber your touch.

…

Be patient with yourself. You ruin everything if you wish to hasten; calmly take each step in turn to be certain of reaching the top; be patient; nature itself works slowly. Follow its example. Your efforts, led wisely, will be honored with success, but if you want to acquire everything too quickly, you would lose time and fail.[2]

1842

It is in vain for me to attempt to express to you the deep and heartfelt emotion you have aroused in me by your rare mark of honor ... The honorable name of *Teacher* of Music (and I refer to music in its grand, complete and *ancient* signification), by which you esteemed gentlemen, dignify me, I am well aware that I have undertaken the duty of unceasing *learning* and untiring labor.[3]

1856

Don't forget to let me have your Methode ... Although I have grown too old and too lazy to improve my piano playing, yet I will get some good out of it for my pupils, amongst whom are two or three really brave, earnest fellows.[4]

Your X is a perfect madman, and I should certainly not advise you to have anything to do with a man like him. He asked me to attend a vocal practice of his pupils, when the poor people had to shout nothing but four or five notes do, de, da! X has entirely surrendered himself to his monomania of method, which to him has become a kind of dram-drinking.[5]

1872

Von Bulow's edition of Beethoven outweighs in the matter of instruction a dozen Conservatories.[6]

1874

It would be a poor luxury to add a third music school to the two schools already existing (meagerly) at Budapest. If one cannot emulate with honor the similar establishments of Vienna, Leipzig, etc.—what is the good of troubling any further about it? Now to give a vigorous impulse to Art among us, we must first unite and fuse into one spirit a set of professors of well-known capability,—a very arduous and ungrateful task, the accomplishment of which demands much intelligence, and a sufficient amount of cleverness and money.[7]

1876

On March 2 I shall start my course of piano lessons with eight or ten pupils of both sexes.[8]

[2] Comments of Liszt noted in the lesson diary of Mme. Auguste Boissier, 1831–1832, quoted in Elyse Mach, *The Liszt Studies* (New York: Associated Music Publishers, 1973), xi.

[3] Letter to the Faculty of Philosophy, University of Konigsberg, March 18, 1842, quoted in La Mara, op. cit., I, 56.

[4] Letter to Louis Kohler, May 24, 1856, quoted in La Mara, op. cit., I, 271.

[5] Letter to Richard Wagner, Dec. 25, 1856, quoted in Ashton Ellis (ed.), *Correspondence of Wagner and Liszt* (New York: Haskell House, 1969), II, 170.

[6] Letter to Otto Lessmann, Sept. 26, 1872, quoted in La Mara, op. cit., II, 220.

[7] Letter to Edmund von Mihalovich, Dec. 8, 1874, quoted in ibid., II, 267.

[8] Letter to Olga von Meyendorff, Feb. 20, 1876, quoted in William R. Tyler (trans.), *The Letters of Franz Liszt to Olga von Mayendorff 1871–1886* (Washington: Dumbarton Oaks, 1979), 234.

I shall remain here quietly until mid-March, teaching a dozen pianists of both sexes at the new Academy of Music. Part of my instruction consists of telling them that several hundred of their profession are already 'in excess' in this world of 'concerts' and harmony trimmed with dissonance.[9]

⁹ Letter to Marie zu Sayn-Wittgenstein, Nov. 20, 1876, quoted in Howard E. Hugo, ed., *The Letters of Franz Liszt to Marie zu Sayn-Wittgenstein* (Cambridge: Harvard University Press, 1953), 205.

1877

Four times weekly I have a class for pianists and pianists, native and foreign. Half a dozen of these distinguish themselves and will be able to grow into capable public artists. Unfortunately there are far too many concerts and concert-players. As Dingelstedt quite truly said, 'The theater is a necessary evil, the concert a superfluous one.' I am trying to impress this sentence on my disciples of the Hungarian Academy of Music.[10]

[10] Letter to Eduard Liszt, Jan. 2, 1877, quoted in La Mara, op. cit., II, 312.

Mme Schumann having in the past been so kind as to play this transcription [*Prelude and Fugue* in A minor] in public, it has been accepted as tolerable, even in the conservatories of the pure conservatories where my name is excluded, and is considered an insult to sound doctrine.[11]

[11] Letter to Olga von Meyendorff, May 20, 1877, quoted in Tyler, op. cit., 276.

The work best praises the Master: in like manner do the pupils, when preparing themselves for pre-eminence, praise their teacher.[12]

[12] Letter to Kornel von Abranyi, July 28, 1877, quoted in La Mara, op. cit., II, 317.

My chief occupation here is teaching the piano to about fifteen people, of whom seven or eight already show remarkable talent; let me name M. de Rossel who comes from Kharkov, as did Joseph Rubinstein five years ago … ; M. Roth, a pupil of Reinecke and several times a prize winner at Leipzig; two Hungarians, Juhary and Agghazy. This whole young generation will be more deserving than in the two preceding ones to which I belong, while at the same time facing more obstacles than these on the road to fame and—to box office receipts. So I do not fail to repeat clearly to young pianists that most of them are superfluous, and that only male and female singers for opera are in demand and hence well paid.[13]

[13] Letter to Olga von Meyendorff, Dec. 9, 1877, quoted in Tyler, op. cit., 302.

1878

My three pianists whom you saw at Weimar, MM. Roth, Pohlig and Brunner, are hard at work here. I give them my brief instructions in the Sala Dante … In my rooms in the Via de' Greci I wish neither to see nor hear any piano.[14]

[14] Letter to Olga von Meyendorff, Oct. 23, 1878, quoted in ibid., 310.

1879

Your *Paraphrases* charm me: nothing can be more ingenious than these 24 Variations and the 16 little pieces ... In short, here we have an admirable compendium of the science of harmony, of counterpoint, of rhythms, of figuration, and ... 'the Theory of Form'! I shall gladly suggest to the teachers of composition at all the Conservatoires in Europe and America to adopt your *Paraphrases* as a practical guide in their teaching.[15]

1880

My pianists (of both sexes) come here three times a week for their treatment. There are ten or twelve, of whom a third are making good progress.[16]

1885

With regret, and a firm conviction, I repeat to you in writing that Khedor Kullak's forgetfulness ought to be made good by his heirs. Otherwise it would be severely denounced as unfaithfulness to his position as an artist. A fortune of several millions gained by music teaching ought not to remain buried without any regard to music students. Unless the heirs prefer to found a Kullak Scholarship, I consider that they are in duty bound to endow the four existing musical scholarships—those in the names of Mozart, Mendelssohn, Meyerbeer and Beethoven—with 30,000 marks each.[17]

1886

I spend a couple of hours a day with my students.[18]

---

[15] Letter to Borodin, Cui, Liadoff and Rimsky-Korsakoff, June 15, 1879, quoted in La Mara, op. cit., II, 353.

[16] Letter to Olga von Meyendorff, Jan. 22, 1880, quoted in Tyler, op. cit., 368.

[17] Letter to the Editor of the *Allgemeine Musik-Zeitung*, Sept. 5, 1885, quoted in La Mara, op. cit., II, 474.

[18] Letter to Olga von Meyendorff, Feb. 24, 1886, quoted in Tyler, op. cit., 492.

28 *Berlioz on Music Education*

HECTOR BERLIOZ (1803–1869) was not only a great composer, as everyone knows, but also a great writer. He is not so well known as a writer only because his vast body of some four hundred lengthy newspaper articles have never been republished. In this essay we will quote from some of those which deal with music education. We can only wish he had written more, for as always he was a careful observer of everything going on around him which dwelt with music.

In 1835 he published an article decrying the fact that music was not part of the education of all children in France. He sarcastically quotes a French slogan of the day, the same we hear from the MENC, that Music is for every child. His point is that we really do not believe that, because we do not teach music to every child.

> It is not necessary to come to [composers] to give us philanthropic theories on the popularity of the arts: music is not made for everyone because of the simple reason that every one is not made for music. We have already said it, and we will not tire of repeating it. That is rigorously true, but it is, especially in France, desperately in evidence. With us, is music a part of the education of the people? Do they teach choral singing and playing of instruments in the public schools? Does the army participate in this teaching? Well, good Lord! Listen to the songs of our workers when they return from the gates on holidays; go into the schools, into the barracks; attend the harmonic frolics of children and soldiers, and tell us if what you hear does not much more resemble the howling of fighting Hurons, than the song of civilized men. With us, the people only retain musical scraps, which it denatures more or less. They have never been able to sing from one end to the other even the shortest tune if it includes the least modulation, the slightest accent different from the practices of vaudeville tunes. As an example, I bear a grudge against 'The Marseillaise.' Out of fifty thousand individuals who think they know that famous national hymn, there are not one hundred, quite certainly, who can sing it to the end without gross errors; they sing easily the beginning and the end, but at the minor,
>
> *Entendez-vous dans les campagnes*
> *Mugir ces farouches soldats!*

> The sentiment of tonality and of melodic form completely escapes them; there is no more than a horrible cacophony that stops short a part of the singers, for the others continue bravely without wondering at the fact that they are singing in three or four different tones, and who only stop at the refrain,
>
> *Aux arms, citoyens.*
>
> What does music have in common with such organizations? Musical art is a power, which, coming from the thought of the composer, addresses, through interpreters, alas too rarely faithful, to certain organs, to certain emotions, to certain ideas of the human being, to move some, excite and ennoble others, in an aim, if not of utility, at least of noble pleasure, high and delicate. How can its action be exercised on a people in whom the organs, emotions and ideas absolutely are lacking? Whether it is a fact of nature, a fault of education, or, what is worse, a vicious education, does not matter; it is sufficient to ascertain it to prove the absurdity of this proposition trafficked by many people in France: 'Music is made for everyone.' After that, in admitting that in the crowd that throngs to open air concerts, one can count on a great number of amateurs made for music, again I would prove, without doing my utmost to hunt for faults in the details of technique, that the principle on which these miserable attempts rest is false and not to be conceded.[1]

[1] *Journal des Debats*, July 21, 1835.

We have no information regarding how much, or little, influence the above article may have had, but one can see Berlioz's delight in the announcement the following year that some music would be introduced into the lower grades.

> It is difficult to foresee when French art will be able to gather the fruit of the recent decision of the Minister of Public Instruction, intended to introduce singing into primary school teaching; the teachers will be lacking yet for a good while. Little by little, however, they will be formed; and when musical sentiment, developed first in the normal schools, finally can issue forth and be communicated to that immense quantity of young students, deprived up until today of the means of instruction, when musical signs have become as familiar as letters of the alphabet to a great part of the nation; then, I think, one will be able to determine the truth of this opinion, already promulgated by several eminent artists: In the wise use of great masses lies the whole future of art.[2]

[2] *Journal des Debats*, July 23, 1836.

During this same month of July, 1836, Berlioz published a eulogy of a musician and teacher, Alexandre Choron (1771–1834). It seems likely, since Choron had been dead for two years, that Berlioz's real purpose was to influence the Minister of Public Instruction during the period when music in the primary schools was under discussion. In any case, Berlioz wrote a loving tribute to the qualities of a great teacher of any age.

Choron, only living through the life of his school: the students were he himself: outside of that, there was no longer any Choron; he offered the most complete realization of the ravishing ideal that the genius of Hoffman could make us love so much in 'The Violin of Cremona.' Uniting to the fantastic sensibility of Antonia all the oddities of Crespel, his soul was not in an instrument, but in a school of music; and, like Antonia dying at the moment when the mysterious violin is broken, so Choron was to die from the blow which struck his school. He was an artist in the highest meaning of the word, one of those fiery, fanatic, devout, jealous artists, martyrs for their faith, whose race becomes rarer every day ... He loved his students, gave them his time, his money; he exalted their merit, inflated their successes, had difficulty in understanding them, and other times, when their rebellious intelligence could not rise promptly to the compass of his own, he overwhelmed them with violent reproaches, with hard epithets, he beat them, he would have killed them for one wrong note too many. He must have suffered cruelly from so many disappointments coming one after another, after such beautiful hopes; he must have died a thousand times before the last time. And yet, he would not have asked for anything better than to live: in his moments of happiness, he was so completely, so profoundly happy. How his face beamed, the poor, great artist, when at the head of his troupe of children and young people of both sexes he left Paris to go for a walk in the fields. Having arrived at the plains of Montrouge, neighboring his dwelling, often in Springtime lost in the burgeoning wheat, how many times the children of harmony astonished the crude peasants with the magic of sublime hymns that the master had taught them ...

Ah! Poor Choron! What a soul! With what expansive force he was gifted! What would his intelligence have been capable of, if it had been understood and appreciated! What an instrument! What a lever for the one who would have known how to make use of it! But his school, calumniated under the rubric of Utility, stricken with reprobation; during the Revolution of July [1830], by the absurd prejudice that was attached to its title as an institution of religious music, little by little, it was seen to that all means of existence were withdrawn. His principal students had already left him to go into the theaters of France and abroad to make use of the excellent method ... others, retained yet for a time by sacrifices of all kinds by means of which Choron tried to stay his crumbling edifice, finally were dispersed, when the unhappy director saw the absolute impossibility of providing for their needs; and the door of the school, once closed on them, was never again opened, except to allow the withdrawal of its founder's casket.[3]

[3] *Journal des Debats*, July 3, 1836.

With regard to higher music education, Berlioz on several occasions argued for bringing the famous Paris Conservatoire up to date. At the time he wrote his *Memoirs,* he reviewed the progress and noted areas where instruction was still not available.

> Our Conservatoire was for long without classes in such essential instruments as double bass, trombone, trumpet and harp. These gaps have been filled in the last few years. Unfortunately many others remain ...
>
> (3) The omission of the basset horn from the syllabus of students of the clarinet was until recently a serious error, for it meant that a great deal of Mozart's music could not be performed properly in France—an absurd state of affairs. But now that Adolphe Sax has perfected the bass clarinet to the point where it can perform everything that lies within the range of the basset horn and more (it can play a minor third lower), and since its timbre is similar to the basset horn's but even more beautiful, the bass clarinet should be studied in conservatoires alongside the soprano clarinet and the smaller clarinets in Eb, F, and high Ab.
>
> (4) The saxophone, the latest member of the clarinet family, an instrument which will prove extremely useful when players have learnt to exploit its qualities, should be given its own separate position in the curriculum, for before long every composer will want to use it.
>
> (5) We have no class in the ophicleide, with the result that of the hundred or hundred and fifty persons in Paris at present blowing this exacting instrument, hardly three are fit to be in a good orchestra, and only one, M. Caussinus, is a really first-rate player.
>
> (6) We have no class in the bass tuba, a powerful rotary-valve instrument differing from the ophicleide in timbre, mechanism and range, its position in the trumpet family being exactly equivalent to that of the double bass in the violin family. Most modern scores include a part for either ophicleide or bass tuba, sometimes for both.
>
> (7) The saxhorn and the piston-valve cornet should be taught in our Conservatoire, both being now in general use, the cornet especially.
>
> (8) No instruction is given in percussion playing. Yet is there any orchestra in Europe, large or small, which does not possess a timpanist? They all have a functionary of that name; but how many are true timpanists, thorough-going musicians, accustomed to every complexity of rhythm, masters of the technique of the instrument—which is less easy than is commonly believed—and gifted with a keen ear sufficiently trained to enable them to tune and change key accurately, and to do so during a performance, with all the noise of the orchestra going on round them? I must positively state that, apart from the timpanist at

the Opera, M. Poussard, I know of only three in the whole of Europe—and I have had the opportunity of scrutinizing a few orchestras in the last nine or ten years. Most of the timpanists I met did not even know how to hold their sticks and were consequently helpless when it came to executing a true tremolo or roll. A timpanist who cannot manage a quick roll in every degree of loud and soft is a man of straw.

All conservatories ought therefore to have a class in percussion, in which students can acquire a thorough proficiency in timpani, tambourine and side-drum at the hands of first-rate musicians. The old convention, now no longer tolerable and already abandoned by Beethoven and one or two others, whereby the percussion was treated perfunctorily or in a crudely insensitive manner, undoubtedly helped to perpetuate its low status. Composers having till recently used it merely as a source of noise (more or less superfluous or actively disagreeable) or as a means of mechanically emphasizing the strong beats of the bar, it was assumed that this modest mission was all that it could or was meant to fulfill in the orchestra, and consequently that there was no need to go into the technique of the thing with any great care or to be a real musician in order to play it. In fact, it takes a very capable musician to play even some of the cymbal and bass-drum parts in modern scores.[4]

[4] David Cairns (ed.), *The Memoirs of Hector Berlioz* (London: Gollancz, 1969), 402.

In this same discussion, Berlioz also mentions problems in violin study and the fact that there were no classes in viola. He also notes the absence of classes in rhythm, music history, instrumentation and conducting.

He returned to this subject again in a newspaper article in 1857, adding some *special* classes for singers!

I still remember the time in the Conservatoire when there were no classes in harp, trumpet, trombone, or even any class in contrabass. Fortunately, we have in France in the highest degree the sense of the needs of musical art, and after having recognized that in all theater and concert orchestras there are contrabasses, trumpets, trombones and harps, the usefulness of these four classes in our great and beautiful school of music was admitted …

We only lack now in our musical instruction a half-dozen other instrumental classes, a class in instrumentation for composers, plus two or three classes in rhythm, a class in pronunciation, another in prosody, another in the French language, another in the history of music and ten or twelve classes of common sense for singers.[5]

[5] *Journal des Debats*, Feb. 3, 1857.

Finally, in an article of 1858, Berlioz brings to the attention of his readers the publication of what may have been the first band method book in France. The principle will seem very familiar to readers today who are acquainted with materials for elementary school bands.

> Mr. Charles Dupart has just published a teaching work which we think is truly useful for musicians who are destined for the military bands. Usually these young people receive hardly more than ten minutes of lessons each, three or four times a week. There are too many students for the number of teachers. To remove this problem, Mr. Dupart had the bright idea to write combined exercises for all the wind instruments. These exercises will at first be in one part and then in two parts written in octave, or double octave, and even in simple harmony. They are, thus, to be played by the flutes, clarinets, saxophones, sax-horns, cornets, horns, trombones, etc. The students, instead of sharing the teacher's time, can study the lesson together, under the teacher's direction. They will also become accustomed to playing together and this advantage is considerable. Mr. Dupart, in composing his *Methode polyphonique*, has thus rendered a true service to the study of wind instruments, and his work can not but encourage the development and progress of military bands in France.[6]

[6] *Journal des Debats*, Dec. 21, 1858.

29 *Wagner on Music Education*

RICHARD WAGNER (1813–1883), as we suppose everyone knows, was not only a very great composer but also wrote enough prose to represent a normal author's life work. Wagner is not easy to read. In German, he invents words, or strings of hyphenated words which then fall among numerous clauses in those endless nineteenth-century German sentences. The English translation by William Ashton Ellis, to whom all English speaking musicians must be indebted, no matter what, suffers from the same problems. Ellis, a ninteenth-century contemporary of Wagner, generally made the well-meaning mistake from trying to mirror the German in English, whereas it would have better honored the greatness of Wagner's mind if he would have made three sentences in English where there was one in German. Also Ellis used now archaic scholastic ninteenth-century English which includes many passages where the real meaning of Wagner's idea is nearly lost.[1] We have taken the liberty of modernizing some of Ellis' English.

Wagner, therefore, needs to be read when you have lots of care-free time, but the effort will be rewarded. Here our purpose is to give only a kind of outline of Wagner's basic ideas on higher music education, with the necessary sources for the reader who wishes to read in depth and give thought to his ideas.

Wagner's most extended writing on higher music education is found in an 1865 document entitled, 'Report to His Majesty King Ludwig II, of Bavaria upon a German Music School to be founded in Munich.'[2] After sending his report to the king, Wagner asked that a commission be formed to study the idea. The king appointed such a committee which met on 24 April 1865, in the persons of Wagner, Franz Lachner, Hans von Bulow and others. The government branch involved decided the entire proposal was too expensive, but two years later a school was founded in Munich with von Bulow as its head. It only took two years until the anti-Wagner forces not only forced von Bulow to resign, but leave town.

[1] As an illustration, for 'performance,' Ellis gives 'rendering.'

[2] Wagner's discussion is found in William Ashton Ellis, *Richard Wagner's Prose Works* (New York: Broude Brothers), IV, 173ff.

From among the ideas which Wagner put forth relative to a higher music school we will focus on just a few which we believe are particularly relevant to our society today.

First, Wagner repeatedly stresses that performance must be at the center of music education. The proposed music school, he writes,

> can be of profit only when it rigidly confines its work to the fostering of the art of performance.

He implies, in the text which follows, that the other studies can only have their meaning when centered in performance.

> The invisible bond, uniting the various branches of study, will always have to be the attendance of the students in performance.[3]

[3] ibid., IV, 196ff.

As an illustration, he points to the study of aesthetics, which we do not even teach today, and says this cannot be done

> through academic lectures, and the like, but here, too, we must strike the purely practical path of direct artistic exercise, under higher guidance for the performance.

And again,

> True aesthetics in music and the only intelligible history of music we must teach in no other way except in beautiful and correct performances of works of classical music.[4]

[4] ibid., IV, 200.

Wagner understood, as did all great composers before him, that music is not of the realm of conceptual data. Music is of the experiential side of the student. All thinking young musicians today must wonder how it was that American music education decided in the 1950s to go in the opposite direction and why the disastrous effects of that decision remain unrecognized by our doctors of education.

In another place,[5] Wagner speaks of this problem with respect to composers. He states that in the finest composer one does not see, or is not aware, of the earlier stages of learning, such as counterpoint. Who, he wonders, ever thinks of Mozart's education when listening to his *Figaro*? But, he sug-

[5] ibid., VIII, 57.

gests, composers often feel impelled to demonstrate the skill they have learned. But this is 'wrong-headed,' for the listener 'enjoys a clear, melodious thought.' In trying to demonstrate his learned skills, Wagner suggests, the composer only ends in 'turgid bombast.'

Another topic Wagner addresses is the tendency in music appreciation courses to add 'stories' to the music in the hope of providing meaning to the student.[6] He suggests that this only has the effect of preventing the listener from having the benefit of the direct communication with the composer, for the 'story' distracts his attention toward a non-musical end.

[6] This discussion is found in ibid., VII, 75ff.

We also appreciate the fact that Wagner draws our attention to the very word, 'conservatory.' It means, he writes, an institution to conserve something, which of course he says is classical music. In this discussion he observes, 'we possess classical works, but as yet no classic [rules of] performance for them.' This is the fundamental fault which he finds responsible for the German audiences of his time being ill-educated and often satisfied with mere entertainment.

Another of his observations, which seems to be related to this one, speaks of accepting the empty for the sound.

> The acceptance of the empty for the sound is desensitizing everything we possess in the way of schools, tuition, academies and so on, by ruining the most natural feelings and misguiding the faculties of the rising generation ... But that we should pay for all this, and have nothing left when we come to our senses ... is abominable![7]

[7] ibid., VI, 147.

Finally, we wish to draw the reader's attention to an example of Wagner's analysis of music, found in a private notebook dating from 1849, for it illustrates powerfully how far we are removed in how we talk about music today. In all other academic fields of art the lectures of professors do not stop with discussion of grammar. Specialists giving a class on the great works of Shakespeare, for example, do not mention the grammar of Shakespeare; they discuss the great themes of the individual plays.

It is *only* in the field of music that we discuss a masterpiece in terms of grammar. And usually that is *all* we discuss. Our hesitancy, if not inability, to discuss what the music is *really* about is why we invent 'stories' for the music appreciation classes.

There are even teachers of conducting who speak mainly of grammar, whereas their primary value to a student should be not in identifying the grammar on the page, but identifying what is not on the page.

In 1855, in Zurich, Wagner heard the amazing C-Sharp Minor Quartet by Beethoven and was deeply moved. He returned to his room to enter his impression in his notebook,[8] but he wrote nothing of Beethoven's grammar. He made no reference to keys and modulations, chromaticism or accidentals or development and variation, etc. Here was Wagner's analysis:

[8] ibid., VIII, 386.

> (Adagio) Melancholy morning-prayer of a deeply suffering heart: (Allegro) graceful apparition, rousing fresh desire of life. (Andante and variations). Charm, sweetness, longing, love. (Scherzo) Whim, humor, high spirits. (Finale) Passing over to resignation. Most sorrowful renunciation.

Illustrations

All artwork, illustrations, and photographs are either in the public domain or covered by a Creative Commons licence. Details of each illustration are below.

1 MUSIC EDUCATION BEFORE PLATO
The three musicians, Tomb of Nakht, Thebes, ca. 1422–1411 BC, Source/Photographer: Plate X, Orbis Pictus volume 30, Payot Lausanne, Printer: Hallwag S.A. Berne, public domain

2 PLATO ON MUSIC EDUCATION
Herm représenting Plato, marble, Roman copy after a Greek original from the last quarter of the fourth century, Artist Unknown, Museo Pio-Clementino, Sala delle Muse, Source/Photographer: Marie-Lan Nguyen (2006), public domain • Bust of Socrates, marble, Roman copy after a Greek original from the fourth century BC, from the Quintili Villa on the Via Appia, Museo Pio-Clementino, Muses Hall, Source/Photographer: Jastrow (2006), public domain

3 ARISTOTLE ON MUSIC EDUCATION
Aristotle teaching Alexander the Great, original source: http://www.mlahanas.de/Greeks/Alexander.htm, public domain • Bust of Aristotle, marble, Roman copy after a Greek bronze original by Lysippos from 330 BC, Ludovisi Collection, National Museum of Rome, Source/Photographer: Jastrow (2006), public domain

4 GREKK VIEWS ON MUSIC EDUCATION AFTER ARISTOTLE
Female musician playing an aulos, detail of a roman mosaic of a street scene with musicians from the Villa del Cicerone in Pompeii. The mosaic is signed by Dioskurides of Samos. Museo Archeologico Nazionale, Naples, public domain

5 MUSIC EDUCATION IN ANCIENT ROME
Title page of Quintilian's Institutio oratoria, ed. by Pieter Burman(n) the Elder, Leiden, 1720, public domain • Frontispiece of Quintilian's Institutio oratoria, ed. by Pieter Burman the Elder, Leiden 1720, the copper engraving by F. Bleyswyk shows Quintilian teaching rhetorics.

6 HOW THE CHURCH REINVENTED MUSIC EDUCATION
Sextus Empiricus, public domina • Medieval illustraion of Anicius Manlius Severinus Boëthius (a late-antique philosopher), public domain

7 MUSIC EDUCATION IN THE DARK AGES
Depiction of the Venerable Bede from the Nuremberg Chronicle, 1493, public domain • Emporer Charlegmagne by Albrecht Dürer, 1512, Location: Germanisches Nationalmuseum, Nuremberg, public domain

8 MUSIC EDUCATION IN THE PRE-RENAISSANCE
Map of Medieval Universities, Source: *Historical Atlas* by William R. Shepherd, New York, Henry Holt and Company, 1923, public domain

9 MUSIC EDUCATION IN THE FOURTEENTH CENTURY
Opening title of *The Dreame of Chaucer*, published 1532, public domain

10 MUSIC EDUCATION IN THE FIFTEENTH CENTURY
Portrait of Franchino Gaffurio, Milan, Leonardo da Vinci, ca. 1490, public domain • Self-portrait of Leonardo da Vinci, Turin, Royal Library (inv.no. 15571). ca. 1510–1515, public domain

11 MUSIC EDUCATION IN SIXTEENTH-CENTURY ITALY
Vincenzo Giustiniani by Nicolas Regner (ca. 1630), public domain • Gioseffo Zarlino, public domain • Gioseffo Zarlino's monochord for 2/7-comma meantone temperament, *Le istitutioni harmoniche* (1558), p. 130, public domain • Pico della Mirandola, 1400s, public domain • Giordano Phillipo Bruno from *Livre du recteur*, 1578, public domain

12 MUSIC EDUCATION IN SIXTEENTH-CENTURY FRANCE
Portrait of Pierre de Ronsard by François-Séraphin Delpech, lithograph, 18th/19th century, public domain • King Charles IX of France by François Clouet, public domain • Marin Mersenne, artist unknown, public domain • John Calvin by Georg Osterwald, 19th century, Source: Bibliothèque publique et universitaire de Neuchâtel - BPUN, public domain • Portrait of Marguerite de Navarre by Jean Clouet, Walker Art Gallery, Liverpool, UK, ca. 1530, public domain

13 MUSIC EDUCATION IN SIXTEENTH-CENTURY GERMANY
Moritz Landgraf von Hessen-Kassel by Matthaeus Merian, 1662, public domain • Philipp Melanchthon by Lucas Cranach, ca. 1537, public domain • Michael Praetorius, 1606, Source: *Die großen Deutschen im Bilde* (1936) by Michael Schönitzer • Titlepage of Michael Praetorius' *Syntagma Musicum*, public domain

14 MUSIC EDUCATION TREATISES OF SIXTEENTH-CENTURY GERMANY
Johannes Cochlaeus, artist unknown, public domain • Adrian Coclico, public domain

15 MARTIN LUTHER ON MUSIC EDUCATION
Martin Luther by Wenzel Hollar (1607–1677), Source: University of Toronto, public domain

16 MUSIC EDUCATION IN SIXTEENTH-CENTURY ENGLAND
Portrait of Henry VIII, Royal Collection, Windsor Castle, ca. 1560–80, after Hans Holbein the Younger, public domain • Title page for *The Compleat Gentleman* by Henry Peacham with elaborate border showing figures of 'Nobilitas' and 'Scientia', engraving by Francis Delaram, 1622, Source: United States Library of Congress, public domain • Sir Walter Raleigh, by 'H' monogrammist (fl. 1588), Source: National Portrait Gallery, London: NPG 7, public domain • Frontispiece of *The Civile Wares* with portrait of Samuel Daniel, 1609, Thomas Cockson, public domain

17 ON MUSIC EDUCATION IN BAROQUE ITALY
Tommaso Campanella by Nicolas de Larmassin, from Isaac Bullart's *Académie des Sciences et des Arts*, livre II, 1682, public domain • Tommaso Campanella, *Civitas Solis* (The City of the Sun), 1623, public domain • Jean-Jacques Rousseau by Maurice Quentin de La Tour, public domain • Il Pio Ospedale della Pietà in Venice, public domain • Antonio Vivaldi by François Morellon de la Cave, public domain

18 ON THE PHILOSOPHICAL ROOTS OF GERMAN MUSIC EDUCATION
Portrait of Johann Mattheson, 1746 (engraving), from the detail of an engraving by Johann Jacob Haid after a painting by J. S. Wahl, and is in the The Andre Meyer Collection, public domain • *Der vollkommene Capellmeister* by Johann Mattheson, Hamburg 1739, public domain • Portrait of Johann Joseph Fux, 18th century, public domain

19 THE MUSIC EDUCATION SCENE IN BAROQUE GERMANY
Heinrich Schütz by Christoph Spetner, Leipzig, ca. 1650/1660, public domain • Kaiser Ferdinand III by Frans Luycx, ca. 1637/1638, public domain

20 ON THE PHILOSOPHICAL ROOTS OF FRENCH MUSIC EDUCATION
Jean-Philippe Rameau by Jacques Aved, public domain • Titlepage of Charles Batteux's *Les beaux-arts réduits à un même principe*, 1746, public domain • *Réflexions critiques sur la poésie et la peinture* (Critical Reflections on Poetry and Literature) by Jean-Baptiste Dubos, 1755, public domain

21 THE MUSIC EDUCATION SCENE IN BAROQUE FRANCE
François Couperin, 1735, Etching by Jean-Jacques Flipart after painting by André Boüys, public domain • Jean-Baptiste Lully by Jean-Claude Chabert, Source: Bibliothèque nationale de France, public domain • Portrait of Louis XIV by Pierre Mignard, public domain • Moliere, Source: *Bibliothek des allgemeinen und praktischen Wissens. Bd. 5*, 1905, public domain

22 THE MUSIC EDUCATION SCENE IN JACOBEAN ENGLAND
George Frideric Handel by Balthasar Denner, National Portrait Gallery, London, public domain • John Playford by David Loggan, 17th century, Source: Bibliothèque nationale de France, public domain • Roger North by Peter Lely, public domain

23 ON MUSIC EDUCATION IN RESTORATION ENGLAND
Daniel Defoe by Michael Van der Gucht, public domain • Title page of Samuel Richardson's *Clarissa*, 1748, public domain • *Spectator,* 1711, by Joseph Addison, public domain • *The Tatler*, British magazine, 1709-1711, edited by Joseph Addison and Richard Steele, public domain

24 SCHUMANN ON MUSIC EDUCATION
Robert Schumann, Wien 1839, Lithographie by Joseph Kriehuber (1800–1876), public domain

25 CHOPIN ON MUSIC EDUCATION
The only known photograph of Frédéric Chopin, ca. 1849, Louis-Auguste Bisson, public domain

26 MENDELSSOHN ON MUSIC EDUCATION
Felix Mendelssohn Bartholdy, Source: Adolph Kohut: Berühmte israelitische Männer und Frauen, Vol.1, Leipzig 1900, bw-photo of the painting by Eduard Magnus, c. 1845, public domain

27 LISZT ON MUSIC EDUCATION
Portrait of Franz Liszt painted by Henri Lehmann in 1839, public domain

28 BERLIOZ ON MUSIC EDUCATION
Photograph of Hector Berlioz by Félix Nadar, Gaspard-Félix Tournachon (1820–1910), public domain

29 WAGNER ON MUSIC EDUCATION
Richard Wagner by Franz Hanfstaengl (1804–1877), ca. 1860, public domain

About the Author

Dr. David Whitwell is a graduate ('with distinction') of the University of Michigan and the Catholic University of America, Washington DC (PhD, Musicology, Distinguished Alumni Award, 2000) and has studied conducting with Eugene Ormandy and at the Akademie fur Musik, Vienna. Prior to coming to Northridge, Dr. Whitwell participated in concerts throughout the United States and Asia as Associate First Horn in the USAF Band and Orchestra in Washington DC, and in recitals throughout South America in cooperation with the United States State Department.

At the California State University, Northridge, which is in Los Angeles, Dr. Whitwell developed the CSUN Wind Ensemble into an ensemble of international reputation, with international tours to Europe in 1981 and 1989 and to Japan in 1984. The CSUN Wind Ensemble has made professional studio recordings for BBC (London), the Koln Westdeutscher Rundfunk (Germany), NOS National Radio (The Netherlands), Zurich Radio (Switzerland), the Television Broadcasting System (Japan) as well as for the United States State Department for broadcast on its 'Voice of America' program. The CSUN Wind Ensemble's recording with the Mirecourt Trio in 1982 was named the 'Record of the Year' by The Village Voice. Composers who have guest conducted Whitwell's ensembles include Aaron Copland, Ernest Krenek, Alan Hovhaness, Morton Gould, Karel Husa, Frank Erickson and Vaclav Nelhybel.

Dr. Whitwell has been a guest professor in 100 different universities and conservatories throughout the United States and in 23 foreign countries (most recently in China, in an elite school housed in the Forbidden City). Guest conducting experiences have included the Philadelphia Orchestra, Seattle Symphony Orchestra, the Czech Radio Orchestras of Brno and Bratislava, The National Youth Orchestra of Israel, as well as resident wind ensembles in Russia, Israel, Austria, Switzerland, Germany, England, Wales, The Netherlands, Portugal, Peru, Korea, Japan, Taiwan, Canada and the United States.

He is a past president of the College Band Directors National Association, a member of the Prasidium of the International Society for the Promotion of Band Music, and was a member of the founding board of directors of the World Association for Symphonic Bands and Ensembles (WASBE). In 1964 he was made an honorary life member of Kappa Kappa Psi, a national professional music fraternity. In September, 2001, he was a delegate to the UNESCO Conference on Global Music in Tokyo. He has been knighted by sovereign organizations in France, Portugal and Scotland and has been awarded the gold medal of Kerkrade, The Netherlands, and the silver medal of Wangen, Germany, the highest honor given wind conductors in the United States, the medal of the Academy of Wind and Percussion Arts (National Band Association) and the highest honor given wind conductors in Austria, the gold medal of the Austrian Band Association. He is a member of the Hall of Fame of the California Music Educators Association.

Dr. Whitwell's publications include more than 127 articles on wind literature including publications in Music and Letters (London), the London Musical Times, the Mozart-Jahrbuch (Salzburg), and 39 books, among which is his 13-volume *History and Literature of the Wind Band and Wind Ensemble* and an 8-volume series on *Aesthetics in Music*. In addition to numerous modern editions of early wind band music his original compositions include 5 symphonies.

David Whitwell was named as one of six men who have determined the course of American bands during the second half of the 20th century, in the definitive history, *The Twentieth Century American Wind Band* (Meredith Music).

A doctoral dissertation by German Gonzales (2007, Arizona State University) is dedicated to the life and conducting career of David Whitwell through the year 1977. David Whitwell is one of nine men described by Paula A. Crider in *The Conductor's Legacy* (Chicago: GIA, 2010) as 'the legendary conductors' of the 20th century.

'I can't imagine the 2nd half of the 20th century—without David Whitwell and what he has given to all of the rest of us.' Frederick Fennell (1993)

www.ingramcontent.com/pod-product-compliance
Lightning Source LLC
Chambersburg PA
CBHW080723300426

44114CB00019B/2467